The Child's Construction
of Language

BEHAVIOURAL DEVELOPMENT
A SERIES OF MONOGRAPHS

Series Editor
RUDOLPH SCHAFFER
University of Strathclyde
Glasgow, Scotland

Furnishing the Mind: A Comparative Study of Cognitive Development in Central
   Australian Aborigines
G.N. SEAGRIM and R.J. LENDON   1980

Acquiring Language in a Conversational Context
C.J. HOWE   1981

The Child's Construction of Language
W. DEUTSCH   1981

BEHAVIOURAL DEVELOPMENT:
A SERIES OF MONOGRAPHS

Series Editor: *RUDOLPH SCHAFFER*

The Child's Construction of Language

Edited by

WERNER DEUTSCH

Max-Planck-Institute for Psycholinguistics
Nijmegen, The Netherlands

1981

ACADEMIC PRESS

A Subsidiary of Harcourt Brace Jovanovich, Publishers

London   New York   Toronto   Sydney   San Francisco

ACADEMIC PRESS INC. (LONDON) LTD.
24/28 Oval Road,
London NW1

United States Edition published by
ACADEMIC PRESS INC.
111 Fifth Avenue
New York, New York 10003

Copyright © 1981 by
ACADEMIC PRESS INC. (LONDON) LTD.

British Library Cataloguing in Publication Data
The child's construction of language.
    1. Language acquisition
    I. Deutsch, W.
    401'.9   P118

ISBN 0-12-213580-6

LCCCN 81-68977

Printed in Great Britain

CONTRIBUTORS

Bierwisch, Manfred *Akademie der Wissenschaften, Zentral-institut für Sprachwissenschaft, Otto-Nuschke Str. 22, DDR - 108 Berlin, German Democratic Republic.*

Braine, Martin D.S. *New York University, Department of Psychology, 6 Washington Place, New York, NY 10003, USA.*

Bruner, Jerome S. *Harvard University, Department of Psychology, William James Hall, 33 Kirkland St, Cambridge, MA 02139, USA.*

Clark, Eve V. *Stanford University, Department of Linguistics, Stanford, CA 94305, USA.*

Deutsch, Werner *Max-Planck-Institut für Psycholinguistik, Berg en Dalseweg 79, NL - 6522 BC Nijmegen, The Netherlands.*

Flores d'Arcais, Giovanni B. *Universiteit Leiden, Psychologische Functieleer, Hooigracht 15, NL - 2312 KM Leiden, The Netherlands.*

Foppa, Nikolaus *Universität Bern, Psychologisches Institut, Gesellschaftsstrasse 49, CH - 3012 Bern, Switzerland.*

Hardy, Judith Atkinson *New York University, Department of Psychology, 6 Washington Place, New York, NY 10003, USA.*

Käsermann, Marie-Louise *Psychiatrische Universitätsklinik der Universität Bern, CH - 3072 Bern, Switzerland.*

Karmiloff-Smith, Annette *Max-Planck-Institut für Psycholinguistik, Berg en Dalseweg 79, NL - 6522 BC Nijmegen, The Netherlands.*

Lemos de, Claudia *Departamento di Linguistica, IEL, Unicamp, Campinas 13100, Brazil.*

Maratsos, Michael *University of Minnesota, Institute of Child Development, 51 East River Road, Minneapolis, MN 55455, USA.*

Schieffelin, Bambi *University of Pennsylvania, Graduate School of Education C1, Philadelphia, PA 19104, USA.*

Schlesinger, Izchak M. *The Israel Institute of Applied Research, 19 George Washington St, P.O. Box 7150, Jerusalem, Israel.*

Schmidt, Hans-Dieter *Humboldt Universität Berlin, Sektion Psychologie, Oranienburger Str. 18, DDR - 102 Berlin, German Democratic Republic.*

Shatz, Marilyn *The University of Michigan, Human Performance Center, 330 Packard Road, Ann Arbor, MI 48104, USA.*

Slobin, Dan I. *University of California, Berkeley, Department of Psychology, Berkeley, CA 94720, USA.*

Sydow, Hubert *Humboldt Universität Berlin, Sektion Psychologie, Oranienburger Str. 18, DDR - 102 Berlin, German Democratic Republic.*

Tyler, Lorraine Komisarjevsky *Max-Planck-Institut für Psycholinguistik, Berg en Dalseweg 79,NL - 6522 BC Nijmegen, The Netherlands.*

PREFACE

That children usually acquire their mother-tongue incredibly
rapidly and almost effortlessly, has become a standard belief.
Even if one would have to restrict this view at a second
glance, there remains the following paradox: what seems to be
a simple task to master for children, poses an extremely difficult problem to solve for the researcher. There is still
controversy as to what the proper preconditions and learning
mechanisms of language acquisition are. Additionally, the
question of the learning mechanisms presupposes an answer to
the question of what in language acquisition is acquired.
And the answer to the second question is in no way trivial,
if "what is acquired" is not looked upon exclusively from a
linguistic perspective.
   The papers in this book contribute to problems that occupy
central importance in contemporary discussions of language
acquisition, namely 1) the function of social interaction in
the acquisition and use of linguistic skills, 2) the structuring and reorganization of linguistic knowledge, and 3) the
analysis of changes in language production and understanding
from a processing perspective. Certainly, the papers cannot
form a coherent and unified theory of language acquisition,
but one can see them as preliminary building blocks of a con-
structivist position that could be augmented by further developments.
   The present book originated from a conference on "Beyond
Description in Child Language". It took place at Kasteel
Heyendael in Nijmegen (The Netherlands) from June 10-17,
1979, and was generously funded by the Ford Foundation, the
Max-Planck-Gesellschaft, and the Netherlands Institute of
Advanced Study.
   If this book's value goes beyond the publication of con-
ference proceedings, then it is clearly a result of the co-

operation with Manfred Bierwisch, Melissa Bowerman, Jerome
Bruner, Robin Campbell, William Levelt, Michael Maratsos,
and Charles Read who shared responsibility in selecting the
contents, and therefore should be regarded as consulting
editors.

Thanks are also due to the contributors who spent so much
time and effort in adjusting their conference papers to the
general structure and theme of the book.

Not least of all I am indebted to my colleagues and co-
workers at the Max-Planck-Institut für Psycholinguistik in
Nijmegen. They have aided me in seeing the problems inherent
in editing such a book and in finding pragmatic solutions to
them.

Nijmegen, June 1981   Werner Deutsch

CONTENTS

INTRODUCTION

WERNER DEUTSCH

*Max-Planck Institut für Psycholinguistik
Nijmegen, The Netherlands.*

> Das Grosse bleibt gross nicht,
> und klein nicht das Kleine.
>
> B. Brecht

The subject of the book is the classical problem of child
language research which has received changing emphasis
throughout the history of this field. What are the basic
developmental mechanisms that move the child from one level
of linguistic functioning to the next one? Does the child
himself play the main role in the acquisition of his/her
mother tongue, or is the process and product of language
acquisition mainly shaped by the social environment of the
child? The latter position emphasizes the *passive role* of
the child, which Wundt (1900, p. 296) summarized as follows: Child
language is "eine Erzeugung der Umgebung des Kindes, an der
das Kind selbst wesentlich nur passiv mitwirkt." (Child
language is a product of the child's environment. During
this process the child basically integrates language in a
passive way.)

Or is language acquisition a kind of reinvention (creation)
in which the child plays a highly *active role*? A representative of this alternative position, Ament, a contemporary
of Wundt, argued that in language acquisition the child
is not imitating the adult's language, but the contrary
holds, namely the adult is imitating the child. This
active view of language acquisition is summarized in the
following statement: "Die Onomatopoetika und die gesamte
Ammensprache überhaupt sind nicht eine Erfindung der Mütter
und Ammen, sondern der ungezählten Kinder von Jahrtausenden,
zu der Mütter und Ammen in keinem anderen Verhältnis als
dem der Fixierer, Überlieferer und Nachahmer stehen" (Ament,
1902, p. 15). (The onomatopoetic expressions and the entire baby

talk is not at all an invention of the mothers and caretakers, but of the innumerable children through millenia in relation to whom the mothers and caretakers have to be seen as fixators, surrenderers and imitators.)

The controversy at the beginning of the century between an active and a passive view of the child's role in language acquisition was temporarily shelved, when Stern and Stern demonstrated that both positions were untenable for both empirical and theoretical reasons. In their book "Die Kindersprache" which appeared in its first edition in 1907 (and which I shall use as a source-book for quotations of insight throughout this introduction), Stern and Stern regarded language acquisition as a process with two basic properties. On the one hand, it was considered an *approximation process* in which the child learns the conventionalized forms of a particular language system. On the other, it was viewed by the Sterns as a *constructive process* insofar as the child generates and tests his own hypotheses about the relationships between form, content, and function of a language system. In short, language acquisition was seen basically as a *convergent process*, in which internal and external forces constantly interact. "Nur in dem ständigen Zusammenwirken der inneren zum Sprechen drängenden Anlagen und der äusseren Gegebenheit der Umweltsprache, die jenen Anlagen Angriffspunkt und Material zu ihrer Realisierung bietet, kommt der kindliche Spracherwerb zustande." (Language acquisition, its predispositions, points of access and material realization take place only by the constant interaction between the internal forces that push the child towards using language and the external circumstances from the language of the environment.)

As the main evidence for their theoretical position, Stern and Stern took material from children's word formations. Their general approach remained a torso, since it had almost no impact upon the later theoretical developments in child language research.

One reason for this is rooted in the leading role at that time of the behaviouristic explanation of learning processes and developmental mechanisms. Within that framework internal processes were considered irrelevant to the question of explaining language acquisition. The latter process was seen as a learning process, determined - as was all learning - by the laws of "classical" and "instrumental" conditioning.

It was Chomsky's (1959) critical review of Skinner's "Verbal Behavior" (1957) that reopened the issue of developmental mechanisms in language acquisition. However, at the outset the problem was revived without a connecting link to historical roots - as for example Stern's book which had

appeared fifty years earlier. In sharp contrast, Chomsky
proposed a nativistic view of language acquisition. According to his model, man's ability to acquire language is a
genetically determined disposition. Its unfolding is relatively independent of the other developmental processes and
progress in the domain of cognitive and communicative functions. Each child is equipped with a so-called *Language
Acquisition Device* (LAD) which allows him/her to generate and
to test hypotheses about the formal (syntactic) structures of
any natural language. The recognition of these structures —
which permit the productive use of language — is possible,
even when and if the received linguistic input is deficient
or incomplete. For a detailed discussion of Chomsky's LAD,
see especially Levelt (1975).

Chomsky's view on language acquisition has been highly
productive in terms of stimulating discussions on some aspects of acquisitional mechanisms. Is language actually a
unique and autonomous representational and communicative
system which can only be acquired by human beings? What
are the commonalities of different languages that allow for
the rapid and effortless acquisition of any of them? Does
the development of language presuppose no particular prerequisites of cognitive and social development, and is language acquisition really an independent autonomous process
from its very beginning? The last issue especially, has led
to a fascinating controversy between Piaget and Chomsky,
which is documented in Piattelli-Palmarini (1980).

There can be no doubt that all these issues touch questions
of acquisitional mechanisms that are basic for language development. However, other questions — that seem to be
equally basic for these mechanisms — have been widely
neglected within the framework of Chomsky's ideas. For example, what are the processes and mechanisms that are underlying children's progress from one level of linguistic functioning to another level which is a step towards what the
adult native speaker of a given community is capable of in
real language use?

What are the developmental changes in the role of linguistic knowledge for the processes of producing and understanding verbal utterances? Which conditions trigger the acquisition of such language-specific knowledge and its transitions?
When does the child reach the adult's linguistic functioning
in language use, and what are the defining criteria for such
an approximation and for the "end" of the acquisition process?

The contributions of this book are mainly concerned with
questions of this type and going beyond those generated or
stimulated by Chomsky's ideas. The questions of the present

book can be considered as an extension of Stern and Stern's
contribution and provide a connecting link to an almost
entirely neglected tradition.

In the following, I want to summarize the common ground
of the contributions to this book by characterizing some
central aspects of developmental changes in language acquisition.

1) In language acquisition the child gradually learns to make
   himself understood and to understand others with less
   dependency on the necessity of extralinguistic cues. By
   this, the linguistic means gradually become relatively
   autonomous from other knowledge sources — pertinent to
   language production and language understanding. This
   'relative autonomy' of linguistic knowledge, however,
   does not imply a functional separation from these other
   sources. It does mean that the linguistic system can take
   over and express many functions of other representational
   and communicative means.

2) What are the basic mechanisms that trigger transitions in
   the linguistic functioning of the child? One obvious
   factor is communicative pressure. Without extensive and
   precise linguistic knowledge many communicative exchanges
   can lead to misunderstandings and misinterpretations of
   what has been intended by a particular message. These
   situations can force the child to draw his attention to
   those linguistic devices that could minimize the occurrence
   of communicative failure (cf. Deutsch and Pechmann, in press;
   Käsermann, 1980). However, the factor of communicative
   pressure is not at all a sufficient explanation for developmental changes in linguistic knowledge. It can play
   a role, but it is probably of minor importance compared
   to another condition. This condition has to do with the
   child's basic attitude toward language. The child from
   the very beginning of the acquisition process regards
   language as an internal problem space per se.

This view has been put forward by Karmiloff-Smith (1979),
and is reflected in many of the contributions to this book.
During language acquisition the child is engaged in discovering the relations between various linguistic forms, their
respective meanings, and their intra- and extralinguistic
functions on different levels of representations.

The acquisition of linguistic knowledge is not merely a
cumulative process, by which the linguistic knowledge increases in terms of completeness and similarity to what the
adult's state is. Yet, this process can be more appropriately

seen as a series of changing organizations and reorganiza-
tional procedures of linguistic knowledge (cf. Karmiloff-
Smith, 1979).

In the preceding paragraph, I have outlined what the main,
most general task is in language acquisition from the child's
point of view, namely to discover the relations between linguistic forms on the one hand and the meanings and functions
that can be represented and expressed by these forms on the
other hand.

This perspective points to a basic difference between describing the structure and the rules of a particular linguistic
system (or of language in general) from the linguist's point
of view, and that of the person acquiring such a system. The
basic difference is as follows. For a systematic and parsimonious description of a given system, it is mostly important
to *separate* particular aspects of the language system by imposing analytical distinctions (cf. Bierwisch, 1979). For the
acquisitional process, however, the *linkage* between differences
in form and corresponding differences in meaning and function
is the essential problem which has highest priority. If one
accepts the latter viewpoint, it would be misleading to take
traditional linguistic distinctions as corresponding aspects
for the acquisition process.

Instead of a division into phonological, syntactic, semantic,
and pragmatic development, we have chosen a different principle
of organization. This principle avoids a type of fragmentation
which would negate the child's real task in language acquisition
that of relating various aspects of language.

Thus, the book is set up according to a "domain of analysis"
principle. Those contributions that share the same "grain"
of linguistic unit involved in the theoretical and empirical
analysis of language have been grouped together. The book is
divided into four parts: "Interaction", "Utterance Sequences",
"Utterances", and "Words".

Part I takes "Interaction" as its domain of analysis and
contains five contributions which consider the structure and
process of dyadic interaction. During the interaction the
communicative roles between the interlocutors can change from
either speaker to listener or vice versa.

In the first chapter of Part I, Shatz provides a general
theoretical framework for the issue of which ways interactive
aspects of communication might illuminate an account of grammatical aspects of language acquisition. She discusses the
relationship between interaction and language under three
aspects: the directness of the relationship itself, the
direction of possible facilitating effects of one system on

the other, and the temporal relation of the acquisition of
social knowledge and linguistic knowledge.

Four positions are outlined in the chapter, namely 1) an
anti-nativist view which assumes direct structural relations
between social interaction and language acquisition; 2) a
neo-nativist view with the assumption of partial or indirect
structural relations; 3) a *process approach*, in which, despite the lack of structural mappings between the systems,
progress in one might have a facilitating effect upon the
other; and 4) a view where the two systems share properties
in terms of the *commonality of learning principles*. Using
available empirical evidence, Shatz evaluates the relative
merits and demerits of each of these positions.

In the second chapter of Part I, Bruner regards the use
of language in natural settings as a social activity between
at least two participants. Its functioning does not only
require a knowledge about the mapping relations between form,
content, and function of linguistic utterances, but also social skills regarding the *coordination of activities* among
the participants involved. The success or failure of communicative exchange is basically dependent on the dyad involved and their interaction. He argues that already pre-
linguistic communication between child and adult takes place
in a highly organized and systematic manner which involves
an agreed-upon outcome. Developmental changes in these
interaction-formats can be described in terms of changing
distribution and control of activities between child and
adult.

In Bruner's chapter an analysis is also made of whether
particular interactional patterns can have a facilitating
effect upon the linguistic skills involved in children's
acquisition of the particular sphere of *indicating* and
requesting. Moreover, Bruner discusses the more general
issue of whether ordered patterns of interactive discourse
could not only *assist* and *facilitate* but also *determine* the
acquisition of grammatical knowledge.

The chapter by de Lemos discusses the status of prelinguistic communicative development in relation to later linguistic
development. She examines the regularities which determine
a particular type of child-adult interaction at successive
points of its evolution, from a prelinguistic period to
early language. The types of interaction considered are
what she terms "*games demonstrative of event-structure*" and
are represented by activities such as object trajectories,
actions on containers, build-and-bash, and so forth. Data
from the acquisition of Brazilian Portuguese are used to
show that the acquisition of *proto-aspectual markers* is

closely connected with the mastery of event-types in social
interaction.

The fourth chapter of the "interaction" section analyses
the interactive discourse between child and adult when *mutual
understanding* is critical. Käsermann and Foppa show that even
very young children are sensitive to an adult's signal of non-
understanding. Such signals (e.g. "Hm?") from the adult usually elicit an "improved" version of the child's first utterance.
Two questions are at the centre of this study:

1) What are the determinants of children's responses to such
   nonspecific adult reactions? Käsermann and Foppa show that
   children tend to repeat complete utterances or to delete
   their redundant elements, and that incomplete utterances
   are disambiguated by making additions or explaining ambiguous parts.
2) If the adult reacts in more specific ways to the misunder-
   standing situation, could this be a relevant condition for
   children's acquisition of linguistic knowledge? The
   results of their analysis show that the adult indeed reacts to the relevant aspects of a child's utterance in
   a meaningful and consistent manner. Thus, it can be
   argued that the adult is providing *some* of the *learning
   conditions* the child needs for eventually internalizing
   the required knowledge.

In the final chapter in Part I, Schieffelin investigates
the constraints of interactive discourse upon the acquisition
of *word order* and *case marking* in an *ergative language*. This
language, Kaluli, requires agentive case marking in only
one of its two possible word-orders. Kaluli children must
learn not only when to use the agentive case marker (Object
Agent Verb sentences only) but also when to use each word
order for the desired pragmatic effect. AOV sentences as,
for example, narrative statements require little from the
listener. OAV sentences, however, indicate that the speaker
wants to do something to an agent. The results of a longitudinal data analysis reveal that children use appropriate word
order pragmatically before they use case marking correctly.
Developmentally, children initially use no case marking on
agents at all, then they add the agentive marker to all agents,
and finally they use correct application.

This chapter thus suggests that the grammatical marking of
pragmatically important aspects of language use precedes the
acquisition of the formal linguistic modulation of meaning.

Part II, "Utterance Sequences", concerns the analysis of
processes in producing and understanding connected utter-

ances. In contrast to the contributions of Part I the communicative role of the child remains constant. The two chapters
in this part are distinctly *process-oriented*.

The first chapter focuses on the processes and developmental changes underlying the production of discourse.
Karmiloff-Smith argues that "Sequences of Utterances are the
appropriate domain for the study of *anaphoric devices*, such
as pronouns. Furthermore, she submits that developmental
changes in the domain of connected discourse cannot be explained by acquisitional models which stress only its social-
interactive aspects. Rather, one has to assume that the
child's construction of language is deeply affected by the
processing procedures the child has to generate for *himself*
to keep track of *discourse relations*.

Karmiloff-Smith reports on a study of children's *elicited
narratives* in which she investigates the psychological processes of the functions and use of pronouns. The results
show that the use and non-use of pronouns serves to organize
the ongoing discourse relations by a procedure of preemption
of initial utterance slot for the "thematic subject". In
later development, non-thematic subjects are also used in
initial utterance slots, but then children apply clear
linguistic markers to this effect. In older children, pronouns are not being used for economy of repetition, but for
the establishment of such intradiscoursive thematic relations.

Karmiloff-Smith argues that the final stage has to be
characterized by a *greater control of the interplay between
various levels of processing*, and not by greater economy.

The second chapter of Part II concerns children's *understanding of spoken discourse*. Tyler explains the general
properties of this process as revealed by earlier studies
on adult language comprehension, namely the different knowledge sources involved and their immediate interactions in
"on-line" processing of utterances. She argues that *on-
line experimental tasks* are uniquely suitable to discover
the precise nature of developmental changes in children's
language understanding.

She reports on two experiments where five-, seven-, and
ten-year-old children are involved in an *identical monitoring* and a *category monitoring* task while listening to different types of prose. The results clearly show that the
general structure of the on-line comprehension process seems
to be the *same* for children as it is for adults. Developmental differences emerge only in the category-monitoring
task. These differences can be interpreted as a developmental lag in the ability to use certain linguistic cues for
discourse mapping. Tyler discusses the consequences that on-

line data should have for the interpretation of "off-line"
experimental data in children's comprehension of spoken discourse.

Part III, "Utterances", contains contributions where special
emphasis is given to the structure and the meaning of *single
utterances*.

The first chapter in Part III is by Slobin. He proposes
that grammatical forms are first acquired in the encoding
of *prototypical events*, and that the early encoding of such
events corresponds to the *canonical sentence forms* available
in the input language. The development of transitive sentences in several different types of languages is offered
as support for his arguments. The prototypical causal event
is one in which an agent carries out a physical and perceptible change of state in a patient by means of direct
body contact or with an instrument under the agent's control.
Such events are encoded in consistent grammatical fashion
by the age of two, whether the means of encoding be regular
word-order, accusative case marking, or ergative case
marking.

Slobin shows that for those languages in which data from
formal comprehension tests are available (English, French,
Italian, Japanese, and Serbo-Croatian), there is evidence
for an early stage in which the child responds consistently
only to sentences which are in canonical form.

Hardy and Braine investigate the role of *semantic concepts*
in children's *grammatical organization of sentences*. What
are the syntactically relevant semantic concepts (i.e. *case
categories*)? How narrow are they represented in the minds
of four- and five-year-old children? Are they narrower
and more concrete than the case categories proposed by
linguists?

As the experimental method for exploring these questions,
children learn to place tokens of different shapes in pictures according to the role they play in a scene. After
the training session, children are presented with new pictures and sentences where they have to place the appropriate
token on the new role exemplars. From children's choices
one can infer what the system of syntactically relevant
semantic concepts is at a particular point of development.
The results show that children's concept of the *actor*, of
the *subject of attribution*, and of the *object of action*
are remarkably similar to the adults' case system in English.
Hardy and Braine conclude that later development does not
concern the organization of the basic system, but the learning
of the relevant exceptions.

The third chapter of Part III is by Schlesinger. In his

paper he outlines developmental changes in the mapping between semantic and syntactic knowledge. He proposes a
"Semantic Assimilation Hypothesis", which impels the child
to reorganize his linguistic knowledge toward a system operating on syntactic structures. Semantic assimilation is described as an extension of already existing semantic categories. By this, not only the *assimilating category* (i.e.
the experiencer), but also the *assimilated category* (i.e. the
agent) retains some of its "semantic flavour". Schlesinger
also discusses whether the child extends his categories
solely on the basis of similarities between linguistic constructions. He argues that such an alternative to semantic
assimilation is not very plausible, because in language use
the child is out for "semantic sense", even if and when he/
she can notice formal resemblances between linguistic constructions. Furthermore, Schlesinger proposes that the
semantic assimilation hypothesis can also account for the
process of *category formation*.

The last chapter in Part III is concerned with children's
construction of formal grammatical categories such as noun
and verb. The basic question is whether these formal categories can arise from semantic ones. Maratsos proposes an
inductive mechanism which can account for the change of
categories over time. This mechanism takes into account
both *semantic* and *structural similarity* in order to determine
whether or not an incoming example will be recognized as an
example of the already extant grammatical category. Maratsos
applies that mechanism to the derivation of mover-movement
and actor-action rules as examples of early semantic-structural rules. He also discusses how and when the nature of
the category and the basis for assimilation of new members
change.

Part IV deals with "Words" as domain of analysis. It contains four contributions. The first chapter is by Flores
d'Arcais. He investigates the acquisition of a particular
class of words which function to connect clauses with a specific meaning as, for example, the concessive connective
although and the temporal connective *while*. In a series of
experimental tasks three main questions are studied.

1) What is the *acquisitional order* in which children differentiate the meaning of the connectives?
2) What is the development of the notion of "*wordness*" the
   child has about connectives?
3) What are the *strategies* the child uses in various linguistic tasks?

The results show that causal and temporal connectives seem

the first to be differentiated, final and consecutive last.
Furthermore, the knowledge that connectives are "words"
develops more slowly than the corresponding knowledge about
nouns and adjectives. In lexical decision tasks the decision latencies for connectives are longer than the latencies
for nouns and adjectives. The analysis of strategies in
dealing with connectives reveals important task-related differences. At a given age the child might be capable of performing correctly in one task, but not yet in another one.

Flores d'Arcais concludes that in the acquisition of the
meaning of connectives different levels of knowledge are
likely to be involved, and that the acquisition process is
not completed by the age of 12.

E. Clark's paper raises the issue of *word innovations* in
lexical development. She shows that from an early age onwards children exploit the word-formation devices of their
language to fill gaps in their current lexicon. Many new
words are *contextuals*, because their intended interpretations
depend critically on the context of their utterance and hence
demand cooperation between speaker and listener. Not only
must children master the conventions governing the meanings
of innovations, but they must also master the appropriate
forms for expressing those meanings.

On the basis of experimentally elicited word-innovations,
Clark discusses the basic principles of *word-formational
devices*, namely the *principle of productivity, the principle
of semantic transparency,* and the *principle of regularization,* and their respective weight for the explanation of
acquisitional order.

The third chapter of Part IV is by Schmidt and Sydow. They
investigate the developmental changes in the representation
of meaning similarities among words. They distinguish two
different types of meaning relations. *Interconceptual relations* represent knowledge about experienced events with case
categories like actor, instrument, etc. as their basic elements. *Intraconceptual relations* refer to logical relations
between featural codes of concepts as, for example, sub- and
superordination.

In a series of experiments concerning meaning comparisons
among nouns, Schmidt and Sydow show that different semantic
relations attain a consistent level of generality at different points of development. Furthermore, they demonstrate
that the ability to identify semantically related noun pairs
relies on specific conditions. They conclude that the nature
of representational cognitive processes and its development
is a highly open issue.

In the last chapter of Part IV, Bierwisch presents a theo-

retical account of the acquisition of word meaning. He analyses which tasks language as a system imposes on the child
in order to produce and to understand words properly. Bierwisch outlines the ways in which the *meaning representation*
of a word has to be connected to *different levels* of representation, dependent on the *structural* and *functional properties of an utterance* or *spans of utterances* in which a word
appears. He discusses what the basic differences are in the
meaning of different word classes, and how these differences
are reflected in acquisitional processes.

All the contributions in this book deal with the acquisition of spoken language and concern the process of first
language acquisition in a variety of different languages,
namely Dutch, English, French, German, Italian, Swiss-German,
Portuguese etc. Thus, the book follows what Stern and Stern
have stated in this vein in 1907: "Und dennoch kann die
Kindersprachkunde mehr als die Analyse individueller Sprachent-
wicklungen sein; denn sie vermag Bildungsgesetze zu formu-
lieren, die in jeder Kindersprache wirksam sing." (But child
language research can be more than the analysis of individual
acquisition processes, because from it general laws of construction can be formulated that are at work in each and
every child's language development.)

REFERENCES

Ament, W. (1902). Begriff und Begriffe der Kindersprache.
  Schiller-Ziehensihe Sammlung von Abhandlungen 5.
Bierwisch, M. (1979). Strukturen und Prozesse im Sprach-
  verhalten. *In* "Psychologische Effekte sprachlicher Struk-
  turkomponenten" (Bierwisch, M., ed.). Berlin: Akademie-
  verlag.
Chomsky, N. (1959). Review of B.F. Skinner "Verbal Behavior",
  Language 35, 26-58.
Deutsch, W. and Pechmann, T. (in press). Social interaction
  and the development of definite descriptions, *Cognition*.
Karmiloff-Smith, A. (1979). "A Functional Approach to Child
  Language: A Study of Determiners and Reference". Cambridge:
  Cambridge University Press.
Käsermann, M. (1980). "Spracherwerb und Interaktion". Bern:
  Huber.
Levelt, W.J.M. (1975). What became of LAD? From: "Ut
  videam: Contributions to an Understanding of Linguistics",
  for Pieter Verburg on the occasion of his 70th birthday.
  Lisse: Peter de Ridder Press.
Piattelli-Palmarini, M. (ed.) (1980). "Language and Learning".
  London: Routledge and Kegan Paul.

Skinner, B.F. (1957). "Verbal Behavior". New York: Appleton-Century-Crofts.

Stern, C. and Stern, W. (1907). "Die Kindersprache". Leipzig: Barth.

Wundt, W. (1900). "Völkerpsychologie". Erster Band: Die Sprache. Leipzig: Engelmann.

PART I: INTERACTION

LEARNING THE RULES OF THE GAME: FOUR VIEWS OF THE RELATION BETWEEN SOCIAL INTERACTION AND SYNTAX ACQUISITION

MARILYN SHATZ

University of Michigan, Human Performance Center, Ann Arbor, Michigan, USA.

1. INTRODUCTION

That language is a phenomenon belonging primarily to the domain of social activities is hardly an arguable point. While one can list non-social uses of language as well as types of social interaction that are not linguistic, the fact remains that the overlap between language use and social interaction, though imperfect, is still considerable. Moreover, some minimal amount of social interaction seems to be necessary for language acquisition to take place. The obvious kinship between language and social interaction suggests the possibility of a relationship between knowledge in the social sphere and the learning of linguistic forms. Yet, the precise nature of that relationship is not so obvious. While researchers have often argued that investigations of the social contexts of acquisition are central to demystifying the process of acquisition (e.g. Campbell and Wales, 1970; Ryan, 1974), few have specified just what the role of interaction in acquisition might be. Despite this lack of clarity, the popularity of the primacy-of-interaction view, as well as the number of studies it has already spawned, is astonishing. For this reason alone, it is worth examining more carefully some possible relationships between social interaction and syntax acquisition, with particular attention to their historical origins and the arguments that can be mounted for or against them.

Given the vagueness with which the interaction-language relationship is often treated in the literature, how can one begin to explicate and evaluate different possible views of that relation? I suggest that one can ask four questions which help to differentiate positions and to provide a system

for organizing data potentially relevant to evaluating them.
First, one can ask whether the acquisition of social knowledge and linguistic knowledge are seen as simultaneous
tasks or whether one is considered to be prior to the other.
Second, are there facilitating effects of one system on the
other and are they unidirectional or bidirectional? A third
question concerns the directness of the relationship. That
is, how much is the relation mediated by the internal properties of the child? Finally, one can ask whether the
relationship is based on structural commonalities between
the two systems and if so, what the nature and extent of
those commonalities are. While the existing data do not
allow us to determine with much certainty or specificity the
actual relationship between social interaction and syntax
acquisition, I contend that we can at least limit the set of
relationships which it is reasonable to investigate further
to those consistent with tentative answers to these four
questions.

As a way of examining the data bearing on the answers to
these questions, I outline and evaluate four different kinds
of relationships between social interaction and syntax acquisition which are distinguishable on the basis of the different sorts of answers they provide to the above questions.
The positions range from a strong one, deriving syntax
acquisition directly from interactionally provided social
knowledge to a weak one, where the relatively autonomous
process of syntax acquisition can be facilitated by the efficient distribution of processing resources. From the discussion of the four positions I shall conclude that the set
of reasonable relationships adheres to the following constraints: First, while some social knowledge is acquired
earlier than linguistic knowledge, it is likely that much of
the acquisition of one system is not prior to the other.
Given this, it is likely that facilitation will be bidirectional, if it occurs at all. With regard to the specific
sort of relations to be found between the two domains, there
is at best only a partial structural commonality, and even
this is relatively indirect, suggesting that internal properties of the child are central to a characterization of
the relation.

One implication of these conclusions is that interaction-
ist, anti-nativist theories of acquisition are incompatible
with reasonable relationships between social interaction
and syntax acquisition, since they discount the importance of
the internal properties of the child. To anti-nativists who
are so often strong advocates of the investigation of the
social interaction context of language acquisition, this

implication is likely to be both surprising and disconcert-
ing. Perhaps they can take solace in yet another conclusion:
that there still appear to be places for social interaction
in the acquisition story, albeit not the one they expected. To
defend these claims, I turn now to the outlines of the four
positions.

2. AN ANTI-NATIVIST VIEW: DIRECT STRUCTURAL RELATIONS

There can be little doubt that the recent interest in the
relationship between social interaction and the acquisition
of language is in direct response to the innateness solution
proposed by transformational grammarians to the puzzling fact
that language development occurs during a time when other
complex cognitive systems do not demonstrate such quick and
general growth. As Bruner (1977) noted,

> The dominant view of the last decade has been, of course,
> Chomsky's, based on his so-called Language Acquisition
> Device. But the central feature of that device — that
> the child in some sense "has a knowledge" from the start
> of the universal rules of language and that he generates
> from this knowledge hypotheses about the local language
> encountered around him — while boldly suggestive, is
> plainly insufficient in the light of the past years of
> research. A more realistic approach to language acquisi-
> tion must surely examine what the child learns that helps
> him pass from prespeech communication to the use of
> language proper, lest we leap too easily to Cartesian
> conclusions about innateness.

A proposed alternative to the innateness solution, then, is
to give the child a prior learned system of knowledge with
which the child can uncover the structure of language. Since
language acquisition goes on in a social context, a good bet
for the known system is interactional knowledge.
    Note that, if the motivation for a system of priors is
to reduce the contribution of the child, then only certain
kinds of prior systems will suffice; namely, those which
directly and clearly provide the structural information necessary for the acquisition of the new system, since any
indirect relation assumes mediation via the internal properties of the child. (We discuss below other sorts of
prior systems not so motivated and without the anti-nativist
constraint that the child be a weak contributor.) More specifically, the notion of facilitation on structural grounds
seems to depend on a view of the child as analogy-maker,
seeing similarities between one system and another (cf.

Shatz,in press). As Gentner (1981) has pointed out, analogy differs from identity in that making analogies always involves selecting some relations and not others as relevant. The ability to be appropriately selective is, of course, a property of mind and would appear to go against the goal of weakening the child's contribution. Yet, to the extent that the analogy between the known and unknown system is a good one, then presumably it requires less on the part of the learner to recognize and understand it. Thus, the issue is whether there exists a "good" analogy between the two systems. Good structural analogies have been described as clear,systematic, and specific (Gentner, 1981). To date, the evidence that the relationship between social and syntactic information has these characteristics has not been forthcoming. Few specific relations have even been proposed and those that have (e.g. Bruner, 1975) have not been successfully defended. For example, while interactions involving actions such as giving and taking may have an inherent order to them, the translation of that order to word order in a given language is not necessarily direct or transparent (cf. Slobin, in press. Likewise, gestures, another source of information in interactive situations that has been proposed as potentially useful to the child (Macnamara, 1977), do not map to grammatical properties of language in sufficiently unique or systematic ways to be taken as good clues to structure (Shatz, in press).

Even if "good" analogic relations could be found, there is a further requirement that would have to be met before acquisition could be claimed to be free of much mediation by the internal properties of the child. Since language acquisition is not instantaneous, the order and rate of development should also be a function of the social environment. There are two alternative ways this requirement could be fulfilled. First, the child might be provided during the prelinguistic stage with all the social information he or she would need to acquire language but only gradually be provided with the necessary interaction-language pairs from which to draw the appropriate structural analogies. The other alternative is that as soon as the child obtained a particular social understanding, the relevant language would immediately be provided and the structural information extracted. In either case, the order of acquisition would depend on the orderly provision of data from sources outside the child.

Consider instead a state of affairs such that, regardless of what mappings were provided for him, the child acquired grammar in a different way from the way the data were presented. Then one would have to concede that there were

internal constraints on the application of the prior system
to the one being acquired. Such constraints might be either
general processing characteristics that limit the young
child's ability to use the data as given or constraints
peculiar to a language acquisition device. Presumably the
former limitation would be more palatable to anti-nativists
than the latter. However, in the absence of a well-docu-
mented theory of processing, it is impossible to determine
which of the internal constraints that might be found stem
from general processing causes. Hence, any evidence for internal constraints is a potential threat to an anti-nativist
position.

Again, the relevant data are not encouraging to the anti-
nativist view. Elsewhere I have addressed at length the
problems of trying to locate the major burden of acquisition
order in the environment (Shatz, in press). Suffice it to summarize those arguments here by saying that the facts of early
mother-child interaction do not support the view that mothers
are so finely tuned to their children's development that they
provide them with an ordered set of regularly changing data
that can account for the order of their acquisitions (also
see Hoff-Ginsberg and Shatz, 1981, for a review). Rather
it appears that children take from the data the information
they are "ready" to utilize. Readiness appears not to be a
function solely of what the child has already been exposed
to but of what the child has already constructed of the
grammar. Whether the child's selectivity is a result of processing limitations or the language acquisition "program", to
the extent that there appear to be internal influences on
acquisition order, then there is less reason to hold to a
strong anti-nativist position.

Still another characteristic of the anti-nativist view can
be called into question. As noted above, social knowledge is
assumed to be the base system generally necessary to the
acquisition of syntactic knowledge, although specific alternative formulations may vary with regard to how much social
knowledge precedes any syntax acquisition. That is, all
relevant social knowledge could be acquired prior to any
syntactic acquisitions during the prelinguistic period, or
"local" advances in social knowledge could be followed by
relevant local acquisitions in syntax. In either case social
knowledge necessarily precedes advances in syntax and the
acquisition of it is conceptualized as a prior and not a
concurrent task.

However, children's interactive behavior can often be shown
to be the result of fairly primitive response strategies, and
the development of their intentional understandings may
depend at least in part on linguistic cues (Shatz, 1978a).

Moreover, the strategies children sometimes develop in interactive situations often seem to be far removed from either
interactive or formal linguistic convention. For example,
we observed the following dialogues between a 25-month-old
child and her mother, who regularly used "hmm" in two ways,
either to acknowledge her child's utterance or to prompt the
child following an unanswered question of her own.

1) M: Can you put the bed in one of the rooms?
       Hmm?

   C: Hmm.

2) M: Who's gonna drive the car?

   C: Hmm.

   M: Who's gonna drive the car?

   C: Hmm.

   M: Is Mommy gonna drive the car?

   C: Hmm.

3) M: What's this?

   C: Doggie.

   M: How does a doggie go?

   C: Woof.

   M: Woof?

       Hmm. Okay.

       Where should the doggie go in the house?

   C: Hmm.

The sequences suggest the child developed an answering
strategy on the basis of her experience with her mother, but
her response behavior indicates that she misinterpreted and
misused the interactional data provided. Such examples have
to make one skeptical about how much a child knows about the
meaning of the interaction she is being engaged in before
she begins to unravel the complexities of syntax.

    In sum then, the interactionist, anti-nativist view answers
the four questions we posed earlier in the following way:
There are direct structural commonalities between the two
areas of knowledge, the contribution of the child is low,
and the social task precedes the one of syntax acquisition,
with the direction of influence flowing from the prior to
the later task. On multiple grounds, such a view does not
seem tenable. It remains to examine other sorts of language-

interaction relationships and the cases that can be made for them.

3. NEO-NATIVIST VIEWS: PARTIAL OR INDIRECT STRUCTURAL RELATIONS

In and of itself a system of necessary priors is not incompatible with an innatist view of language acquisition. Indeed, recent theories of syntax acquisition which postulate rich innate linguistic mechanisms also stipulate the need for meaning representations of input sentences in order for syntactic analysis to proceed (Wexler and Culicover, 1980; Pinker, in press). To the extent that such representations are derived from events occurring in a social context, then social information becomes prerequisite to the syntax acquisition enterprise. While one sort of knowledge still takes temporal precedence over another, these systems differ from the anti-nativist view on several grounds. Most importantly, the relation between prior knowledge is presumed at best to be either indirect (Wexler and Culicover, 1980) or partial (Pinker, in press). Indirect or partial mappings suffice because these views postulate in addition some kind of innate apparatus rich enough to operate on such inputs to create the necessary linguistic structures. Hence, for Wexler and Culicover, prior semantic representations generate (by an unspecified process) deep structural representations which are then the base to which surface strings are associated such that SS-DS strings can be analysed in accordance with universal grammar principles to accomplish the construction of a particular grammar.

An alternative role for semantic information is suggested by Pinker (in press). In his theory, semantic correlates to syntactic constructions are necessary initially to begin the learner's task of fixing parameters for innate syntactic schemata. Once some parameters are set, however, the syntactic system can bootstrap itself, with syntactic information even fed back into the further development of the semantic system. The relationship of semantics to surface syntax may be more direct in Pinker's theory than in Wexler and Culicover's, yet his approach differs from the anti-nativist views discussed above in that, like Wexler and Culicover, he maintains that syntactic entities are givens to be interpreted in light of, rather than derived from, prior information. Hence, both Pinker's and Wexler and Culicover's positions are to be distinguished from the first view on two grounds: they grant the child more innate linguistic apparatus, and whatever link there is to social interaction is maintained via semantic representations.[1†]

To the extent that these nativist views assume an understanding of what is said solely on the basis of contextual
information, they are subject to some of the same criticisms
as the anti-nativist view; namely, that there is little
evidence the child has much understanding on non-linguistic
grounds alone. The more these views reduce dependence on
prior knowledge, the more they avoid this objection. Unfortunately, neither view is sufficiently well specified on
these grounds to be able to evaluate them much further.
Wexler and Culicover do not address the question of the origins of the semantic representations, nor do they consider
the extent to which semantic representations must be present
before syntactic analysis proceeds. It is unclear what the
implications would be for their model if semantic readings
for only some subset of input sentences were available to
the child, thus limiting the set of sentences on which syntactic analysis could initially be done. As noted above, such
a limitation seems compatible with Pinker's approach, although
the details remain to be worked out. Indeed, depending on
the nature of bootstrapping and feedback operations, it is
possible that the learning of language could itself facilitate an understanding of the social system in which linguistic experience itself is embedded. In other words, such a
system would be bidirectionally facilitative.[2]

One virtue of these more recent nativist approaches is that
they avoid a criticism of the earlier nativist view; namely,
that it ignored the socio-cognitive context of acquisition.
In so much as these approaches take that context into account
while at the same time arguing against an isomorphism between
prior forms of knowledge and syntactic knowledge, they seem
more reasonable in general than either earlier nativist or
current anti-nativist accounts. However, evaluating particular proposals for the relation between innate capacities
and mechanisms for utilizing non-linguistic information in
the acquisition process must await better specification of
these aspects of the theories.

4. THE PROCESS APPROACH: THE ALLOCATION OF RESOURCES

The two previous views assume that facilitation of syntax
acquisition is accomplished via some structural analogues
between a system of priors and the to-be-learned system.

---

† Superscript numerals refer to notes which are to be found
at the end of the chapter.

They differ in the degree of relation between the two systems
and the extent to which one derives from or is subsequent to
the other. A third alternative is one that focuses less on
structural relationships and more on how, despite the lack
of clear structural mappings between the two systems being
learned, progress in one might facilitate progress in the
other. This alternative takes as a given that in any conversational situation young children have essentially two tasks,
one to create a productive grammar on the basis of the
language they are exposed to, and the other to function as
active participants in their social worlds. To the extent
that the interactive task can be accomplished with relative
ease, then more resources can be allocated to the analytic
task. Thus, the crucial difference between this view and
the previous ones is that facilitation occurs via the easy
resolution of one of two tasks rather than via structural
analogies.

There are two ways in which solutions to interactive tasks
can be found easily. One is actually to have the social
knowledge on which to base interactive responses. Yet, as
we have seen, the attribution of much social knowledge to
such young children is a troublesome assumption. A second
possibility is that children develop primitive heuristics
for staying in interactions. That is, they have interactive
strategies which result in relatively acceptable behavior
before they fully understand what is being said to them or
what is expected of them. The advantage to the proposal of
heuristics is that it avoids the troublesome attribution of
social knowledge to the child while still providing a means
of making the interactional task "easy" from the perspective
of the expenditure of resources. Thus, the process approach
maintains the possibility of facilitation while neither depending on structural relationships nor on a high level of
prior social knowledge.

Two kinds of facilitation are possible in this view. The
most obvious sort is rather general. Just about any strategic behavior which fulfills the requirement that a response
occur without much analysis of the conversational demands
should result in resources remaining for other tasks. It is,
of course, possible that some strategies are more efficient
than others. That is, they use demonstrably less resources
in their execution than others and hence are even more facilitative. Even so, they should simply result in more general
facilitation on the rate of as opposed to changes in the mode
of acquisition.

The second sort of facilitation is more direct and specific.
While it is clear that children progress through the acquisi-

tion process at different rates, it is as yet unclear whether
modes of acquisition differ interestingly among children or
whether such differences are at all related to interactional
behavior. One can speculate, however, on how diverse interactional strategies might have more specific effects on syntax acquisition. First, it is possible that a given interactional strategy focuses attention on particular aspects of
the speech stream, making it more available to analysis. For
example, some children apparently imitate the most recent
words they hear as a way of producing a response in an interaction. It may be that one consequence of the attention
focused on the ends of utterances is that they gain preferred
status for early syntactic analysis as well. Secondly, since
strategic behavior is embedded in an interactive situation,
one consequence of it is that it has a role in eliciting
further input to the acquisition system. Insofar as different interactive strategies result in different subsequent
turns by the conversational partner, then the child may be
exposed to different but especially salient information depending on his particular behavior. For example, consider
the child discussed earlier who had learned to respond to
his mother with "hmmm." Such responses on his part were
often followed by his mother reformulating her question to
him or asking a second question. Contrast that sort of input with the behavior of a mother whose child often responded
"that" to just about any sort of question she asked. Her
response to those often inappropriate responses was to name
an object she thought might be the referent for the child's
utterance. Hence, these two children were getting differential amounts of different inputs as a consequence of their
response strategies. If the mechanisms of syntactic analysis
are at all sensitive to frequencies of different types of
input, then these sorts of differences could have an effect
on the acquisition process.
   The process approach has several advantages over the anti-
nativist position in that it avoids two major difficulties
of the latter view. One is the postulation of direct structural relationships between the social sphere and the syntactic one; the other is its dependence on external factors as
the major determinant of the rate and course of acquisition.
The process position avoids these problems first by taking
no stand on the issue of structural relationships; they are
not crucial to the proposed facilitation mechanism. On the
other hand, in so far as some structural relations, either
partial or indirect, may be necessary for syntactic analysis
to proceed, the view is not incompatible with the nativist
positions discussed earlier. Secondly, the mechanism of

resource allocation maintains a role for the environment but gives the child a larger role in the determination of rate and order of acquisition. To the extent that resource allocations are functions of strategic behaviors developed in and having consequences for interactions, then the determinants can be said to be truly interactive, rather than wholly external or internal to the child. Thus, this position avoids the criticism that can be made of the anti-nativist view that the environment has to operate in a manner finely tuned to the child's capacities without a clear exposition of the means for achieving that tuning or empirical evidence for it (cf. Shatz, in press).Still another advantage to the process approach is that it allows for bidirectional facilitation. Presumably syntactic analysis would result in a greater degree of linguistic performance in interactive situations, possibly fostering the engagement of the child in more sophisticated social interactions, with increased opportunities for social learning.

With regard to evidence for the process approach, much of it is on the level of feasibility arguments rather than actual demonstrations of facilitation. For example, the notion of limited resources has a reasonably long and respectable history in cognitive psychology. Moreover, it has on several occasions been recruited to explain children's linguistic and communicative behavior (Bloom, Rocissano and Hood, 1976; Knapp, 1979; Shatz, 1978b). One possible difference between these previous uses of the notion and the one here is that in the prior cases, while researchers argued that the performance of one task could interfere with the performance of another task, the two tasks drawing on the same pool of resources seemed alike in that they both involved the execution of cognitive processes, for example;understanding utterances, producing syntactically complete strings, and so on. In the present case, one could argue, the claim is somewhat different; namely, that it is a performance task and a learning task which are hypothesized to share the same resource pool. Furthermore, it could be argued that there is less evidence in the cognitive literature for these sorts of tasks sharing limited resources than for ones in like domains doing so. The counter to this argument is that in the absence of full understandings of learning and cognitive processes, it is unclear how different or separate the two sorts of tasks are. At least at present, there seem to be neither theoretical or empirical reasons to reject the proposed extension of the limited resources argument out of hand.

As for the existence of conversational strategies, the evidence in favor of them seems reasonably solid. Not only

are there many anecdotal reports of the sort quoted in our
examples above, but more systematic work has confirmed the
existence of various sorts of response heuristics in young
children. Shatz (1978a, c; Shatz, Bernstein and Shulman,
1980) found that children had a tendency to produce action
in response to ambiguous utterances. Allen and Shatz (1981)
described children who took any sort of "what" question as
an opportunity to make responses based on their experience
with their own mothers' question routines, and imitation as
a conversational response strategy has been suggested by
Rees (1975) and reported by Boskey and Nelson (1980). Such
research suggests that children develop consistent ways of
responding to conversational demands on the basis of only
partially understood or analysed information about either
the linguistic or communicative constraints on the messages
addressed to them.

To my knowledge, there have been no direct tests of a
process facilitation model. However, a bit of suggestive
data is available from a study done on the relationship of
children's behavior in response to language under different
conditions of contextual support (Shatz, Allen and Raizman,
in prep.). In this study children aged 18 to 26 months were
asked a variety of questions like "What says woof-woof?",
and "What does a dog say?" The same questions were asked
three times, once with a gesture at a relevant object (in
this case, a toy dog), once with a gesture at an irrelevant
object, and once with no gesture at all. We found that the
14 subjects could be divided into three groups: five who
had more tendency to produce verbal imitations as responses,
five who had virtually no tendency to do so, and four who
occasionally imitated. In other words, we seemed to have
children with different sets of strategies for operating in
unfamiliar conversational settings. The question of relevance here is whether these children differed in their linguistic knowledge in ways that suggested their different
strategies of interaction might have led them down divergent
paths of linguistic development.

Before proceeding, it is important to point out that the
groups were unequal in that by and large, the imitators tended to be found among the younger children. Hence, overall
differences in general measures of language development
such as mean length of utterance were expected, although
the correlation between MLU and frequency of imitation was
low once age was partialled out ($r=-0.19$). Of more interest
is the possibility that the generally less advanced group
had some knowledge not possessed by the more advanced group.
In particular, imitators may have been more sensitive to

words likely to appear at the ends of utterances and therefore might have learned more about constructions appearing
in last position than would non-imitators. One of our question types was the sort of construction requiring a progressive verb, e.g. "jumping", in response to questions like "What
is the girl doing?" Thus, we could examine whether imitators
were better at this sort of response form than non-imitators.
In fact, only one imitator produced any syntactically canonical responses to such utterances, as did one non-imitator.
Nor was imitators' performance on this utterance type any
better than on the other sorts of utterances where facilitation via an imitation strategy might not have been expected.

Given the age differences in the subject groups, one might
argue that imitation is a characteristic strategy of an early
stage which our non-imitators had already progressed through.
If so, they would have already achieved benefits from it and
could not be expected to look worse on this measure than
children still in that stage and in the process of acquiring
those benefits. There are two reasons to discount this argument. First, there is little reason to believe that all or
even most children go through a stage of imitation (Bloom,
Hood and Lightbown, 1974). Secondly, most of the non-imitators
failed to produce canonical progressive responses; hence, if they
did pass through a stage of imitation, they apparently
learned little about progressive verbs while in it. In
sum, neither non-imitators nor imitators do well on a construction that might reasonably be expected to be facilitated
by an imitation strategy.

Obviously, the data presented above are only suggestive.
They neither address the issue of general facilitation nor do
they unequivocally disconfirm the possibility of specific
influence. They do suggest, however, that conversational
strategies may have little effect on the progress of syntax
acquisition, and that the two tasks being accomplished by
the child may go on relatively independently of one another.

It is important to point out that even if specific process
facilitation was proved, it would have few implications for
the etiology of linguistic structures. Because no assumptions of structural analogies are made in the process approach,
the architecture of the syntactic system is assumed to be derived from other sources, either innate linguistic or possibly cognitive in nature. Facilitation, should it occur,
is primarily on rate, and on order for those places in the
system where the order in which parameters are set has no
consequences for the structure of the system. Thus, the process facilitation view does little in and of itself to assuage
anti-nativist qualms concerning innate constraints on linguis-

tic structure. As already noted, the process view is compatible with nativist proposals. It is also compatible with
the final view to be presented, one in which the possibility
of structural relationships exists, not because of one system
depending on or deriving from the other, but because the
acquisition of the complex systems of both social and syntactic knowledge are subject to the same constraints inherent
in the learning device.

5. A RELATIONSHIP WITHOUT FACILITATION: COMMONALITY OF LEARNING PRINCIPLES

The previous views have all in one way or another assumed some
sort of facilitation, either unidirectional or bidirectional,
as a function of the relationship between social and syntactic
systems. Yet, the possibility of a relationship between the
two systems does not depend on the occurrence of facilitation.
It may be that the systems share properties in common such
that the investigation of one can lead to insights into the
acquisition of the other without the actual acquisition of
one leading to facilitation of acquisition of the other. In
other words, the analogy between the systems may more appropriately be at the level of the researcher's analysis rather
than at the level of the child's. The proposal to be considered here is that the shared properties have to do with
the common principles operating in the acquisition of complex
knowledge systems.
     There are several reasons for suggesting that there may be
common properties to the acquisition of both social and syntactic knowledge. First, while structural relations between
the systems have been difficult to confirm, there is little
doubt that both are complex, rule-governed systems. Both,
for example, are characterized by multiple form-function
mappings. In language, one syntactic structure can serve
more than one function and multiple forms can express a
single function. Similarly, a sequence of interactive behavior can serve multiple social purposes, and particular
purposes can be expressed in multiple ways. Secondly, both
systems seem to have some universal properties as well as
others that are culture or language specific.
     As for developmental considerations, rapid progress on
both tasks is made early in life, when general cognitive
limitations of the child are presumably at their greatest.
Finally, in both the social and the linguistic spheres, it
appears that the systems to which children are exposed are
somewhat modified and adjusted to the child's capacities
(Ratner and Bruner, 1978; Snow, 1977; Snow, Dubber and

de Blauw, 1980). In the case of syntax, the modifications do
not appear to solve all the problems of acquisition (Newport,
1976; Shatz, 1979). While it is less clear to what extent
the early interactions in which parents engage their children
ease the problem of learning the social rules of the culture,
our "hmm" example at least suggests that early interactions
are not always transparent. Furthermore, the large within-
culture and cross-cultural variations in the degree to which
parents provide direct tuition in social behavior also suggest that the acquisition of social knowledge is not fully
under environmental control.[3] In short, to the extent that
children are confronted at the same point in time in their
general development with sets of complex data that are non-
obvious with regard to the organization of the systems,
then one might expect that children bring to the acquisition
of such systems a common set of devices for dealing with the
input data. While the discovery of such common acquisition
principles, if they exist, is sure to be an arduous task, I
suggest below a few examples of the kinds of commonalities
I am proposing.

At a fairly elementary level, one can draw parallels between
the acquisition stages of the two systems with regard to the
occurrence and role of rote learning. In both the social
and linguistic domains, children are engaged early on in
rather rigid sequences of routinized behavior. There are
several reasons why routines might be crucial to the acquisition of complex systems composed of multi-constituent sequential behavior. For one, the routines may have consequences for the ease of processing in that their practice
may enhance the accessibility of responses in sequence.
Moreover, without requiring much creativity or knowledge on
the part of the child, they foster participation in extended
patterned sequences, providing information on the pacing and
time parameters for standard sequences.

It has been argued that even some of the structural aspects
of the systems to be learned can be demonstrated in series of
routine sequences by varying the units which share privileges
of occurrence within sequences, by transforming elements
systematically, or by varying the occurrence of optional elements (Bruner and Sherwood, 1976; Ratner and Bruner, 1978).
However, the learner must be able to take advantage of such
information displays. In so far as any learning in either
the social or the syntactic spheres takes place on the basis
of such demonstrations, it is likely that both systems recruit
common cognitive procedures for characterizing the displayed
information on the basis of optionality, privileges of occurrence, permissible transformations, and so on. Moreover, it

seems reasonable that the necessary cross-sequence comparisons
in both systems would be subject to the same memory limitations.

It is important to note that this view differs from the
anti-nativist one in that no direct structural analogies
between the two systems are being suggested. Rather, the two
systems are both constrained by their dependence on a set of
common cognitive procedures. There is no stipulation that
all available procedures be utilized for the acquisition of
every complex system, nor is it necessary that there be a
unique procedure for any analysis that must be done. Therefore, a partially unique solution to its overall acquisition
problem may be achieved within each knowledge domain. One
would not predict isomorphic relations between any two complex systems, any more than one would expect isomorphic specific grammars in two languages commonly constrained by principles of universal grammar. As in languages, the only
place where isomorphic properties would be expected is where
there would be a unique solution to a commonly required
analysis. It would be foolhardy to speculate at this time
on the location of such intersections of the two complex
systems being considered here.

Moreover, it is reasonable to suggest there may be uniquely
linguistic procedures among the set of procedures, if all
that is meant by the suggestion is that there exists at least
one procedure which applies only to linguistic data. Such
procedures may exist either because humans do not fully utilize their capacities to create a complete range of possible
complex systems or because those procedures are appropriate
only to structures functioning within one particular system
and no other. This latter possibility is at the heart of
traditional nativist claims, but the question of which procedures are shared by systems should be as interesting as
whether there are ones unique to language. It is the investigation of the former question that might facilitate the
understanding of the acquisition of complex systems generally.

The argument that children have procedures for analysing
complex data in order to construct a solution for an internal problem space has been elegantly presented for the language domain by Karmiloff-Smith (this volume). She suggests
that much of what passes as error in children's speech can
be understood as indications of the internal analyses children perform. She takes as evidence for her position several
cases in which children move from producing forms correct by
adult standards to some consistent alterations of these forms
and then back to more standard ones. A related example of
analytic behavior is reported by Newport (1981). She notes

that deaf children learning sign go through stages of marking
the decomposition of signs into their morphemic elements.
Thus, instead of producing the sign for "cut with a scissors",
which is made by projecting the hand through space while
simultaneously moving the index and middle fingers in a scissoring motion, the children first make the scissoring motion
and then move the hand through space. My suggestion here
is that any complex rule-governed system will require an internal problem space for the accomplishment of acquisition,
and that certain stages in the development of complex systems
will resemble each other in so far as the analytic procedures
utilized in those problem spaces are common ones. Thus, it
would not be surprising to find evidence in the development
of children's social knowledge of a stage at which they do
the equivalent of morphemic analysis. Indeed, the anecdotal
reports of reduplicative phrases like "boy brother" or
"mommy lady" may be attempts to mark separately each of the
relevant dimensions along which distinctions in the child's
social world are drawn.

In summary, then, the commonality of learning principles
view provides the following answers to the questions posed
above. The tasks of acquiring social and syntactic knowledge
are seen as being mainly simultaneous, primarily because the
facts suggest that much of both are learned over the same
time period in development. There is no necessary temporal
relationship between them. Nor is there reason to suppose
that the acquisition of one facilitates the acquisition of
the other. Obviously, learning how to use one's language
appropriately in social situations may be closely tied to
social knowledge, but it is the acquisition of syntax in
particular that is our concern here, and not pragmatic development. Third, the basic proposals of this position grant
the child procedures for analysing data in internal problem
spaces. Hence, the role of the child as a mediator between
the environment and the knowledge system is an important one.
Finally, the existence of direct structural commonalities is
compatible with, but not necessary to the view. While the
rules of the games may be different, the rules for learning
the rules may not be.

6. SUMMARY

Table 1 presents a synopsis of the kinds of answers the four
positions described above give to the questions posed earlier.
I have argued that the weight of the evidence is against an
anti-nativist position which depends on direct structural
commonalities and prior social sophistication to support its

TABLE 1 *Four views of the relation between social interaction and syntax acquisition*

Characteristics	Positions			
	Anti-nativist	Neo-nativist	Process Facilitation	Learning Principles
Concurrent tasks?	No	No	Yes	*
Facilitation?	Yes, Unidirectional	Yes, Bidirectional	Yes, Bidirectional	*
Child's Contribution?	Low	High	High	High
Structural Commonalities?	Yes, Direct	Yes, Partial or Indirect	*	Only if based on learning principles

* For these questions, no one answer is central to the position. For example, structural commonalities are compatible with but not necessary to the process facilitation approach.

stance that the child's contribution is low. By acknowledging a high contribution from the child, the other views cope better with the current evidence on these issues. However, the views differ as to the specific nature of the child's contribution. The neo-nativist position argues for uniquely linguistic mechanisms to account for syntax acquisition. The learning principles view leaves open the question of how many procedures involved in syntax acquisition are uniquely linguistic, while the process view is compatible with both the neonativist and learning principles positions. In the absence of better-specified positions and with little relevant data, it is inappropriate to speculate on the relative worth of the neo-nativist and learning principles views. Indeed, it is possible that they may turn out to be closer to one another in their more elaborated versions.

It is perhaps reasonable to defend the exposition of these various positions despite their deficiencies in specificity and, undoubtedly, veridicality. The fact that interaction as a level of analysis has gained equal status with the sentence and the word in a volume of this sort is indicative of the time and effort being expended on research on interaction and language. Some of that work is motivated by other interests than a desire to explain the acquisition of syntax. But often motivations are so unclear or the relation of such work to syntax acquisition is left so amorphous that erroneous conclusions are easily drawn. I have argued that "if the field of language acquisition is to get beyond the level of phenomenal description of behavior, the theoretical question of relations among kinds of knowledge must be addressed more explicitly" (Shatz, 1978d). The above is an attempt to provide a framework in which such a discussion can proceed.

ACKNOWLEDGEMENTS

The current version of this work was prepared during my tenure as a John Simon Guggenheim Memorial Foundation fellow. Thanks are due to Bolt Beranek and Newman and Harvard University for providing me with support services in Cambridge and to Dedre Gentner for her comments on the manuscript. The research of my colleagues and myself alluded to herein was sponsored by the National Institute of Mental Health, Grant No. 5RO1-MH30996.

NOTES

1   The Pinker and Wexler and Culicover views are distinct from the views (e.g. Schlesinger, 1971) that suggest syn-

tactic structures evolve from semantic structures without
benefit of further innate constraints. Since for these
latter views too, semantic representations may depend
to some extent on interactional experience, then they
appear to be related but non-nativist characterizations
of a social interaction-syntax relation. However, such
views are not presented here because they suffer other
difficulties as viable theories of acquisition (see
Marantz, 1980, for a review).
2 The position that language is a vehicle for providing the
child with a social world view is a popular one in anthropological circles (cf. Harré, 1980; Schieffelin, 1979).
Such a position helps remind us that it was possibly the
enticingly controversial nature of nativist claims, as
well as a kind of ethnocentricity, which led developmental
psycholinguists to consider social knowledge the prior and
language acquisition the mystery to be explained in terms
of it rather than the other way round.
3 See Schieffelin (1979) and S. Joslin (1958) for examples
of direct tuition in different cultures.

REFERENCES

Allen, R. and Shatz, M. (,981). "'What says meow?' The role
of context and linguistic experience in very young children's responses to 'what' questions." Unpublished manuscript, University of Michigan.

Bloom, L., Hood, L and Lightbown, P. (1974). Imitation in
language development: if, when, and why. *Cognitive Psychology* 6, 380-420.

Bloom, L., Rocissano, L. and Hood, L. (1976). Adult-child discourse: developmental interaction between information processing and linguistic knowledge. *Cognitive Psychology* 8,
521-552.

Boskey, M. and Nelson, K. (1980). "Answering unanswerable
questions: the role of imitation." Paper presented at
Fifth Annual Boston University Conference on Language
Development, October, 1980.

Bruner, J.S. (1975). The ontogenesis of speech acts. *Journal
of Child Language* 2, 1-20.

Bruner, J.S. (1977). Early social interaction and language
acquisition. *In* "Studies in Mother-Infant Interaction"
(H.R. Schaffer, ed.). London: Academic Press.

Bruner, J.S. and Sherwood, V. (1976). Early rule structure:
the case of peekaboo. *In* "Play: Its Role in Evolution and
Development" (J.S. Bruner, A. Jolly and K. Sylva, eds).
New York: Basic.

Campbell, R. and Wales, R. (1970). The study of language
acquisition. *In* "New Horizons in Linguistics" (J. Lyons,

ed.). Harmondsworth: Penguin.

Gentner, D. (1981). Are scientific analogies metaphors? *In* "Metaphor: Problems and Perspectives" (D.S. Miall, ed.). Sussex: Harvester Press.

Harré, R. (1980). Colloquium presented at the Graduate School of Education, Harvard University, December, 1980.

Hoff-Ginsberg, E. and Shatz, M. (1981). "Linguistic input and the child's acquisition of language: a critical review". Unpublished manuscript, University of Michigan.

Joslin, S. (1958). "What Do You Say, Dear?" New York: Scholastic Books.

Knapp, D. (1979). "Automatization and the child's acquisition of language". Unpublished dissertation, University of California, San Diego.

Macnamara, J. (1977). From sign to language. *In* "Language Learning and Thought" (J. Macnamara, ed.). New York: Academic Press.

Marantz, A. (1980). "On the acquisition of grammatical relations". Unpublished manuscript, M.I.T.

Newport, E.L. (1976). Motherese: the speech of mothers to young children. *In* "Cognitive Theory" (N. Castellan, D. Pisoni and G. Potts, eds). Vol. II. Hillsdale, NJ: Erlbaum Associates

Newport, E. (1981). Constraints on structure: evidence from American sign language and language learning. *In* "Minnesota Symposium on Child Development, V. 14" (W.A. Collins, ed.). Hillsdale, NJ: Lawrence Erlbaum Associates.

Pinker, S. (In press). A theory of the acquisition of lexical-interpretive grammars. *In* "The Mental Representation of Grammatical Relations" (J. Bresnan, ed.). Cambridge, MA: M.I.T. Press.

Ratner, N. and Bruner, J.S. (1978). Games, social exchange and the acquisition of language. *Journal of Child Language* 5, 391-402.

Rees, N.S. (1975). Imitation and language development: issues and clinical implications. *Journal of Speech and Hearing Disorders* 40, 339-350.

Ryan, J. (1974). Early language development: towards a communicational analysis. *In* "The Integration of a Child into a Social World" (M.P.M. Richards, ed.). Cambridge: Cambridge University Press.

Schieffelin, B. (1979). Getting it together: an ethnographic approach to the study of the development of communicative competence. *In* "Developmental Pragmatics" (E. Ochs and B. Schieffelin, eds.). New York: Academic Press.

Schlesinger, I.M. (1971). Production of utterances and language acquisition. *In* "The Ontogenesis of Grammar" (D. Slobin, ed.). New York: Academic Press.

Shatz, M. (1978a). On the development of communicative understandings: an early strategy for interpreting and responding to messages. *Cognitive Psychology* 10, 271-301.

Shatz, M. (1978b). The relationship between cognitive processes
and the development of communication skills. *In* "Nebraska
Symposium on Motivation, 1977" (C.B. Keasey, ed.). Lincoln:
University of Nebraska Press.

Shatz, M. (1978c). Children's comprehension of question-
directives. *Journal of Child Language* 5, 39-46.

Shatz, M. (1978d). Describing the developing conversationalist:
a review of "Child Discourse". *Contemporary Psychology* 23,
718-720.

Shatz, M. (1979). How to do things by asking: Form-function
pairings in mothers' questions and their relation to children's responses. *Child Development* 50, 1093-1099.

Shatz, M. (in press). On mechanisms of language acquisition:
Can features of the communicative environment account for
development? *In* "Language Acquisition: The State of the
Art" (L. Gleitman and E. Wanner, eds). Cambridge: Cambridge
University Press.

Shatz, M., Allen, R. and Raizman, C. (1981). Show doesn't
lead to tell: The effects of dual input on children's
responses to test questions. (In prep.)

Shatz, M., Bernstein, D. and Shulman, M. (1980). The responses of language disordered children to indirect directives in varying contexts. *Applied Psycholinguistics* 1,
295-306.

Slobin, D. (in press). Universal and particular in the acquisition of language. *In* "Language Acquisition: The State of
the Art" (L. Gleitman and E. Wanner, eds). Cambridge:
Cambridge University Press.

Snow, C.E. (1977). Mothers' speech research: from input to
interaction. *In* "Talking to Children" (C. Snow and C.
Ferguson, eds). Cambridge: Cambridge University Press.

Snow, C., Dubber, C. and deBlauw, A. (1980). "Routines in
mother-child interaction". Unpublished manuscript, Harvard
University.

Wexler, K. and Culicover, P. (1980). "Formal Principles of
Language Acquisition". Cambridge, MA: M.I.T. Press.

THE PRAGMATICS OF ACQUISITION

JEROME S. BRUNER

Department of Psychology and Social Relations, Harvard University, Cambridge, Mass., USA.

1. INTRODUCTION

These past years have seen many changes in the study of
language acquisition. The most recent of these has been
toward pragmatics, particularly the analysis of how mother-
infant interaction shapes and constrains the acquisition
process. To some extent, the shift has led to certain con-
fusions and imprecisions, but even the most formalistic and
syntactically orientated among us would not deny that the
new pragmatic emphasis has been useful. Studies of speech
acts and their acquisition, of developing sensitivity to
presupposition, of deixis, of repair, etc. have all brought
a new liveliness to the enterprise. A functional dimension
has been added, and while perhaps interest has broadened to
concern with communication rather than with formal language
alone, the change is overdue.
  Yet difficulties have arisen in the train of this new
research. Key concepts have often been left fuzzily defined
and discovery procedures for instantiating key concepts in
speech samples have, for their part, been equally fuzzy. Two
good examples are "intention" and "mutual knowledge," both
of them central to Grice's account of how occasion meanings
are established. It is not that people who work on pragmatic questions are slack or unmindful of the difficulties.
Rather, at this stage of the game, the concepts seem inherently difficult to make precise either empirically or
formally. It has even been claimed that the trouble is not
a temporary result of working on a new frontier, but rather
inheres in the nature of the pragmatics itself. Grice (1975)
has suggested that it is in the nature of pragmatics that
its principles do not have binding entailment, but can be
expressed only in the form of maxims — as in his own

Cooperative Principle. It is still difficult to know whether
Grice is correct and whether, if he is, linguistics will be
disarrayed by having one of its branches, pragmatics, more,
let us say, like anthropology than like formal logic. Perhaps linguistics will have to live with an assemblage of
three parts as in the nursery rhyme — how ladies ride, how
gentlemen ride, and how farmers ride. I am not sure that
syntax goes daintily at a trot nor that semantics gallops,
but I *am* sure that pragmatics goes like hobbledehoy!

I would like to suggest that parts of the confusion through
which we are living comes neither from the inherent nature of
pragmatics nor from its new-found exuberance. There appear
to be two difficulties besetting us that are historical
rather than essential. One of these derives from the uncertain relation between the rules governing sentences, i.e.
grammar, and the rules governing discourse. In so far as
pragmatics is concerned with context, presupposition, deixis,
and the like, its proper data base is discourse and its rules
will be discourse rules. Yet most linguistic description is
based not upon discourse or upon conversational exchange, but
upon sentence parts, the products of grammatical analysis.
We tend therefore to formulate our discourse-related rules
in terms of sentence based grammatical concepts that were
constructed to be as discourse independent as possible. And
so we ask questions about, say, the role of such sentence
features as passivization, clefting, article choice, lexical
selection, or whatever. And this habitual procedure in linguistics has paid off handsomely — but only up to a point.

It is plainly important to know what functions are served
by sentence parts in given contexts — that a variety of grammatical rules will yield well formed strings that can look
after the foregrounding intentions of a speaker, for example.
But this may be only a small part of what pragmatics might be
looking for, small both in the ordinary sense and in the special sense that it might be the small detail of pragmatics.
For sentence parts defined grammatically are the small detail
of speech. Keeping to the linguistic categories of sentence
grammar, the pragmatician may in fact cut himself off from
such discourse issues as, for example, under what conditions
one says something as compared to staying silent, what are
the essential and other conditions on various classes of
utterances in different contexts. Indeed, it is even arguable that a full specification of the priveleges of occurrence
of certain grammatical transformations is not possible without
an account of discourse setting. I have in mind, of course,
Wason's (1965) demonstration of what he has called "contexts
of plausible denial." In any case, what I would want to say

is that if the pragmatician must depend in his trade upon grammatical categories that boast a high degree of context independence, he is going to generate rules that may be even weaker than what he would do if he had a linguistics of discourse to fall back upon.

Fillmore (1977) comes close to what I have in mind with his concept of *perspective*. He distinguishes between the "nuclear elements" in a sentence and the "perspective" produced by their assembly. The function of perspective is to alter "salience." In sentences containing the verb *to hit*, one can bring into salience either the agent and the affected object (1) or the agent and the instrument (2).

1) I hit the fence with the stick.
2) I hit the stick against the fence.

He asks not only about the devices that one can use to bring something into a desired perspective, but what are the conditions that lead to perspective alteration. This is in much the same spirit as Keenan, Schieffelin, and Platt's (1976) discussion of topic as discourse dependent, and their effort to delineate the rules for what they call "questions of immediate concern."

Let me mention, finally, a second historical difficulty of pragmatics. Pragmatics, for all its linguistic pedigree, probably can never be an exclusively linguistic concern. It is too rooted in principles of human action and interaction. As Fillmore puts it, "whenever we pick up a word or phrase, we automatically drag along with it the larger context or framework in terms of which the word or phrase we have chosen has an interpretation," (1977, p. 74). The "context or framework" is almost certainly broader than language. And that creates a second horn for the dilemma of pragmatics. Unfortunately, social psychology has not been much concerned (until very recently) with the relation between action, intention, belief, etc. on the one side, and language use on the other.

So it may be the case, alas, that pragmatics is being hindered on the one side by its too close association with a linguistics dominated by ideas of context-free grammars, and by its lack of support from the other side, from social psychology that, until recently, left that most social of human activities, language, exclusively to the linguists. Perhaps if pragmatics took heart, it could lure linguistics toward social psychology and social psychology toward linguistics. I propose to try something of that order in what follows.

2. A VIEW OF COMMUNICATIVE INTERACTION

I shall limit myself to the specialized problems that arise
in adult-child interaction, though I know they are asymmetrical in terms of the power and knowledge and skill of
the participants. I do this because I am principally interested in the early stages of acquisition where the asymmetry
is very marked, at least at the start.

First with respect to the general motivation to communicate,
I think that it is there from the start. That much I think
is clear from the findings of Stern (1977) and of Bateson
(1975) on turn taking and gestural and vocal phrasing. This
is very far from saying that linguistic intent is there from
the start. We know precious little about how the child-
adult pair go from their spontaneous, mutually contingent
exchanges to something like the Gricean cycle where both
parties are using non-natural or conventional means to communicate an intent and each knows that the other knows that
they are doing so with this in mind. The interested reader
is referred to Denkel's (1978) excellent account of the philosophical dilemmas involved in tracing this progress. All that
we need note here — and we shall return to the point later —
is that the progress appears to depend at the outset upon the
child learning the appropriate pragmatics of indicating,
requesting, or whatever, before ever he learns grammatical
forms, and that it may well be that the pragmatics is constitutive with respect to his grammar. That is to say, he
may learn grammar much as he learns a tool kit — the latter
to get things done with things, the former to get things done
with words.

I think that it is possible to say a good deal more than
that there is an initial motive or "push" to communicate.
Indeed, there appears from the start to be a two-step differentiation in this early communicative push. The first is
a differentiation, a very critical one, between communication
to achieve *joint attention* with another and communication for
achieving *joint action* with another. This is basically the
differentiation between what Halliday (1975) calls the mathetic and the pragmatic functions of communication. I find it
very difficult to believe, for reasons I shall relate, that
this differentiation is not well on its way by the sixth or
seventh month by which time the child is able to comprehend
the significance of and to follow another person's line of
regard. But more of this presently.

Once the child begins to construct a manageable representation of events in the world, he begins to distinguish *actual*
from *possible* states and events. The referential activity
that constitutes the greater part of his achievement of joint

attention can now encompass possible objects — "missing" objects that are not in their canonical place, playful imaginary objects, etc. With respect to communicating for establishing joint action, the child now is able to establish play routines involving variations on the possible. Both the mathetic and the pragmatic functions become much richer in the range of events they can encompass in child-adult communication.

At roughly the same time, during the second half of the first year, the infant also begins to make a distinction between the extrinsic or "message" function of his communicative acts and their "affiliative" or regulatory function — that aspect of communication that has to do with maintaining a transactional relationship with another. This, of course, is a crucial distinction for the mastery of "speech acts" in the sense that it involves mastering the distinction necessary for grasping the preparatory, essential and sincerity felicity-conditions on utterance.

One may ask — probably in vain! — when the push to communication becomes, properly speaking, an intention. When one calls something intentional (rather than "pushed" or "driven," say), what is implied is: (a) persistent directionality, in which (b) alternative or optional means are deployed (c) to achieve an end which (d) is foreseen and which (e) when reached terminates the action. And (f) when the end foreseen is not achieved directly, there is repair and substitution of means. How much more has to be stipulated about consciousness is always a moot point. The full complexity of the specification is brilliantly set forth in Anscombe's monograph (1957). What is much more to the point is that there be an opportunity for the members of a communicating pair to begin responding to each other's signalled intentions — regardless of how conscious the signaller may be. For this is what creates the conditions for conventionalization of the means of communication. Let me turn to that next.

Conventionalized procedures for exchanging messages of different levels of differentiation begin to develop very early. Even early crying patterns are quickly conventionalized, we know from Pratt's (1978) work. The mother from the start treats the child's cries as if they were intended to be more or less particular messages. One of the first changes in the child's crying pattern is short pausing during which he scans to see whether anything is happening. Where things do happen, the child gradually reduces cry intensity and also develops characteristic modes of crying for different contexts and to express different needs. The

mother responds to the child by continuing to read his cries
as if intended communications, and then imputing intentions
to them to which she responds. This is a transactional process of convention-making. It is not surprising then that
Ainsworth and Bell (1974) show that mothers with the greatest
responsive sensitivity to their children during the first
quarter of their first year are the ones with the most linguistically advanced children at the end of the fourth quarter.
And later on as well, Cross (1978) finds that children whose
mothers are most finely tuned to their baby talk are the ones
who progress fastest linguistically.

We know from the past decade's research that adult speech
to infants is highly orderly and highly correlated with the
infant's level of speech (e.g. Snow and Ferguson, 1977). The
regularity of this relationship is greatly aided by the establishment of *formats* for interaction between mother and
child, formats with a high degree of constraint on variability. There is no limit aside from capacity upon the content of the format; they may be attention sharing formats,
request formats, pretend play, whatever. A format provides
a means for structuring and conventionalizing the exchange
of messages about intentions. Insofar as a format becomes an
"expectable way" of doing things together, it provides a
basis for establishing shared presuppositions as well as
ways for calibrating one's messages.

Above all, a format is a device for framing communication,
for locating it in a particular piece of social reality to
which intentions and conventions relate. By cutting down on
the number of degrees of freedom with which mother and child
must deal in communicating with each other, it probably does
a great deal by way of increasing successful exchanges and
cutting down frustration. It can, therefore, provide an excellent test frame for trying out new forms that might place
too great a strain on the child's capacities if they occurred
in less familiar settings. In a study by Ninio and Bruner
(1978) for example, the first signalling of the given-new
distinction (by intonation) occurred in a highly familiar
naming format before it was carried over into less established settings. Similarly, Fausta Campos (1979) has shown
that new items in the child's lexicon may first appear in a
particular format and remain there for some time before being
extended to other contexts.

A format, of course, is quintessentially transactional: what
one party does is contingent on what the other has done and
what each anticipates the other will do. By being small in
compass and familiar in form, the format allows the child to
use his processing capacities for new combinations rather

than for dealing with the unfamiliar (cf. Shatz, 1978). By
having a more or less fixed sequential structure, moreover,
the format provides the child with a sense of the direction
of the discourse, what Vogt (1978) has called *sens*. The
child is enabled to steer discourse and to learn to correct
and repair his own part in the discourse when he fails to
achieve his end.

3. THE LANGUAGE ASSISTANCE SYSTEM (LAS)

Eventually the child transcends the props and formats that
scaffold his early communicative acts. Rather than having
his formats imposed by the environment (and particularly by
his mother) he must now impose formats on communicative situations himself. Imposing formats constitutes, of course,
learning how to perform speech acts in a fashion that as-
sures that there is uptake of the child's message by interlocutors in his environment. A speech act, on this view,
comes into being once the child is able to internalize and
then generalize a format. Initially, then, speech act mastery is, so to speak, from the outside in. The transfer of
initiative from adult to child is gradual and, as research
of the last decade has shown, extraordinarily well ordered.
It is this ordered pattern of transfer of initiative that I
wish to call the Language Assistance System, or LAS.
    The first thing to note about the adult role in this system
is the adult's willingness to share or even hand over control
to the child once he has learned to fulfill the conditions on
speech. However obvious this may seem, it is a *sine qua non*
of the adult's role in the system. In point of fact, it can
be shown in at least two ways to be quite a non-universal
feature of tutorial support systems - by its absence in some
and its late flowering in others. It is certainly *not* a
feature of the form of tutorial by which adults teach children the moral precepts of the culture, and when there is a
shift toward greater permissiveness, it is even called a
revolution. Secondly, and for all that four-year-olds modu-
late their speech in a fashion appropriate for two-year-olds
(Shatz and Gelman, 1973), there is evidence that indicates
that older children can help younger children solve practical
problems, but they do not seem to be able to hand over or
even properly demonstrate the skill required for the younger
child to do it on his own (McLane, 1980). Ease of "handover"
may well be inherent in the reciprocal or dialogic nature of
speech, in the sense that speech in its nature requires each
party to take their turn, and a turn of one's own means an
opportunity to share control. Whatever it is, it is ubiqui-
tous from the start in discourse.

The most striking evidence, of course, comes from the work, already cited, of Stern (1977), Bateson (1975), Trevarthen (1980), Brazelton and Tronick (1980), and Brazelton, Koslowski and Main (1974). As soon as the infant is aroused and ready to communicate, the adult hands over a turn and shapes her behaviour to conform with the contour of the exchange. They will even take over the "lexicon" of gestures and expressions that the infant brings to the exchange and, as Trevarthen points out, at the early stage of communication, adult imitation of the child is perhaps more in evidence than the reverse. There is also a marked tendency for the initiative in certain game-like sequences involving signalling (like peekaboo and various exchange games like give-and-take) for the initiative in starting to shift from adult to child, with the adult often acting as a scaffold to assure continuity in the child's emerging control (e.g. Bruner, 1978; Ratner and Bruner, 1978).

A second interesting feature of the system is the extent to which, from the start, it is based upon the assignment or attribution of communicative intent. I think it is probably an extension of an old point made by Lorenz (1965) that any species treats all species as if they were members of their own species. For even during the first hours in the life of a child, the mother treats his cries and gestures as indicating some intended message (Macfarlane, 1977). And the mother, moreover, assigns meaning to the message in the light of the prevailing context, and as Shatz (1978) has shown, the mother's response to the child is based on the action context. The obvious way to sum all this up is to say that adults treat children before their speech is fully developed as if they were trying to operate by the rules governing fully developed speakers. But for all that, as we know from Cross's (1978) comprehensive review of the literature, the complexity of mother's speech is closely correlated or "fine tuned" to the level of complexity of the child's speech. There is ample evidence that mothers also update their expectancies with respect to the child's speech so that once he has made a step forward linguistically, regressions are not acceptable. We do not accept a "bad day" in the child's language as we do, say, in his management of frustration.

LAS has, of course, a "modelling" feature, but it is not necessarily based on the expectation that the child will imitate adult speech. Rather, the adult models by a system of exaggerating or highlighting distinctions in the language. As Garnica (1977) notes, there is an exaggeration of stress and marking to highlight phrase markers or high-information-yield elements in a sentence, etc. In this respect, it would

seem that LAS is closely tuned to any innate readiness of
the Language Acquisition Device, LAD, to recognize grammatical distinctions.

Similarly in dialogue, the mother "models" such crucial
requirements as topic maintenance by filling in for the child
when he is unable to maintain topic, until finally fewer and
fewer maintenance "turnabouts" by the mother are required
(Kaye and Charney, 1980). A turnabout is a relevant response
made to the previous speaker's utterance that "turns it
around and sends it back" for response by the other. At the
end of the second year, mothers exceed their infants seven-
fold in such turnabouts, yet a couple of years later they
are about even.

In case it seems as if the mother is "consciously" acting
as a language tutor for a good part of her time — and
mothers, when asked, say they do not feel that is what they
are up to — I would like to mention one point, a suggestion
of Goffman's (1979). The mother, rather, sees her role as a
socializer, as somebody trying to get her baby to be "civi-
lized." Language lessons are a fall-out from this other
function. And indeed, when one looks closely at mothers'
roles, that is not a bad description. Our own studies of
the ontogenesis of request (Bruner, Ratner and Roy, 1981),
for example, show our mothers to be far more preoccupied with
the child learning the preparatory, essential and sincerity
felicity-conditions on request than his learning the correct
syntactical forms for their utterances. The mothers, moreover, are particularly occupied with developing formats in
which the child can understand the conditions on his utterances, and it is not surprising that Reeder's (1979) $2\frac{1}{2}$- and
$3\frac{1}{2}$-year-old children were able readily to recognize formats
indicating offers and those indicating requests. As Cross
(1978) notes, mothers are tuned to the child's "general
psychological comprehension" of situations, not to his grammatical competence.

Let me say a word specifically about the child's progress
toward imposing formats rather than, so to speak, simply
being imposed on by them. If you follow the same children
over a period of time, you find that there is an interesting
extension and transformation of formats. What first surfaces as peekaboo, resurfaces later as a game of hiding and
finding objects with many of the same expressions and segment markers. Later still it reappears — after months of
absence — as a more formal hide-and-seek, and still later
as a game of guessing in which hand an object has been hidden. Characteristically, this early play involves role exchanges and object substitution in various established rou-

tines. In the process, there is negotiation over agency,
action, object, locus, instrument and other referents of
case grammatical forms (Bruner and Sherwood, 1976; Ratner
and Bruner, 1978). It is an odd way to put it, but the
child seems to be abstracting the arguments of action in carrying out his exchanges before he has mastered the grammatical case forms for expressing them. This must, as I have
argued elsewhere (Bruner, 1981), give the child rich cues in
the real world about distinctions he will have to master in
the world of speech. Something comparable seems to be happening in the case of other grammatical distinction yet-to-
be-made. One striking example is aspect, or perhaps one
should call it "proto-tense." As Farwell (1977) and deLemos
(1979) have noted, goal and action toward a goal are early
abstracted and generalized across formats — in play formats,
ones involving eating, bathing, etc. The child's sensitivity
to initiation of action, completion, continuation, resump-
tion, deviation, etc. is signalled by such expressions as
there, all-gone, uh-oh, more, again, and, as deLemos has
shown, even in the adoption of a postposition in Portuguese,
-bo for completion.

Let me now turn to two examples of acquisition where the
role of pragmatics is rather clear in detail. This will
enable me to fill in the rough picture I have been sketching.

4. INDICATING AND REQUESTING AS EXAMPLES

I choose indicating and requesting as examples because they
represent, as already noted, the most primitive differentiation in the infant's communicative system. They serve to
illustrate in a more connected way the points I have tried
to make in the preceding sections.

Indicating, as Ninio and Bruner (1978), Ninio (1980), and
Bruner (1981) have put it, involves a conventional procedure
in which one party is attempting to bring a topic to common
attention with another. It is technically difficult to
establish "when" indicating starts because of the asymmetry
of the early indicating situation. Collis and Schaffer (1975)
have indicated, for example, that the mother spends a good
deal of time following the child's line of regard, using her
hypotheses about where the child's eye lights to shape her
comments on what she takes to be the "topic" of his attention.
There is nothing conventional or "non-natural" about indicating the target of one's attention by direction of gaze, nor
could anybody say for sure whether the child's looking is
intended to let the mother know what he has at the focus of

attention. In like vein, Scaife and Bruner (1975) have
shown that children begin following the line of regard of
adults at about five or six months and are well into doing
so habitually by a year. The anomaly in all this is that
the two partners, adult and child, gradually build a convention by exploiting expectancies built up on the basis of
quite natural and non-intentional indicating cues — orientation, line of regard, physical manipulation, etc. The
child's exclamation of notice, often some variant of *da*
which may or may not be conventional, is very early uttered
in the expectancy that the adult will in fact look at the
target of the infant's line of regard. And the mother's
first efforts at naming are geared into where the child
happens to be looking.

By the time pointing appears on the scene — around the
end of the first year — there is a highly elaborated system of indicating already in operation, involving distinctive
if idiosyncratic intonation patterns to distinguish indicating and requesting (e.g. Halliday, 1975), such manoeuvers
as "handing" an object toward a viewer, etc. Where we have
been lucky enough in a few cases to observe the onset of
pointing in children being followed longitudinally, one
gets the impression that pointing appears not simply as an
indicating gesture, but as a *marking procedure* in the clas-
sic linguistic sense. Pointing was reserved for three
classes of "referent": old objects in a new context, new
and especially vivid objects, and in some way not easily
specified, hypothetical objects or uncertain loci. One of
our subjects, Richard, pointed upward and pronounced his
idiosyncratic word for "bird" sitting on the floor quietly
after dinner, after he had spent a day out of doors quite
excited by flights of magpies. It is difficult to know, of
course, just what role the marked-unmarked distinction
plays in such early communication, or whether it is in fact
the genuine distinction that is being made. Yet it is striking that pointing in these early appearances appears to be
principally given over to this end and only later becomes
extended in use, as for example in indicating a requested
object, a quite late use of pointing.

Indicating by lexical means is, of course, ordinarily
part of an exchange process — the familiar pair of adult
dominated games, "Where's the X?" and "What's that?" Like
most adult interventions, it is introduced very soon after
the child is able both to point and to comprehend semanti-
city in words used by the parent. It is interesting for the
light it throws on LAS that when the child begins to use
non-standard lexical items, adults very often imitate them

in attempting to indicate something to the child — handing
over even before the child has achieved correct forms.

Ninio and I (1978) have described in detail the rich
interactions that attend the later developing of "naming"
and the building of a lexicon that occurs in "book-reading"
formats. Mothers typically establish exchange sequences,
in this case an initial attentional vocative which the
child fulfills by directing attention to the object, then
the familiar "What's that?" which is then followed by adult
naming if the child does not succeed. It is, of course, an
artificial or at least a "pedagogical" procedure, but it is
typical of long-lived formats in the sense that the mother
holds to it very steadily over months as the child becomes
better able to meet the standard requirements imposed. Each
time he makes a step forward, the mother raises the criteria by which she judges adequacy. And as the format becomes routinized by the child's increasing skill, the
mother adds elements to it. So that, for example, when she
wishes to signal to him that she knows that he knows certain
words, she changes the intonation contour on her "What's
that?" from rising to falling. Or once the child becomes
letter perfect in being able to name a particular whole
object, she will now add a topic-comment addendum to her
cycle, asking after the correct naming by the child, "And
what's the doggy doing?" with a terminal rising intonation,
indicating that she is again after the new (rising) as compared with the given (falling). And one then also begins
to see the entry of "preparatory conditions" on indicating,
very reminiscent of the "questions of immediate concern"
discussed by Keenan, Schieffelin, and Platt (1978) — "You
know what?"

The ontogenesis of requesting goes through a similar
pattern of development, except that in certain crucial
respects it has an even stronger pragmatic context, for
requesting, after all, requires not only that somebody
turn their attention toward your preselected target, but
that they do something about it in your behalf. There is,
consequently, more emphasis on meeting what I referred to
earlier as the affiliative conditions, maintaining the
right relations with the requestee. But in the main,
there is the same kind of differentiation occurring, and
again with the same sort of support system established between the child and parent.

Because a request is more costly for the requestee than
simply turning his attention to a matter of concern to
somebody else, there is a great deal of early emphasis on
its so-called speech-act conditions. For unlike indicating

(which runs on a surprisingly free track) requesting demands
careful preparation (Garvey, 1977), as well as the usual requirements of sincerity and relevance. (The essential condition seems to give little trouble, save to philosophers!)
To our surprise (Bruner, Ratner, and Roy, 1981), there were
even some conditions that speech-act theory had not quite got
round to. There is, for example, an implicit requirement
that requests meet a disclosure condition. We discovered
this when one of our young subjects started developing a
"successive guidance" strategy for dealing with requests
that were too complicated for him to articulate in advance
of the action required of the requestee - e.g. *Get up*. (R)
Go there. (R) *Open door*. (R) *Get telephone*. The mother in-
sisted that she must know the goal in advance.

But in so far as requesting involves not only indicating
that you want, but indicating *what* you want, it also creates
extraordinarily complex situations in which the child must
combine the two basic formats, with indicating being subordinated to requesting. These combinations often involve
highly productive manoeuvers. Children, for example, often
want something that is not in sight, and unless there is
some highly familiar routine involved from which the mother
can infer the target of their request, the child must use
either a lexeme or some even more complicated means to
manage the remote reference. In these cases, it is very
striking the extent to which the child leans on the presup-
positional structure built up in past encounters as a basis
for using deixis as a source of reference, with the willing
collaboration of the parent. A good example of this is the
use of canonical locus as a means for indicating an object
that is desired: indicating the place where it is expected
ordinarily to be while also signalling request for it.
Children in these predicaments behave much as the children
in the Deutsch and Pechmann studies (1980) on referential communication.   They give as few indications as needed to get
a response from the adult that they understand or that they
need more guidance. It is by no means the case that the
child learns to handle such complex requests by one utterance, so to speak. They early on learn that they can count
on the adult guiding them as to what more information is
needed. That, I think, is the heart of the negotiatory process that is so prominent a feature of the Language Assistance System.

I must comment finally on how little "language teaching"
goes on in requesting — in contrast to the indicating
mode where there are games and forms of "picture reading"
principally designed to teach words. And there were no

instances at all in our studies of efforts to get the child
to say what he wanted to in grammatically "correct" form.
But then our children were only two when we finished. What
we were observing instead was a great deal of practical
teaching of scripts, in the sense of Schank and Abelson
(1977). There is also, as noted earlier, a good deal of
perspective making and of saliencing at a primitive level
not requiring the grammatical procedures that Fillmore (1977)
mentions in this connection. And particularly with respect
to requests, one encounters the kind of discourse constraint
that eventually leads the child to appreciate the cultural
constraints on requests (in the manner of Goody, 1978).
All of this suggests that the child is indeed learning a
heavily pragmatic set of discourse rules well before he can
appreciate a grammar of sentence parts. It is as if the
dynamics of language, in the sense of its *sens* or direction
in speech acts, is being learned first in some preliminary
way to guide the child in his construction of utterance.

This leaves quite moot the question whether in any way the
rules of discourse determine or are constitutive of the
rules of grammar that, in time, the child learns to use in
producing and comprehending sentences. I do not think we
can answer the question yet. All that we can say is that
the pragmatic base, whose acquisition seems to be made possible by the Language Assistance System, appears to be a
necessary condition for the operation of the Language Acquisition Device, whatever form it may eventually turn out to
have (see Bruner, 1981). My own intuition is that there
will turn out to be some of the same duality of patterning
between discourse rules and sentence grammar as there is between sentence grammar and the lexicon or between lexemes and
phonemes — complicated, highly top-down, difficult to
characterize, but fruitful to study.

REFERENCES

Ainsworth, M.D.S. and Bell, S.M. (1974). Mother-infant
    interaction and the development of competence. *In* "The
    Growth of Competence". (K. Connally and J.S. Bruner, eds).
    New York and London: Academic Press.
Anscombe, G.E.M. (1957). "Intention". Ithaca: Cornell
    University Press.
Bateson, M.C. (1975). Mother-infant exchanges: the epi-
    genesis of conversational interaction. *In* (R. Rieber
    and D. Aaronson, eds). *Annals of the N.Y. Acad. Sci.* <u>263</u>.
Brazelton, T.B., Koslowski, B. and Main, M. (1974). The
    origins of reciprocity: the early mother-infant inter-

actions. *In* "Origins of Behavior: The Effect of the Infant on its Caregiver" (M. Lewis and L. Rosenblum, eds). New York: Wiley.

Brazelton, T.B. and Tronick, E. (1980). Preverbal communication between mothers and infants. *In* "The Social Basis of Language and Thought" (D. Olson, ed.). New York: Norton.

Bruner, J.S. (1978). Learning how to do things with words. *In* "Human Growth and Development" (J. Bruner and A. Garton, eds). Oxford: Oxford University Press.

Bruner, J.S. (1981). The social context of language acquisition. *Lang. & Comm.* 2 (to be published).

Bruner, J.S. and Sherwood, V. (1976). Early rule structure: the case of "Peekaboo". *In* "Life Sentences: Aspects of the Social Role of Language" (R. Harre, ed.). London & New York: Wiley.

Bruner, J.S., Ratner, N. and Roy, C. (1981). The beginnings of request. *In* "Children's Language" (K. Nelson, ed.), Vol. 3. New York: Gardner Press.

Campos, F. (1979). The acquisition of *porque* in Brazilian Portuguese. PhD Thesis, University of Campinas, Dept. of Linguistics.

Collis, G. and Schaffer, H.R. (1975). Synchronization of attention in mother-infant pairs. *Journal of Child Psychology and Psychiatry* 16, 315-20.

Cross, A.G. (1978). Mother-infant interaction in the study of child language development. PhD Dissertation, University of Melbourne.

DeLemos, C. (1979). Prelinguistic games and the development of proto-aspectual "words". Paper presented at the conference "Beyond Description in Child Language", Nijmegen, June 1979.

Denkel, A. (1977). Communication and meaning. D. Phil. Thesis, Oxford University.

Deutsch, W. and Pechmann, T. (1980). Form and function in the development of reference. Paper presented at the XXII International Congress of Psychology, Leipzig, July 1980.

Farwell, C.B. (1977). The primacy of *goal* in the child's description of motion and location. *Papers and Reports on Child Language Development* (9th Chld. Lang. Forum), Dept. Linguistics, Stanford University, Stanford, 1977.

Fillmore, C.J. (1977). The case for case reopened. *In* "Syntax and Semantics" (P. Cole and J. Sadock, eds), Vol. 8. New York and London: Academic Press.

Garnica, O. (1977). Some prosodic and paralinguistic features of speech to young children. *In* "Talking to Children: Language Input and Acquisition" (C. Snow and C.A. Ferguson, eds). Cambridge: Cambridge University Press.

Garvey, C. (1977). "Play". Cambridge, MA: Harvard University Press.

Goffman, E. (1979). Personal communication.

Goody, E. (1978). "Questions and Politeness". Cambridge: Cambridge University Press.

Grice, H.P. (1975). Logic and conversation. *In* "Syntax and Semantics" (P. Cole and J. Morgan, eds), Vol. 3. London and New York: Academic Press.

Halliday, M.A.K. (1975). "Learning How to Learn". London: Arnold.

Kaye, K. and Charney, R. (1980). How mothers maintain "dialogue" with two-year-olds. *In* "The Social Contract of Language and Thought" (D. Olson, ed.). New York: Norton.

Keenan, E.O., Schieffelin, B.B. and Platt, M. (1978). Questions of immediate concern. *In* "Questions and Politeness" (E. Goody, ed.). Cambridge: Cambridge University Press.

Lorenz, K. (1965). "Evolution and Modification of Behavior". Chicago: University of Chicago Press.

Macfarlane, A. (1977). "The Psychology of Childbirth". Cambridge, MA: Harvard University Press.

McLane, J. (1980). Personal communication.

Ninio, A. (1980). Ostensive definition in vocabulary teaching. *Journal of Child Language* 7, 565-574.

Ninio, A. and Bruner, J.S. (1978). The achievement and antecedents of labelling. *Journal of Child Language* 5, 1-15.

Pratt, C. (1978). The socialization of crying. D. Phil. Thesis, Oxford University.

Ratner, N. and Bruner, J.S. (1978). Games, social exchange, and the acquisition of language. *Journal of Child Language* 5, 391-401.

Reeder, K. (1979). The early recognition of offers and requests. (Privately circulated.)

Scaife, M. and Bruner, J.S. (1975). The capacity for joint visual attention in the infant. *Nature* 253, 265-266.

Schank, R.C. and Abelson, R.P. (1977). "Scripts, Plans, Goals, and Understanding". Hillsdale, NJ: Erlbaum Associates.

Shatz, M. (1978). On the development of communicative understandings. *Cognitive Psychology* 10, 271-301.

Shatz, M. and Gelman, R. (1973). The development of communication skills: modification in the speech of young children as a function of the listener. *Monographs of the Society for Research in Child Development* 38.

Snow, C. and Ferguson, C.A. (1977). "Talking to Children: Language Input and Acquisition". Cambridge: Cambridge University Press.

Stern, D. (1977). "The First Relationship: Mother and Infant". Cambridge, MA: Harvard University Press.

Trevarthen, C. (1980). The foundations of intersubjectivity: the development of interpersonal and cooperative understanding in infants. *In* "The Social Basis of Language and Thought" (D. Olson, ed.). New York: Norton.

Vogt, C. (1978). Por una pragmatica da representacao. *Proc. III Encuntro Natl. Ling.*, Rio de Janeiro.

Wason, P.C. (1965). The contexts of plausible denial. *Journal of Verbal Learning and Verbal Behavior* 4, 7-11.

INTERACTIONAL PROCESSES IN THE CHILD'S CONSTRUCTION OF LANGUAGE

CLAUDIA DE LEMOS

State University of Campinas, Brazil.

1. INTRODUCTION

In spite of the large amount of recent research on the pragmatics of language acquisition, the problem of relating
early mastery of social interaction to the processes whereby
the child acquires the semantics and the morphosyntactic
systems of his language remains virtually untouched. It
seems to me that those difficulties, i.e., the difficulties
faced by transactional theories on language acquisition in
providing evidence for *continuity* from pre-linguistic development and the child's later linguistic abilities, must be
related to theoretical problems concerning the "status" of
entities or units such as interactional formats and utterances or their formal representations.
  As posed by Bretherton and Bates (in press):

  the case for continuity would be satisfied if it could be
  shown that behavioral and organizational skills which
  an infant has acquired in one period of development are
  used in the construction of more complex behavioral and
  organizational skills later (op.cit.: 3).

It is, consequently, plausible to say that any statement on
continuity made within the framework of transactional
theories on language acquisition are ultimately dependent
on demonstrating that some of the properties, rules or processes characteristic of *interactional formats* are, at least
partially, constitutive or determinative of properties,
rules or processes involved in building up utterances or,
more generally, in operating with linguistic units.
  Given the relationship holding between theories on language acquisition and linguistic theories, it follows from
the above considerations that transactional theories on

language acquisition are ultimately dependent on demonstrating
that some of the properties, rules or processes characteristic of *interactional formats* are, at least partially, constitutive or determinative of properties, rules or processes
involved in building up utterances or, more generally, in
operating with linguistic units.

Given the relationship holding between theories on language
acquisition and linguistic theories, it follows from the
above considerations that transactional theories on language
acquisition are only compatible with discourse theories,
namely, theories which take the discourse and not the sentence,
as a basic unit. The need for considering discourse as an
operational space in accounting for some of the child's
linguistic skills has been pointed out recently by authors
such as Shugar (1977), Keenan, Schieffelin and Platt (1979)
and, in this volume, by Karmiloff-Smith.

Moreover, the points I have just made could be taken as
being also relevant to explain why speech-act theories and
even Gricean conversational postulates have not really set
the grounds for establishing the necessary evidence for continuity between pre-linguistic communicative development
and the child's later linguistic skills. In spite of dealing with questions concerning discourse roles and the interpretation of utterances in discourse units, their views
seem far to provide the basis for relating interactional
formats to discourse processes and discourse processes to
the construction of utterances.

The data to be presented and discussed attempt to demonstrate the possibility of looking at interactional formats
as at least partially constitutive of the processes whereby
the child acquires linguistic units and operate with them
in their way to utterance-construction. Though being mainly
concerned with the acquisition of proto-aspectual markers
in Brazilian Portuguese, I hope to provide some evidence on
how the semantic and morphological "status" of those markers,
as well as their combinatorial or syntactic potentiality in
early child speech, seem to result from the child's operating with formats as basic units, in a process which could
be described as involving both intra-format and inter-format
operations.

2. THE PRAGMATIC ROUTES OF COMPLETION MARKERS

Studies on the acquisition of Brazilian Portuguese have
shown that the emergence of tense-forms is governed by very
strict *linguistic* (semantic) and *extra-linguistic* restrictions (cf. de Lemos, 1975).   Indeed, perfective tense

forms would first appear with accomplishment verbs and exclusively as markers of completion of the child's own actions,
while perfective tense forms of achievement verbs, such as
break, fall down would occur in contexts where the child
seems to be attending to changes of state resultative of
unobserved processes. As for progressive forms, they first
occurred only with *activity verbs*, such as *jump, dance* in
contexts where the child was calling attention for the activity he was engaged in. Moreover, imperfective tense forms
which emerged much later, during the first half of the
child's third year, occurred at first only with state and
activity verbs in imaginary contexts such as pretend-play
and story telling formats. Similar restrictions on the
emergence of perfective and imperfective tense forms have
been described by Antinucci and Miller (1976) as holding in
the acquisition of verbal inflections of Italian.

The extra-linguistic restrictions just mentioned showing
the close relationship between *format-types* and the emergence of verbal inflections, appeared to me as providing
enough motivation for attempting to reconstruct the pragmatic routes of verbal inflections or aspectual markers in
pre-linguistic or social interaction. Furthermore, Bruner's
mention of a completive or terminal marking as the most
usual form of signalling in intention-oriented interactions
between the mother and the infant and, mainly, his view on
it as possibly serving "as an initial step in primitive
semantic segmentation, the forming of units", seemed to
point towards the heuristic or even cognitive function communicative formats can have in the child's development
(Bruner, 1975; 3).

Two sets of data have been used for pursuing this initial
motivation. The first one, already presented and discussed
in a previous work (de Lemos, 1978) has been extracted from
videotaped interaction, in natural setting, of two mother-
child dyads, an English one and a Brazilian one. Eight
video-tapes of Richard's interaction with his mother from 8
to 15 months and twelve from Tiago from 1;0 to 2;0 have
been used. Tiago had his interaction with mother, caretaker
and his 10-year-old sister also audiotaped weekly during
the same period, contextual notes being made on those occasions.

The second set of data comes from non-identical twins,
Renata and Augusto, in interaction with their mother and
covers the period from 1;0 to 2;5 of the children's life.
They consist of 4 video-tapes from 1;3 to 1;6 and another 4
from 1;9 to 2;2, plus weekly audio-recorded sessions from
1;0 to 2;5, contextual notes having been taken in every
recording session by two observers.

Though I will concentrate the discussion on the twins'
data, I shall be presenting some data and conclusions made
in the previous work on Tiago and Richard, since they will
help to set up points which are relevant for the discussion
of the former.

Both in Richard's and in Tiago's corpus the marking of
segments of action by the adult and, mainly, the use of
completion-markers was most frequently related to the instantiation of a type of social game which I have called
games demonstrative of event structure. Those games defin-
able as actions on containers (put x into y/ take x out of
y, hide/find x in y) and *build-and-bash* could be described
as *joint-attention formats* in which *joint-action formats*
are embedded, since it was the adult who, at first, introduced into the child's attention an action accomplished by
himself, a complementary role being taken by the child at
the completion of the adult's turn. The child's role in
those games was characteristically reversive in the first
phase: M hides x in y/ C finds x in y; M builds a tower and
C knocks it down.

Those games can, indeed, be seen as focal instances for
the presentation of events and event structure to infants,
as Naming Games are, as far as objects are concerned. As
a matter of fact, *events* cannot be held, shown and labelled
in the same way as *objects* can be. As Lyons points out in
his distinction between first-order and second-order entities (cf. Lyons, 1977), objects and events are differently
related to space and time and one could say that events
exist through their phases. Moreover, as far as Portuguese
is concerned, the task of labelling an event implies the
task of marking its phase and its location in time.

The idea that the mother, through the instantiation of
those games, was providing the child with events as objects
of contemplation is not as speculative as it could appear.
Her previous clearing of the ground, the *neutral* character
of the objects used to build or to hide (blocks, cubes,
beakers — rarely labelled on those occasions) the "staccato"
or "rallentato" rhythm of her doing, allow for such interpretation. Moreover, the emphatic linguistic marking of
preparatory, progressive and completive phases of the adult's
actions and of the reversive action of the child, could be
interpreted as a segmentation device or a display of the
event structure.

However, the markers used in those games did not seem to
share the same segmentation or display "status": with the
exception of that falling on the reversive phase, namely, on
the child's completion of his reversive turn, all the others
could be deleted.

The development of *build-and-bash* formats seems to be related to this obligatory marking of game-completion or completion of the child's action. Richard's corpus, where 18
instantiations of *build-and-bash* are present, shows that at
15 months he has not yet incorporated neither the mother's
role in the building part of the game, nor her completion-
marker *all gone*, but he is already trying "to help" in the
construction and starts to vocalize as he knocks it down.
As for Tiago's corpus, where 40 instantiations of *build-and-
bash* type of game were found, it shows that at 1;6 he has
already incorporated the two-person structure of the game.
He builds silently, only asking for help when facing a difficulty, and uses his mother perfective tense forms after
completing the reversive phase. His utterance, on the other
side, generates another two-person structure within the
game format. As soon as he says *caiu* ("fell down"),
desceu ("got down"), *acabou* ("finished", "all gone"), the
adult takes it to produce a confirming response — "Caiu,
Tiago?" — to which he would later answer: "Caiu". Successive one-word utterances and two-word utterances emerge
later in this new "locus" of the game structure generated
by his uptake of his mother's completion marker, process
which could be described as *specular* on the child's part and
complementary on the adult's side. From 1;3 to 2;0 perfective tense forms become the most frequent non-nominal
expressions in Tiago's speech and their productivity appears
to be related to the child's migration from specific games
and non-play formats to other non-play and play situations
(cf. Ferrier, 1977, and Booth, 1978 for similar data on
"routines").
    The data on the twins' acquisition of proto-aspectual
markers will allow me to clarify points which have been
left obscure in the brief presentation of Tiago's data.
Their relevance, however, lies in the fact that they represent an adult-child situation which cannot be seen as
favouring either the instantiation of social games or that
of highly structured formats, as was the case for Tiago
and Richard. I hope to be able to show how aspectual markers and, mainly, completion-markers developed within this
particular situation and gradually became integrated into
their semantic and morphosyntactic developing systems.
I will attempt to do it by presenting the data in three
phases: a first phase, from 1;0 to 1;6, which is characteristically that of adult marking; a second phase, from
1;6 to 2;2 which shows the emergence of the children's
marking and the changes in the mother's markers, and the
third phase, from 2;2 to 2;5, when the combinatorial possibilities of those markers are explored by the children.

At the beginning of this first phase — from 1;0 to 1;3 —
Renata and Augusto are still in a pre-linguistic period, at
least as far as production is concerned. Mother-child and
nanny-child interactions are fairly well established as far
as requests for nearby objects are concerned. Non-request
formats are, indeed, the area where their data differ crucially from those from Richard and Tiago. Occasions for
joint-attention and, mainly for joint-action, are shorter
and less available. Thus, completion markers in the twins'
"corpora" occur rarely in games and basically in situations
when the child is acting with or without objects, but on
his/her own. So, instead of those markers being agreed
conventions in a sequence of turns as in demonstrative
games, it is their very use which imposes a format on the
child's behaviour. In other words, they segment "the current of life", to apply Wittgenstein's expression (1953) to
the stream of exploratory behaviour of Renata and Augusto
at that period.
   The linguistic types of realization of completion-marking
by the adult in this phase are:

a) perfective tense forms in the third person singular,
   mainly those of the first conjugation ending by the
   stressed suffix /-o/: *jogou, pegou, achou, acabou*, etc.,
   inserted into an intonational matrix which could be
   described as a short-rising and long-falling contour;
b) monosyllabic segments such as /a/, /ta/, inserted into
   the intonational matrix described above;
c) a gesture which can be described as opening arms and
   hands downwards, co-occurring with a) and b) in a subset
   of contexts.

   Perfective tense forms, and mainly *acabou* ("finished") and
quebrou ("broke") occurred also in two other format-types:
an attention-format, similar to naming-game formats, where
the attention of the child was directed to an object out of
its canonical or normative state, such as broken toys and
empty containers; and a verbal routine or verbal game, consisting of the adult's question *Cadê X?* ("Where is X?"), X
being usually a family member, such as Daddy, absent at
the moment, plus the answer, produced by the adult him/her-
self after a pause: *Cabô!* ("Finished!" or "All gone!").
   In both format-types, the perfective tense forms are inserted into an intonational matrix different from that characteristic of completion-markers, namely, a short-rising
and a short-falling contour. The same gesture described
above could co-occur with perfective tense forms in both
format-types.

Besides the distributional characteristics of those forms along three different types of formats — action, attention and verbal games — one should bring into notice the subtypes of action-formats where those completion markers are used. Seventy-three per cent of their occurrences fall at or around the endpoint of actions performed by the child on objects (e.g., opening a box) and 18% at or around endpoints of actions performed by the mother on the child, on the child's request (e.g., sitting the child up onto a chair). It is important to notice also that endpoints of actions performed by the adult on the child, but unrequested by him/her (e.g., tying his/her shoelaces) are either left unmarked or receive a different marker - *Pronto* ("ready"), inserted into a different intonational contour.

This distributional pattern and the fact that it represents only a subset of contexts where adult perfective tense forms can occur, force me somehow to discuss an issue which is both controversial and familiar to linguistic and psychological theories, namely, the problem of intentionality or of assigning intentions to the child's behaviour.

In order to do it, four features of that distribution must be considered:

1) Changes of state/place brought about by *non-intentional processes*, such as the incidental falling of an object, are virtually left unmarked by the adult.
2) Activities which do not involve change of state or do not have an inherent locative goal, such as cuddling a doll, are marked in a different way by the adult.
3) Changes of state brought about by *unobserved processes* are much less frequently marked and, besides belonging to different formats, are inserted into different intonational matrices.
4) The high frequency of completion-markers in actions performed by the child.

One is not allowed to go as far as to look at those features, or at this distribution, as practical lessons given by the mother to the child on the Aristotelian distinction between telic and atelic events. A reasonable or plausible interpretation of it could be the following: by the use of completion markers the mother frames those among the child's behaviours to which *terminal points are possible to be ascribed* and *intentions are possible to be attributed*. Indeed, the adult's markers fall, in this first phase, both on the child's behaviour in which persistence in a means-end structure is clear (e.g. struggling to open a box) as well as on fuzzy intentional behaviour such as looking into a toy-box

apparently without any particular toy in mind, and on apparently unintentional behaviour, such as walking around and
suddenly picking up an object from the floor.
   In opposition to social games where there is a previous
agreement on a goal, action plan and intention, in opposition
to joint-action formats where intentions can be negotiated,
the action formats just described seem to be instantiated
or framed by the mother's use of a completion-marker. The
incorporation by the mother of the child's action - *one per-*
son structure - into an interactional format - *a two person*
structure - can, thus, probably be taken as having some role
in the segmentation of events in the world and in the shaping
of intentions (cf. de Gelder, 1979, for theoretical arguments
favouring this view).
   The embedding of the child's action into a two person
structure is a format with two turns at the beginning of this
first phase. A third turn is provided sometimes by the child:
he/she looks/smiles to the mother or looks back to the object,
in a sort of acknowledgement. At the second part of this
phase, i.e., from 1;3 to 1;6, eight instantiations of completion markers are present in Augusto's corpus. Most of
them are monosyllabic segments /a:/, /o:/, /pa:/,
/ba:/, etc. inserted into the same intonational matrix
found in the mother's completion markers and are used exclusively to mark completion of his own actions: throwing a
ball, nesting a cube, standing up from a difficult position.
The completion or disappearance gesture occurs twice in the
verbal routines already described.
   As for Renata, at 1;6 she uses that gesture, already instantiated in two verbal routine formats,in an unpredictable
context, namely, after insistently pointing to a large spot
on the carpet, where her brother had spilled orange juice.
   Notice that in all those instantiations of either the intonational component of mother's completion markers or of the
gesture which sometimes accompanied them, a new "locus" in
the two person structure format is generated and filled in
by the adult with a confirming utterance, i.e., a perfective
tense form to which the child does not respond in the first
phase.

1) R holds up a packet of playing cards above her head, looks
   at Ma, her nanny, and *lets the cards drop onto the floor.*
   R:p͡â   Ma: Pá! Caiu, né?
                        ("Pa! It fell down, didn't it?")

   R picks up a card from the floor.

The second phase is characteristically that of the children's

uptake of the adult's role in marking the completion of their
own actions and in signalling non-canonical states of objects.
However, this incorporative process is realized at a morphological level via a process of reduction of the perfective
tense forms used by the adult to a sort of general completion
and non-canonical state marker /-bo/. Three main factors can
be seen as interacting in this reduction process:

a) a large number of the perfective tense forms used by the
adult have a stressed /-o/ suffix and this explains its perceptual saliency (cf. Slobin, 1973);
b) the most frequent verbs for signalling non-canonical
states are *acabar* and *quebrar*, whose perfective tense forms —
acabou and *quebrou* - end by /-bo/, since *quebrou*'s version
/ke'bo/ is found in the speech of even older children:
c) *acabar*, i.e., its perfective tense form *acabou* or /aka'bo/
("finished") has a completive content which accounts for its
high frequency both as a completion marker and in signalling
non-canonical states in the adult's speech to the children.

The distribution of *bo* in Renata and Augusto's speech from
1;6 to 2;1 covers, at the beginning, the same types of formats where perfective tense forms occurred in the adult's
speech to them, namely, for marking completion of their own
actions, for calling attention to non-canonical states of
objects and in answers to *Cadê X?* ("Where is X?") questions
in verbal routines.

Given that those three contexts share a resultative change
of state/place feature, it could be said that this was the
meaning of *bo* for Renata and Augusto. However, its intra-
format values seem to be loosely related: their *bo*- answers
in verbal routine were often incorrect.

2) R, A, Ma. in the living room. Two observers (C and Cl).
   R is playing with toy kitchen-tins.

> Ma: Cadê a tia Cláudia, Renata?
>   ("Where is Aunt Claudia, Renata?")
>
> R (opening arms and hands downwards) bô:
>
> Ma: Não acabou não. Olha a Cláudia aí.
>   ("No, she isn't all gone. Look at
>   Claudia there.")

> R looks at Claudia.

Furthermore, *bo* was rarely used to encode achievements,
i.e., incidental changes of state/place, and positive accom-
plishments were still distinguished from non-canonical states
by the intonational patterns found in the adult's speech to

them and in their first phase. Part of the way *bo* has to
make in the direction of the broader semantic range of perfective tense forms in Adult Portuguese (e.g., the encoding
of cessation of states/activities, and achievements) starts
at the end of the second phase and in the third phase. Augusto and Renata used *bo* sometimes as a completion marker of
an action done by the adult on his/her request and to comment
on the disappearance of objects involving both an accomplishment and a non-canonical state, as in (3):

3) A picks up a small doll and locks it inside a toy-wardrobe.
   Then, looking at E (Obs.):

   A: abo! (opening arms and hands downwards)

   E: Acabou, Augusto?
      ("All gone, Augusto?")

   A: bo

The morphological status of *bo*, at this second phase, is
still that of an intra-format element. If one brings to
notice the fact that other "verbal" forms in the same period -
abi ("open"), *po ~ põe* ("put") and *tia ~ tira* ("take off") can
be traced back to adult imperative forms and occur exclusively
in request-for-action formats, one can argue for a primary
opposition between formats governing the emergence of those
forms. Evidence for such interpretation seems to be the
later occurrence in the same phase and in the third one of
sequences such as (4) where an action is embedded into a
request-format:

4) R holds a box to Ma.

   R: á: á: abi, abi
      ("a: a: open, open")

   Ma: Você que que eu abra, filha?
       ("Do you want me to open, honey?")
   Ma takes the lid off the box.

   R: bo:

Notice that the request is made with a verbal unmarked form
and its completion with this sort of general and isolated
morpheme. Another source of evidence for the unbound or relatively independent status of *bo* and/or *-o* is found in the
speech of another subject in the same research project (cf.
Gebara, 1979; 5):

5) Ra pushes a toy bird up to the top of the metal stick to
   which the bird is partially fixed. Ra looks at its basis
   or support and up to the bird.

Ra: $\overset{\frown}{\text{ey}}$ vay $\overset{\longrightarrow}{\text{la}}$:
   ("It goes there")

Ra observes the trajectory of the bird sliding down the metal stick.

Ra: $\overset{\frown}{\text{ey}}$ vay $\overset{\longrightarrow}{\text{la}}$:
   ("It goes there")

Ra smiles as the bird gets to the basis, looks at the endpoint of the trajectory and touches it with her right hand:

Ra: $\overset{\frown}{\text{vai}}lo$

   ("It goes thered")

The way *bo* enters successive one-word utterances and the first two-word utterances at the end of the second phase also involves intra-format and inter-format processes. In order to describe them, I have to come back to the adult's role in the development of action- and attention-formats where the adult's perfective tense forms have firstly occurred. Figure 1 is a schematic representation of such development.

If one compares the first phase formats represented in 1 to the second phase ones, represented in 2a and 2b, one can see how the uptake by the child of the adult's marker in the second phase generates a two-person structure or complementary turns in a primitive dialogue. The first form of this dialogue, represented in 2a and illustrated by (1) above, is better described as the incorporation by the adult of the child's marking into her turn, or into her confirming utterance. At this point, the child may or may not take the next turn by producing a sort of further confirmation or assent. This process, which is *complementary* as far as turn-taking is concerned, is characteristically *specular* at a linguistic segmental level, since the same unit, or, in this case, the same marker, can be carried along three turns. The same specular process is present in 2b, although the introduction of a yes/no question in the adult's turn increases its complementary character, as illustrated in (6):

6) R has found a toy cup with a broken handle. She looks up to M and, as M looks at her, R shows M the cup:

R: $\overset{\searrow}{\text{bo}}$ $\overset{\searrow}{\text{bo}}$

M takes the cup from R's hand.
M: Quebró, filha?
   ("Did it break, honey?")

R: $\overset{\searrow}{\text{e}}$ $\overset{\searrow}{\text{bo}}$ ("Yes, *bo*")
M: Ah! ("Oh!")

FIRST PHASE
1 C's action

           Ad's marking

SECOND PHASE
2a C's action

          C's <u>marking</u>[1]
             Ad's <u>confirming utterance</u>

2b C's action

          C's <u>marking</u>
             Ad's yes/no <u>question</u>
                (C's <u>answer</u>)[2]

2c X's action
  x's state

          C's <u>marking</u>
            (Ad's yes/no <u>question</u>)
                (C's <u>answer</u>)
                   Ad's <u>Wh-question</u>
                   Ad's answer

2d X's action
  x's state

          C's <u>marking</u>
            Ad's <u>Wh-question</u>
                   C's* <u>answer</u>
                   C's* <u>answer</u>
                   C's answer

2e X's action
  x's state

          C's <u>marking</u>
            Ad's <u>Wh-question</u>
                   C's bo/N
                   C's N/bo
                   C's bo+N
                   C's N+bo

FIG. 1. *C child; Ad Adult; X Any person familiar to C including C and Ad; x inanimate objects.*

[1] The underlining signals the turns whose linguistic components are partial or total repetitions or the previous turn of the same turn in a previous phase.
[2] The parentheses have been used to indicate that the turn in question may or may not be instantiated in the sequence.

An important change in the development of dialogue construction occurs in the same phase and is represented in 2c
and 2d: the introduction of a wh-question mainly *quem* ("who")
and, less often, *o que* ("what")- at the adult's second turn,
the answer being provided by the adult him/herself at the
beginning, as shown in 2c. When Augusto and Renata start to
take the turn generated by the adult's wh-question, their
answers are either repetitive of part of the adult's turn
(cf. C's answer in 2) or nouns which constitute inadequate
(cf. C's answer in 2d) or adequate (cf. C's answer in 2d)
responses to that question. Examples of such sequences are:

7) A is concentrated in fastening up and down the zipper of
   the observer's pencil case. At a certain point the
   zipper's clip stops sliding and A turns to D, his older
   brother:

   A: bo abo

   D: Quebrô? O que quebrou?
      ("Broken? What is broken?")

   A: tata
      ("Tata" (R's nickname))

8) R shows a broken toy cup to E, one of the observers.

   R: bo bo ebo

   E: Quebrô, é? Quebrou?
      ("Did it break, did it? Did it break?")

   R: e ebo
      ("Yes, *ebo*")

   E: Quem quebrou a xícara?
      ("Who broke the cup?")

   R: bubu
      ("Bubu" (A's nickname))

The format or dialogue types represented in 2d and 2e are
the main contexts where Augusto and Renata produced successive one-word utterances and two-word utterances. Notice,
for instance, that *bo*-structures such as the one instantiated
in (9) below follow from sequences such as (8):

9) Following from (8). R looks up to C, the other observer,
   and points to the broken toy cup.

   R: bubu obo tita
      ("Bubu *obo* cup")

However, there are not empirical bases for saying that an

Agent-Action-Object or even an Agent-Action structure resulted
from their interactional skills at that period. Answers such
as the one found in (10) would provide counter-evidence for
such a view:

10) R puts a toy lamb inside a toy barn and closes the barn's
    door, looking at A.

    R: bȯ abȯ

    C: Acabou? Acabou o quê?
       ("Finished? Finished what?")

    R: abȯ bubu abȯ

   Furthermore, the only "agents" referred in those formats are
themselves, i.e. in Renata's answers *Bubu* (Augusto's nickname)
is the answer for the adult's <u>who</u>-questions and in Augusto's
utterances, *Tata* (Renata's nickname) is the most probable
"agent".
   A reasonable proposal would be, instead, to relate the production of those early multi-word utterances by the children
to their mastery of the complementary processes operative in
the dialogue construction by the adult in 2d and 2e. This
is tantamount to saying that the utterances represented in
the child's second turn in 2e can be seen as a product of
the incorporation by the child of the linguistic components
of previous complementary turns in adult-child prototypical
dialogues. Such a view, i.e. the view that *horizontal constructions* are derived from *vertical constructions* in early
syntactic development, has already been put forward by other
authors (cf. Greenfield and Smith, 1976, Scollon, 1977) and
strongly stated by Ochs, Schieffelin and Platt (1979; 252)
who see "...competence as a move away from sequential organizational towards syntactic organization of propositions".
   However, the intra-format processes and operations discussed above are not the only factors which account for the
emergence of successive one-word utterances and two-word
utterances in Renata and Augusto speech in the second phase.
Inter-format processes seem also to be operative in the
same period, as shown by (11) and (12):

11) A has been playing around while R is drawing with the
    observer's pen. A observes R for a moment and then
    reaches for the observer's pencil case on the floor. The
    pencil case is empty. A looks at R, touches her arm and,
    as she looks back, takes the pen from her right hand:

    A: da bȯ
       ("Give. *Bo*.")

12) A has a record in his right hand. R goes toward A, opening her hand in a request gesture.

R: dí dí dí
("Record. Record. Record.")

A hides the record on his back.

A: nãw abo   abo di
("No, *abo*. *Abo* record.")

Both the successive one-word utterances of (11) and the two-word utterance of (12) can be seen as resulting from the embedding of *bo*-format into a request sequence. In (11), Augusto's comment on the non-canonical state of an object takes the function of justification of his request[2], while in (12) the same type of utterance functions as a justification of his refusal to comply to Renata's request.

Another important aspect of the twins' speech at the end of the second phase is the development of *bo* action- and attention-formats into telling or reporting formats where the adult sets up the linguistic grounds for the child to report past experiences shared by both of them - adult and child - to a third interlocutor and/or to the adult him/herself[3]. A typical instantiation of this sort of "telling-games" is (13):

13) M: Fala assim: O que aconteceu com o carro do vovô.
Conta pra tia Ester.
("Say such and such: what happened to Grandpa's car.
Tell aunt Ester.")

A: Ahm?
("Uh?")

M: O carro do vovô.
("Grandpa's car.")

E: O que aconteceu, Augusto?
("What happened, Augusto?")

M: Com o carro do vovô. O que aconteceu?
("With Grandpa's car. What happened?")

A: abo u tarru vovô.
("*Abo* Grandpa's car.")

M: Quebrô!
("It has broken!")

E: Quebrou o carro do vovô?
("Has it broken, Grandpa's car?")

This is the longest utterance produced by Augusto in the second phase, in the same way as *bubu obo tita* (cf. (8) above) is Renata's longest one. Both are built up by the incorporation of part of the adult's precedent turns and are "directed" to a third interlocutor or to an interlocutor who did not participate in a previous dialogue on the same topic (cf. (7) and (8)).

The third phase, as far as the morphological and semantic status of *bo* is concerned can be characterized by the gradual replacement of *bo* in action-formats by perfective tense forms, which, interestingly enough, do not have /-o/ suffixes, such as *pois* ("put on/up"), *adiu-caiu* ("fell down") and *abiu* ("opened").

From a syntactic point of view, the third phase shows an increase of two-word and three-word utterances with *bo* and its variants *abo, ebo* and *obo*. However, differently from the second phase, they do not occur only in contexts of reporting past experiences shared by the adult interlocutor and do not result from the partial incorporation of the adult's precedent turns. Some of them are, indeed, reports of events observed only by the child and are used to initiate the dialogue. Examples of this transition to "displaced speech"[4] or to the informative function of language are:

14) M, A, R and the two observers are in a corner of the living-room. A stands up, runs to a large window on the left. A draws the curtain a little and looks at the street outside. A car passes by. A runs to M:

A: abo u tarru u mo
   (*"abo* the man's car")

M: Acabou o carro do moco?
   ("All gone the man's car?")

15) A, M, E and C, the two observers, in the living-room. R comes from her bedroom, where her toys are kept.

R: á á á ádi
   abo adi a tata

E: Cabô o que?
   ("Finished what?")

R: abo adi

C: O disco?
   ("The record?")

R: abo tata

M: Disco? A Tatá acabou o disco?
   ("Record? Tata finished the record?")

Although further research is needed to reconstruct the way utterances such as the ones exemplified above develop from telling-formats such as (13), there seems to me that they are related through the same specular and complementary processes which have been posited as accounting for the first horizontal constructions found in the second phase. Moreover, the fact that those multi-word utterances represent a more advanced linguistic stage relatively to the precedent ones should not be necessarily based on the mastery of grammatical rules by the child, as many authors have proposed. In my opinion, the progress made by the child at his/her first multi-word stage is basically related to the mastery of prototypical or primary dialogue turns which allows him/her to construct utterances which are not subsequent to those of his/her interlocutor but based on a representation of that interlocutor in that particular situation.

3. CONCLUSIONS

I hope to have given at least some evidence for the view that interactional formats are an operational space for the child's construction of semantic, morphological and syntactic relations. I also believe that a claim for continuity - from format to dialogue and discourse - is plausible within such a framework, since the processes of incorporation of the adult's turn by the child have been demonstrated to be characteristic of adult-child pre-linguistic interaction, by the literature on role-taking and turn-taking (cf. Schaffer, 1977; Kaye, 1977; and Bruner and Sherwood, 1976). Moreover, the specular, complementary and reciprocal nature of the processes whereby vertical constructions grow and develop into horizontal constructions has already been shown, in which concerns adult-child and child-child social interactions in the work of Camaioni (1979). Thus, it is not unreasonable to conclude that what the child brings to the task of learning his/her language are, at least partially, processing skills which are required by the very construction of discourse.

It could be said that this is far from being enough, since the child has still a long way to go for the acquisition of horizontal syntax and I quite agree with it. However, as far as complex sentences are concerned, there seems to be many reasons to believe that their emergence and development are governed by the same processes, as shown in the work of Campos and de Lemos (1979) and as suggested by Keenan, Schieffelin and Platt (1979). As for the construction of the so-called basic syntactic relations, Ruth Clark's view

on the child's operations on "stored fragments" of adult
utterances (R. Clark, 1978) as a way to rule-formation,
allows for the compatibility of the hypothesis I have put forward with the hypotheses the child can make about sentence-
constituents and construction.

Yet, it could be argued that those processes of mutual and
direct incorporation presented as constitutive of adult-child
formats and dialogues are absent from the adult discourse.
It seems to me, however, that notions such as presuppositions, topic and comment, perspective and focus involve a
representation of the interlocutor in the speaker's construction of his utterance and that such representation can be
seen as the outcome of those processes of mutual incorporation. The work by Ducrot (1972) and Vogt (1977; 1979) provides theoretical arguments and empirical evidence for such
a view.

Such interpretation seems to allow for the tentative conclusion that the child must go through the process of enter-
ing a two-person structure with an empirical interlocutor in
order to build up his representation of himself and of the
Other as interlocutors, which enables him to become a player
of many "language games". This is not far from Vygotsky's
claiming that:

> From the very first days of the child's development his
> activities acquire a meaning of their own in a system of
> social behaviour.... The path from object to child and
> from child to object passes through another person. This
> complex human structure is a product of a developmental
> process deeply rooted in the links between individual
> and social history.
>
> (Vygotsky, 1978; 30)

NOTES

1 This research has been carried out with the aid of a grant -
   76/1384 by the Fundacão de Amparo à Pesquisa do Estado de
   São Paulo, to the Research Project on Child Language Acquisition of the Department of Linguistics, IEL, State University of Campinas. Part of the work presented here has
   been done by the author at the Netherlands Institute for
   Advanced Studies, in Wassenaar, Holland, and was finan-
   cially supported by the same Foundation, grant 78/1530.
   The author wishes also to thank Jerome Bruner and Luigia
   Camaioni for their fruitful comments on an earlier draft
   of this paper, and both Carlos Vogt and Jerome Bruner for
   the endless discussions which have influenced and encouraged

the author to pursue the line of research shown, though still preliminarily, in this paper.
2 Cf. Campos and de Lemos (1979) on similar processes operating on the emergence of complex causal sentences.
3 Cf. similar data presented by Simões (1978) on "telling-games" as precursors of narrative discourse.
4 Cf. Campbell (1977) on arguments favouring the view that the emergence of utterances expressing propositions is related to the child's ability to use "displaced speech".

REFERENCES

Antinucci, F. and Miller, R. (1976). How children talk about what happened. *J. Child Lang.* 3, 167-189.
Booth, D.A. (1978). Language acquisition as the addition of verbal routines. *In* "Recent Advances in the Psychology of Language" (R.N. Campbell and P.T. Smith, eds), pp. 219-241. New York and London: Plenum Press.
Bretherton, I. and Bates, E. (1979). The emergence of intentional communication. *New Directions in Child Develop.* 4, 81-100.
Bruner, J.S. (1975). The ontogenesis of speech acts. *J. Child Lang.* 2, 1-9.
Bruner, J.S. and Sherwood, V. (1976). Peekaboo and the learning of rule structures. *In* "Play - Its Role in Development and Evolution" (J.S. Bruner, A. Jolly and K. Sylvia, eds), pp. 277-284. New York: Basic Books.
Camaioni, L. (1979). Child-adult and child-child conversations: an interactional approach. *In* "Developmental Pragmatics" (E. Ochs and B.B. Schieffelin, eds). New York: Academic Press.
Campos, M.F.P.C. and de Lemos, C.T.G. (1979). Pragmatic routes and the acquisition of "causal" expressions (In prep.)
Campbell, R.N. (1976). Propositions and Early Utterances. *Salzburger Beiträge zur Linguistik* 2, 247-259.
Clark, R. (1976). Some even simpler ways to learn to talk. *In* "The Development of Communication" (N. Waterson and C. Snow, eds), pp. 391-413. New York: Wiley.
de Gelder, B. (1979). "Intentions and Mother-Child Interaction". Mimeo.
de Lemos, C.T.G. (1975). "The use of *ser* and *estar* with particular reference to child language acquisition in Brazilian Portuguese". Unpublished Ph.D. Dissertation, University of Edinburgh.
de Lemos, C.T.G. (1978). "Joqos demonstrativos da estrutura de eventos no periodo pré-linguistico: seu estatuto como pré-requisito do desenvolvimento da linguagem". Paper pre-

sented at the III Encontro Nacional de Linguistica, PUC-
Rio de Janeiro.

Ducrot, O. (1972). "Dire et ne pas dire; Principes de séman-
tique linguistique". Paris: Hermann.

Gebara, E.M.S. (1979). "O papel da intonacão na emergência
do aspecto: duas estratégias diferentes". Paper presented
at the XXXI Reunião da Sociedade Brasileira para o Pro-
gresso da Ciência, Fortaleza, Brazil.

Greenfield, P.M. and Smith, J.H. (1976). "The Structure of
Communication in Early Language Development". New York:
Academic Press.

Kaye, K. (1977). Towards the origin of dialogue. In "Studies
in Mother-Infant Interaction" (H.R. Schaffer, ed.). New
York: Academic Press.

Keenan, E.O. (Schieffelin, B. and Platt, M. (1978). Questions
of immediate concern. In "Questions and Politeness: Strategies of Social Interaction" (E. Goody, ed.), pp. 44-55.
Cambridge: Cambridge University Press.

Lyons, J. (1977). "Semantics". Cambridge: Cambridge University Press.

Ochs, E. Schieffelin, B. and Platt, M. (1979). Propositions
across utterances and speakers. In "Developmental Pragmatics"
(E. Ochs and B. Schieffelin, eds), pp. 251-268. New York:
Academic Press.

Schaffer, H.R. (1977). "Studies in Mother-Infant Interaction".
New York: Academic Press.

Scollon, R. (1973). A Real Early Stage: an Unzippered Condensa-
tion of a Dissertation on Child Language. *Working Papers in
Linguistics* 5(6), 67-81.

Shugar, G. (1976). Text analysis as an approach to the study
of early linguistic operations. In "The Development of Communication" (N. Waterson and C. Snow, eds), pp. 227-251. New
York: Wiley.

Simoes, M.C.P. (1978). "Ensaiando Narrativas: do "jogo de
contar" às proto-narrativas". Paper presented at the III
Encontro Nacional de Linguistica, PUC-Rio de Janeiro.

Slobin, D.I. (1973). Cognitive prerequisites for the development of grammar. In "Studies of Child Language Development"
(C. Ferguson and D.I. Slobin, eds). New York: Holt, Rinehart
and Winston.

Vogt, C. (1977). *O Intervalo Semântico*. São Paulo: Ática.

Vogt, C. (1978). Por uma pragmática das representacões". Unpublished paper.

Vygotsky, L.S. (1978). "Mind in Society: The Development of
Higher Psychological Processes" (M. Cole, V. John-Steiner,
S. Scribner and E. Souberman, eds). Cambridge, MA: Harvard
University Press.

Wittgenstein, L. (1953). "Philosophical Investigations". New
York: Macmillan.

SOME DETERMINANTS OF SELF CORRECTION: AN INTERACTIONAL STUDY OF SWISS-GERMAN

MARIE-LOUISE KÄSERMANN* and KLAUS FOPPA**

*Max-Planck-Institut für Psycholinguistik, Nijmegen, The Netherlands, **Psychologisches Institut der Universität Bern, Switzerland.*

1. THE THEORETICAL STATUS OF SELF-CORRECTIONS

The present chapter intends to show that by analysing *self-corrections* embedded in specific contexts one can obtain information about two central questions in child language development, namely about *what* constitutes the child's knowledge about language at a given point in time as well as *how* she/he could have acquired this knowledge.

Although the scientific reconstruction of the child's knowledge about language is an interesting endeavour in its own right, it is also a precondition for tackling the question of how the child could have learnt what he knows. Accounting for how the child's linguistic capabilities change in time presupposes a characterization of what it is that is changed. Furthermore, this conception has to be such that against this background the question of acquisition can be tackled. There are important phenomena for approaching the task of reconstructing that kind of knowledge about language for which consequently a plausible developmental account can be given, e.g. self-corrections as such, and as parts of specific interaction sequences. These claims shall now be elaborated in turn.

The task of representing the child's knowledge about language at a given point in time is by no means as trivial as to select that model of description which covers the respective corpus in the most inclusive and unequivocal manner. Rather, one should be able to develop procedures which in some way or other make use of the fact that ulti-

* Now at: Psychiatrische Universitatsklinik, Bern, Switzerland.

mately it is the child himself who is the criterion for what
he knows or does not know about language. Therefore the task
of representation demands finding possible candidates of
"linguistic" evaluation in what the child does or says. Spontaneous and triggered self-modifications or self-corrections
can be treated as such a sign because the occurrence (v. the
kind) of these modifications presupposes that the child con-
trols his own utterances. In fact they are treated in this
way by several authors (Clark, 1978; Marshall and Morton,
1978; Slobin, 1978; Valian and Wales, 1976, etc.). Furthermore, at least part of the kinds of modification resulting
from the monitoring imply the child's awareness of correct
(in comparison with the adult model) forms. Thus self-corrections are evidence for, and give access to, the child's knowledge about standards.

If one assumes that knowledge about language can be described as processing (producing as well as understanding)
speech according to standards (e.g. of grammaticality), then
it seems adequate to analyse self-corrections in specific
ways (Foppa and Käsermann, 1980) in order to infer what the
child knows about language at a given point in time. The
question of how the child has acquired what he knows then
amounts to accounting for how these standards became determinants of speech. However, although the conception of knowledge about language as a set of standards determining speech
processing may be sufficient to predict and describe the *form*
of utterances, it does, in our opinion, provide only part of
a framework which would also allow for an account of acquisition mechanisms. This is so because in such a framework (e.g.
Marshall and Morton, 1978), standards are but necessary parts
of an internal structure that should explain the observed phenomena (self-corrections). In terms of psychological processes this implies that they are observed by a speaker for
no other reason than their existence. Their existence, as
such, is not questioned and not questionable. Yet, it seems
that having some notions about how these standards came to be
determining factors equals having some hypotheses about how
they could have been acquired.

Before turning to developing an augmented view of standards,
two short digressions should be made. Firstly, it is clear
that language acquisition understood as a succession of stages
could easily be described by what has been developed so far.
Yet, given one is not so much interested in this kind of
developmental account, but rather in how acquisition seen
as transition works, then one has to deal with mechanisms.
Secondly, being concerned with acquisition mechanisms as
learning mechanisms does not imply that one denies any innate
endowment.

Approaching the question of acquisition mechanisms one has
to assume that standards are not only structurally justified,
but also have an aspect of instrumentality. That is to say,
observing standards is not a value in itself but could be instrumental in achieving some goals. It is not hard to list
examples of goals which could be involved in speaking, e.g.
one speaks in order to get something done by somebody else,
or in order to be understood by some people but not by others,
or in order to compose an argument. While heterogeneous,
these goals seem to have one thing in common: underlying the
actual utterances there are specific expectations which have
to be fulfilled by these utterances. If one assumes the function of utterances is to realize such expectations — generally
speaking to express underlying communicative intentions — then
an instrumental conception of standards is plausible for several
reasons. To begin with, to make someone comply with one's
wishes speaking grammatically is sometimes not just desirable
but a necessary precondition to attain this goal. So the form
of an utterance has to map accurately its underlying communicative intention. Still another point is that there probably
does not exist a one-to-one relationship between a specific
communicative intention and its optimal realization by an
utterance. Rather, there are many ways to express one thing,
and which expression is optimal depends not only on the "good-
ness of fit" between a given communicative intention and its
expression, but also on the relationship between a set of possible expressions and the actual situation (defined by parameters of time, place, addressee, verbal context, etc.) in
which one of them actually happens to be uttered. So whether
someone complies with one's wishes might depend, e.g. on whether one keeps in mind he is hard of hearing. Again in choosing an expression which is optimal under actual given conditions standards seem to play an instrumental role. Another
way of stating the instrumentality of standards is to draw attention to the fact that some of them need not be taken into
account under certain conditions (e.g., syntactic completeness is not required in case of elliptical utterances). Thus
the optionality of standards is an argument for their instrumental character.
    Against this background one can now try to explain in which
ways such a broadened view of standards may contribute to
working on the problem of how the child could acquire such
knowledge. For this one can assume that one function of
utterances is to be *understandable* and standards are instrumental in monitoring the realization of that goal. "Understandability" in this context is not so much conceived of as
an inherent feature of utterances but is a value attri-

buted to utterances by a speaker in the following way. An
utterance which expresses a specific communicative intention
is judged to be understandable (or an optimal realization of
its underlying communicative intention) if an interpretation
of that utterance (by a hearer and/or the speaker himself)
in a specific situation reconstructs exactly the communicative intention in question. The relationship between a communicative intention and its reconstruction by interpretation
yields the value of the utterance's understandability. This
value may be optimal, that is to say the communicative intention is adequately reconstructed by the interpretation in
the given situation. It may also be less than adequate. In
case of such a discrepancy one could expect the speaker, while
keeping constant his initial communicative intention, to re-
formulate his utterance, thus producing self-corrections.

To conceive of understandability in this way has a methodological as well as a theoretical consequence. Firstly, if
one assumes that discrepancies occur in a dialogic interpre-
tation-loop then one should be able, by arbitrarily signalling lack of understanding, to provoke reformulations. The
adequate unit of analysis therefore is such a dialogue sequence characterized by a specific signal of non-understanding
(see in more detail below). Secondly, the interlocutors who
normally provide and feed back interpretations of children's
utterances are as a rule linguistically more mature than the
children themselves. They are also the ones who incorporate
the norms that constitute understandability in that speech
community. They, therefore, are in a position to signal
deviance as well as to provide for more adequate expressions.
Seen in this light it might be possible to find evidence for
how this standard knowledge — which first has to be shown as
being existent — could be transmitted in dialogues, thus
pinning down some mechanisms of learning.

2. THE EMPIRICAL ANALYSIS OF SELF-CORRECTIONS

Against this background the following results are pertinent
to the questions:

1) whether self-corrections indeed may be provoked by signalling non-understanding;
2) if so, whether the observed corrections are systematic
   and what kind of standards seem to be the determining
   factors;
3) and how such standards could have been acquired.

2.1 Occurrence

The prediction of a speaker being led to reformulation of
his utterance by a signal of non-understanding from his
interlocutor has been tested in the course of several investigations (Käsermann, 1977, 1978, 1980 and other members of
the Bernese Group of Language Development, see Foppa, 1978;
and independently Gallagher, 1977, 1978). This was done by
a quasi-experimental intervention-technique of inserting
every now and then unspecific questions like /hm?/ in the
course of dialogues between an adult and a child. In this
way it has been shown with thousands of instances of provoked non-understanding that with children of different
ages (at least from 16 months on; see Straumann, in prep.),
with different social background (Meyer, 1980), with different mother tongues (Amstutz, 1977), and with and without
language disturbances (Huber, 1978), there is a tendency to
respond in a specific way: in most cases (80% to 90%)
children either repeat the "non-understood" utterance verbatim, shortened or with an otherwise modified surface
structure. These facts will be elaborated more fully later.
For the present purpose it is sufficient to say that the expectations expressed as to the notions of communicative intention and of understandability are supported: children
have indeed to be credited with having a notion of communicative intention and with being able to react in a generally
meaningful way, that is saying again a similar thing, to a
partner-initiated evaluation of an utterance.
  Certainly more evidence is needed in order to feel confident that these modifications tap in any but the most general
sense the child's knowledge about language. Were it to turn
out that the modifications themselves are random events then
one would not want to attribute any theoretical relevance to
them. But provided one can show that they are systematic
with regard to given standards and under certain actual
conditions one would be prepared to admit the child's awareness of some linguistically relevant distinctions.

2.2 Kind of Standards

With regard to the question whether modifications indeed are
systematic with regard to certain postulated standards it
has been shown (Käsermann, 1978, 1980) that children as young
as 20-24 months in non-understanding sequences with their
mother change sounds in words significantly more often towards
an adult model than away from it. The same holds true for
words within utterances: some of the structurally missing

elements are added, redundant or false elements are deleted
and word order is also revised. These results show that
even at an early stage children's revision behaviour seems
to be guided by their awareness of standard word-forms,
standard word-order and so forth.

2.2.1 Data analysis In the same manner the data to be
described in more detail below are analysed with regard to
questions about whether observed modifications are random or
systematic events, and, if they prove to be systematic, which
kinds of standards are the respective determinants. However,
the material to be investigated stems from and older age
group and consists of dialogues between children and an experimenter instead of the mother. These dialogues were recorded in the following way : Sixteen 4 to 5-year-old
children were visited in their homes. Half of the children
were from middle-class families, and half of them from
working-class families. The experimenter brought a set of
picture books with her and the child was free to choose which
one he/she wanted to look at. Most of these sessions lasted
for about one hour, some of them for up to an hour and a half.
In the course of these dialogues the experimenter intervened
every now and then by asking /hm?/ thus producing what had
been established as a modification provoking non-understanding
signal. The tape recordings were transcribed using a broad
transcription.

From what is known already it was expected that at least
some of the observed modifications would indeed be systematic.
However, the kind of determining standards would hopefully
have changed as a function of the children's age. On the
basis of earlier observations one could assume that there
could be one dominant factor determining the children's
responses. Whenever a child's utterance preceding the nonspecific /hm?/ might be called "complete" and/or "correct"
children should either have repeated it unchanged or in a
shortened version (with redundant elements deleted). Conversely, if the utterance was "incomplete" the children
should in some way or another explain what had been unclear
or add those parts which had been missing. In cases where
the utterances were inadequate (*referentially* or *grammatically*
invalid) the children should correct their mistakes. Thus
one could hypothesize that the occurrence and kind of modifications to be observed should be meaningful with regard to
the postulated standards of "completeness" and "correctness".

Utterances were identified as *complete* if they were in fact
complete and unambiguous ("The sun is shining") and also if
they were incomplete but could easily be completed or dis-

ambiguated by reference to something said earlier or with respect to both partners' shared knowledge (*conversational completeness*). The utterance "That is a pity!" may thus be "conversationally complete" when it is clear what "that" refers
to from the context. *Incomplete utterances*, on the other hand,
were those which carried too little information or could not
be disambiguated by reference to the context. They might be
incomplete with respect to some of their referents ("That's
a pity!" could be such a case if it remained unclear what was
meant by "that"; one then would speak of *referential incompleteness* or *semantic indeterminateness*); or with respect to
some missing grammatical parts (*grammatical incompleteness*).
The identification of inadequate or incorrect utterances
rested on the assessment of referentially or grammatically
invalid usage.

The structure of the dialogue-sequences analysed was the
same as in the other cases reported thus far: an initial
child utterance (CU_1) is followed by an unspecific adult
question /hm?/ (---) which in turn is followed by the critical utterance (CU_2). To demonstrate how the utterances were
categorized and what categories were used to test the predictions an example of each category is given below. Two
remarks, however, should be made in advance.

The English versions are to be seen as rough equivalents
at best. Furthermore, each utterance may be categorized in
more than one way. Note that for the antecedent utterance
(CU_1) that category was chosen which was taken up in CU_2,
that means: if a referential incompleteness (semantic indeterminateness) of CU_1 was *explained* in CU_2 this category
was chosen for CU_1 regardless of whether other deficiencies
were present or not. This procedure may appear as rather
problematic since the categorization of responses is performed in such a way as to maximize the probability of confirming the underlying hypothesis. Although this is true in
principle, one should bear in mind that it is by no means
self-evident that the child will repair deficiencies of his
utterances at all. So, if he takes up at least one of them
this would already be a "result". It would clearly be of
interest whether the child, having potentially the choice
between several inadequacies in a given utterance, displays
any systematic revision preferences, and whether the number
and type of inadequacies revised changes as a function of
time. However, in the context of the present paper such a
developmental account is not striven for.

In the following some examples are given for the relationship between inappropriate utterances (CU_1) and repairs (CU_2).
These examples are classified according to the category of

inappropriateness and the type of repair (critical parts of CU_1 and CU_2 are underlined).

	Swiss German	English equivalent	Categorization
1) CU_1:	und da wott er dä siesse. u nächär nimmt er ne aus wäg. u... u da tuet er ne siesse	and there he wants to shoot him. and then he takes him everything away. and...and then he does shoot him.	*referentially incomplete/ semantically indeterminate*
CU_2:	da...u da tuet ne...dr gross Has tuet ne da siesse	there...and there does...the big rabbit does shoot him there.	*explanation of reference*
2) CU_1:	-Frosch - cho u - i die abe- gumpet u...u het's gholt.	-frog came and jumped in there and...and fetched it.	*grammatically incomplete*
CU_2:	nächär...nächär isch dr Frosch cho u isch dri abegumpet u het's gholt.	then...then the frog has come and has jumped into it and fetched it.	*addition of grammatical elements*
3) CU_1:	mit sine länge Schueh, da	with his large boots there	*referentially inadequate*
CU_2:	oder...vo de länge Schueh gheit si um	or...from (in the sense of: because of) the large boots she falls down	*correction of referential aspect*
4) CU_1:	nächär si...si das wider usecho	then they...they has come out again	*gramatically inadequate*
CU_2:	nächär is das wieder usecho	then it has come out again	*correction of grammatical aspect*
5) CU_1:	was het denn d'Muetter gsait, wo si haimcho isch?	what has the mother said when she came home?	*complete*
CU_2:	was het denn d'Muetter gsait, wo si haimcho isch?	what has the mother said when she came home?	*verbatim repetition*

	Swiss German	English equivalent	Categorization
6) CU$_1$:	u da brönnts <u>jetze</u>	<u>and</u> there it burns <u>now</u>	*complete*
CU$_2$:	da brönnts	there it burns	*deletion of re-dundant elements*
7) CU$_1$:	nächär...ghört si öppis gränne	then...she hears something cry	*complete*
CU$_2$:	nächär geit si das Schtägli ab u geit ga luege u nächär isch es...ds Büssi	then she goes down the stairs and goes to look and then it is...the kitty	*no adequate response*

2.2.2 Results Tables 1a, b and 2a, b show the results for
the two subgroups. The overall picture seems to be very
similar despite minor differences with respect to some details. In both groups (Tables 1b, 2b) the tendency to react
to the intervention at all by either producing a verbatim
repetition or a somewhat modified version is above chance
(namely 90.5% for the middle-class and 85.8% for the working-
class children respectively). Thus the reaction rate of
these children lies within the range reported in earlier
investigations.

Furthermore, the main prediction as to the contingencies
of repetitions and deletions in CU$_2$ on a complete and correct
CU$_1$ and of modifications in CU$_2$ on a somewhat inappropriate
CU$_1$ respectively is fulfilled (Tables 1a, 2a).

Finally, a more finely grained analysis of the kind of
compensations of specific inappropriatenesses of the described
varieties shows that children indeed repair the identified
deficiencies of CU$_1$ on an above chance level: referentially
incomplete/semantically indeterminate parts of the utterance
were explained, missing grammatical elements were added,
grammatically or referentially incorrect parts of the utterances were corrected (Tables 1b, 2b). The numbers in brackets
give the values to be expected on the basis of the distributions of sums and it may easily be seen that the observed
distribution would render a highly significant χ^2 if this
statistic had been computed. Since this statistical test —
and by the way each other inference test, regardless of
whether it is parametric or not — is not without problems
when applied to data where the observations are not independent (and where it therefore is not clear for what kind of
population the results should be generalized) it was decided
to dispense with it.

TABLE 1a *Relation between the presence vs. absense of inade-*
quacies in CU_1 and the presence vs. absence of subsequent
modifications in CU_2. Middle-class children (n=8)

CU_1	CU_2			
	Modifi-cations	Repetitions & deletions	no adequate responses	Total
Inadequate	$179^{(126)}$	$80^{(140)}$	$35^{(28)}$	294
Complete and correct	$90^{(143)}$	$220^{(160)}$	$25^{(32)}$	335
Total	269	300	60	629

( ) = expected values

Besides these main results there are still some additional
points which deserve mention with respect to the total group.
First the high proportion of verbatim repetitions or deletions of redundant elements whenever CU_1 is complete (linguistically or conversationally speaking) is remarkable (67%
for both groups). Nevertheless in 15% of all complete CU_1, CU_2
had to be classified as "explanation of reference". Closer
inspection, however, reveals that in these cases what had
been categorized as "explanation of reference" in fact should
have been described as "explanation of cause" since it were
predominantly *reasons for CU_1* which were given by the children in CU_2. This seems to be a very plausible strategy:
whenever a non-understood utterance in the speaker's view
is perfect and neither a hypothesis that because of external
noise nor the suspicion that because of his inattentiveness
the partner has missed the message holds, it is reasonable
to assume that the nonspecific question was motivated by the
listener's interest as to *why* the utterance was made.

2.2.3 Discussion In relating the reported results to
theoretical concerns one could state that in tackling the
problem of the systematicity of modifications one in fact
is dealing with at least three different aspects of the
child's knowledge about language. First, it seems clear
that triggered repairs since they are systematic, are dependent on the *existence* of certain standards. Secondly, the
kind of standards involved in these children's repair strategies seem to belong to at least two analytically distinguishable classes: on the one hand, there seem to be standards
of inherent linguistic import like grammatical correctness.

TABLE 1b *Relation between characteristics of CU₁ and the observed modifications in CU₂ following signals of non-understanding ("nam?"). Middle-class children (n=8)*

	CU₂							
CU₁	Explanation of reference	Addition of grammatical element	Correction of referential aspects	Correction of grammatical aspects	Repetition	Deletion of redundant elements	No adequate response	Total
Referentially incomplete	55(20)	5	4	-	25	8	8	105
Gramatically incomplete	7	50(10)	3	2	5	10	16	93
Referentially inadequate	4	-	25(5)	-	12	6	8	55
Grammatically inadequate	1	1	1	21(2)	9	5	5	41
Complete and correct	52	11	24	3	177(94)	43(38)	25	355
Totals	119	67	57	26	228	72	60	629

42.77%   90.46%   47.69%   9.54%

( ) = expected values

TABLE 2a *Relation between the presence vs. absence of inadequacies in CU_1 and the presence vs. absence of subsequent modifications in CU_2. Working-class children (n=8)*

	CU_2			
CU_1	Modifications	Repetitions & deletions	no adequate responses	Total
Inadequate	$229^{(179)}$	$119^{(179)}$	$69^{(59)}$	417
Complete and correct	$47^{(97)}$	$156^{(96)}$	$22^{(32)}$	225
Total	276	275	91	642

( ) = expected values

And, on the other hand, there are standards (e.g. required level of explicitness) whose implementation seems to be dependent on an evaluation of the actually given situation. The 4 to 5-year-old children under observation are guided by these standards in a non-random fashion. Thus their knowledge about language can be characterized as comprising of language internal as well as dialogically relevant features. (By the way: noticing the parallel between this approach and others - e.g. Gallagher, 1977, 1978; Campbell and Wales, 1970 - which operate with the distinction between the child's structural and conversational rule-systems may sharpen one's awareness of the difference in the treatment). However, interpreting the results in this manner immediately leads to asking still another question. If it is correct to assume the existence of two kinds of standards (or of linguistic standards which are somehow weighted in actual speech) one would like to know more about their possible interplay. Without having yet made any attempt to investigate this question, it nevertheless seems to be worthwhile to indicate the direction of the argumentation, not only because this eventually should lead to a more differentiated picture of the child's knowledge about language but also because exactly these considerations seem to be relevant to approaching the question of *how* the child could have learnt what he is obviously capable of doing.

3 ACQUISITION OF STANDARDS

The mere fact that in CU_2 modifications do occur, and with respect to their being standard approximations can be judged

TABLE 2b *Relation between characteristics of CU_1 and the observed modifications in CU_2 following signals of non-understanding ("mm?"). Working-class children (n=8)*

CU₁	CU₂							Total
	Explanation of reference	Addition of grammatical element	Correction of referential aspects	Correction of grammatical aspects	Repetition	Deletion of redundant elements	No adequate response	
Referentially incomplete	62[19]	–	7	–	14	10	14	107
Grammatically incomplete	7	68[18]	4	1	22	14	29	145
Referentially inadequate	6	2	35[7]	–	20	10	14	87
Grammatically inadequate	5	1	3	28[3]	11	18	12	78
Complete and correct	32	10	5	–	119[65]	37[31]	22	225
Totals	112	81	54	29	186	89	91	642

42.99% 85.82% 42.83% 14.81%

( ) = expected values

as "corrections", implies that somehow deficient forms are
used by the child in CU_1 as well. Although it is quite evident that while some forms would be judged to be deviant by
any standard one might care to invent, others clearly are
deficient by some standards but not by others. Take as an
example the child saying "a needle": this utterance is deficient if measured against an absolute standard of syntactic
completeness but it is not deficient by a conversational
standard if it happens to be an (elliptical) answer to the
question "And what does she hold in her paw?" or if it is
accompanied by pointing. Therefore,for a given communicative intention there are two forms (e.g. elliptical and syntactically complete utterances; pronouns and corresponding
noun phrases) which with respect to that communicative intention could be seen as free variants ("synonymous")but
which are not equally appropriate in each kind of situation.
The investigation of this realm should reveal the interaction
of the two types of standards and, moreover, it should shed
light on the mechanisms involved in learning to pay attention
to them. It is this latter question which will be approached
now.

3.1 The adult's responses to inadequate and incomplete utterances

If one asks *how* children could have acquired this ability to
evaluate an utterance and — if necessary — to compensate
for specific deficiencies, then one possible assumption is
that the relevant information is transmitted to the child
through the adult's verbal behaviour in dialogue. Possibly
some of the adult's verbal responses to the described inadequacies of a child's utterance could provide the child with
that information, on the basis of which he then could induce
what is eventually to become the knowledge guiding his capacity to spontaneously produce understandable utterances,
and to adjust inappropriate ones.
   Since the following analyses set out to find evidence for
exactly this assumption, a few remarks to both legitimize
and qualify it seem to be called for. The assumption that
the growth of children's linguistic verbal capability is the
result of the verbal input provided by more competent speakers
(esp. adults) is obviously not an original one. For example,
this stance is taken by many attempts to investigate the in-
stigating and directional effect of so-called expansions immediately following a child's utterance. Nor does it seem to
be a particularly successful hypothesis. Although the matter
has been widely investigated (see Cazden, 1965; Brown and

Hanlon, 1970; parts of Snow and Ferguson, 1978; and many
others), the large body of equivocal results seems to be
sufficient to inhibit anyone from thinking along these lines.

However, the usual expansion-approach conceives of expansions as having a very direct effect by making available surface structure information and especially lacks any theoretical considerations as to why this kind of information should
be of any significance to the child. In contrast, there are —
even empirical — reasons (Käsermann, 1979) to establish the
possible relevance of expansions if they are seen as forming
part of a sequence of functionally related dialogue contributions. It is this functional embeddedness which under certain conditions could allow the child to judge occurring expansions against his communicative intentions and — given
certain relationships — assimilating not only new forms to
it but also realise the conditions under which these forms
are adequate. Without elaborating this point any further
such a different conception of expansions makes one more confident of finding some positive evidence of their effect.

With the background of these considerations one then can
ask whether potential inadequacies of CU within the range of
the four described varieties are verbally taken up by the
adult and whether his responses are such as to compensate
for these inadequacies. A second question addresses the point
brought up in discussing our results above. There it was
suggested that the child had to realize that some forms are
deficient by some standards but not by others. So if it is
the case that children not only acquire standards but also
learn to differentiate between actual conditions under
which considerations of these standards is either obligatory
or optional, then this also puts some constraints upon the
adult's responses which one would wish to observe if they
were to transmit relevant information. In this case one
would expect that adult verbal responses not only do occur
sometimes after inadequate child utterances but also do
model some kind of systematicity with regard to features
of the context. Posing this second question at all, is
dependent on the results to the first question. As long as
it turned out that the adult reacted to these inadequacies
either always or not at all the initial assumption for different reasons would be hard to maintain. If the adult
never reacted one could no longer assume that the child had
induced the prerequisites for his repair strategies from the
adult's behaviour in discussion. And if the adult always
reacted (thus at best transmitting some absolute standards)
it would remain unclear how the child could have acquired
his ability to discriminate between different conversational
constraints.

To tackle these questions four out of the 16 transcripts
that formed the data base for the preceding part were analysed. Two children from each of the two educational back-
grounds were selected. Then each pair of utterances consisting of a child utterance and the consequent adult utterance were compared.

Firstly, the child's utterance was coded as to the presence
of one or more of the described inadequacies and then there
followed a check as to whether these parts were verbally
responded to by a compensatory adult utterance. It is worth
pointing out that coding potential inadequacies of CU, without being circular, presupposes some kind of criteria which
are independent of the consequent adult reaction. (Alternatively, one could do the categorization of the CU without
knowledge of the following adult utterance.) In the case
of grammatically invalid CU, such a criterion is given by
the language system itself. In the case of referentially
adequate CU (or parts of CU), too, the decision as to what
forms a false or a right expression with regard to a given
situation is not difficult to make, given the accessibility
of that situation. Yet with regard to the remaining two
categories there exists no such simple and straightforward
solution. This is so because each utterance regardless of
its given elaboration could always be even more elaborate
(e.g. through the embedding of additional clauses) and more
specific than it is. In other words there exists neither a
structural nor a situational upper limit on possible explicitness. Furthermore the adequacy of the level of explicitness
depends very much upon the respective interlocutor's expectations. Although it is feasible in principle to take into
account the complexity of that matter, no general solution
was attempted in this context. Rather the analyses restricted themselves to utterances for which a clear decision could
be made as to whether they *contained enough information to be
understood if they were presented in the absence of any verbal
and situational context.* In accordance with this criterion,
syntactically incomplete (with regard to a simple sentence)
utterances and any pronoun use were judged to be grammatically and referentially incomplete respectively. This criterion amounts to applying what has earlier been termed an
"absolute standard". However, in treating the second question some modifications of this criterion will be necessary
(see below).

Bearing on the first question as to the occurrence (vs. non-
occurrence) of the adult's responses the following results
were obtained: In each of the four children's corpora there
were instances of the four types of inadequacies (total

number of utterances N = 838). With three of the four
children the rank order of the frequencies of the inadequacies was: referentially incomplete/semantically indeterminate
(54.9-64.1% of the total number of inadequacies), grammatically incomplete (19.9-28.4%) and — with a certain overlap —
referentially inadequate (9.3-13.5%) and grammatically inadequate (3.5-10.7%). For the fourth child — the "weakest"
speaker out of the four — grammatically incomplete instances
covered 52.9% followed by 26.1% referentially incomplete,
10.6% referentially inadequate and 10.4 grammatically inadequate utterances. The percentage of referentially inadequate
utterances has to be handled with care as an optimal record
of the situation of utterances was not available. Nevertheless these figures certainly provide a background which is
probably ordinally correct for the analysis of the adult's
verbal responses which here are of central interest.

The adult reacted to each type of inadequacy with each child;
moreover her reactions were not unspecific but precisely
aimed at compensating for the given inadequacies. This
result (elaborated below) shows that expansions indeed occur
as a consequence of the described inadequacies and that they
model the respective standards. It might be objected though —
and this objection would hold for all the results to be yet
presented — that the experimenter's readiness to take up
these children's verbal inadequacies is not representative
either for adults in general or possibly for the mothers of
the tested children. Although there is a sign of the experimenter's responding being dependent on the children's respective level of speech proficiency (to be reported presently)
this objection, of course, could only be invalidated by investigations.

However — and this is already part of the answer to the
question whether the adult reacts differentially to deficiencies
in CU — the adult's verbal response does not occur whenever
there is an opportunity to, but only in a certain percentage
of all possible cases. The mean percentage reactions, over
all children, is highest with instances of referentially
(65.8% of all cases in this category) and grammatically
(42.4%) inadequate utterances while referentially (28.6%) and
grammatically incomplete (26.2%) instances are taken up less
frequently.

From one point of view part of these results is just a
reaffirmation of the Brown and Hanlon remark that adults
seem to be preoccupied with teaching children THE TRUTH rather
than anything else. But from a slightly different point of
view the fact that the adult especially corrects CU for this
aspect seems to be less interesting than the fact that some-

times he doesn't! It is exactly the adult's differential reaction taking place to a greater or lesser extent with regard
to each of the types of inadequacy which — if systematic —
could be a potentially meaningful teaching device.

There is still another aspect of the frequency-of-uptake[2]
data which could be seen as a hint in exactly the same direction: within any of the four categories, the frequency of the
adult's uptake does not remain constant but varies between
the four children, thus suggesting that the expansion behaviour
under examination is not just a fixed idiosyncratic feature
of that experimenter. Moreover, if one rank-orders the four
children as to their speech proficiency (subjectively assessed
on the basis of their length of utterance), the percentage
of uptake are negatively correlated with this order with regard to all categories except the one of grammatical incompleteness.
In other words the frequency of uptake seems to be determined
to some extent by the child's individual level of speech development.

3.2 Determining Features

Having shown that (a) the experimenter sometimes does and
sometimes does not react to verbal inadequacies and that (b)
the determinants of this behaviour do not lie entirely within
the adult herself but are subject to change dependent on the
respective child's speech proficiency, one now can tackle the
question whether there are any systematic differences between
utterances in situations which are or are not taken up by
the adult. To answer this question two groups of inadequacies (grammatically incomplete and a sub-group of referentially incomplete utterances, namely utterances with personal
pronouns) and the corresponding adult's verbal uptake are
analysed more closely. That is to say CU with this type of
inadequacy which are taken up by the adult are compared to
those of the same type but without adult expansion.

3.2.1 Features determining the uptake of grammatically in-
complete utterances As a rule the children's grammatically
incomplete utterances are not completed by the adult's consequent utterance if their completion can be inferred either
from the *situation*, or from the *verbal context* in which they
occur. So, on the one hand, an utterance like "now another
one" does not get expanded (to "now you want to look at another picture book") if it is clear from the situation (including perhaps even the child's gestures) that this is exactly what the child wants. On the other hand, if the grammatically incomplete CU occurs within a verbal context where
it is either:

a) an elliptical answer to the adult's question;
b) a specification of one of the adult's or the child's own
   preceding utterances;
c) or if it fits into a slot of a previously established
   sentence frame as in a labelling situation where the
   child or the adult utter just once the fully explicit frame
   (e.g. "This is a lion" with the continuation "a tiger", "a
   monkey", etc.)

This verbal context seems to be sufficient as a completion
of the given utterance and therefore expansion does not
occur. Note that it is precisely this relationship between
an utterance and its context — termed "conversational completeness" before — that has also been shown to be a determinant of children's own repair strategies.

However, grammatically incomplete utterances are taken up
and are completed if at the same time there are some alternatives in the situation or in the verbal context. That is
to say, if a grammatically incomplete utterance could refer
to two or more facts, or if it could be completed by two or
more verbal contexts, or if there are alternative modes of
expressing parts of an utterance, then expansions do occur.
To get an impression of the kind of situations and verbal
contexts which seem to call for an adult's uptake consider the
following examples for the conditions of syntactic completion.

If, for instance, a predication is left implicit, which as
such is obvious from the situation but holds true for at
least two referents then the utterance gets expanded:

	Swiss German	English equivalent
8) CU:	dä het emu äuwä nid...	that one probably doesn't have...
AU:	nei, dä het nid Zahnweh	no, that one doesn't have toothaches

If the adult asks a question in using two formats, after
the child's elliptical answer, she selects one of the frames
and fills in the child's answer.

9) AU: aber d'Hüehner, was choi die mache, Tue da, was git's da?   but the chickens what can they do, look there, what is ob-tained here?

   CU: Eier   eggs

   AU: jo, die tüe Eier lege   yes, they do lay eggs

If the child's incomplete utterance is referentially indeterminate or false, the adult's specification or correction

respectively is embedded within a complete utterance. An example of the adult's reaction to a *referentially indeterminate* child utterance is the following:

	Swiss German	English equivalent
10) AU:	was git's jetz do us däm?	what is now becoming of that one?
CU:	das	this/that done
AU:	jetz isch's e Ballon!	now it is a balloon!

The same pattern occurs in an adult's response after a *referentially false* child utterance:

11) AU:	was macht d'Frou?	what is the woman doing?
CU:	schlafe	sleep
AU:	jo, die het nume d'Ouge zue, die tuet nid schlafe, die tuet schaffe, lue.	yeah, she has only her eyes closed, she doesn't sleep, she does work, look.

In other words, elliptical answers which as a rule are not taken up get expanded under the condition of their referential indeterminateness or incorrectness.

If there is a possible categorial or structural ambiguity within a child's utterance or if there is evidence that the child himself has syntactically different, though not necessarily correct ways, of expressing essentially the same message then the adult expands the CU and in doing so selects one of the alternatives or integrates them.

12) CU:	dsä Bett	??? bed
AU:	hm?	hm?
CU:	es Büssi	a kitty
AU:	hm?	hm?
CU:	das is ou Bett	this is bed, too
AU:	jo, ds Büssi isch ou im Bett	yes, the kitty is in the bed, too

Summarizing, one could say that the adult obviously differentiates between the so-called conversationally complete and the conversationally incomplete utterances and takes up only the latter type. The concept of conversational completeness that up to now remained vague can be defined with regard to situational and verbal contextual features of an utterance. For an utterance to be conversationally incomplete means

that there exist alternatives which if not resolved might
affect the understandability of an utterance. From this
pattern of adult responses the child could have induced the
awareness he obviously partly has access to (see above).
This aspect of knowledge consists in observing that speaking
in as elaborate and complete a manner as possible is not to
be striven for under all conditions but is only necessary
under specific conditions of potentially hampered utterance
understandability.

*3.2.2 Features determining the uptake of a subclass of
referentially indeterminate CU* The adult's verbal responses
with regard to personal pronouns will now be discussed in a
more detailed fashion. As is the case with grammatically
incomplete utterances, there is a possibility to treat personal pronouns from a somewhat absolute point of view, as
inherently indeterminate. On the basis of this criterion,
personal pronouns were included to describe the overall frequency characteristics of the adult's uptake. However, as
the data from triggered modifications have shown, the child
does not act in accordance with an absolute standard of
maximal explicitness but usually tunes his level of explicitness to "conversational" requirements. Therefore, if there
is any connection between the child's repair strategies and
the adult's uptake one should expect the adult not to expand
each occurring personal pronoun but only selectively react
to these pronouns which are conversationally indeterminate,
that is either in their relation to the situation or to the
verbal context.
    To tackle this assertion the values of the independent
variable (the child's use of conversationally indeterminate
vs. determinate pronouns) as well as the dependent variable
(the adult's uptake) are defined in the following way:
    A personal pronoun is conceived of as being sufficiently
determinate:

a) if it refers to some bit of shared knowledge of the
   dialogue partners and furthermore does so in an unequivocal manner, or
b) if by its use it creates, unequivocally, some new bit of
   shared knowledge.

On the other hand, if a pronoun is used in a way that violates this principle then it is termed indeterminate. To
specify what is meant by this statement examples of each of
the several levels at which a pronoun can be identified as
being indeterminate are given. This is the case:

a) if a pronoun functions as a substitute for a *label* (e.g.
   within the frame of the child saying "That's a dog, a
   cat and a ... this one", "this one" referring to a parrot
   is indeterminate);
b) if a pronoun is ambiguous with regard to a given *situation*.
   In "Flurina knits a cap for *her*" the pronoun is ambiguous
   if the utterance refers to a picture in which one can
   see Flurina with *her* mother and *her* puppet;
c) if the pronoun is ambiguous with regard to conventions
   which have been set up in the preceding *dialogue*. Thus
   if both partners agreed in referring to a certain fact by
   uttering /he/ the use of /he/ referring to a different
   person may potentially be ambiguous. Also if a speaker
   misjudges the memory span of his partner, or if he does
   not take into account the level of expected explicitness
   that is set up for instance, by a question of his partner,
   the used pronoun will be relatively indeterminate.
d) if the pronoun occurs in a *verbal context* of another pronoun or a noun in such a way that by the canonical interpretation (anaphora) it refers back to this part without
   really intending this reference. Thus in the utterance
   "There he wants to shoot him, and there he does shoot him"
   the canonical interpretation leads one astray because the
   first /him/ refers to the rabbit and the second one to
   the hunter. (This text was uttered by a child while looking at a well known story "Der Jäger und der Hase" out
   of the "Struwwelpeter");
e) if the pronoun is part of a construction which is *structurally ambiguous* like "da het's" with the possible meaning of "there is" or "it has"; or "da faht's a" with the
   possible meaning of "something starts" or "it (the child)
   starts doing something".

On the side of the dependent variable, each adult's substitution of a pronoun by the respective noun phrase, or each
specific question aimed at eliciting a CU which is more
determinate with regard to the part in question, is counted
as an adequate verbal response. For the point to be studied
it is not essential whether the adult's substitutions refer
to the referent intended by the child. As the child is
not supposed to learn in the first place specific lexical
items, but a set of conditions which require explicitness,
as well as the principle of remedy for possibly occurring
failures of that type, it is sufficient to assume that the
adult's responses, at least sometimes, just have the character of suggestions.

The results for each child separately and for all children
together are presented in Table 3. From the distribution

TABLE 3 *Relation between levels of determinateness and occurrence of adult's verbal response with respect to pronouns.*

	Child	Adult Adequate verbal response	No adequate verbal response
Referentially indeterminate	M.U.	14	1
	H.J.	1	0
	W.H.	8	1
	S.A.	3	1
	overall	26	3
Referentially not indeterminate	M.U.	2	130
	H.J.	2	55
	W.H.	0	39
	S.A.	0	9
	overall	4	233

frequencies in this contingency table it is clear that in each case the frequencies of either of the two expected outcomes (cells a and d) outweigh the two others. Overall the adult responds to 10 (38.5% of all expected responses) dialogically indeterminate, labelling and verbal contextually indeterminate each 6 (23.1%), situationally and structurally indeterminate pronouns each 2 (7.7%).

In the following some examples are given for the relationship between an inappropriate pronoun usage and the consequent uptake-utterance of the adult. The critical parts in CU and AU are underlined.

	Swiss German	English equivalent	Categorization
13) CU:	Dä louft emu. U da flügt er furt. Mit <u>däm</u>.	This one walks. And there he flies away. With <u>this</u>.	*indeterminate pronoun*
SU:	Jo. Da het's eso ne starche Luft gä, nächär het er em grad furtgwäiht, <u>mit em Schirm</u>.	Yes, there is stormy weather/strong wind and it has carried him away, <u>with the umbrella</u>.	
14) CU:	<u>däm</u> het s <u>Flurina</u> grüeft (däm = Fuchs oder Vogel)	That <u>one</u> Flurina <u>has called</u> (that one = fox or bird).	*situationally ambiguous pronoun*
AU:	het dr Fuchs s <u>Vögeli</u> greicht?	has <u>the fox</u> taken away <u>the bird</u>?	

Swiss German	English equivalent	Categorization
15) AU: oder isch <u>es</u> scho vorhär uf dr Änte obe gsi? (es = s Büssi)	or has <u>it</u> been on the bac<u>k</u> of the duck already? (it = the kitty)	*dialogically ambiguous pronoun*
CU: ja, lueg, hie isch'<u>s</u> im Wasser	yeah, look, here <u>it</u> is in the water	
AU: jo, ds <u>Änteli</u>	yes, <u>the duck(y)</u>	
16) CU: Nächär go si$_1$ mit ihm i <u>Garte</u> Nächär tüe si$_2$ tanze (si$_1$ = alle Tiere) (si$_2$ = die Katzen)	Then <u>they$_1$</u> go to the garde<u>n</u> Then <u>they$_2$</u> do dance (they$_1$ = all animals) (they$_2$ = the cats)	*inappropriate pronoun in the present context*
AU: ja, <u>d Büsseli,</u> gäu	yes, <u>the cats,</u> isn't it	
17) CU: do <u>het's</u> no es chl<u>īses</u> (het's = "gibt es" oder "besitzt es")	there it has also a small one (it has = "there is" or "it possesses")	*structurally ambiguous pronoun*
AU: jo, dasch ds Bäbeli, am <u>Meiteli</u> sis.	yes, this is the puppet, the <u>girl's</u> (puppet).	

In other words the occurrence of the adult's verbal responses is predictable if one defined "indeterminate pronouns" in the way described above. However, it is clear that the adult's modelling of exactly the same kind of behaviour which is contained in the child's repair strategies does not *prove* any causal relationship between these two events. It could well be the other way around, too. Nevertheless that there is a correspondence at all makes one feel confident to search for such a mechanism by more detailed investigations.

So far it has been shown that there are striking parallels between the conditions under which the child is induced to repair his initial utterance in a meaningful way and the conditions under which the adult responds to and expands the respective inadequacies. Knowing that much, one starts wondering whether in these children there is any sign of taking into account, *spontaneously*, some of these conditions as well. To answer this question one naturally would not

want to register utterances which are correct already since
— for obvious reasons — they could be adequate just by chance.
However, instances of self-corrections of initially inadequate
usage would provide exactly the data looked for.

Spontaneous self-corrections, or self-expansions of pronouns used inadequately, were registered for two out of the
four children. The respective proportions of corrections
(C) and non-corrections (nC) reveal that the children are
most proficient in spotting dialogically indeterminate pronouns (19C: 11nC). This fact has its counterpart in the above
mentioned adult's preference to verbally take up exactly this
kind of indeterminacy.

However, with regard to the other categories there is no
such direct correspondence. As the numbers in each of these
categories are small one should perhaps not try to interpret
them with regard to the adult's behavior. Overall one has the
impression that the children are better in detecting difficulties in utterances if the diagnosis is supported by situational and dialogic cues (27C: 14nC) while they are worse
if they have to rely entirely on inherent linguistic cues as
might be the case with the categories of verbal contextual
and structural indeterminateness (5C: 12nC).

Finally, one should take notice of the category of grammatically inadequate pronouns. At first it seems incompatible with
the initially reported results concerning dialogically induced
repair strategies that the children should be unaware of these
instances. Yet, there is still another possible interpretation
of this phenomenon: consider the categories of dialogically and
verbal contextually dependent pronoun correction. Part of the
problem using these instances correctly, and unequivocally,
stems from something which could be paraphrased as "referent
and corresponding pronoun agreement". While a more or less
proficient adult speaker has at his disposal several linguistic means to use the same pronoun with different referents in
an unequivocal way, 4- to 5-year-old children in the absence
of these mechanisms (e.g. reliance on case marking, semantics
of the verb etc.) would lead one to expect that they have some
problems in coping with this situation. Judging from several
instances of self-corrections one gets the impression that instead they work with a heuristic of the following type: "If I
myself or my partner refers to the *same referent twice* I should
use the same pronouns. Furthermore, if I refer to different referents for which the same pronouns could be used if they occur
in isolation I have to change one of the pronouns either by sub-
stituting a noun phrase or a different pronoun". Such a principle should lead exactly to self-corrections of the following
type:

EU: und <u>die</u> dlaine brüele   and <u>these</u> small ones cry, too
    au (<u>die</u> = Känguruhs)   (these kangaroos)

CU: und <u>die</u>...<u>die Luusbue</u>   and <u>these</u>...<u>the rascals</u>...
    ...<u>die fräche Buebe</u>   the <u>saucy boys</u> do laugh
    tüen lache.

And it also should lead to the conservation of some linguistically speaking inadequate pronouns like the following ones:

18) CU: tüen *si ihn* ufpumpe   do *they* inflate *him*
        (tüen *si si* ufpumpe =   (do *they* inflate *they*/them =
        richtig)   correct)

19) CU: do will *si ihn* go   there *she* wants to shoot *him*
        verschiesse
        (do will *er ihn* go   (there *he* wants to shoot
        verschiesse)   *him*)

Such a principle could well be an overgeneralization formed
on the basis of the experience of being not (or not unequivocally) understood, or of being corrected for instance where
the same pronoun was used for different referents — as in
"There he$_1$ wants to shoot him$_2$ and there he$_2$ does shoot him$_1$".
Against this background the preservation of grammatically inadequate pronouns (as in the examples above) could be interpreted as a *compensatory* strategy.

4. CONCLUSIONS

It has been shown that the children repair their utterances
in the *presence* as well as in the *absence* of any *communicative
pressure*. Hence, it is not just the actual need of successful
communication but also *an enduring aspect of the child's knowledge about language* which determines the form of utterances.
The correspondence between the children's induced and spontaneous repairs and the adult's modelling behavior point in
the direction of *how* the children could have acquired their
abilities. Moreover, the clearly inadequate usage of some forms
seems to be interpretable by some kind of rules which ultimately could be rooted in the adult's expansion behavior as well as
in his difficulties sometimes to understand what the child
wants to say. However, far more detailed investigations are
needed to find out how the child's awareness of functional on
the one hand and formal aspects of utterances on the other hand
interact in order to allow for a progression in the acquisition
process.

ACKNOWLEDGEMENT

We would like to thank Roger Wales and Jürgen Weissenborn for
discussing a draft version of this chapter with us. Roger
Wales also corrected the English, but should not be held responsible for the specific variant of the idiom.

REFERENCES

Amstutz, B. (1977). "Sprachmodifikationenen bei Zweisprachigen".
  Master thesis, Bern.
Brown, R. and Hanlon, C. (1970). Derivational complexity and
  order of acquisition in child speech. *In* "Cognition and the
  Development of Language" (R. Hayes, ed.), pp. 155-207. New
  York: Wiley.
Campbell, R. and Wales, R. (1970). The study of language
  acquisition. *In* "New Horizons in Linguistics" (J. Lyons,
  ed.) pp. 242-260. Penguin.
Cazden, C. (1965). "Environmental assistance to the child's
  acquisition of grammar". PhD dissertation, Harvard University.
Clark, E. (1978). Awareness of language: some evidence from
  what children say and do. *In* "The Child's Conception of
  Language" (A. Sinclair, R.J. Jarvella and W.J.M. Levelt,
  eds), pp. 17-54. Berlin, Heidelbert, New York: Springer.
Foppa, K. (1978). Language acquisition - a human ethological
  problem? *Social Science Information* 17, 93-105.
Gallagher, T.M. (1977). Revision behaviors in the speech of
  normal children developing language. *Speech and Hearing
  Research* 20(2), 303-318.
Gallagher, T.M. (1978). Conversational aspects of language-
  disordered revision behaviors. *Speech and Hearing Res.*
  21(1), 118-135.
Huber, M. (1978). "Sprechstrategien bei sprachgestörten Kindern
  im Vorschulalter". Master thesis, Bern.
Käsermann, M.L. (1977). "'Hm?' - Sprechstrategien von Kindern
  in Nicht-Verstehens-Situationen". Paper read at the Schweizer-
  ische Tagung experimentall arbeitender Psychologen, Zürich,
  1977.
Käsermann, M.L. (1980). "Spracherwerb und Interaktion". Phil.
  dissertation, Bern; Bern: Hans Huber.
Käsermann, M.L. (1979). "Mutter-Kind-Dialoge: Determinanten
  der Wortwahl und Wortordnung kindlicher Äusserungen in
  Nicht-Verstehens-Situationen". Paper read at the 21. Tagung
  experimentall arbeitender Psychologen. Heidelberg, 1979.
Marshall, J., and Morton, J. (1978). On the mechanics of
  EMMA. *In* "The Child's Conception of Language" (A. Sinclair,
  R.J. Jarvella and W.J.M. Levelt, eds). Berlin, Heidelberg,
  New York: Springer.

Meyer, S. (1980). "Schichtspezifisches Dialogverhalten bei 4-jährigen Kindern. Master thesis, Bern.

Slobin, D.I. (1978). A case study of children's ideas about language. *In* "The Child's Conception of Language" (A. Sinclair, R.J. Jarvella, and W.J.M. Levelt, eds), pp. 45-54. Berlin, Heidelberg, New York: Springer.

Snow, C. and Ferguson, C. (eds) (1978). "Talking to Children. Language Input and Acquisition". Cambridge, London, New York, Melbourne: Cambridge University Press.

Straumann, R. (1981). "Der Einfluss unspezifischer Interventionen auf den Grad der Verständlichkeit von Äusserungen eines 16 Monate alten Kindes". Master thesis. (In prep.)

Valian, V. and Wales, R. (1976). What's what: talkers help listeners hear and understand by clarifying sentential relations. *Cognition* 4, 155-176.

A DEVELOPMENTAL STUDY OF PRAGMATIC APPROPRIATENESS OF WORD ORDER AND CASEMARKING IN KALULI*

BAMBI B. SCHIEFFELIN

University of Pennsylvania, Philadelphia, USA.

1. INTRODUCTION

Children all over the world acquire their conversational skills in the context of social interaction. In these contexts they are learning not only the structure of their language, but the culturally preferred conventions of interaction and language use. This in turn helps guide the acquisition of linguistic forms. What a child says in everyday situations can be seen as influenced by what society selects as significant, what is socially or culturally a priority. When one takes interaction as a major context of language acquisition, what a child chooses to say, as well as *how* a child chooses to say it, must be seen as culturally, linguistically and cognitively conditioned. It is important within this type of perspective to take into account whether young children's utterances are not only syntactically correct, but whether they are pragmatically appropriate in the specific contexts in which they are used. Competence in interaction involves both.

In this chapter I will describe two related phenomena in young Kaluli children's conversation: the acquisition and use of pragmatically appropriate word order and the development of correct agentive casemarking. The Kaluli language is an especially revealing one in which to examine syntactic

* Research for this paper was sponsored by the National Science Foundation and the Wenner-Gren Society for Anthropological Research, New York. Many thanks to the following friends for their helpful suggestions on earlier versions: M.S. Ammon, L. Bloom, A. Duranti, B. Lavandera, E. Ochs, E.L. Schieffelin, M. Silverstein and D. Slobin.

phenomena within a pragmatic framework given the relationships between word order, casemarking and pragmatic conventions.

The Kaluli children whose language development I shall be
discussing live on the Great Papuan Plateau in the Southern
Highlands of Papua New Guinea. The Kaluli are traditionally
nonliterate tropical forest subsistence horticulturalists.
They reside in long house communities made up of 60-100
individuals separated by an hour or so walk over forest
trails (E.L. Schieffelin, 1976).

Kaluli, one of five languages of the Bosavi family, is a non-
Austronesian language. In several important ways it resembles
some other non-Austronesian (or Papuan) languages that have
been described in Papua New Guinea. These languages, as reviewed by Li and Lang (1979), have the following general structural characteristics. They are verb-final languages marking
case relations postpositionally on nouns. Modifiers generally
follow the head noun and the genitive construction typically
has the order Genitive + Head. Verb morphology tends to be
complex and often irregular. Information about transitive
and intransitive subjects is cross-referenced in the verb
through agreement. In Kaluli this applies to all tenses
except those marking past and habitual for which there are
single forms. This subject-verb agreement shows a nomina-
tive-accusative pattern.

In terms of marking the semantic functions of nouns,
Kaluli has a mixed word order and inflectional system.
That is, sometimes word order and other times casemarking is
used to indicate semantic functions. Li and Lang point out
that "those Papuan languages which have case systems are
mostly ergative" (1979; 309). In Kaluli casemarking on
nouns follows a semantically motivated split ergative system.

Before presenting the data on acquisition, some linguistic
facts drawn from family conversations will be provided on the
pragmatics of word order, followed by a short description of
the casemarking system.

2. THE PRAGMATICS OF WORD ORDER AND CASEMARKING IN KALULI

Kaluli has two allowable word orders, AOV (Agent Object Verb)
and OAV (Object Agent Verb), each of which is used for pragmatic focus. In this analysis I follow Givón's definition of
focus, "the constituent with the most salient or important
pragmatic information" (1975; 185). For Kaluli this means
that the preverbal position, the position directly preceding
the verb indicates what is in focus, what is the "issue" or
what is being contrasted by the speakers in any discourse.

In other words, the preverbal position has the relatively
new information focus for the utterance. Therefore one
would expect that in sentences with OAV order agents would
be in focus. In sentences with AOV order, agents would not
be in focus. This is precisely what we find when we examine
utterances in on-going conversation.

Furthermore, given the pragmatics of these orders, each
one is selected and used by speakers in different speech
genres or registers, for different speech acts. OAV, with
the agent in focus, is used in a variety of speech acts,
such as making requests, teasing, tattling, and in arguments
concerning who shall perform a certain action. Utterances
with AOV order, with the agent not in the focused position,
are used to announce or report an action, in narratives,
stories, or when the speaker is focusing on or contrasting
objects. We examine utterances taken from family interactions in order to see more clearly the pragmatics of word
order in Kaluli.

1) Three people are sitting around and one spots a cucumber.
   Reaching for it -
   Speaker 1: yagan   -ɔ ni   diɛno.   I will take
               cucumber   I   take   the cucumber.

   Speaker 2: A! yagan   -ɔ nisa diɔl.   No! I (not you)
               no   I   take   take the cucumber.

In this first example Speaker 1 is the potential agent and
uses OAV order in claiming the cucumber. However, Speaker 2
challenges the claim, and uses another focused subject pronoun (I not you) and keeps the agent in preverbal position.
To compare the pragmatics of word order we look at another
OAV utterance where the speaker refers to a third person as
agent.

2) A group of children are eating salt, a prized commodity.
   Abi, a 3 year old boy, is taking more than his share.
   His older sister (aged 9) tattling on him calls out to
   her mother -

   sɔlu -wɔ Abi - yɛ nɛlab.   Abi keeps eating salt.
   salt   abs   ERG   eat

Here the agent, Abi, is in focus; the issue concerns *who*
is eating the salt. The speaker uses OAV order since she is
focusing on the agent as the issue. Here, the speaker wants
the listener (the mother) to do something, or say something
to the agent, since the agent is acting in a problematic way.

We next examine AOV utterances and their pragmatic force
in discourse. As was mentioned, in this word order the agent

is *not* in focus.   Speech acts used with AOV include reports
and announcements of action.

3) A woman is sitting with a group of people. Getting up
   she says -
   ne   de   gilimɛnigo.   I am going to light a fire.
   I   fire   light

The speaker (agent) is simply reporting her action, and does
not expect anyone to do anything about what she has said.
The agent is not in focus, and is placed before the object.
In the next example the speaker uses the same order (AOV) and
refers to a third person agent.

4) Abi's older sister (aged 9) sees him drinking dirty water.
   Calling to her mother to inform her -
   Abi   -yɔ   hɔn   mogago-   wɔ   nab. Abi drinks <u>bad water</u>.
         N   water   bad   N   eat/drink

It is all right for Abi to drink, but not dirty water. The
object upon which he is acting is problematic, in focus, and
in this utterance it is placed directly in front of the verb,
AOV.

   In these four examples we can see how the pragmatic concerns of the speaker are reflected in the way in which elements of the utterance are arranged. Pragmatic concerns and
context determine the word order selected by individual
speakers. In turn, word order selection communicates the
concerns of the speaker to the listener.

   In referring to the self as agent (or potential agent)
speakers only use personal pronouns. Kaluli has several
pronominal sets which co-occur with these two word orders
(B.B. Schieffelin, in press). However, in referring to third
person agents, a variety of proper and common nouns, pronouns,
and demonstrative forms are available. Once a word order is
chosen, a corresponding case system is called into operation
to mark the agent of the utterance.

   Given the fact that transitive sentences have the understood semantic equivalent of two noun phrases in so-called
"case relations" to a predicate, languages provide ways to
signal which is of one kind, agent, and which is of the
other, patient or object. Casemarking on nouns is one way
to do this. In an ergative schema of casemarking, the casemarking on the agent noun phrase of transitive verbs, (such
as <u>give</u>, <u>hit</u>) is different from that of the subjects of intransitive verbs (such as come, go, sit) which is the same as
the objects or patients of transitive verbs.

   In recent discussions on ergativity (Comrie, 1978; Dixon,
1979; Silverstein, 1976) it has been pointed out that in all

ergative languages the casemarking system applies under certain conditions, and not under others, e.g. word orders,
tenses, person/number of agents. Samoan, for example, uses
ergative casemarking in VAO and VOA orders, but not in AVO
utterances (Ochs, in press). Kaluli similarly uses two casemarking systems, each related to word order. OAV follows an
ergative casemarking system. AOV follows both an ergative and
a neutral casemarking system. The selection of one or the
other in AOV depends on the hierarchy of nouns used to encode
agent and object.
    In OAV utterances in which the agent refers to a third
person casemarking on nouns is realized as follows:

          Nominal casemarking - Ergative/Absolutive

          - ɛ   ERG (agents of transitive verbs)
          - ɔ   ABS (subjects of intransitive verbs)
                     (objects of transitive verbs)

          phonologically conditioned alternation

          -ɛ/-yɛ/-wɛ   -ɔ/-yɔ/-wɔ

As in many other non-Austronesian ergative languages, only
full nouns, that is proper nouns, common nouns, deictics and
demonstratives that refer to animate agents receive casemarking. Personal pronouns do not receive casemarking except
for locative and dative case. Instead they change form completely. Example 2 above illustrates the ergative and absolutive casemarkers and how they are used in OAV utterances
with third person nominal agents. The ergative marker -yɛ is
obligatory on the agent (Abi) which is in preverbal position.
The absolutive marker (-wɔ) is attached to the object, salt.
    Compare this to Example 4, AOV (third person agent). Notice
that there is no ergative casemarker on the agent, again Abi.
Instead, most third person AOV utterances are marked with
neutral case (-ɔ) on either or both nouns as follows:

          Nominal casemarking - Neutral

          -ɔ   N (agents of transitive verbs)
                    (subjects of intransitive verbs)
                    (objects of transitive verbs)

          phonologically conditioned alternation

          -ɔ/-yɔ/-wɔ

The neutral casemarking is the "unmarked form", identical
to the absolutive and the form given as a citation form in
elicitation. In casual or fast speech, such as commonly
spoken in family interactions, these neutral casemarkers are

often omitted. This is consistent in both adults' speech to children and adults' speech to each other. While most AOV utterances follow a neutral case paradigm, there is one exception which is related to the types of nouns representing agent and object. Table 1 displays the rules of selection in AOV utterances.

TABLE 1 *Rules of casemarking selection in AOV utterances*

	Agent	Object	Transitive verb
A	proper name kin term + ERG	proper name kin term + ABS	trans verb
B	proper name kin term + N	animate/inanimate noun, pronoun, deictic, demonstrative + N	trans verb
C	animate noun pronoun + N	proper name/kin term, animate/inanimate noun, pronoun, deictic, demonstrative + N	trans verb

In condition B and C the neutral forms can be used on both nouns as in Example 4. Condition A is the exception.

Dixon (1979) and Silverstein (1976) have discussed what types of lexical items are most likely to occur as agents. A hierarchy of agents, from most likely to least likely, shows that first and second person pronouns are highest in this animacy hierarchy. Animate common nouns follow, while inanimate common nouns are the lowest (Dixon, 1979; 85). Proper nouns fall in the middle of this continuum; that is, they are just as likely to be acted upon by an agent as they are likely to be agents.

In Kaluli when both agent and object are expressed by proper nouns (names or kin terms, condition A) this can be seen as the context of maximum ambiguity in the animacy hierarchy. The ergative paradigm is used to indicate which equally potential agent is in fact controlling the action. The ergative marker grammatically disambiguates the function of each proper noun in the utterance. Thus we have clear evidence that the ergative marker is not simply a focusing device, since it is possible to have an agent "out of focus" with the ergative marker indicating that it is the agent. In fact, in condition A it is obligatory.

5) Abi - yε Mεli- yɔ sandab.   Abi hits Mεli.
        ERG   ABS hit

To summarize the word order/casemarking relationship, in OAV
(third person agent), the ergative marker is *obligatory*. In
AOV it must not be used on sentence initial agents, or it is
incorrect, except in the one condition, specified as A in
Table 1, where there is maximal ambiguity in terms of the
animacy hierarchy. Pragmatics and context mutually interact
with word order determining which order communicates the
speaker's intentions, and casemarking is determined by word
order.

The following stretch of discourse illustrates how word
order is used by two participants in an interaction. (Child
speech is on the right, adult speech and context is on the
left. Age is in months and weeks.)

6) Mɛli (28.3) is naked, and her mother wants her to put on
   a skirt. Instead she gets a pubic cover (abbreviated pc).

[1]Mother → Mɛli: kɛn   kama,
                  skirt put on, IMP

      dabale   we   kadesa
      pc   this give up IMP
      Put on (a) skirt; give up this pc.

                              [2]a!/
                                 no!/

[3]mɔ!
   No!

                      [4]mɔ! dabale · dabale
                         no! pc   pc

                         kɛmɛnɔ   wɛ/
                         wear FUT-I   EMPH
                         no! I will wear (the) pc!

[5]wa?
   huh?

                      [6]ne   dabale kɛmɛnɔ/
                         I   pc   wear
                         I will wear (the) pc.

[7]a! kɛn   kɛlan - balo
   no skirt wear HAB EMPH
   no! you wear skirts.
   dabale S - wɛ   kɛlan
          ERG   wear HAB
   S. wears (a) pc.

                      [8]ne dabale kɛmɛnɔ/
                         I pc   wear

[9]ge   kalu - wɔ
   you boy   QST
   Are you (a) boy?

[10]ne dabale kɛmɛnɔ/

[11]kɛn   kɛlan, dabul-ɔ gi   kɛlan
skirt   wear   belts   you   wear
You wear skirts, you wear belts.

[12]nɔ!   dabale kɛmɛnɔ/
mother!

In line 1 mother says, "Put on a skirt. Give up this pubic
cover (abbreviated pc)." Notice that in both utterances,
the objects "skirt" and "pubic cover" are directly before the
verb and the subject is deleted. Mɛli's response (line 2)
is "no, (I) will wear the pubic cover." The object, pubic
cover, again is in preverbal position, indicating it is the
issue in contrast. Information indicating that the subject
is the speaker is cross-referenced in the verb. The agent (I),
which is not in focus, is deleted, a pattern common to both
adult and child speakers. Mɛli's words are met with a clarification request from her mother. She responds (line 6) "I
will wear the pubic cover", this time adding the(nonfocused)
subject pronoun (previously deleted) to the left, keeping
the object in preverbal position. For Mɛli the issue concerns
the object, the pubic cover as opposed to the skirt. (Children
and adults rarely inserted a constituent (in this example,
the subject pronoun) between the verb and the preverbal noun
phrase in responses to clarification requests or in repetitions of their own utterances.) In line 7 Mɛli's mother restates her position, that Mɛli should wear a skirt, contrasting "skirt" to Mɛli's preferred "pubic cover". She introduces a new topic in referring to Mɛli's brother Seligiwɔ
(marked S), pointing out that *he* wears a pubic cover. Here
the focus is on the agent, Seligiwɔ , in preverbal position.
The agent is marked with the obligatory ergative marker.
Mɛli maintains her position and word order throughout. (A
more sophisticated speaker at this point could have used OAV
order putting "I" agent in preverbal position to contrast
who wears the pubic cover.) Her mother asks (line 9), "Are
you a boy?!" and Mɛli simply restates her position. Her
mother adds (line 11) "you wear skirts" (object in focus,
OV) "skirt belts *you* wear" (OAV), contrasting 'you' with her
earlier assertion about Mɛli's brother.

This interaction illustrates the relationship between word
order and the pragmatic concerns expressed through it. As
with any linguistic form/meaning relationship, word order is
socially motivated by what each of the participants wants in
the situation. It is used to express concerns and issues of
importance for each speaker.

3. THE DEVELOPMENTAL PROGRESSION OF THE ACQUISITION OF WORD
ORDER CONVENTIONS AND CONCOMITANT CASEMARKING IN THREE
CHILDREN

The data come from an 18-month field study on the development
of communicative competence (B.B. Schieffelin, in press).
For the present analysis I have examined the longitudinal
tape-recorded and transcribed conversations I collected from
3 Kaluli children. At the beginning of the study these children, 2 boys and a girl, were about 24 months old. Samples
were collected at 4-6 week intervals and consisted of an
average of over 3 hours per sample. The language was recorded
in the every-day familial settings in which it was being
learned, so as to document the contexts of language acquisition as well as the acquisition process itself. The language
that comprises these samples therefore is naturalistic and
spontaneous, and captures the communication of the child with
those people with whom he or she regularly interacted. Extensive contextual and ethnographic notes were taken both
during and after recordings. These were used to understand
and interpret the meanings of utterances as well as the meanings of interactions.
    To analyse the relationship between word order and case-
marking in children's spontaneous transitive declarative
utterances with third person agents, we examine utterances
which express an agent, object, and verb, but not necessarily
in that order.

3.1 Acquisition of the Ergative Casemarker in OAV Order

Recall that in adult speech this casemarker is obligatory in
OAV for marking the agent. Once children begin producing
3-element utterances with third person nominal agents, they
go through 2 stages in acquiring the obligatory casemarker.
First, they leave it out; the agent is expressed before the
verb with no casemarking at all. Next, they add it in obligatory contexts.

7) Wanu (27.3) had been playing with and talking about a
   bag of salt. He says to his mother -

   *sɔlu- wɔ Babi-∅ dimi-lɔb/   <u>Bambi</u> gave the salt.
   salt   give EVID

The agent, Bambi, is in focus and correctly placed before the
verb. However, the obligatory ergative marker is absent.
The agent of the verb "give" usually appeared in OAV order
because social and cultural conventions dictated that the
agent — the "giver" — is focused on and made explicit

in any type of transaction. When children omitted an obligatory ergative marker, mothers often told them to say it
again properly after providing the correct model for them to
imitate.

   Mɛli, at 26 months, also produced utterances with this type
of error.

8) Mɛli had been requesting salt from her mother, who wasn't
   responding. Finally after looking and not finding it she
   says to her mother (referring to her cousin, named Mama) -

   *sɔlu-wɔ   Mama-ø diabe/   <u>Mama</u> took the salt.
    salt   take

Mɛli had already mentioned the salt, and the issue in focus
was the agent, Mama. The word order, as in Example 7, is
pragmatically appropriate, determined by the discourse and
context history, but the obligatory grammatical casemarker is
missing.

   After a period of producing OAV without agentive (ergative)
casemarking, the 3 children started producing OAV third person utterances with the ergative casemarker on the agent.
Children used this word order with its concomitant case system correctly to contrast agents within their own turns as
well as across speaker turns. Examples 9 and 10 show how
children were using word order and ergative casemarking
correctly.

9) Mɛli (27.3) is taking one sandal, and her brother
   Seligiw (S) is taking the other one. She speaks to
   her mother -

   Nodo - wɔ   nisa   diɔl/   <u>I</u> take one.
   one side   I   take

   Nodo - wɔ   S-wɛ diab/   <u>Seligiwɔ</u> takes one.
               ERG   take

Notice that Mɛli is contrasting agents, I and Seligiwɔ, within her own turn, using OAV order and marking the third person
agent with the obligatory ergative marker. Children also
used OAV word order when contrasting agents across speaker
turns which was important in arguments.

10) Wanu (31.) and his sister are talking. She is hold-
    ing a bag.

    Sister: as -ɔ we Daibo -wɛ dimiabe. <u>Daibo</u> gave this bag.
            bag   this   ERG give

    Wanu: we   Babi - yɛ dimiabe. <u>Babi</u> gave this.
          this   ERG

Wanu counters his sister's claim that D. had given the bag, retaining the OAV order that she had used.

These examples illustrate the child's developing skill in constructing pragmatically appropriate and grammatically correct arguments. The same effect could have been accomplished with stress in English; Kaluli instead uses word order.

One might assume from these examples that children are marking only proper nouns (names, kin terms) with the ergative marker when they appear before the verb. This is not the case. Children marked a variety of animate agents, referring to them with common nouns as well as deictics and demonstratives.

11) Abi (33.2) talking about his missing knife, says -

    Enɔ num   -ɛ afa di/   <u>Someone</u> stole it.
    it   someone ERG steal

Thus far we have seen examples where the child initially omits the ergative marker and then puts it on agents correctly. Interestingly, in only one example in the entire corpus of OAV third person (77 tokens) is the absolutive casemarker used incorrectly on an agent in the position of focus, that is, before the verb.

3.2 Development of Children's AOV Utterances with Third Person Nominal Agents

Recall that for adult speech, AOV order uses neutral casemarking on both nouns, in most contexts — that is, both nouns are marked identically, and word order signals function. In casual speech one or both of these neutral, unmarked case suffixes may often be omitted. Only when both nouns are expressed as proper nouns must ergative marking be used with sentence-initial agent. To mark agents in any other way is incorrect.

Children essentially go through 3 stages once they start producing 3-element AOV utterances. First, agents are not marked at all; then the ergative marker is added to sentence-initial agents, producing incorrect utterances. Next the ergative marker is restricted to OAV order, and only those infrequent occurrences of the special condition.

12) Abi (25.1) is watching me eat pandanus, a tropical vegetable, and announces to his mother -

    Babi oga   nab/   Bambi eats pandanus.
          pandanus eat

This is the correct word order since he is reporting an event.
Neither noun is marked. Wanu and Mɛli produced similar constructions.

For 2 of the 3 children, within a month of producing correctly marked sentence-medial agents there was an overgeneralization of the ergative marker to agents in sentence initial
position. Wanu did not follow this pattern exactly, but he
was using the ergative marker with 2-element (AV) constructions, which might have influenced his incorrect extension
of the ergative marker in sentence-initial position. None of
the children produced utterances in which both nouns were proper nouns at this time. Instead, all sentence-initial agents
were being marked incorrectly. All three children produced
this type of error.

13) Wanu (29.) is with his father, who is taking salt out
    of a box. Wanu says to his sister -

    *do   -wɛ sɔlu diab/   My father takes salt.
    my father ERG salt take

The word order is correct since he is reporting his father's
action. However, the ergative casemarker is on the agent in
sentence initial position, followed by the object, and this
is incorrect. The ergative casemarker in Kaluli is homophonous
with and instrumental to the genitive casemarker. This is common in many ergative languages (Allen, 1964).

14) Mɛli (31.2), watching her mother prepare bananas for
    cooking, a common event, says to her cousin -

    *nɔ   -wɛ magu sofɛnigab/ My mother is about to
    my mother ERG banana cook   cook bananas.

Again, word order is correct, but casemarking has been incorrectly over-applied to the agent. Mothers did *not* correct
the children when they used the ergative on sentence initial
agents as they had when it was omitted.

As with OAV, AOV orders were pragmatically correct except
for very few instances, two of which were related to a specific discourse context — children's difficulty in answering
who (agent) questions, which are structured Obj + who + Vb.
The answer must follow the same order, and the information
answering "who" must have the ergative marker.

The exceptional condition in AOV (2 proper nouns) which
used the ergative paradigm was rare in both adult and child
speech. It could not have been the basis upon which children
were overgeneralizing in their production of incorrect sentence initial, ergatively marked agents. In fact, given the
40 AOV utterances produced by the three children, only one

TABLE 2 *Acquisition patterns for casemarking agents.*
A = agent, O = object, V = verb, $-$ ɔ = casemarking for the
object of transitive verbs, $-$ε = casemarking for the agent of
transitive verbs (OAV).

Sample no.	Age	$OA^{-ε}V$	$A^{-ɔ}OV$ (conditions B & C)
		Abi	
I	(25.1)	-	$A^{∅}OV$
II	(25.3)	-	$*A^{-ε}OV$
III	(27.2)	$OA^{-ε}V$	-
IV	(28.2)	$OA^{-ε}V/*OS^{∅}V$	$A^{-ɔ}OV/*A^{-ε}OV$
V	(30.0)	-	$A^{-ɔ}OV$
VI	(31.2)	$OA^{-ε}V$	-
VII	(32.2)	$OA^{-ε}V$	-
VIII		$*OA^{∅}V/OA^{-ε}V$	-
		Mεli	
I	(24.1)	-	-
II	(24.3)	-	-
III	(26.0)	$*OA^{∅}V/OA^{-ε}V$	$A^{-ɔ}OV/*A^{-ε}OV$
IV	(27.3)	$OA^{-ε}V$	$A^{-ɔ}OV/*A^{-ε}OV$
V	(28.3)	$*OA^{∅}V/OA^{-ε}V$	-
VI	(30.2)	$*OA^{∅}V/OA^{-ε}V$	$A^{-ɔ}OV$
VII	(31.2)	$*OA^{∅}V/OA^{-ε}V$	$*A^{-ɔ}OV$
VIII	(32.2)	$*OA^{∅}V/OA^{-ε}V$	$A^{-ɔ}OV$
		Wanu	
I	(24.1)	-	-
II	(25.1)	-	$A^{∅}OV$
III	(26.3)	-	-
IV	(27.3)	$*OA^{∅}V$	$A^{-ɔ}OV$
V	(29.0)	$*OA^{∅}V$	$*A^{-ɔ}OV$
VI	(30.3)	$OA^{-ε}V$	$A^{-ɔ}OV$
VII	(32.1)	$OA^{-ε}V$	$A^{-ɔ}OV$

such utterance was produced in the child data, by Wano, 32.2, and it was correctly marked.

Table 2 summarizes the acquisition patterns for the 3 children for casemarking agents in both OAV and AOV orders. (Ages in months and weeks.)

Wanu and Abi produced AOV (third person) before OAV (third person). Mɛli produced them simultaneously. By 32 months all three were consistently controlling both word order and the casemarking system. These Kaluli children used word order pragmatically appropriately before using casemarking correctly. Ergative casemarking was used independent of word order to mark transitive Agent. All three overextended its use in AOV utterances, producing grammatically incorrect utterances before learning to restrict its use to the correct word order, OAV. However, the ergative marker was never extended to the subjects of intransitive verbs, keeping separate the transitive/intransitive verb distinction important in an ergative language. This suggests that these children do not have a general notion of actor/agent.

4. DISCUSSION

First, children used word order pragmatically appropriately before they used grammatical casemarking correctly. There is strong evidence from earlier 2-word utterances that children were encoding Agent + verb when the agent was in focus. When it was not in focus they encoded Object + verb.

Second, only verb-final utterances (AV, OV, OAV and AOV) were produced by Kaluli children, keeping with the adult model of verb-final syntax. In addition, like adults in similar contexts, children produced OAV utterances with greater frequency than AOV, not surprising since OAV utterances are used in arguments, requests, teasing and tattling, all part of family interaction.

Third, Kaluli children did *not* overgeneralize the ergative marker to subjects of intransitive verbs. In other words, they keep the two verb categories which are important in an ergative language, transitive and intransitive, distinct.

This distinction has been reported by two other researchers studying the acquisition of Quiché (Mayan) and Samoan, both of which are ergative languages. Pye (1980) investigating morphological development in Quiché, a verb-initial ergative language, found no instances where a child used an ergative marker for the subject of an intransitive verb. Similarly, Ochs (pers. comm.) reporting her research on the acquisition of Samoan, also a verb-initial ergative language, found that overgeneralization of the ergative marker to intransitive subjects did not take place.

For example, when producing an utterance with an intransitive verb such as "mother goes", Kaluli children consistently used the absolutive casemarker (or none) on "mother". They *never* marked it with the ergative. This was different from the way they would mark "mother" in an OAV sentence such as *"mother hits the dog"*. This suggests that Kaluli children do not have a general notion of agent/actor which is applied across verb categories. Children did produce a sufficient number of intransitive verbs with both proper and common nouns to which they *could* have added the ergative marker but *didn't*. In addition to not adding the ergative marker to subjects of intransitive verbs, children never marked direct objects with this "marked" form, in spite of the fact that subject-verb agreement follows a nominative/accusative paradigm.

One may speculate as to why the acquisition of pragmatic usage in word order precedes grammatical casemarking. When word order serves such marked pragmatic functions, it is more salient in that alternative word orders are more obvious than the presence or absence of a one-syllable casemarker. Any language (such as Kaluli) which uses word order for pragmatic purposes will have an interaction between discourse and syntax. These data suggest that children from an early age are sensitive to that interaction and the meaning conveyed by different word orders. However, to become competent speakers, children must use the morphological devices of their language as well. This ergative language provides a natural experiment on how children acquire a linguistic system which marks agents. We see that the acquisition of agent marking is just as salient and reasonable as the early acquisition of accusative markers in a nominative/accusative language.

REFERENCES

Allen, W.S. (1964). Transitivity and possession. *Language* 40(3), 337-343.
Comrie, B. (1978). Ergativity. *In* "Syntactic Typology" (W. Lehmann, ed.). Austin: University of Texas Press.
Dixon, R.M.W. (1979). Ergativity. *Language* 55(1), 59-139.
Givon, T. (1975). Focus and the scope of assertion: some Bantu evidence. *Studies in African Linguistics* 6, 185-205.
Li, C. and Lang, R. (1979). The syntactic irrelevance of an ergative case in Enga and other Papuan Languages. *In* "Ergativity: Towards a Theory of Grammatical Relations" (Frans Plank, ed.). London: Academic Press.
Ochs, E. (In press). Ergativity and word order in Samoan child language: a socio-linguistic study. *Language*.
Pye, C. (1980). The acquisition of person markers in Quiché Mayan. *In* "Papers and Reports on Child Language Development"

Vol. 19, pp. 53-59. Stanford, CA: Department of Linguistics, Stanford University.

Schieffelin, B.B. (In press). "How Kaluli Children Learn What to Say, What to Do and How to Feel". Cambridge University Press.

Schieffelin, E.L. (1976). "The Sorrow of the Lonely and the Burning of the Dancers". New York: St. Martins Press.

Silverstein, M. (1976). Hierarchy of features and ergativity. *In* "Grammatical Categories in Australian Languages" (R.M.W. Dixon, ed.). New Jersey: Humanities Press.

PART II: UTTERANCE SEQUENCES

THE GRAMMATICAL MARKING OF THEMATIC STRUCTURE IN THE DEVELOPMENT OF LANGUAGE PRODUCTION*

ANNETTE KARMILOFF-SMITH

*Max-Planck Institute for Psycholinguistics, Nijmegen,
The Netherlands and Developmental Psychology,
Cognitive Studies Programme, University of Sussex, UK.*

1. INTRODUCTION

The chapters in Part I of this book stressed the role played by linguistic and non-linguistic interaction in the development of children's language. Indeed, in recent years, much research emphasis has been placed on what has been called "child discourse" (e.g. Ervin-Tripp and Mitchell-Kernan, 1977), and I of course endorse the accent placed on the essential contribution which interpersonal exchanges make to language acquisition. However, one of the arguments of the present chapter will be that some — if not many — developments in children's language cannot be explained by reference to the addressee's interaction with the child. Rather, I shall submit that processing demands from the *child's* own point of view must also be invoked in any explanatory model of language acquisition or of the child's use of other representational systems (Karmiloff-Smith, 1979a).

---

* This chapter is an expanded version of a paper given at the MPG/NIAS Conference on "Beyond Description in Child Language", Nijmegen, Holland, June 1979. It is a revised version of a paper which appeared in J. Kreiman and A. Ojeda (eds) "Papers from the parasession on Pronouns and Anaphora", Chicago: Chicago Linguistic Society, April 1980, 231-250, under the title "Psychological processes underlying pronominalization and non-pronominalization in children's connected discourse". Relevant portions are reprinted here with permission of the CLS. W. Deutsch, S. Garrod, R. Reichman and M. Silverstein are warmly thanked for comments on that paper.

The term "discourse" has been used in both linguistics and psycholinguistics in rather different ways. On the one hand, as referred to above, authors use it to cover the inter-personal, interactional aspects of language — what might be termed "conversational discourse". The units of such discourse can be formed — but not necessarily are formed — of very short (e.g. one word, one sentence) utterance exchanges. Clearly, children do concentrate efforts not only on inter-active dialogic rules, but also on very basic linguistic properties (e.g. word order, morphological marking, rela-tional categories, and so forth) of the single utterance and parts thereof, as discussed in depth in Part III of this book. Language is multifaceted. The term "discourse" has also been used to cover *spans* of a single speaker's utter-ances, i.e. of some undefined length, but at least beyond the sentence. Another, and central argument of the present chapter will be that in certain aspects of children's lang-uage — and, indeed, of adult language too — it is essential to take as one's unit of analysis "spans of utterances", what might be termed "connected discourse", rather than the single sentence. The expression "spans of utterances" seems to be the most neutral way in which to describe this unit of analy-sis since, as mentioned above, the term "discourse" has been given several different connotations. Moreover, the term "text", used for both written and spoken spans of discourse (e.g. Halliday and Hasan, 1976; Lyons, 1977), none the less appears to imply a somewhat static notion. The discussion in this chapter attempts to place upon a speaker's spans of utterances the psycholinguistic notion of a *dynamic, on-going construction* which the speaker monitors as she pro-cesses the connected utterances she produces.

Thus, the psycholinguistic investigator should, in my view, explicitly justify both theoretically — from the point of view of the *functions* of a given linguistic category — and methodologically, the unit of analysis selected for study. A review of existing psycholinguistic literature — in the case of interest to this chapter, that of anaphoric devices such as pronouns — tends to show that in none of the tasks used is the question raised as to *why*, say, pronominalization is a feature of language, nor of when subjects *do* and *do not* use pronouns in their speech.

The main bulk of experimental work in developmental psycho-linguistics has been restricted to testing linguistic hypo-theses in comprehension tasks, production data mainly coming from natural corpora. There is in my view a profound problem stemming from comprehension approaches to psycholinguistic research. This has been discussed at length elsewhere under

the term "the experimental dilemma" (Karmiloff-Smith, 1979b)
but briefly is as follows. If, on the one hand, a comprehension task is set up including all the pragmatic, intralinguistic, paralinguistic, and extralinguistic cues available in normal discourse, then it is nigh impossible to observe developmental differences or, even where such differences
do occur, it is particularly difficult to establish upon which
of these cues, or combination thereof, children of different
age groups are basing their performance. On the other hand,
when such aspects of normal language use are eliminated from
the task, in order to test some "pure" linguistic category,
then it is my conviction that researchers are often observing
children's *ad hoc*, experiment-generated behaviour, frequently
quite asymptomatic of the processes subjects normally use in
interpreting the language they hear.
    Furthermore, the kind of experimental items devised for
such comprehension tasks are usually in the form of a series
of disconnected, adult-like structured sentences, inspired by
written language. (The distance between written and spoken
English may be relatively small, but in French the written
and spoken versions are like two entirely different languages.)
In the area of concern to this chapter, i.e. inter alia the
use of pronouns, a further constraint inserted into such experimental sentences has been that anaphoric pronouns carried
a degree of indeterminacy of reference, with the aim of un-
covering "strategies" used by subjects in interpreting such
potentially ambiguous sentences. But, as Cromer (1976) has
cogently argued, the so-called "strategies" are often useful
tools for the psycholinguist only for as long as the child
is making "errors" in interpretation with respect to some
adult norm. Once children perform as adults do in such comprehension tasks, then the researcher usually has no way of
describing the processes underlying the behaviour. It is not
obvious that the same outcome in behaviour is the result of
the same underlying processes (see Karmiloff-Smith, 1979b, for
discussion). In studying children's language development, it
is my contention that we are completely deluding ourselves
by imagining, when a sentence such as:

1) The president addressed the reporter and he left the room

is converted into a sentence such as:

2) The dog pushed the cat and it ran away

that, by the mere introduction of lexical terms and a pragmatic situation which children can understand, access will
be gained into the processes children use to interpret language. The interdependency of lexical choices and construc-

tion types is such that the two contribute jointly to the
semantic representation the child produces. Thus, tasks which
purport to test "pure" syntactic structures and the models
derived therefrom may be entirely misguided with respect to
language acquisition. Moreover, how often is language used
for asking an addressee to choose between two pictures or to
act out a scene with little animals! And even in the case of
pronoun assignment tasks with adult subjects, I would contend
that often such experiments are tapping experiment-generated
procedures, drawn from subjects' general problem-solving
procedures, and are not necessarily symptomatic of adults'
language processing procedures in normal discourse. How
often do we actually speak in isolated, decontextualized
sentences, leaving our pronominalized referents intralinguis-
tically and/or extralinguistically underdetermined for the
addressee? This is, of course, as much a criticism of some
of my own earlier work as of that of other researchers.
   Before discussing the experiments used for the present
study, let us first briefly run through some of the strategies singled out by researchers as relevant to the way in
which anaphoric pronouns are assigned a referent. The list
is not intended to be exhaustive, but rather to pinpoint the
type of strategies invoked, with the aim of later demonstrating that none of these explanations can be used to model
subjects' *actual use* and *non-use* of pronouns:

a) *parallel function strategy* (e.g. Grober, Beardsley and
   Caramazza, 1978; Kail, 1976; Sheldon, 1974) where the
   pronoun in the second conjunct of a complex sentence is
   interpreted as being co-referential with the noun phrase
   that has the parallel grammatical function in the first
   conjunct;
b) *conservation of semantic role* (e.g. Ferreiro *et al.*, 1976)
   where the child subjects are considered to be attempting
   to conserve the same semantic role (agent or patient)
   across the referents of two clauses in a complex sentence;
c) *minimum distance principle* (e.g. Chomsky, 1969) where subjects are considered to be interpreting the pronoun in a
   complex infinitive sentence as referring to the last-
   mentioned noun phrase;
d) *use of non-ambiguous gender distinctions*(e.g. Grober *et al.*,
   op.cit.) where in sentences such as:

   3) Tom telephoned John because he wanted some information

   4) Mary telephoned John because he wanted some information

the feature (+ male) marked explicitly in the surface structure of the pronoun "he" in (4) suffices, according to these

authors, to eliminate all ambiguities. I shall question such
assumptions later in this chapter.

Many of the preceding comments are in fact criticisms of
experimental work which stems — explicitly or implicitly —
from a deep commitment to the competence/performance distinction in linguistic theory. But, as mentioned before, language
is multifaceted. Researchers have also shown that strategies
such as the ones referred to above can be violated if, say,
stress is added to the pronoun (e.g. Maratsos, 1973), or,
say, the semantics of the verbs used in the two clauses
favour an alternative interpretation (e.g. Caramazza and
Gupta, 1979; Kail and Léveillé, 1977). Indeed, there have
been lengthy discussions on the topic of anaphoric pronoun
assignment in both adult and child language literature, but
the various nuances introduced have concerned issues involving
the *sentence*.

My intention is to challenge the usefulness of the above
interpretations when we wish to explain subjects' actual
use of anaphoric pronouns, since work was based on isolated,
decontextualized sentences which I believe to be erroneous as
the unit of analysis in this domain. Once again we may ask,
how often do we speak in isolated sentences, containing potentially ambiguous pronouns, with no extralinguistic or discourse cues as aids to referent assignment? What relation do
such isolated, ambiguous sentences have to children's *normal
input*? It would be hard to maintain that the latter has *no*
effect on the development of children's interpretative and
production procedures. The claim is not, of course, that *all*
aspects of language should be analysed at the "beyond the
sentence" level (e.g. the reflexive pronoun in "John washed
himself" would seem to be a clear counterexample), but rather
that some aspects of language may be totally misconceived if
an explanation is sought at the isolated sentence level.

Up to this point, much criticism has been made of the majority of comprehension tasks used with children. Thus, an
obvious solution would be to set up production tasks. However, it is well known that the experimental psycholinguist
is beset with many problems in getting subjects to produce
the particular linguistic category under study, since paraphrase, lexicalization of syntactic forms or vice versa
may be produced correctly instead. One solution — in
many respects similar to data used by some linguists — is
for the psycholinguistic researcher to use spontaneous speech
samples for analysis. However, whilst such spontaneous data
are excellent material for generating hypotheses (and this
was the case for the present study), for the *experimental*
psycholinguist a further step is required, i.e. tasks must

be devised in which we can actually render our hypotheses —
and, hopefully, our counter-hypotheses — empirically testable.

Thus, three major issues will be pursued in this chapter:
1) that the unit of analysis for studying children's use of
anaphoric devices such as pronouns should go beyond the sentence to spans of connected utterances; 2) that the internal
pressures on children's processing of the spans of utterances
they produce are such that models of language acquisition which
stress only its interactive aspects are incomplete; and 3)
which follows from the second issue, that developmentalists
have in my view centered their research questions far too
much on *whether* and *at what age* children can understand or
use a certain linguistic category, rather than on *how*, i.e.
on the *processes* involved in such use and understanding.
To my knowledge, the only work in developmental psycholinguistics raising these processing issues in comprehension
tasks is that of Tyler (1979, and this volume) and for adult
work, particularly that of Marslen-Wilson and Tyler (1980).
There have, I believe, been no attempts in developmental
psycholinguistics at building processing models of data
emanating from production tasks, almost as if processing
were only involved in language comprehension and not in
producing it!

2. PRONOMINALIZATION IN DISCOURSE

In this chapter, I shall discuss the results of a study of
children's elicited narratives, which represents an initial
attempt to answer my earlier questions: why do subjects
pronominalize sometimes and not others, what therefore are
the functions of pronouns and the psychological processes
involved in their usage, and how do these processes develop
in the growing child's language?

Let us first enumerate the linguistic hypotheses underlying the empirical work to be discussed, then describe the
study itself, and finally make an attempt to model the psychological processes involved. I have argued that the sentence
is not the most valid unit of analysis in seeking an explanation of anaphoric pronominalization. I shall thus submit that
an analysis of *spans of a speaker's connected utterances*, via
the elicitation of narratives, can be used to demonstrate
that there exist constraints at a broader or higher thematic
level which determine whether subjects pronominalize or not.
It is thus particularly important, both linguistically and
psycholinguistically, to analyse occurrences of *non-pronominalization* in cases where, from a local sentential point of
view, it would have been syntactically and semantically legi-

timate to use an anaphoric pronoun and yet subjects repeat full referring expressions. These cases will be contrasted with ones where, from a sentential analysis, one would predict that subjects should *not* pronominalize, due to intervening sentences in which the referent in question has not been mentioned again. Yet despite this, subjects actually do pronominalize and these pronouns are totally unambiguous for the addressee (unless, of course, the latter is a punctilious linguist!) Thus, the unit of analysis for explaining anaphoric pronouns should be broader than a sentence, or even than two or three juxtaposed sentences, in order to offer an explanation for both pronominalization and non-pronominalization, i.e. the dynamic interplay of various referential expressions, as subjects move from, say, the use of noun-pronoun reduplication, to full noun phrases, to pronouns and to zero anaphora, in their production of a span of connected utterances. It should be added that a cross-linguistic comparison (e.g. French and English) is revealing in this respect.

Furthermore, languages offer several devices which can render a pronoun unambiguous and these have been used in experimental design, e.g. animate/inanimate distinctions (he, she/it), natural gender distinctions (he/she), grammatical gender for inanimates (le/la in French), number (le, la/les) and so forth. None the less, my argument will be that subjects do not necessarily "cash in" on the devices languages offer and that their use of pronouns and other referring expressions is governed by the thematic constraints mentioned above and discussed in detail later in the chapter. In other words, I contend that subjects rarely place a heavy communicative burden on, say, the gender of a pronoun, despite the fact that the gender distinction would allow for unambiguous retrieval of the referent by the addressee.

From a psychological viewpoint, my hypothesis is that anaphoric pronominalization functions as an implicit instruction to the addressee *not* to recompute for retrieval of an antecedent referent but rather to treat the pronoun (or, par excellence, zero anaphora) as the default case for the thematic subject of a span of utterances, and to take it that deviations therefrom will be marked clearly linguistically by use of full noun phrases.

The above hypotheses will be tested against the results of micro- and macro-developmental changes in children's narratives, i.e. differences between the processes used by different age groups as well as spontaneous repairs occurring in a session by any particular child.

Let us first examine an example of child speech which appears to be an obvious case of the use of anaphora:

5) That's a dog. The dog's barking.

6) That's a dog. It's barking.

Must one necessarily conclude that the child's definite
article ("the") or the inanimate pronoun ("it") are being
used anaphorically? I should like to submit that although
this would seem obvious to us as addressees, because *we* are
linking up the child's utterances, it may not necessarily
be the case for the child. It could be that the child has
one procedure for naming: "that's a + N", juxtaposed with
quite a separate procedure for making reference, i.e. the
use of the definite article or the pronoun *deictically*. The
early use of definite referring expressions as carrying a
predominantly deictic component has been well documented
(Karmiloff-Smith, 1979b; Tanz, 1980; Warden, 1976). If it
can be shown that small children are not necessarily linking
up a series of sentences, but rather juxtaposing them, then
researchers may have been overinterpreting children's use
of pronouns as containing a truly anaphoric component. Moreover, various degrees of anaphoric linking may exist, thereby
suggesting the need for a much subtler analysis of early
child speech.*

The existence of an anaphoric component in children's use
of pronouns was tested in a narrative production task in
French, involving a conflict between the grammatical gender
of nonce terms and the natural gender of the extralinguistic
referent to which the nonce term referred (Karmiloff-Smith,
1979b). It should be noted that even natural gender is not
a foolproof predictor of grammatical gender in French. Thus,
"*la* recrue" is a feminine word referring to a male recruit,
"*le* professeur" is a masculine word used to refer to a female
or male professor, "*la* victime" is a feminine word referring
to a victim be the latter male or female. There are no systematic semantic criteria for predicting gender (e.g. two
synonyms may have different gender: "*la* bicyclette" and "*le*
vélo"). The most productive system in French gender is
based on morphophonological distinctions on word endings,
such as the following:

---

* See also Michael Silverstein: "Cognitive Implications of a
Referential Hierarchy", Manuscript for paper given at Max-
Planck Institute for Psycholinguistics, Nijmegen, November
1980, for a discussion of anaphoric linkage and types of
referentiality in language in general.

masculine	*feminine*
-on	-one
-in	-ine
-ois	-oise
-ant	-ante

However, whilst the word ending is a good predictor because
it applies across several different linguistic categories
(e.g. proper names, nouns, adjectives, demonstratives, etc.),
it is not entirely foolproof because again exceptions exist.
Thus, for instance, "flu*te*" is feminine in gender but
"parachu*te*" is masculine; "tap*is*" is masculine but "fourm*is*"
is feminine: "Coch*on*" is masculine but "leç*on*" is feminine,
and so forth. None the less, despite exceptions which are
often very common words, word ending changes are the most
consistent system, and it has been shown that very young
children of 3 years perform consistently in their attribution
of gender based on word endings (Karmiloff-Smith, 1979b).

Using the fact of this early acquisition of lexical concord,
a narrative task with nonce terms was set up to test the
hypothesis that early use of pronouns is not necessarily anaphoric. Without going into details here (see op.cit.),
suffice it to state that a potential conflict was established
between, on the one hand, word endings (e.g. "bicron"
where "-on" is a typical masculine ending; "goltoise" where
"-oise" is a typical feminine ending; "fadiste" where "-iste"
could be of either gender) and, on the other hand, the sex of
the extralinguistic referent. Thus, for example, "goltoise"
was used to refer to a male and "bicron" to a female. The
child's task was to tell stories of her/his own invention
about one of two "goltoises", one of two "bicrons", etc. in
a series of narrative situations in which the experimenter's
utterances contained no cues as to gender (e.g. neutral words
such as "ça"; "deux" etc. were used which contain no distinctive gender marks). The interest of such a design was
to see how children pronominalized once they had introduced
the nonce term with a full NP. Thus, after using for one of
the "goltoises" the feminine indefinite article ("une
goltoise"), would children continue the discourse with the
feminine pronoun "elle" because of the gender attributed to
the word "goltoise", or would they continue the discourse with
the masculine pronoun "il" because the extralinguistic referent
was male? The same questions apply, mutatis mutandis, to the
other terms used, such as "bicron".

The results clearly showed that youngest subjects were
using pronouns deictically. In other words, although all
age groups gave the same gender to a nonce term ("goltoise"

was attributed feminine gender; "bicron" masculine gender),
the youngest ones pursued their narrative with the pronoun
appropriate for the extralinguistic referent. They were
unperturbed by the lack of internal cohesion when juxtaposing
"une goltoise" followed by "il". Older subjects, however,
were sensitive to intralinguistic cohesion and used the pronoun consistent with the gender they had attributed to the
nonce term. Thus, they were in fact referring anaphorically
to prior discourse properties and continued to do so unless
the experimenter's interruption purposely created a conflict.
In other words, if the child had been saying something like:

Example 7
La goltoise, elle est partie en vacances.
Elle voulait voir ...

and the experimenter interrupted asking: "elle, c'est qui?",
the older child would then point to the extralinguistic
referent, and start self-corrections which were particularly
revealing with respect to anaphora and internal cohesion,
as shown in Example 8 below:

Example 8
Elle, c'est cette goltoise ... ah non, lui, ce goltois
vert, c'est un garçon, je suis bête!

What is to be noted in this, and other analogous examples,
is the older child's use of pronouns anaphorically and the
changes introduced by the child to the lexical terms (e.g.
"golt*oise*" is changed to "golt*ois*") when the pronoun is
changed to match the natural gender of the referent. By
contrast, such repairs did not occur in younger children's
productions, clearly denoting the deictic nature of their
pronominalization procedures. For the older child, the pronoun is anaphoric, but a deictic component can be inserted
(e.g. "goltoise" then becomes "goltois").
  Whilst this study was done with nonce terms, similar problems arise in natural French. Take a newspaper report about
a car accident involving a man. Referring to "la victime"
(always feminine gender), should one continue one's discourse
with "elle" because the word is feminine, or with "il"
because the victim is a male? Although in some cases of
literary writing, the pronoun is made to concord with the
lexical term despite the natural gender of the referent, more
frequently, and particularly in spoken French, speakers tend
to find compromise solutions, e.g. interjecting in the above
example, for instance, something like "ce pauvre homme" and
then pronominalizing with "il" (see Lyons, 1977 for a discussion of these issues).

It should be recalled that the gender narrative task contained nonce terms and children could invent stories as they
pleased. The next step, therefore, was to devise more
natural narratives with normal French lexical terms, yet at
the same time constrain the content experimentally so as to
allow for comparisons and the testing of counter-hypotheses.
Furthermore, the gender study merely allowed for an analysis
of the passage from deictic to anaphoric use of pronouns,
but could not answer my present question regarding the *processes* involved in the use of pronominalization.

3. STUDIES OF THE THEMATIC STRUCTURE OF NARRATIVES

The narrative study covered 350 children, 170 of whom were
seen in narrative production tasks, and 180 in a task involving the production of single utterance to describe one
depicted event. The first part of the study covered English
and French children between 4 and 9 years, tested individually in four different story-telling tasks. Each picture
book was designed with specific characteristics to test the
hypotheses and counter-hypotheses discussed above:

Story type (a): one central character, a momentary interven-
                tion of another character, and subsequent
                return to the initial one;
Story type (b): three characters initially, then one is in-
                volved alone in an event, then another be-
                comes central throughout;
Story type (c): two characters from the start and remaining
                together in almost all events;
Story type (d): a series of pictures (bound together as a book
                like the other story types) but with no ob-
                vious link between the different pictures.

This design was based on hypotheses regarding the functions
of pronominalization and non-pronominalization, use and non-
use of the fact that pronouns are gender-marked, that English
marks the difference between animates and inanimates, the
functions of topicalization structures such as noun-pronoun
reduplication in French, and so forth. The purpose was to
demonstrate that the functions of these categories may be
very different when used in spans of connected utterances in
contrast to functions which may obtain for these categories
in isolated sentences. Thus, for instance, pronominalization
and zero anaphora should occur in story types (a) and (c),
because a thematic subject emerges, whereas the counter-
hypothesis is tested in story types (b) and (d) where no clear
thematic subject obtains and children therefore should not

make use of pronouns in the same way, if the underlying
hypotheses are correct. Furthermore, story type (b) allows
us to see if children make use of the fact that a gender
mark can render a pronoun totally unambiguous, since one of
the characters is of different sex to the other two. Story
type (d) was introduced into the design to observe whether
subjects made any attempt at all to give some internal coherence to the group of pictures, since here they were faced
with a true juxtaposition of events and not a "story".
Thus, if children are sensitive to the notion of a narrative
as a whole unit, then there should be signs of this in their
attempts to deal with story type (d).
    The most revealing data in this study come from story type
(a) in which there is an initial central figure, a momentary
introduction of a second, and then a return to the initial
one. The results from story types (b), (c) and (d), (see
brief comments towards the end of the chapter), in which
children did *not* pronominalize or topicalize in the same way
as they did in story type (a), render plausible the general
interpretation offered for this particular narrative.
    A neutral rendering of the six pictures in story type (a)
is as follows:

Picture 1: a little boy, dressed in bright red, is walking
           along a road;
Picture 2: the boy sees a balloon vendor in the left-hand
           corner of the picture and points at him;
Picture 3: the balloon vendor gives the boy a green balloon
           (or, the boy takes a green balloon from the balloon
           vendor);
Picture 4: the boy walks off alone with the balloon;
Picture 5: the balloon flies off into the sky (or, the boy
           lets go of the balloon);
Picture 6: the boy starts to cry.

Each child was presented with a bound book of six pictures
for each of the story types (rather than series of isolated
picture cards), and asked to tell the experimenter "what was
happening". The child did not see all the pictures in advance, but rather the experimenter turned over the pages at
an even pace, children's output being that of normal speech
rate, thus avoiding juxtaposed descriptions of single pictures.
    The following are all typical illustrations of children's
narratives in this study. It should be stressed that in the
first analysis, I have only brought forth the processes involved in the use of various referential expressions placed
in *initial utterance slot*. Clearly, this is inadequate since
it misses the dynamics of the interplay between the latter

and occurrences of pronominalization and non-pronominalization
in other sentence parts. However, this study is the first part
of an entire research programme in which many other analyses
are required of the present data and many other parameters
need to be manipulated in future tasks (e.g. length of story,
changes of episode within the same story, use of narratives
without the concrete support of story books, narratives re-
counted to an addressee who does not share the same referential
information, comparison with other languages and so forth).
However, I believe that this first analysis does give insight
into some of the processes involved in reference maintenance
and points to directions for further analyses. For convenience
of reading the examples, initials have been added in brackets
after each pronominalization in initial utterance slot: (B)
standing for the little boy, (M) for the balloon vendor, and
(GB) for the green balloon. It should be recalled that the
pronoun "he" may refer to the boy or to the man and, while
English marks the distinction between animates and inanimates
(the balloon can be referred to unambiguously as "it"), the
pronoun "il" in French may refer to the man, the boy or the
balloon since the word for balloon is masculine in gender.

Examples (9) and (10) below are typical of a large number of
the subjects under the age of six, a group which stands apart
from other age groups with respect to the function of their
use of pronouns:

Example 9
He's (B) walking along...and he (B) sees a balloon man...
and he (M) gives him a green one...and he (B) walks off
home...and it (GB) flies away into the sky. So he (B) cries.

This gives the initial utterance slot pronoun pattern as follows:

$$B - B - M - B - GB - B$$

Example 10
Là il (B) se promène. Là il (B) voit un bonhomme avec
des ballons. Là il (M) lui donne un ballon...un vert. Là
il (B) part chez lui ou à l'école. Là il (GB) s'envole
loin, très loin. Bien, là il (B) pleure.

Literal translation of Example 10
There he (B) takes a walk. There he (B) sees a chap with
some balloons. There he (M) gives him a balloon...a green
one. There he (B) goes to his house or to school. There
he* (GB) flies off far, very far. Well, he (B) cries.

---

* In the literal translation, the pronoun for balloon has purposely been translated as "he" to point out the potential ambiguity in French with the references to both the boy and the
balloon vendor.

This gives the initial utterance slot pronoun pattern as follows:

$$B - B - M - B - GB - B$$

First, it should be recalled that the children were not presented with separate pictures but a bound book and it was stressed by the experimenter that each contained a whole story. Despite this, it is clear that the young children's narratives are held together by the spatial deictics or by frequent paralinguistic gestures (pointing, eye gaze, head movements, etc.) which accompanied their pronominalization, as well as by the extralinguistic context to which they refer. However, since in the experimental design the experimenter and the child on purpose share exactly the same referential information (the picture book visible in front of both of them, the child and the experimenter sitting next to one another on the same side of a table), the deictic pronouns with the paralinguistic gestures are totally unambiguous *provided the addressee treats each utterance as a separate unit and attempts to make no intralinguistic cohesion across pronouns in the different utterances*. If intersentential linkages are made, then the pronouns are inappropriately used and ambiguous. However, nothing tells us that the *child* is linking up her utterances linguistically. This seems clear from Example (10) where the child starts off each utterance with a spatial deictic, pointing out at the extralinguistic context. Moreover, the only over-six-year-old in the population to use pronouns deictically was one nine-year-old boy, but all his connectives were temporal in nature (e.g. "and *then* he..."). In another pilot study, children were asked to repeat the stories from memory, rather than with the turning of the pages in front of them, but whilst the spatial deictics disappeared from the young children's narratives, they still used pronouns deictically. Furthermore, in my view, even the connective "and", which occurs throughout Example (9) and others from this age group, may not be functioning as an utterance connective but rather as something like an "action connective", implying something like "I haven't finished yet". Indeed, the fact that two linguistic acts of uttering follow upon one another does not imply ipso facto that they are being monitored by the child as part of a "linguistic whole" even if they are part of a "behavioural whole".

It should also be noted in the examples from the under-six-year-olds that these young children *did* make use of the unambiguous inanimate pronoun "it" in English to refer to the balloon and did place the balloon vendor in utterance initial slot, with the deictic pronoun "he". This contrasts with the narratives of older children, as will now be seen.

The next narrative productions to appear developmentally, and quite massively, bear witness from now onwards to children's growing use of pronouns anaphorically and to their sensitivity to reference maintenance and intralinguistic, cohesive devices in general. In the first group discussed below, children are making use of a simplified processing procedure whereby the main character is introduced and then the initial slot of all subsequent utterances is pre-empted for reference to that character. Thus, these children reserve pronominalization in initial slot of utterances exclusively for the thematic subject of the narrative. Examples (11) and (12) below are typical of this type of behaviour:

Example 11
A little boy is walking along. He (B) sees a balloon seller. He (B) wants a green balloon. He (B) gets one. He (B) walks off in the sunshine. He (B) lets go of the balloon and then he (B) starts crying.

This gives the initial slot pronoun pattern:

B - B - B - B - B - B

Example 12
C'est un petit garçon qui se promène devant son immeuble. Il (B) rencontre un marchand de ballons, alors il (B) prend un ballon vert. Puis il (B) s'en va. Il (B) laisse tomber son ballon. Il (B) a pas fait exprès. Et puis il (B) rentre à la maison en pleurnichant.

Literal translation of Example 12
It's a little boy who is taking a walk in front of his apartment building. He (B) meets a balloon vendor, so he (B) takes a green balloon. Then he (B) goes off. He (B) lets go of his balloon. He (B) didn't do it on purpose. And then he (B) goes back home sobbing.

This gives the initial slot pronoun pattern:

B - B - B - B - B - B

Note should be taken in the above examples and others of a similar type of the lexical choice of verbs such as "want/have/receive/take/ask/choose", etc. and their French equivalents. The choice of such verbs enables children either to avoid mention of the balloon vendor or to keep the vendor out of initial utterance slot. The use of the verb "get" could be argued to be functioning as the equivalent of a passive construction. Note should also be taken of the fact that older subjects also keep the balloon man out of the subject slot, i.e. they do not take advantage of the unambiguity of the inanimate pronoun "it" in English. This is to be contrasted with the results of the under-six-year-olds who, it will be recalled, used deictic pronouns and did mention the balloon vendor, did place reference to him in initial utterance slot and did use unambiguous "it".

In my view, in the examples which fall under the category discussed here, i.e. narratives in which the boy is kept in initial utterance slot, we are dealing with the underlying notion of "thematic subject" and not with that of, say, "agency". Several investigators have suggested that children interpret pronominal sentences by making pronoun assignment co-referent with the "agent" of the preceding clause, aiming at conserving the same role for referents across clauses. However, in the narratives studied here, whilst the initial sentence slots were occupied by references to the boy, this referent changed roles from, say, experiencer (wants), to agent (takes, chooses), to possessor (has), etc. All the verbs used by children before and after picture 3 in story type (a) were analysed and many role changes are to be noted. To maintain a hypothesis that the child is trying to conserve "agency" in initial utterance slots, one would then have to predict that the balloon vendor would be referred to as giving the boy a balloon. This was not the case in the spans of utterances making up the narratives discussed here, although it did occur massively in a follow-up experiment concerning an isolated picture with an isolated sentence response (see below).

The follow-up experiment simply involved the key picture from story type (a) - picture 3 - in which the balloon vendor is handing a green balloon to the little boy dressed in bright red. Ninety English-speaking and 90 French-speaking subjects, different to those used in the main study but from the same age groups (4 to 9 years), were asked to say "what was happening" in the isolated picture. It is important to note that identical instructions were given as in the narrative tasks, i.e. the child was always asked "what is happening" rather than, say, "what is in the picture", the latter being suggestive of a descriptive statement.

The results of the follow-up task were very clear. Eighty-two per cent of the children tested said something like: "the balloon-man is giving a balloon to the little boy" (or the French equivalent), i.e. they placed the balloon vendor in the initial utterance slot and used the verb "to give" (a small percentage using the verb "to sell"). There were no spontaneous repairs at all, and the French-speaking children never used noun-pronoun reduplication in describing this

isolated picture. This contrasts greatly with the narrative
productions in which this same picture was included. Whatever the reasons may be for children to describe the isolated
picture in terms of the balloon vendor giving the boy a balloon,
rather than in terms of the boy receiving/taking a balloon
from the vendor (e.g. left to right decoding, perceptual
saliency of the balloon vendor, the fact that the man is
still holding the balloon as he hands it to the boy, hierarchy of age between man and boy, etc.) is totally irrelevant to the arguments I shall invoke for explaining the narrative productions. The essential point is that this *identical* picture was described very *differently* when children produced a single utterance, as compared to the way in which it
was described when the utterance was part of a span of
connected utterances.

The analysis of Examples (11) and (12) could be considered
as highly interpretative on my part if we did not have access
to the results of the follow-up experiment just discussed,
but more particularly to microdevelopmental spontaneous repairs in the narrative task which point in the same interpretative direction, as can be seen from Examples (13), (14)
and (15) below:

Example 13
A little boy is walking along. He (B) sees a balloon-man.
The balloon m...he (B) asks for a balloon and (B) goes
off happily. The balloo...he (B) lets go of the balloon
and (B) starts to cry.

This gives the initial slot pronoun pattern:

$$B - \overset{(M)}{\underset{\searrow}{}}B - B - \overset{(GB)}{\underset{\searrow}{}}B - B$$

Example 14
(lengthy introduction of boy with details of clothes etc.)
He (B) walks up to a balloon-man. He (B) asks if he (M)
could give him...if he (B) could have one. He (B) goes
off with it.

This gives the initial slot pronoun pattern:

$$B - B - \overset{(M)}{\underset{\searrow}{}}B - B$$

First, it should be stressed that in Examples (13) and (14),
spontaneous repairs are always in favour of placing the thematic subject, i.e. the boy, in initial utterance slot. It
should also be noted that zero anaphora in English occurred
only for the thematic subject. In none of the narratives
collected in the whole study was there zero anaphora in the
case of references to the balloon vendor or the balloon, even

if in a few instances the vendor was pronominalized within an
utterance boundary containing a connective.

It is essential to note from these examples of spontaneous
repairs, that in each case the child could have continued
her utterance as it had been started. The utterance would
have been semantically and syntactically appropriate and communicatively clear from a sentential point of view. Thus,
the only explanation for the repairs, in my view, is that
the child is monitoring her narrative for its intralinguistic
cohesion and for the functions attributed to anaphoric pronouns. Such monitoring is achieved by these children by
imposing on the narrative a rigid macro-thematic structure
pre-empting initial utterance slots for references to the
boy, or, as in Example (15) below, by the use of a postposed
disambiguator but for certain referents only:

Example 15
Alors là c'est un petit garçon, il (B) se promène, et
puis tout d'un coup il (B) voit un marchand de ballons.
Puis il (B) demande si il (B) peut en avoir un... Puis
alors il (M) lui donne un, le marchand. Et puis après
il (B) continue son chemin tout content avec le ballon
dans la main. Puis tout d'un coup il (B) le lâche et
puis il (GB) part très loin, le ballon. Et puis lui
alors il (B) pleure.

Literal translation
Well there there's a little boy, he (B) is taking a
walk, and then all of a sudden he (B) sees a balloon
vendor. Then he (B) asks if he (B) could have one. And
then he (M) gives him one, the vendor. And then afterwards he (B) continues on his way very happy with the
balloon in his hand. Then all of a sudden he (B) lets go
of it and then he (in French, il = balloon) goes off very
far, the balloon. And then therefore, he (B) cries.

This gives the initial slot pronoun pattern:

B - B - B - B - (M+NP) - B - B - (GB+NP) - B

Example (15) warrants a number of comments. First, it should
be stressed that whilst the literal translation of the example sounds heavy in English, this is very typical of spoken
French. Second, it is a clear-cut example of how children
clarify any pronouns which occupy initial utterance slot but
which are *not* referring to the thematic subject, with a
postposed definite cross-referencing noun phrase. It can be
noted that each time the boy is pronominalized in initial
slot, there is no definite referring expression added in
postposition. By contrast, each time the balloon vendor or

the balloon are pronominalized in initial slot, postposed
definite referring expressions are always added. This can
only be explained by the fact that the child is monitoring
her use of pronouns, not at the local sentential level, but
at the macro-thematic level. The clarification by placing
nominals in postposition cannot be explained by potential
ambiguity, because the pronouns referring to the boy are
just as potentially ambiguous at the local, intersentential
level. Moreover, the joint attention of both child and experimenter to the extralinguistic context is the same in
all cases. Thus Example (15) is particularly illustrative of
the hypothesis that the child's *use* and *non-use* of pronouns,
i.e. the interplay of various referential devices, is a
function of the macro-thematic structure she has created
and imposed upon her narrative.

It is also worth noting that noun-pronoun reduplication in
this and other similar examples has a different function
than is normally suggested at the isolated sentence level
where it is often used as an emphatic focussing device. For
example, "le garçon il dort" means literally "the boy he is
sleeping" (and presupposes that it is not, say, the girl that
is the topic of interest). This contrasts with "il dort le
garçon" which means literally "he is sleeping the boy"
(and presupposes that he is not, say, reading). In one case,
the noun is topicalized, in the other case it is the verb.
It was seen in our narratives, however, that noun-pronoun
reduplication can have other functions when used in spans of
utterances. Noun-pronoun reduplication was used by French-
speaking children in story type (b) to introduce a new
focus, for instance, and in story type (a) it appears to be
functioning to place a referent in low, non-thematic focus
(see also Reichman, 1978, for a discussion of focussing
devices in English in adult spontaneous conversations). I
would submit that when postposing a noun-pronoun reduplication referring to the balloon vendor, as in Example (15), the
child is not stressing the *content* "balloon vendor" but
rather the *organizational structure*, i.e. initial utterance
slot is not occupied by the thematic subject.

Once children have imposed a rigid structure on their
narratives, by pre-empting the initial utterance slot for
the thematic subject, they can be said to "have a handle" on
the narrative as a whole unit. They are then in a position
to render their narrative structures more mobile. Pronominalization is still pre-empted for the thematic subject at
the discursive level. However, children now appear to have
a hold on the interplay between the discursive organization
and the more local sentential organization. Other characters

are sometimes placed in initial slot. However, when doing
so, children will clearly (and often redundantly) mark the
fact that the initial utterance slot is occupied by a referent other than the thematic subject. Pronominalization
for non-thematic subjects is rare, and usually only occurs
within sentence boundaries with connectives. In utterance
initial slot, if there is a pronoun, it still refers prefer-
entially or by default to the thematic subject, with no need
for re-introduction by a definite noun phrase of the thematic
subject even if there have been intervening utterances with
other referents in that slot. Examples (17) and (18) below
illustrate this level:

Example 17
A little boy is walking along on a sunny day. He (B)
sees a balloon man. The balloon man gives him a
balloon. He (B) walks off home. The balloon suddenly
flies off into the sky and he (B) starts to cry.

This gives the pattern:

$$B - (NP=M) - B - (NP=GB) - B$$

Example 18
Y a un petit garçon qui s'amuse dehors et puis il (B)
voit un marchand de ballons. Alors il (B) demande s'il
(B) peut avoir un de ses ballons. Le marchand il lui
donne le ballon vert. Il (B) repart tout content mais
le vent se leve et tout d'un coup il (B) lâche son
ballon qui part dans les nuages. Il (B) est triste et
il (B) s'en va en pleurant....ben, comme un bébé!

Literal translation
There's a little boy who is having fun out of doors and
then he (B) sees a balloon vendor. So, he (B) asks
if he (B) can have one of his ballons. The balloon
vendor he gives him the green balloon. He (B) goes off
again really happy but the wind picks up and suddenly he
(B) lets go of his balloon which goes off into the clouds.
He (B) is really unhappy and he (B) goes off crying...
well, like a baby!

This gives the pattern:

$$B - B - B - (NPR=M) - B - B - B - B$$

The use of NPR, e.g. "le marchand il..." in initial utterance slot is to be noted in Example (18). It is clear that
the child is not using the NPR for emphatic focussing purposes, but rather to mark the fact that the initial utterance slot is occupied by a referent in non-thematic focus

and not by the thematic subject which would always have been
pronominalized.

From a number of the above examples and the other narratives
in this study, it can be seen how such "strategies" deduced
from research using isolated sentences (e.g. "minimum distance principle", "parallel function strategy", etc. - see
p. 133 above) cannot be used to explain speakers' use of
pronouns. In some cases, the boy is pronominalized despite
intervening utterances where no reference is made to him;
in others, the balloon vendor is not pronominalized although
the latter has just been mentioned (e.g. "He sees a balloon
man. The balloon man gives him a balloon"). Why do children
not use a pronoun here, when it would be unambiguous from a
local sentential viewpoint and the semantics of the verb "to
give" render it even more redundantly clear. It follows
therefore that a broader thematic organization must be invoked to explain why subjects use anaphoric pronouns sometimes and not at others. The use and non-use of anaphoric
pronouns appears therefore to be governed only marginally
by intrasentential constraints or, even, by local intersentential constraints. Rather, in spans of connected utterances, pronominalization and non-pronominalization, the use
of various referential devices, are governed by a broader or
higher level of organization, i.e. the existence or not of a
thematic subject and the procedures which are generated
therefrom. Gradually children become capable of monitoring
the interplay between the discursive and sentential levels
of a span of discourse.

The above analyses are also rendered plausible by the results of the other story types. For example, when there are
initially three characters, older children did *not* pronominalize the character who was subsequently alone in an event
even when the character was the last mentioned in the previous utterance and when the gender of the pronoun would have
rendered reference to that character completely unambiguous.
In these cases, children used a second definite referential
expression, which was not the case in the balloon story where
the boy was immediately pronominalized after the initial
existential expression. In the case of story type (b)
just referred to, clearly children were awaiting the emergence
of a thematic subject before opting for pronominalization.
Local sentential constraints cannot provide an explanation
of the non-pronominalization. It is also worth noting that
in the case of story type (d) where no "story" exists, none
the less the oldest subjects, who were sensitive to the narrative as being a whole unit, endeavoured to introduce an external observer, for instance, who saw each of the juxtaposed

events as he went walking, thus allowing them to relate the
pictures of what was actually merely a series of juxtaposed
events. By contrast, the youngest subjects treated story
type (d) in much the same fashion as they did story type (a)
and the others, i.e. by using deictic pronouns and paralinguistic gestures for all.

4. CONCLUDING REMARKS

In summary, an attempt is made below in the figure to
model the psychological processes involved in the grammatical marking of the interplay of reference maintenance devices. After the initial period of the use of deictic pronouns by the youngest subjects in this study, children
generate a series of procedures for coping with narratives
as a unit. This takes place, it is suggested, as shown in
Fig. 1. First, children introduce a referent with an existential expression or, if the referent is already shared
knowledge with the addressee, then with a definite referring
expression or a proper name. The child then raises implicitly the following question: is there a main protagonist
involved in a sequence of events? If the answer is affirmative, the child creates a "thematic subject" which will then
generate reference maintenance procedures. She thus pre-
empts initial utterance slots solely for reference to the
thematic subject. This is followed by an instruction to
pronominalize and to pre-empt pronominalization and zero
anaphora for the thematic subject at the discursive level.
As the narrative unfolds, this becomes an implicit instruction to the addressee *not* to recompute for retrieval of the
pronominal referent (i.e. there is no "looking back" for an
antecedent) but rather to take it by default to be the
thematic subject. Such a processing procedure places constraints on the lexical choice of verbs and on voice (e.g.
"wants", "gets", and so forth in story type (a)) because the
initial utterance slot is occupied by the thematic subject.
It also constrains the types of referring expressions and the
positioning of non-thematic subjects, which was particularly
notable from the spontaneous repairs.
  Thus, I would argue that repetition of a full noun phrase
is not used to avoid ambiguity, nor is a pronoun used to
avoid uneconomic repetition. Rather, the use and non-use
of pronouns and other referring expressions serves to organize the ongoing discursive relations by a simple processing
procedure of pre-emption of initial utterance slot for the
thematic subject. This analysis questions the notions of
"substitution", "economy of mention" and so forth which have
often been used in discussions of pronominalization.

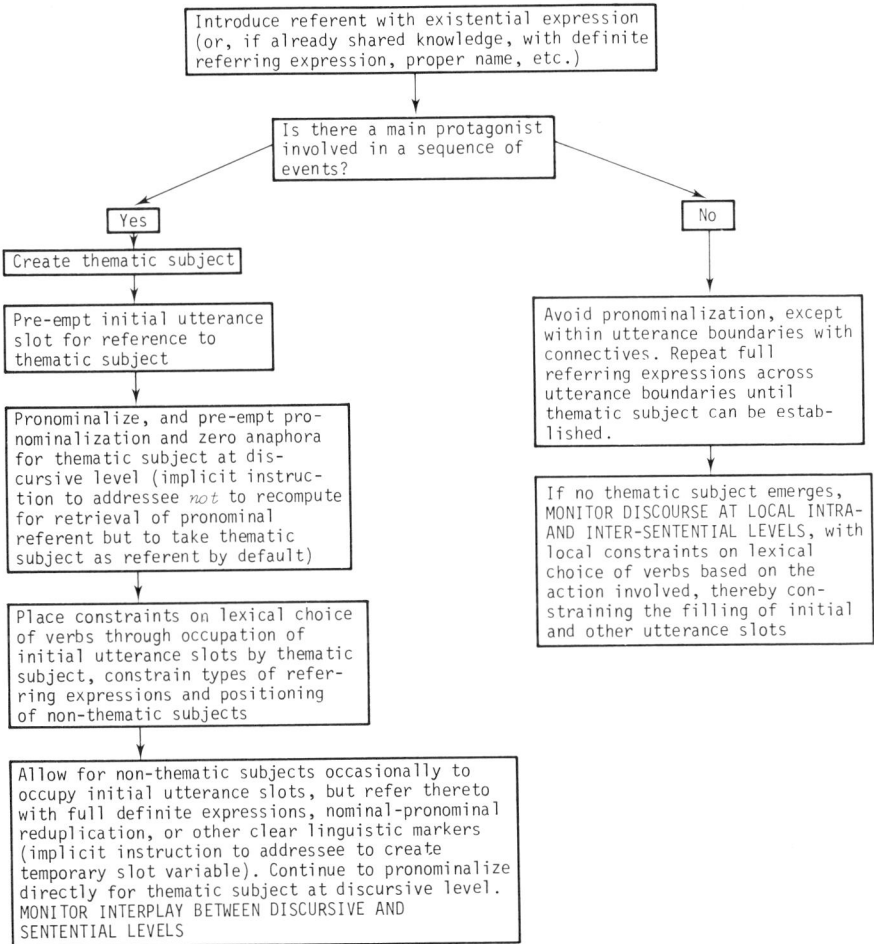

FIG. 1 *Procedures used in the development of linguistic marking of the referential cohesive structure of narrative discourse.*

With development, and once the child has a handle on the span of utterances as a treatable unit, she allows non-thematic subjects occasionally to occupy initial utterance slots. However, when doing so, children use clear linguistic markers to this effect. These are an implicit instruction to the addressee to create a temporary slot variable, but none the less to hold open interpretation of direct pronominalization for the thematic subject as the default case. Indeed, speakers continue to pronominalize directly for the thematic subject, despite intervening sentences, but they carefully monitor the interplay between the discursive and local sentential levels. Thus, again, as far as the older children are concerned, pronouns are not being used for economy of repetition, compliance with minimum distance principles etc., but rather they play a dynamic role in the establishment of intra-discursive thematic relations.

If the answer to the earlier question regarding a main protagonist involved in a sequence of events is negative (see flowchart), then the internal instruction appears to be to avoid pronominalization except within utterance boundaries with connectives. In this case, children tend to repeat full referring expressions for the same referent across utterance boundaries until a thematic subject can be established. If no thematic subject emerges, the child monitors her narrative at the local intra- and inter-sentential levels. Then, it is the action involved which dictates the lexical choice of the verb (e.g. "gives" in the single picture task, or other verbs in the other story types) and it is the verb choice which constrains the filling of utterance slots and the positioning of referents.

Obviously, the analysis of the grammatical marking of thematic structure in language production is merely a part of the broader issue of cohesive devices in general. The use and non-use of pronouns as reference maintenance devices in the very short narratives in this study is, of course, only a small fraction of a very complex part of language acquisition involving spans of utterances. In the spontaneous narratives of my own two children from which the hypotheses for this experimental study were developed, it was clear, for instance, that the thematic subject did get reintroduced by a full noun phrase if there was a change in the episodic organization or if the string of pronouns had been very long. It is as if the default can only be valid for a certain span of time. Moreover, in the field of cohesive devices such as anaphora, clearly pronouns and noun phrases are not the only linguistic markers available. Intonational chunks, voice pitch, lexical cohesion (e.g. the use in French

of the verb "aller" followed later in the narrative by a
slightly unusual usage of a verb such as "re-aller" gives
linkage to two utterances) are amongst the various ways in
which subjects can render their span of utterances a unit
rather than a series of disjointed pieces. Many more
analyses of the present data must be made, as suggested on
p.   above, and many other parameters need to be manipulated before a fuller explanation can be furnished, but
it is clear from the present study that very dynamic processes
are at work when children — or adults — use sentences and
particularly when they go beyond the sentence to produce spans
of connected utterances.

Insights are thus to be gained into language acquisition by
analysing data which extends beyond the sentence to spans of
connected utterances. But insights are also to be gained by
raising questions regarding the *processes* involved in language production and comprehension, rather than concentrating
age group/success levels. Indeed, process-oriented questions
should be raised not only in language acquisition but in
children's cognitive development in general (Karmiloff-Smith,
in press). Furthermore, data from *spontaneous* repairs seem
to offer particularly illuminating ways of understanding such
processes. Clearly some of the developments in children's
linguistic output are due to their interactions with
addressees. However, the final point I wish to stress in
this chapter is that many of the changes encountered in
children's behaviour, be it linguistic or other, cannot be
explained by external pressures from failure to be understood by an addressee or failure to succeed in a task.
Rather, something else is also pushing the child towards
change. In this present study, it would be difficult to
maintain that children progress because they are seeking,
for instance, greater "economy". If that were the case,
then in situations where speakers share the same referential
information, the child should make use of simple deictic
pronouns or, at the very least, if greater economy were the
child's goal, then development should have stopped at the
simple procedure of pre-empting the initial utterance slot of
narratives for the thematic subject. Such a procedure is an
important step for the *child*. It allows her to simplify the
task by creating a single procedure which makes it possible
to keep easy track of reference relations and thus to have a
good grip on the flow of her output of connected utterances.
But, on the contrary, children go on to monitor both the discursive and intra- and intersentential levels, involving
complex procedures, and this can hardly be explained by invok-
ing their desire for clarity towards an addressee. Rather,

I would contend that the child's progress stems, not from a desire for economy, but from one for greater *control* of the simultaneous interplay of various levels of processing - the constant trade-off between discursive organizational features, local sentential relations and lexical choices. Language is not a series of sentences, just as sentences are not just a series of words. Language is a dynamic interplay of many facets, involving just the right balance between information content and processing procedures. In this sense, developmental psycholinguistics never ceases!

RFFFRENCES

Caramazza, A. and Gupta, S. (1979). The roles of topicalization, parallel function and verb semantics in the interpretation of pronouns. *Linguistics* 17, 497-518.
Cromer, R. (1976). Developmental strategies for language. *In* "The Development of Cognitive Processes" (V. Hamilton and M.D. Vernon, eds). New York: Academic Press.
Chomsky, N. (1969). "The Acquisition of Syntax in Children From Five to Ten". Cambridge, Mass.: M.I.T. Press.
Ervin-Tripp and Mitchell-Kernan (eds) (1977). "Child Discourse". New York: Academic Press.
Ferreiro, E., Othenin-Girard, Ch., Chipman, H. and Sinclair, H. (1976). How do children handle relative clauses? *Archives de Psychologie* 172, 229-267.
Grober, E.H., Beardsley, W. and Caramazza, A. (1978). Parallel function strategy in pronoun assignment. *Cognition* 6(2), 117-133.
Halliday, M.A.K. and Hasan, R. (1976). "Cohesion in English". London: Longmans Group Limited.
Kail, M. (1976). Stratégies de compréhension des pronoms personnels chez le jeune enfant. *Enfance* 3-4, 447-466.
Kail, M. and Léveillé, M. (1977). Compréhension de la coréférence des pronoms personnel chez l'enfant et l'adulte. *Année Psychologique* 77, 79-94.
Karmiloff-Smith, A. (1979a). Micro- and macro-developmental changes in language acquisition and other representational systems. *Cognitive Science* 3(2), 91-118.
Karmiloff-Smith, A. (1979b). "A Functional Approach to Child Language". Cambridge: Cambridge University Press.
Karmiloff-Smith, A. (1979c). Language as a formal problem space for children. Paper given at MPG-NIAS Conference on Beyond Description in Child Language. June 1979. Nijmegen, Holland.
Karmiloff-Smith, A. (In press). Modifications in children's representational systems and levels of accessing knowledge. *In* "Knowledge and Representation" (B. de Galder, ed.) London: Routledge and Kegan Paul.

Lyons, J. (1977). "Semantics". Cambridge: Cambridge University Press.

Maratsos, M.P. (1973). The effects of stress on the understanding of pronominal coreference in children. *Journal of Psycholinguistics* 1, 1-8.

Marslen-Wilson, W. and Tyler, L.K. (1980). The temporal structure of spoken language understanding. *Cognition* 8, 1-71.

Reichman, R. (1978). Conversational coherency. *Cognitive Science* 2(4), 283-327.

Sheldon, A. (1974). The role of parallel function in the acquisition of relative clauses in English. *Journal of Verbal Learning and Verbal Behavior* 13, 272-281.

Tanz, Ch. (1980). "Studies in the Acquisition of Deictic Terms". Cambridge: Cambridge University Press.

Tyler, L.K. (1979). On-line structural and interpretation processes in children's understanding of spoken language. Paper given at MPG-NIAS Conference on Beyond Description in Child Language. June 1979. Nijmegen, Holland.

Warden, D. (1976). The influence of context on children's use of identifying expressions and references. *British Journal of Psychology* 67(1), 101-112.

SYNTACTIC AND INTERPRETATIVE FACTORS IN THE DEVELOPMENT OF LANGUAGE COMPREHENSION

LORRAINE KOMISARJEVSKY TYLER

Max-Planck Institute for Psycholinguistics, Nijmegen, The Netherlands.

1. INTRODUCTION

The theme of this chapter will be the development of children's ability to use the structural syntactic and interpretative properties of utterances as they comprehend spoken language. Its emphasis will be upon those comprehension processes which occur as the listener hears an utterance — that is, on the nature of the mental processes involved in immediate (or "on-line") comprehension as they occur over time.

This emphasis reflects my own particular perspective on problems in language acquisition; that is, a perspective derived from a model of the end-state of the acquisition process — of adult language comprehension. I will begin, therefore, by sketching the outlines of this adult model, since it gives the framework within which the developmental questions will be discussed.

The adult model I have assumed (called the "on-line interactive" model) is one which evolved from the results of extensive on-line processing experiments with adult subjects (e.g. Marslen-Wilson, 1975; Marslen-Wilson and Tyler, 1980a; Tyler and Marslen-Wilson, 1977). The basic claim of the model is, first of all, that the processing of an utterance is always conducted with immediate reference to the discourse context in which it occurs. From the first word of an utterance the listener is constructing what we can call an interpretative representation of this utterance. This interpretative representation is the outcome of an on-line interaction between linguistic and non-linguistic analyses. That is, listeners are integrating together constraints derived from the specific discourse context and from their general knowledge of the world, with their analysis of the linguistic

properties of the utterance itself. As each word is heard
and recognized, its semantic and syntactic properties become immediately available and are mapped onto this developing interpretative representation. This means that the
syntactic and semantic properties of utterances, as linguistically defined, do not correspond during processing to computationally distinct syntactic and semantic "levels of analysis". The listener's syntactic knowledge is not realized
during processing as a computationally distinct level of
syntactic analysis of the input, rather, syntactic knowledge
functions during processing to guide the assignment of structural relations within the developing interpretative representation.

The model does not assume that there is also a semantic
interpreter of the classical type — that is, a processor
which operates on word-meanings and syntactic relations to
produce a semantic representation which is then, and only
then, integrated with pragmatic variables and the discourse
context (cf. Fodor, Bever and Garrett, 1974; Kintsch, 1974;
Clark, 1976). This is because there is assumed to be no stage
of processing during which the semantic properties of words
are being analysed independently of their interpretation in
some "context of use". This is not to say that no formal
distinction can be drawn between the semantic and pragmatic
aspects of meaning, but that this distinction is not one that
corresponds to functional subdivisions in the processing
system. Given the lexical semantic information made available when words are being recognized, this information is
directly pragmatically interpreted in its discourse context,
subject to the available syntactic constraints. (For a detailed discussion of this model, see Marslen-Wilson and
Tyler, 1980a.)

Within this general framework, the following basic developmental questions need to be asked. First, we need to
establish whether the general structure of the comprehension
process is the same for children as it appears to be for
adults. That is, do the same types of immediate interactions
between syntactic and interpretative analyses form the basis
for on-line sentence processing? Secondly, are there developmental changes in the extent to which different sources of
processing information contribute to the child's comprehension of an utterance? That is, are there relative imbalances
across ages in the role of lexical, syntactic and interpretative analyses?

These questions concerning the on-line properties of language processing in children depend critically upon obtaining
data from experimental tasks which tap these basic processes.

Processing data derived from such experiments allow us to
address questions about the detailed structure of on-line
processing events — namely *what* processes occur *when* as a
sentence is being heard. This kind of data has clear implications for the study of language acquisition, since a theory
of language development needs to include an account of the
language processing procedures that children are mastering
as they acquire language. Learning to understand spoken
language is to learn how to perform some kind of mapping between sound and meaning, and on-line experimental tasks are
uniquely suitable for studying the properties of this mapping
process.

Despite the relevance of these questions to a model of
language acquisition, few attempts have been made to collect
the appropriate kind of processing data. In this respect, the
research which will be reported in the final section of this
chapter differs from much of the work in developmental psycholinguistics, which has primarily been concerned with rather
general comprehension effects. In such studies, the issue
is invariably one of determining whether a particular linguistic variable — such as the particular syntactic properties
of an utterance — does or does not affect the child's overall ability to comprehend an utterance. Given this approach,
comprehension is typically measured at the end of an utterance, rather than as it is being heard (cf. Bever, 1970a;
Slobin, 1978a; Maratsos, 1974).

Although such studies have little to say about the internal
structure of processing events, they do tell us whether
children use particular types of information at all in their
interpretation of an utterance. Therefore, I will begin by
discussing some of this work; in particular, those studies
which have examined the role of structural syntactic, "semantic" and "pragmatic" sources of information in language comprehension. The first two sections of the chapter will focus
on language comprehension between 2 and 5 years of age. In
the first of these sections I will concentrate upon studies
which have looked at the extent to which young children are
able to use syntactic cues to structural organization. The
second section of the chapter will focus on experiments which
have looked at the role of "semantic" and "pragmatic" information in the comprehension processes of children under five.
Language comprehension after the age of five will be discussed
in the third section, and in the final two sections I will
describe some of my own work on 5- to 11-year-olds (carried out
in collaboration with William Marslen-Wilson), which looks
more directly at the ways in which these various types of information are used in the immediate interpretation of spoken
language.

2. THE USE OF SYNTACTIC STRUCTURAL INFORMATION

A basic question we want to answer when we study the development of language comprehension is the following: How do children get from a string of words to some sort of interpretation
of an utterance? It is clear that they have to know the meanings of the words they are recognizing — and at least some
of the structural relationships between them. Therefore,
they have to know what the relevant markers of these structural relationships are. In English, the ones which have
been most extensively studied in young children are word
order, markers of structural relationships between clauses,
and syntactic markers of the passive. In this chapter, then,
I will discuss the research covering these syntactic cues.
An important point to be kept in mind throughout the discussion, is that the fact that children use these syntactic cues
does not necessarily mean that they thereby construct a distinct syntactic level of representation. It simply means that
children use them to help them to put together words in an
utterance into some structured relationship. How this structural relationship is described is irrelevant for the moment.
And, in fact, although the experiments I am going to discuss
do show that young children use certain syntactic structural
cues, they do not tell us about the kind of representation
which is derived from them.
  Perhaps the best known work on children's sensitivity to
particular syntactic cues during comprehension is the series
of experiments reported by Bever (1970a). These experiments
tested children between the ages of 2 and 5 years, and used
the "acting-out" paradigm.
  In one experiment, Bever wanted to determine whether children
as young as two years could distinguish active from passive
sentences, when their only cues were the syntactic markers
which signalled the passive. So, for example, he found that
when children heard passive sentences of the form:

1) The dog was chased by the cat

where either of the two entities could plausibly carry out
the action specified by the verb (i.e. reversible sentences),
two-year-olds correctly acted out the sentence about 50% of
the time, whereas they were correct about 90% of the time on
actives. On the basis of this difference Bever argued that
even two-year-olds could at least distinguish between different syntactic constructions since, if this had not been
the case and they had systematically interpreted passives as
actives by taking the first noun to be the subject, then they
would have been as bad on passives as they were good on
actives.

However, an important point to stress here is that even if
two-year-olds can successfully distinguish between active and
passive sentences, this does not necessarily reflect their
ability to interpret passives correctly. It could be the
case that the syntactic markers of the passive merely signal
to the child that the utterance cannot be interpreted as an
active, but he has yet to learn how to interpret the structural relationships within a passive construction. This would
result in two-year-olds performing essentially randomly on
passives, in the sense that they would not apply any consistent strategy. It is, in fact, plausible to interpret Bever's
data in just this way — as showing that children respond
randomly on passives. Similar claims for the random nature
of two-year-olds' responses to passives have been made by
de Villiers and de Villiers (1973), who obtained data which
parallelled Bever's.

Bever's data also show that between the ages of two and
three performance on passives appears to be random, even when
there are semantic constraints to aid interpretation (i.e.
irreversible sentences). Between the ages of three and four,
however, children improve both in their ability to exploit
semantic information and to correctly interpret reversible
passives. But this general improvement drops off at four
years of age when children systematically misinterpret reversible passives. Bever suggested that this is because children
use a "perceptual strategy" of taking the first NP of any
sequence to be the actor and thereby interpret passives as
though they were actives. This phase only lasts about six
months, however, and at the age of $4\frac{1}{2}$ to five children correctly interpret the passive 65-70% of the time.

It is not clear, however, to what extent this account of
the acquisition of the passive maps onto the use and comprehension of this construction in normal situations. In most
studies, children are presented with isolated sentences and
therefore a significant function of the passive — namely,
its discourse function — is ignored. Thus, the experimental
situation might encourage erratic and inconsistent behaviour
on the part of the child as he tries to find a discourse interpretation of the passive when there is no prior discourse context. If sentences were presented to the child in a discourse
context, it is possible that a different, or at least smoother,
pattern would emerge.

The interesting issue raised by these experiments, but only
minimally addressed by them, is — what sources of information
do children use when they interpret passives? To answer this
question we, first of all, have to consider what discourse
function is served by the passive in normal usage.

It is commonly argued that an utterance heard in a discourse context is organized into a topic-comment structure. The topic can be defined as "the person, object or event about which something is said, and comment as the information conveyed about this person, object or event" (Grieve and Wales, 1973). Given that speakers usually put what they want to talk about at the beginning of a sentence (Clark, 1965), then this suggests that a speaker uses a passive when he wants to focus on the logical object. Thus, the passive allows the logical object to become the theme of the discourse or its "conceptual focus" (Tannenbaum and Williams, 1968).

On this account, adult listeners who hear a passive sentence will interpret the first NP as the topic of the discourse, but given their knowledge of the linguistic cues which mark passive constructions, they will also interpret the first NP as the logical object or patient of the action denoted by the verb. With young children, however, the picture is somewhat different. If, as has been argued elsewhere (Tyler and Marslen-Wilson, 1978a; Chapman, 1978), the pragmatic aspects of language are primary in development, then young children, who have not yet mastered the linguistic devices which mark the logical relations in passive constructions, will base their interpretation on its discourse structure. That is, they will assume that, since the first NP is the discourse topic it is also likely to function as agent. And this will be their strategy even when the sentence is heard in isolation since this is, in a sense, the unmarked case.

This emphasis upon young children's dependence upon the discourse properties of language is indirectly supported by an experiment by Dewart (1975). She found that the performance of children who could not correctly interpret passives in isolation was severely disrupted when a passive was preceded by an inappropriate context sentence. In contrast, children who could correctly interpret isolated passives were relatively unaffected by the context sentence. This finding suggests, then, that when children have not yet mastered the relevant linguistic cues, they rely upon their knowledge of the discourse properties of their language.

Apart from investigations of the acquisition of the passive construction, several studies have looked at the children's ability to comprehend a variety of subordinating conjunctions. However, most of these experiments will not be discussed here because they are concerned with interpretation of particular lexical items (e.g. "before", "after", etc.) rather than with how they are used as cues to structure (cf. Clark, 1971; Weil and Stenning, 1978). There are surprisingly few experiments that fall into the latter category. From among these, those

which have looked at embedded relatives bear most directly
on the issue of the acquisition of syntactic devices which
serve as cues to structural organization (Bever, 1970a, b;
Slobin and Welsh, 1973; Smith, 1970).

In these experiments, two- to three-year-olds are typically
presented with embedded relatives of the form:

2) The cow that jumped walked away

Children of this age appear to make use of the relative clause
marker, since in Bever's experiments, they acted out or repeated the main clause and ignored the subordinate clause. These
results have been replicated by Smith (1970) and Slobin and
Welsh (1973) using an elicited imitation task. Their subjects
frequently produced only the main clause, but occasionally re-
produced the sentence as two clauses joined by a coordinating
conjunction. Moreover, in Slobin and Welsh's experiment, when
the relative pronoun was omitted in the model sentence presented to the child, she produced incoherent imitations in
which neither the meaning nor the word order of the original
was necessarily maintained, thus strengthening the claim that
the relative pronoun was functioning as a marker to organize
the utterance into two clauses or propositions. Similar
conclusions were drawn by H. Brown (1971) who found that comprehension was improved in four- and five-year-olds when a
relative pronoun was present in the sentence.

These experiments, then, show that children as young as two
to three years are sensitive to the syntactic structural
function of relative pronouns, since if they had ignored the
pronoun and had been operating on the basis of a word order
strategy (i.e. taking the first NP to be the agent and the
first VP as the action performed by the agent), then they
would have responded to the relative clause instead of the
main clause.[1]*

The other main focus of research into young children's use
of cues to syntactic structural relations has centred upon the
role of word order information. In a typical experiment, two-
year-olds hear simple reversible active sentences such as:

3) The cow kisses the horse.

They normally act out such sentences correctly (Bever, 1970a;
de Villiers and de Villiers, 1973; Slobin, 1978a), suggesting
that they are using a canonical word order strategy of taking
the first NP as the agent of the action.[2]

---

* Superscript numerals refer to notes which are to be found
at the end of the chapter.

This claim is supported by an experiment by Dewart (1979), using a rather different technique in which children had to choose the appropriate toy out of a selection of different toys. She found that when a nonsense word was placed before a verb, it was usually interpreted as the agent or mover of the action — and therefore as animate. Thus, in the absence of semantic cues, the child uses a word order strategy to determine relationships within a sentence.

Another method for investigating how children use word order information is to violate the normal order and measure how comprehension is affected. An experiment by Wetstone and Friedlander (1973) examined the effects of word order disruptions on comprehension in two- to three-year-olds. The children were given simple questions and commands which varied in the extent to which word order was distorted. For example, they heard normal sentences of the form:

4) Open up the box

and "misplaced" sentences, such as:

5) Open the up box

where the correct order of function words was violated, but the position of nouns and verbs was not changed. These two sentence types were compared with scrambled sentences of the form:

6) Box the open up.

They found that "nonfluent" children — that is, those who were in the holophrastic or so-called telegraphic stages of language production — responded just as appropriately to all three sentence types. In fact, they appeared to be totally unconcerned by these rather gross violations of syntactic organization. Their strategy was presumably to construct what seemed to them to be a reasonable interpretation of the material just based upon the meanings of individual words, and the extralinguistic context in which they were heard. However, there was a tendency for "fluent" children (who had an average MLU of 3.5) not to respond to the scrambled sentences — suggesting that they at least noticed that the word order irregularities were inconsistent with the most reasonable interpretation of the words. Therefore, longer MLUs are, unsurprisingly, correlated with greater sensitivity to syntactic variables.

What these experiments taken together seem to show is that by the age of two to three years, children are able to use some syntactic cues of word order and subordinate markers. Their interpretation of word order is confined to a strategy

of taking the first NP as the agent of the verb. It is only
when children reach the age of $4\frac{1}{2}$ to five that they are reliably responsive to more complex syntactic cues which signal
syntactic constructions other than the active.[3]

3. THE USE OF INTERPRETATIVE INFORMATION

It is clear that a sentence cannot be understood on the basis
of syntactic cues alone. To understand an utterance the child
has to interpret the input in terms of what he knows about how
particular entities and events function in the world. Studies
of language comprehension which have looked at non-syntactic
structural factors have focused on what are usually called
semantic and pragmatic variables.

The standard psycholinguistic definition of semantics is
the combination of word-meanings and the relationship they
can enter into with each other, given the selection restrictions attached to each word (cf. Fodor *et al*., 1974). Semantic
interpretation is assumed to be distinct from pragmatics which
is considered to be knowledge about entities and their contexts
of use in the world, and external to the semantic structure of
the sentence itself.

Although this distinction is frequently drawn in the literature, it is a rather difficult one to maintain in processing
models, and even in some linguistic theories (see Chomsky,
1979). In the context of the language comprehension process
it is not clear that knowing the meaning of an expression can
be distinguished, in practice, from knowing how that expression is interpreted in the world. Although it might be the
case that some limited aspects of meaning can be expressed in
strictly linguistic terms, there are strong arguments in
favour of the claim that the meaning of a linguistic expression involves extralinguistic sources of knowledge (cf. Chomsky,
1979; Nunberg, 1977). There is, furthermore, experimental evidence which suggests that there is no separate processing
stage which corresponds to the computation of the logical form
of a sentence as distinct from its semantic interpretation
with respect to knowledge of the world (Marslen-Wilson and
Tyler, 1980a). Thus, there are both psychological and linguistic arguments for collapsing the distinction between different types of semantic representation in language comprehension. In order to avoid terminological confusion, we have
used the term "interpretative" representation to refer to the
on-line representation of an utterance which combines these
various notions of semantics in a single processing stage
(Tyler,1981a; Marslen-Wilson and Tyler, 1980a).

It is clear from a number of studies that these interpretative variables are involved in even very young children's

language comprehension. For example, another experiment by Bever (1970a) compared children's understanding of "probable" active sentences, such as:

7) The mother pats the dog

with that of "improbable" actives, of the form:

8) The dog pats the mother.

Even for two-year-olds, performance on probable sentences was better than on improbable sentences. Since the syntactic structure was identical for both types of sentence, comprehension must also have been based upon interpretative analyses. Similar results were subsequently obtained by Strohner and Nelson (1974) who found that two- to three-year-olds try to interpret improbable events as though they were probable.[4]

These experiments provide a good illustration of the difficulty we would get into if we tried to construct an explanation of the results in terms of either pragmatics or semantics. On a semantic account, the improbable sentence was made improbable by the fact that a selection restriction on the verb "pat" was violated. Therefore, the argument would run, performance on improbable sentences is poorer only because of linguistic factors. Although it may indeed be the case that a selection restriction is violated, it is also true that this improbable sentence involves a violation of extralinguistic knowledge. For our experience of the world tells us that it is usually only humans who pat, and not dogs. This rather simple example illustrates the difficulties involved in drawing a distinction between pragmatic and semantic factors in normal language use.

Further data about the nature of the interpretative variables which influence children's speech comprehension comes from a study carried out by Chapman and Miller (1975). In this experiment, children had to act out sentences which contained either an animate or inanimate subject or object, with the result that they almost always identified the animate entity as the subject and the inanimate entity as the object of the sentence. This knowledge of what kind of entity can best function as subject presumably comes from children's real-world experiences in which animate entities are usually agents.

The rather general picture which emerges from these experiments is that around two years of age, children tend to focus on words they know in utterances and construct a reasonable interpretation of them which fits the situational context in which they occur. However, in situations where entities can equally well function as the agent or patient of an action (reversible actives), they are perfectly able to pay attention to word order information, and in general tend to take the first mentioned noun as the agent. This ensures correct interpretation of reversible active sentences, but poor performance on reversible passives. As children get older they make more appropriate use of syntactic structural information in utterances. That is, they are clearly sensitive to some aspects of syntactic structural information at an early age, but here it seems to serve as a signal to the child to modify the heuristics he normally uses for interpretation. It is only as children get older that they discover the specific structural information that a particular syntactic marker carries.

4. THE USE OF SYNTACTIC AND INTERPRETATIVE INFORMATION AFTER FIVE YEARS

From the studies which have been discussed so far, we can construct a general picture of the changes which take place in language comprehension in the pre-school years. But what happens after five years of age? Although language development after five is a relatively neglected area of study (see Palermo and Molfese (1973) and Karmiloff-Smith (1979a) for reviews), there are a few experiments which in general employ somewhat different techniques from those used with younger children. Once again, the experiments I am going to describe here are only those which have focused on the relative contribution of structural syntactic and interpretative variables during comprehension.

In general, these studies suggest that there are developmental changes in the relative contribution of syntactic and semantic sources of information to the comprehension process. However, as I will point out, the data do not force such a conclusion, since there are problems both with the experimental materials and with the paradigms used. Furthermore, since some of these experiments depend upon the doubtful distinction between semantics and knowledge of the world mentioned earlier, they do not constitute evidence for developmental changes in the child's use of a strictly linguistic type of semantic knowledge, of the kind proposed by Katz (1972).

First of all, there is a rather inconclusive series of studies by McNeill (1965) and Entwisle and Frasure (1974) which investigate the claim, originally made by McNeill, that the ability to use semantic information improves between the ages of 5 to 8, whereas the use of syntactic information remains stable. Both experiments used an immediate memory paradigm and the same stimuli, which consisted of "normal" sentences, such as:

9) Wild Indians spear heavy buffaloes

syntactic prose sentences (that is, sentences which are syntactically normal but semantically anomalous), for example:

10) The quickly ticking restaurant pleased streets

and random word order sentences, of the form:

11) Needed coloured gently the car time.

The two experiments, however, differ somewhat in their results. McNeill, for example, found that recall of syntactic prose and random sentences remained stable between five to eight years of age, whereas performance on normal sentences improved considerably as children got older — thus lending support to his claims. However, although Entwisle and Frasure found the same improvement for normal sentences with age, they also found an increase in performance on syntactic prose sentences. They argue from this that children's ability to use syntactic cues in processing sentences does improve after five.

But it is not clear how we should interpret these results, since all of the children clearly found the task extremely difficult. Even the oldest children recalled the five-word normal proce sentences with less than 50% accuracy, and the younger children's performance was much worse than this. I find this particularly odd, since in my own experiments (Tyler and Marslen-Wilson, 1978a, b) five-year-olds recall ten to twelve word sentences with 80% accuracy. This discrepancy is even more striking, given that in my experiments children did not know in advance which particular sentence in a story they were going to reproduce, whereas in the McNeill, and the Entwisle and Frasure experiments, children were presented with sentences in isolation and so they were prepared to recall each sentence they heard.

There are a number of plausible explanations for the poor levels of recall obtained in these experiments. Firstly, it is probable that the children found the sentences so difficult to remember because function words were almost entirely omitted. Function words are an important source of structural syntactic information, and it is reasonable to assume that five-year-olds are able to exploit this information since by that age they are sensitive to the distinction between function and content words (Swinney and Cutler, 1979).

Another potential source of the poor level of recall could have been the fact that sentences were presented in isolation. An advantage of presenting isolated sentences is that children know exactly what they have to remember and recall, but its disadvantage is that there is no discourse or pragmatic context with respect to which each sentence can be interpreted. Therefore, given that the task, or more likely the materials,

were so difficult for the children, it is not at all clear
what the results of these experiments tell us about normal
performance — and, in particular, normal sentence processing.

In spite of these problems with both McNeill's and Entwisle
and Frasure's experiments there is some evidence from an experiment by James and Miller (1973) which is frequently cited
as support for McNeill's claim that knowledge of semantic
selection restrictions improves with age. James and Miller
(1973) were specifically interested in the question of whether
children's comprehension of sentences would be impaired when
there were minimal violations of selection restrictions. To
test this, they asked five- and seven-year-olds to tell them
whether sentences they heard were "okay" or "silly". The
sentences were either normal, or they contained one selection
restriction violation. For example, if the normal sentence
was:

12) The pretty girl smiled at the man

the "anomalous" version was:

13) The furry girl smiled at the man.

They found that older children were better at distinguishing
between normal and "anomalous" sentences than the younger
children, and argued that this was because as children get
older more selection restrictions are added to the words in
their lexicon. But, once again, we are faced with the problem
that a selection restriction violation also violates real
world knowledge, and therefore we cannot argue on the basis of
this kind of experiment for developmental changes in the
child's use of semantic as opposed to extralinguistic information during sentence comprehension.

The evidence, then, for changes in the child's ability to
use syntactic and interpretative constraints as they get
older is rather inconclusive. Apart from the difficulties with
the McNeill, and the Entwisle and Frasure experiments mentioned
earlier, there is an additional problem associated with their
use of sentences in isolation. As David Greene (1977), for
example, has shown, the operations involved in processing a
sentence for the purpose of memorizing it can be quite different from those involved in processing it for comprehension
purposes. Therefore, these experiments are of limited value
in elucidating the comprehension processes we are interested
in here.

However, the memory paradigm developed by Jarvella (1971)
avoids many of these problems. Subjects hear sentences in
discourse contexts, and they are not told in advance which
sentence they are going to have to recall. Consequently,

this task is more appropriate for investigating comprehension processes as opposed to self-conscious memory processes. For these reasons I used this paradigm in a series of experiments looking at the role of syntactic and interpretative information in five- to eleven-year-old children's comprehension. I will describe these experiments in the next section of the paper.

5. SYNTACTIC AND INTERPRETATIVE INFORMATION IN LANGUAGE PROCESSING: SOME IMMEDIATE MEMORY EXPERIMENTS

In a first experiment, (Tyler and Marslen-Wilson, 1978a), five-, seven- and 11-year-olds listened to a story, and at unpredictable intervals the story was stopped and the children were asked to repeat back verbatim the last sentence they heard. The five-year-olds differed from the older children and adults in the extent to which their recall was dominated by the syntactic clausal structure of the two-clause test sentences. In particular, their recall did not show the double bow-shaped serial position curves (one for each clause) that was typical of adult performance and that were produced by the 7- and 11-year-olds. Instead, the pattern of their responses was best described by a single bow-shaped serial position curve covering the entire sentence.

This lack of clausal structuring of recall, together with the fact that the meaning of the original sentence was preserved, suggested that the five-year-olds were responding on the basis of a unified representation of the sentence as a whole. This claim was supported by the further finding that when the five-year-olds heard a "syntactic prose" story — which retained the syntactic structure of the original normal prose story but had no coherent meaning — then clear clausal segmentation was observed. Thus it was not the case that the five-year-olds could *not* use syntactic structure to organize their recall, but rather that a syntactically-based representation was rapidly superceded by a more global — presumably interpretative — representation when such a level of representation was available. The 7- and 11-year-olds, although clearly also interpreting and understanding the test-sentences, did not show this rapid loss of the clausal syntactic structure of the material.

This analysis, stressing the role of interpretive variables in five-year-olds' comprehension, is supported by a second experiment which explicitly manipulated the extent to which two clauses could be interpretatively integrated (Tyler and Marslen-Wilson, 1978b). Thus, test sentences were classified as being either of High or Low semantic cohesion. A High

Cohesion sentence was one in which the agent and patient were the same in both clauses and the actions in each clause were part of the same general event. In Low Cohesion sentences, agent, patient, and actions in each clause were as unrelated as possible without making the sentence as a whole incomprehensible. It is important to remember that since the sentences were heard in a story context, we were manipulating the relative degree of cohesiveness rather than making an all-or-none contrast. An example of each type of sentence is given below:

14) High Cohesion:
    Sarah was sad about the news and she cried a little bit.

15) Low Cohesion:
    Sarah tried to make him better and the children ate their sweets.

Using the Jarvella paradigm, we found that five-year-olds' recall of the High Cohesion sentences did not preserve its syntactic clausal structure. In contrast, recall of the Low Cohesion sentences was clearly clausally segmented. This difference was not due to differences in the overall per cent of words correctly recalled for the two types of sentence, since overall recall was very similar in both cases — 84% for High Cohesion sentences and 80% for Low Cohesion sentences. For older children, recall of both sentence types continued to reflect the syntactic clausal structure of the material.

However, in a later experiment, it became clear that differences between High and Low Cohesion sentences in five-year-olds' recall were not merely due to the interpretative factors within a sentence, but rather to the ease with which the test sentence could be integrated into the prior discourse. Thus, High Cohesion sentences were closely related to the preceding context and could be rapidly interpreted within that framework. But Low Cohesion sentences invariably marked or contained a transition from one event to another and were less rapidly assimilable into the prior discourse.

This final experiment, then, indicated that the five-year-olds' performance was primarily determined by the discourse properties of the test sentences, so that recall primarily reflected the products of a sentence's integration into its discourse context and the loss of its syntactic organization. In contrast, the seven-year-olds' recall always preserved the syntactic (clausal) structure of the test sentences while, at the same time, being sensitive to discourse relations.

However, since these results were based on recall data, they do not allow us to distinguish between explanations of the results in terms of differences either in immediate sentence processing operations, or in memory processes. Clearly, one plausible interpretation of these differences in recall is that they reflect differences in five-year-olds' versus older children's dependence on syntactic as opposed to interpretive factors during the original processing of the material. This suggestion is, in fact, congruent with the conclusions drawn from McNeill's study which was mentioned earlier. Taken together, the experiments discussed in this section at least raise the possibility that children aged between five and 11 differ in their use of various sources of information during comprehension. However, they do not provide a coherent picture of what these differences might be. To answer questions about the processes underlying the immediate comprehension of spoken language we need to use experimental tasks which reflect these processes more directly.

I decided, therefore, to try to resolve some of the ambiguities involved in the interpretation of the memory data by constructing an experimental situation in which I could examine the extent to which the syntactic and interpretative properties of utterances are used by children in their on-line processing of spoken language. In the following section these experiments will be described in some detail.

CHILDREN'S ON-LINE PROCESSING OF SPOKEN LANGUAGE

The study of immediate spoken language processing in young children does not have a long or rich history. Apart from my own work, I know of only three other experiments which have been carried out, and all of them in the past couple of years (Foss, Bias and Starkey, 1978; Swinney and Cutler, 1979; Cole and Perfetti, 1980). Each of these experiments deals with a different, and somewhat restricted, aspect of language processing phenomena.

In Foss, Bias and Starkey's (1978) experiments they investigated the effect of a particular syntactic configuration — namely, embedded that-complement clauses — on on-line processing in five-year-olds. Their results were somewhat equivocal, but suggested that, for some five-year-olds at least, monitoring for target words occurring within an embedded relative clause took longer than monitoring for target words occurring within main clauses. This result is consistent with earlier claims that the relative pronoun functions as a syntactic marker for young children (cf. Bever, 1970a).

A similar emphasis on the role of syntactic information during on-line comprehension is evident in the work of Swinney and Cutler (1979). The framework for their research was a model of adult language processing which claims that adults have a specialized word recognition device to facilitate the processing of closed class items which, given that they are usually poorly articulated, would otherwise pose problems for the word recognition system. Due to this specialized device, it is argued, open and closed class items present equivalent processing loads to the processing system.

The issue raised by Swinney and Cutler (1979) was whether children as young as five years of age also show evidence of this specialized device. Using a word monitoring task, with monitoring targets being either open or closed class items, they found that monitoring reaction times to open class items were faster than to closed class items for children between the ages of five and eight. Given that adults show no such difference, they argued that the special closed class recognition device does not develop until after the age of eight.

What this claim presumably means is that before the age of eight, children should have difficulty in recognizing closed class items in normal speech. This in turn would imply that these children would not be able to exploit fully the proposed major function of closed class items during on-line processing — that is, "to support syntactic analysis by permitting the assignment of major category membership" (Bradley, Garrett and Zurif, 1980). Consequently, we would expect to find some evidence of developmental changes in children's ability to use the syntactic structural properties of utterances in the on-line comprehension of spoken language. However, as we will see, the data from my own on-line processing experiments do not support such a position.

A third experiment, by Cole and Perfetti (1980), attempted to determine whether there were developmental changes in the extent to which contextual information facilitates word recognition processes. Children ranging in age from $4\frac{1}{2}$ to 11 years monitored a story for words containing a mispronunciation. All children detected more mispronunciations when the mispronounced word occurred in a predictable context. Reaction times to detect mispronunciations were also obtained from seven- to 11-year-olds, and a corresponding increase was found in the speed of detection for predictable words.

My own research has also focused on the role of contextual information during language comprehension. Its aim was to develop a picture of the general structure of the on-line comprehension process in children between the ages of five and 10 and to determine whether it differed in significant ways from that of adults. In particular, I wanted to examine the nature of the interactions between syntactic and interpretative sources of information, and to assess the relative contribution of each of them in on-line processing.

These developmental processing issues were investigated using a word-monitoring task which we had previously used with adults (Marslen-Wilson and Tyler, 1975; 1980a). This is a task in which a subject listens to a sentence for a word target specified in advance and presses a response key when he hears that word. Our adult research showed that the task is sensitive to the on-line interaction of syntactic and interpretative analyses with word recognition processes. This meant that the word monitoring task could be used to investigate the availability and relative importance of syntactic and interpretative analyses during on-line sentence processing.

The task was made appropriate for young children by presenting the target word in picture form. Thus, each child was presented with a picture of a common object and asked to name it. He was then told that the word would occur in a sentence he was about to hear and that he should press the response key as soon as he heard the word. In order to assess the role of syntactic and interpretative information during sentence comprehension, children heard sentences which varied in the availability of these sources of information. Thus, monitoring target words occurred in three types of prose context, which we can label Normal Prose, Syntactic Prose and Random Word Order. Each trial consisted of pairs of sentences, rather than sentences in isolation, and the target always occurred in the second sentence of each pair.

In Normal Prose, the sentences had a normal syntactic structure and allowed the development of an interpretative representation. That is, the first sentence set up a small scenario which provided a background for the interpretation of the second sentence. An example of a Normal Prose sentence-pair, with target word emphasized, is:

16) John had to go back home. He had fallen out of the *swing* and had hurt his hand.[5]

In Syntactic Prose, only the syntactic constituent structure was preserved and no coherent interpretative representation could be constructed. An example of one of these sentences is:

17) John had to sit on the spoon. He had lived out of the *swing* and had enjoyed his kitchen.

Finally, Random Word Order merely consisted of an unstructured string of words. For example:

18) The on sit spoon to had John. His lived had and out *swing* the he of had enjoyed kitchen.

Using similar materials in experiments with adults (Marslen-

Wilson and Tyler, 1975; 1980a), we found that monitoring
latencies were significantly facilitated in Normal Prose
relative to Syntactic Prose, and in Syntactic Prose relative
to Random Word Order. This reflected the respective effects
of interpretative and syntactic analyses on the word recognition processes underlying word monitoring performance.
   The basic developmental question here is, first of all,
whether this adult pattern is obtained at all age levels, and
second, if it is, whether the effects differ in magnitude
across ages. The data, shown in Table 1, clearly establish
that that adult pattern does hold across ages, and that there
are no overall developmental differences in the extent to
which syntactic and interpretative information is used during
processing. For all age groups, word monitoring in normal
sentences was faster than when the targets occurred in Syntactic Prose. This advantage of Normal over Syntactic Prose
was essentially the same for all ages — 83 ms for the five-
year-olds, 95 ms for the seven-year-olds and 91 ms for the
10-year-olds. There was also a smaller, but consistent,
increase in reaction times from Syntactic Prose to Random
Word Order for all ages. This pattern of reaction times
suggests that word recognition decisions in children between
the ages of five and 10 years are sensitive — and to the
same extent — to both the syntactic and interpretative properties of language.

TABLE 1   *Mean reaction times in identical monitoring (ms)*

Age Group (years)	Prose type		
	Normal Prose	Syntactic Prose	Random Word Order
Five	421	504	527
Seven	316	411	459
Ten	271	362	387

   However, to establish that the experiment is genuinely
tapping interpretative analyses, and not just a within-
sentence "semantic" analysis, a second major variable was
included; that is, the position of the target words in the
test sentences. The target words were distributed evenly
from the third to the eleventh word position in the second
sentence of each sentence-pair.

In the adult studies, where the target words were similarly distributed (Marslen-Wilson and Tyler, 1980a), Normal Prose had a significant advantage of 50-60 ms over Syntactic Prose right at the beginning of a sentence, and this advantage remained constant across word positions. When the same stimuli were tested with the lead-in sentence of each sentence-pair omitted, this early advantage of Normal Prose over Syntactic Prose disappeared. This established, then, that the early advantage of Normal Prose derived from the first sentence of each sentence-pair, which provided an interpretative context on to which each incoming word of the test sentence could be mapped.

These effects in Normal Prose can be contrasted with the effects in Syntactic Prose and Random Word Order (the comparison between these materials measures the contribution of syntactic analyses alone). There was no difference in monitoring latencies for these materials early in the sentence, the word position curves for the two materials did not significantly diverge until several words had been heard, and removing the lead-in sentence had no effect on the relationship between the two types of prose. Thus, syntactic analyses alone could not have produced the early advantage of Normal Prose, which depends instead upon the interpretability of a normal sentence in its discourse context.

The developmental question here is whether all children between the ages of five and 10 will show a similar advantage of Normal Prose over Syntactic Prose from the beginning of the sentence, thus showing evidence of the immediate construction of an interpretative representation.

For each of the three groups of children we tested the pattern of reaction times across word positions for each prose type was similar to the pattern obtained for adults in our earlier experiment. In Normal Prose and Syntactic Prose, reaction times became progressively faster throughout the sentence, indicating that monitoring latencies were facilitated by the syntactic and interpretative constraints which develop as more of the sentence is heard. In contrast, Random Word Order monitoring latencies remained stable across word-positions, reflecting the absence of any developing constraints on word recognition decisions.

A more direct measure of the development of syntactic and interpretative analyses across the sentence can be obtained, however, by taking the differences between prose contexts across word positions. This procedure eliminates word-position effects due to different words, and provides a relatively pure measure of the effects of contextual variables across the sentence. Furthermore, it removes any differences

due to absolute differences in reaction times for each age
group. Because of the constraints on the number of sentences
which could be presented to a child in an experimental session,
there were only a few words at each word-position. Therefore,
word-positions were collapsed into four word-position groups,
with an average of seven words in each group.

The differences between Normal and Syntactic Prose at each
word-position group for each age group are plotted in Fig. 1.

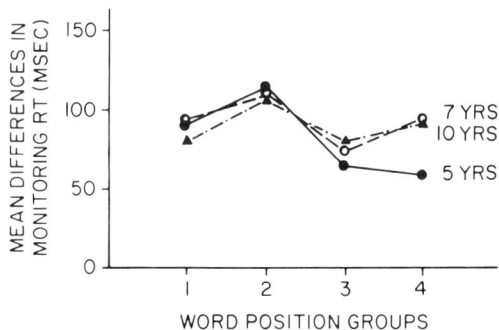

FIG. 1 *Mean advantage of Normal Prose over Syntactic Prose
across word positions in Identical monitoring. Word position
group 1 corresponds to the third and fourth word positions in
the test sentences, group 2 to word positions five and six,
etc.*

This graph shows the advantage of hearing a word in an interpretative context. There are two points to note here. First,
the three age groups show identical advantages across the first
three word-position groups (the slight fall-off in the last
word-position group for the five-year-olds is not significant).
Second, the degree of facilitation for the early word-positions
is just as great as for the later positions — exactly as we
found for adults (Marslen-Wilson and Tyler, 1980a).

These results suggest that when a normal sentence is heard
in a context, word recognition processes are facilitated to
the same extent by the listener's interpretative representation, whether the word occurs at the beginning or at later
points in the sentence. When a sentence is heard in isolation,
as the earlier adult experiment showed, these facilitatory
effects take some time to develop and are minimal at the early
word-positions. The early and strong effects which we find
in the present experiment (and with adults) are clearly derived from the prior discourse context, which provides an
interpretative representation in terms of which subsequent

material can be immediately analysed. Furthermore, the
strength of these effects both remains constant throughout
the course of the sentence, and does not vary as a function
of age.

In contrast to the fairly constant effects of interpretative
facilitation across the course of a normal sentence, syntactic
constraints take some time to develop and do not exert de-
tectable facilitatory effects on word recognition decisions
at the beginning of a new sentence. This is reflected in
Fig. 2, which plots the differences between Syntactic Prose
and Random Word Order at each word-position group. This
graph, then, shows the advantage over word-positions of hearing
a target word in a syntactically organized string rather than
a scrambled string. What we see here also is essentially
the same pattern for all age groups, and the same pattern as
was obtained for adults. That is, there are no significant
differences early in the test sentence, and the advantage of
Syntactic Prose over Random Word Order increases across the
course of the sentence. Thus, purely syntactic facilitation
builds up relatively slowly over a sentence, and does not
show any carry-over effects from the context sentence.

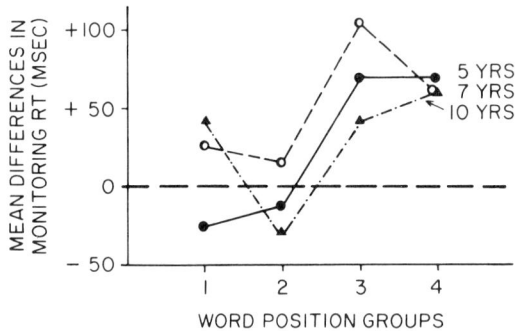

FIG. 2 *Mean advantage of Syntactic Prose over Random Word
Order across word positions in Identical monitoring.*

These results, taken together with our earlier adult data,
suggest that there are no developmental changes after the
age of five years in the basic processes underlying spoken
language comprehension. When the children we tested heard
a normal sentence in context, they attempted to map the input,
word-by-word as they heard it, onto some form of developing
interpretative representation that included information derived
from the prior context. If this had not been the case, then

we would not have obtained the strong facilitatory effects on
word recognition decisions early in a normal sentence, and
throughout the entire course of the sentence. There was no
evidence in these data that even the five-year-olds performed
this mapping process less readily than older listeners, or
that they obtained any less benefit from any of the available
sources of processing information.

This is a picture of the processes involved in spoken
language understanding that is consistent with those approaches
to language acquisition which emphasize the pragmatic aspects
of language comprehension (Karmiloff-Smith, 1979b); that is,
which stress the basic importance in language use of the
listener's knowledge of the world, and of the discourse context.

Furthermore, there is no sign in the present data that syntactic knowledge should be given some special developmental
precedence. There is no evidence, in particular, that the
child's ability to exploit syntactic information is more fully
developed at age five, and that other components are still,
as it were, catching up (cf. McNeill, 1970). The on-line processing data obtained here provides no support for the earlier
claims (McNeill, 1970; Entwisle and Frasure, 1974), based on
memory experiments, for developmental changes beyond age five
in the relative balance between syntactic and semantic (interpretative) knowledge in language comprehension.

This monitoring experiment, then, provides a picture of
the general structure of the processes involved in on-line
language comprehension between the ages of five and 10 years.
In a subsequent study we used a different task, called *Category* monitoring, to probe the ways in which the accessing
of word-meanings interacts with the process of constructing
an interpretative representation of the input. In this task,
children were shown a picture containing many members of a
particular taxonomic category. After they had named the
category, they heard a sentence containing a word which was
a member of that category, and they pressed a response key
when they identified the word. We used this task to obtain
basic data about how five- to ten-year-olds access the semantic
properties of words in different prose contexts.

Category monitoring is clearly a more complex task than
Identical monitoring. As our research with adults showed,
Identical monitoring is essentially a single-stage task, in
which once the listener has identified the word, he can immediately make his monitoring response. However, Category
monitoring involves two stages. The first stage is a word-
identification stage, which we assume to be mediated in
exactly the same manner as the word-identification stage in
Identical monitoring. A second stage is then required, in

which the semantic attributes of the identified word are
searched in order to determine whether they include the
specified taxonomic category membership. Subtracting the
Identical monitoring reaction time from the overall Category
monitoring reaction time provides an estimate of how long this
additional process of category attribute matching takes.

The important point here is that, as the adult research
shows, the semantic attribute matching component of Category
monitoring interacts with the prose context in which the target word appears. Optimal Category monitoring performance
is achieved when a target word occurs in Normal Prose test
sentences which are preceded by a discourse context. This is
because recognizing a word in Normal Prose involves assessing
the semantic attributes of the word against the developing
interpretation of the utterance. This makes the semantic
attributes of the word immediately available for the semantic
attribute matching stage of the Category monitoring task.
This can be contrasted with the situation in Syntactic Prose
or Random Word Order. In these materials there is no interpretative representation within which the semantic attributes
of the word are being evaluated for their contextual appropriateness. This produces considerable delays in the semantic
attribute matching stage of the task.

The developmental question here is whether the presence or
absence of an interpretative representation will interact with
the process of accessing the semantic properties of a word in
the same way for all age groups.

To answer this question we have to look, first of all, at
the mean monitoring latencies for each prose type and age
group. These data are presented in Table 2. Just as for the
Identical monitoring data, the overall picture looks very
similar for all age groups. Reaction times in Normal Prose
are faster than in Syntactic Prose, but the difference between Syntactic Prose and Random Word Order was not significant. These results suggest, then, that category monitoring
responses were facilitated by interpretative constraints, but
not by syntactic constraints alone.

However, unlike in Identical monitoring, there are some
age-related differences in the Category monitoring data.
Namely, there was a larger difference between Normal and Syntactic Prose as children got older. That is, there was an
increase with age in the degree to which monitoring reaction
times were facilitated by interpretative constraints.

Moreover, these age-related differences in the degree of
facilitation derived from interpretative constraints were
clearly related to the position of the target word in the
sentence. That is, there were large differences between ages

TABLE 2 *Main reaction times in category monitoring (ms)*

Age Group (years)	Prose type		
	Normal Prose	Syntactic Prose	Random Word Order
Five	646	772	776
Seven	503	662	679
Ten	400	580	616

in the degree of facilitation at the beginning of the sentence, with five-year-olds exhibiting the least and 10-year-olds the most facilitation. But there was no evidence of differential facilitation with age towards the end of the sentence.

We were, furthermore, able to determine that these age-related differences were specifically due to an interaction of interpretative constraints with the semantic attribute matching stage of the category monitoring task. We did this by subtracting the differences between Normal Prose and Syntactic Prose across word positions in Identical monitoring (Fig. 3) from the differences between Normal and Syntactic Prose in Category monitoring. The outcome of this manipulation is displayed in Fig. 3. As this graph clearly shows, the five-year-olds appear to show no facilitation of interpretative analyses upon the processes involved in semantic attribute matching for the first two word-position groups. And seven-year-olds show reduced facilitation in the first word-position group relative to the 10-year-olds. By the third word-position group, all ages show the same amount of facilitation upon semantic attribute matching.

To evaluate the developmental significance of this effect, we have to consider two distinct issues. First, why do we find this difference only in Category monitoring and not in Identical monitoring, and second, why is the five-year-olds' performance worse only over the first two word-position groups and not later in the sentence?

In the research into children's memory for sentences in story contexts (Tyler and Marslen-Wilson, 1978b) which I described earlier, we observed that five-year-olds were more restricted than older children in the types of textual linkages they could readily exploit. My argument here is that it is restrictions of this sort that produce the five-year-olds' decrement in performance early in a sentence. In particular, recent research by Karmiloff-Smith (this volume) on

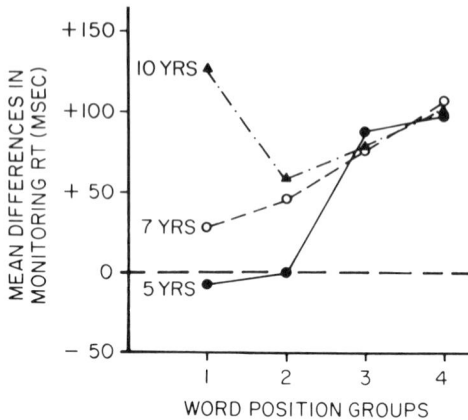

FIG. 3 *Estimated facilitation of semantic attribute matching across word positions (Normal Prose advantage in Identical monitoring subtracted from Normal Prose advantage in Category monitoring).*

children's use of anaphoric pronouns, and current research of my own on children's processing of anaphoric devices (Marslen-Wilson and Tyler, 1980b), suggest that children below the age of six years have not fully mastered the use of anaphoric pronouns. Karmiloff-Smith's data show that five-year-olds' use of pronouns fails to observe inter-sentential linguistic constraints on pronominalization, so that it is often only the non-linguistic context that disambiguates the correct antecedent for the listener. By the age of eight, however, children are becoming more sensitive to discourse constraints on the use of pronoun anaphors. These production differences are paralleled in a recent on-line experiment which examined five-, seven- and 10-year-olds' processing of words which were preceded either by an unambiguous anaphoric pronoun, or by an anaphoric full noun phrase. The results showed that the seven- and ten-year-olds' performance was equally good under both conditions, whereas the five-year-olds' performance was significantly impaired in the pronoun condition relative to the full noun phrase condition. Given the design of the experiment, this suggested that the pronoun was not functioning to indicate its antecedent as well as the full noun phrase.

A preliminary interpretation of these various results is that five-year-olds have not yet fully mastered the use of the inter-sentential linguistic cues which guide the mapping

of an utterance onto its discourse context. Their interpretation of pronouns appears to be much more dependent upon
pragmatic inferences than would be the case for older children and adults. Turning to the present experiment, we observe that 75% of the Normal Prose test sentences had anaphoric pronouns in subject position early in the sentence.
If the five-year-olds cannot make as much use of the linguistic cues to the interpretation of these anaphors, then this
suggests that the beginnings of such sentences will make
greater processing demands on them than will be the case for
seven- and ten-year-olds. Thus, given that Category monitoring is a more demanding task than Identical monitoring
because of the extra response stage involved, then this would
explain the pattern of results we obtained.

We now have in progress further experiments, investigating
in more detail just what the problem is here for the five-
year-olds. However, given that in the Identical monitoring
data we find the same pattern of immediate discourse mapping
early in the sentence as we did for adults, this suggests
that young children, just as much as adults, are conducting
their on-line analysis of an utterance within the framework
of its discourse context. Thus, their problems in the present experiment are unlikely to be caused by a general failure to relate utterances adequately to the context in which
they are being heard. Instead, it seems likely that young
children's construction of a discourse-level interpretation
of an utterance is primarily guided by pragmatic and inferential processes, and that there is a developmental lag in the
ability to use other cues for discourse mapping.

CONCLUSIONS: SOME ADVANTAGES OF PROCESSING APPROACHES

In the previous section I described two experiments designed
to investigate the general structure of on-line language processing in children between the ages of five and ten years.
The data from the Identical monitoring experiment showed that
all children map the syntactic and semantic properties of
the words they hear onto an interpretative representation of
the utterance which includes information derived from the discourse context. There were no signs of any age-related differences in the general structure of this process. The only
developmental differences were those which emerged in the
Category monitoring experiment, and we attributed those to
developmental changes in the child's ability to use linguistic cues to discourse mapping.

Analyses of this type, which include details of the nature
and time-course of interactions between various sources of

processing information would not be possible without on-line processing data. In general, the value of on-line tasks is that they allow us to determine when certain forms of analysis of the speech input can become available to the listener. The speech input is necessarily ordered in time; thus, at any given moment one can determine exactly how much of the input the listener could have heard. Given a response tapping his internal representation of the input at some given moment, we can then hope to capture the properties of the forms of internal representation that develop as the input is being processed.

It is clear from the studies reported in the previous section that experimental access to these developing internal representations is not confined to research with adults, but also includes children as young as five years of age. These experiments confirm the viability of carrying out certain kinds of on-line tasks with five-year-old children. We can use these tasks, then, to obtain the kind of data we need in order to construct a model of the development of immediate comprehension processes. The Identical and Category monitoring experiments, in particular, can be seen as a first step in studying the development of the structure of these processes.

I might conclude by pointing out that the perspective on children's language processing provided by the on-line data has consequences for the way in which "off-line" data about younger children's should be interpreted. Research on two- to three-year-olds, for example, shows strong effects of pragmatic and extralinguistic context upon the interpretation of utterances. However, no attempt is made to account for these effects in terms of the processing mechanisms involved, in spite of the enriched descriptions which a processing approach can provide. A processing approach requires us not only to ask questions about whether certain sources of information are used at all in language comprehension, but also about how they are used and when they become available to the listener. Without some attempt to develop an account of the processing mechanisms involved, it is not clear what explanatory force claims about the effects of extralinguistic context on language comprehension in two- to three-year-olds really has. At this point we are not in a position to offer a coherent processing account of language comprehension in such young children, but the aim of this chapter is to make clear why it might be important to begin to do so.

NOTES

1   An interesting issue which emerges from these experiments
    is why children frequently respond to only a single pro-
    position in a complex sentence. Is it due to some general
    processing or memory capacity limitation (cf. Slobin,
    1978b; Bever, 1970b), or to an inability to relate the two
    clauses together into a meaningful representation? Un-
    fortunately, there is currently no data which allows us
    to distinguish between these two possibilities.
2   Such experiments, however, invariably do not distinguish
    the type of category which the child is deriving from word
    order cues. That is, whether the first NP of a sequence
    is interpreted in its syntactic role of subject, or its
    semantic role of agent. Some experimental attempts to
    disentangle this vexed issue have recently been reported
    by Marantz (1980). His data suggest that the youngest
    children he tested — namely, three-year-olds — appear
    to order elements in a sentence on the basis of their
    semantic roles, but by the age of five, children interpret
    word order on the basis of the grammatical relational roles
    of words. He argues from these developmental differences
    that it is only by the age of five that children have
    acquired the grammatical relations which "mediate the map-
    ping between semantic relations and their surface expres-
    sions".
3   Contrary to the view that word order serves a grammatical
    function for young children, Slobin (1978a) has argued,
    in keeping with Brown and Bellugi (1964), that word order
    regularities cannot necessarily be taken as evidence of
    grammatical competence. It may just be the case, he
    argues, that SVO word order is what the child has heard
    and it is only later when he acquires more sentence forms
    that word order actually has a grammatical function.
4   It is not clear, however, that children of this age
    actually construct an interpretation of the sentence as a
    linguistic object, or whether they merely construct a
    pragmatically appropriate interpretation of the individual
    words which they know.
5   Since the original test sentences were in Dutch, there are
    word order differences between the Dutch originals and the
    English translations.

ACKNOWLEDGEMENTS

This chapter was written when the author was a Sloan Fellow
at the Center for Cognitive Science at MIT, April-July 1980.

I would like to thank Roger Wales and William Marslen-Wilson for carefully reading earlier drafts of this chapter.

REFERENCES

Bever, T.G. (1970a). The cognitive basis for linguistic structures. *In* "Cognition and the Development of Language" (J.R. Hayes, ed.). New York: Wiley.

Bever, T.G. (1970b). The comprehension and memory of sentence with temporal relations. *In* "Advances in Psycholinguistics" (G.B. Flores d'Arcais and W.J.M. Levelt, eds). Amsterdam: North-Holland Publishing Company.

Bradley, D., Garrett, M. and Zurif, E. (1980). Syntactic deficits in Broca's aphasia. *In* "Biological Studies of Mental Processes" (D. Caplan, ed.). Cambridge: MIT Press.

Brown, H.D. (1971). Children's comprehension of relativised English sentences. *Child Development* 42, 1923-1963.

Brown, R. and Bellugi, U. (1964). Three processes in the child's acquisition of syntax. *Harvard Educational Review* 34, 133-151.

Chapman, R.S. and Miller, J.F. (1975). Word order in early two and three word utterances: does production precede comprehension? *Journal of Speech and Hearing Research* 18, 355-371.

Chapman, R. (1978). Comprehension strategies in children. *In* "Speech and Language in Laboratory, School and Clinic" (J.F. Kavanagh and W. Strange, eds). Cambridge, Mass.: MIT Press.

Chomsky, N. (1979). "Language and Responsibility". Sussex: The Harvester Press.

Clark, E.V. (1971). On the acquisition of the meaning of "before" and "after". *Journal of Verbal Learning and Verbal Behavior* 10, 266-275.

Clark, H.H. (1965). Some structural properties of simple active and passive sentences. *Journal of Verbal Learning and Verbal Behavior* 4, 365-370.

Clark, H.H. (1976). "Semantics and Comprehension". Janua Linguarium, The Hague: Mouton.

Cole, R.A. and Perfetti, C.A. (1980). Listening for mispronunciations in a children's story: The use of context by children and adults. *Journal of Verbal Learning and Verbal Behavior* 19, 3, 297-316.

Dewart, M.H. (1975). "A psychological investigation of sentence comprehension by children". PhD Thesis, University College, London.

Dewart, M.H. (1979). Children's hypotheses about the animacy of actor and object nouns. *British Journal of Psychology* 70, 525-530.

de Villiers, J. and de Villiers, P. (1973). Development of the use of word order in comprehension. *Journal of Psycholinguistic Research* 2, 4, 331-341.

Entwisle, D.R. and Frasure, N.A. (1974). A contradiction resolved: children's processing of syntactic cues. *Developmental Psychology* 10, 6, 852-857.

Fodor, J.A., Bever, T.G., and Garrett, M. (1974). "The Psychology of Language". New York: McGraw-Hill.

Foss, D.J., Bias, R.G. and Starkey, P. (1978). Sentence comprehension processes on the pre-schooler. *In* "Recent Advances in the Psychology of Language" (R. Campbell and P. Smith, eds). New York: Plenum Press.

Green, D.W. (1977). The immediate processing of sentences. *Quarterly Journal of Experimental Psychology* 29, 1-12.

Grieve, R. and Wales, R. (1973). Passives and topicalisation. *British Journal of Psychology* 64, 2, 173-182.

James, S.L. and Miller, J.F. (1973). Children's awareness of semantic constraints in sentences. *Child Development* 44, 69-76.

Jarvella, R.J. (1971). Syntactic processing of connected speech. *Journal of Verbal Learning and Verbal Behavior* 10, 409-416.

Karmiloff-Smith, A. (1979a). Language development after five. *In* "Language Acquisition" (P. Fletcher and M. Garman, eds). Cambridge: Cambridge University Press.

Karmiloff-Smith, A. (1979b). "A Functional Approach to Child Language: a study of determiners and reference". Cambridge, Cambridge University Press.

Katz, J.J. (1972). "Semantic Theory" New York: Harper and Row.

Kintsch, W. (1974). "The Representation of Meaning in Memory". Hillsdale, New Jersey: LEA.

Maratsos, M. (1974). Children who get worse at understanding the passive: a replication of Bever. *Journal of Psycholinguistic Research* 3, 65-74.

Marantz, A. (1980). "On the acquisition of grammatical relational concepts". Unpublished manuscript, MIT.

Marslen-Wilson, W.D. (1975). Sentence perception as an interactive parallel process. *Science* 189, 226-228.

Marslen-Wilson, W.D. and Tyler, L.K. (1975). Processing structure of sentence perception. *Nature* (London) 257, 784-786.

Marslen-Wilson, W.D. and Tyler, L.K. (1980a). The temporal structure of spoken language understanding. *Cognition* 8, 1-71.

Marslen-Wilson, W.D. and Tyler, L.K. (1980b). Towards a Psychological basis for a theory of anaphora. *In* "Papers

from the Parasession on Pronouns and Anaphora" (J. Kreiman
and A. Ojeda, eds). Chicago Linguistic Society, Chicago.

McNeill, D. (1965). "Is child language semantically consistent?" Unpublished manuscript, Harvard University.

Nunberg, G. (1977). "The Pragmatics of Reference". PhD
Thesis, The City University of New York.

Palermo, D.S. and Molfese, D.L. (1972). Language acquisition
from age five onward. *Psychological Bulletin 78*, 409-428.

Slobin, D.I. and Welsh, C.A. (1973). Elicited imitation as a
research tool in developmental psycholinguistics. *In*
"Studies of Child Language Development" (C.A. Ferguson
and D.I. Slobin, eds). New York: Holt, Rhinehart and
Winston.

Slobin, D.I (1978a). Universal and particular in the acqui-
sition of language. Paper presented at the conference on
"Language Acquisition: State of the Art". University of
Pennsylvania.

Slobin, D.I. (1978b). *Psycholinguistics.*

Smith, C.S. (1970). An experimental approach to children's
linguistic competence. *In* "Cognition and the Development
of Language" (J.R. Hayes, ed.). New York: Wiley.

Strohner, H. and Nelson, K.E. (1974). The young child's
development of sentence comprehension: Influence of event
probability, nonverbal context, syntactic form, and
strategies. *Child Development 45*, 567-576.

Swinney, D. and Cutler, A. (1979). "Effects of sentential
stress and word type upon children's comprehension". Paper
presented at Mid-Western Psychological Association, Chicago.

Tannenbaum, P.H. and Williams, F. (1968). Generation of active
and passive sentences as a function of subject or object
focus. *Journal of Verbal Learning and Verbal Behavior 1*,
246-250.

Tyler, L.K. and Marslen-Wilson, W.D. (1977). The on-line
effects of semantic context on syntactic processing. *Journal
of Verbal Learning and Verbal Behavior 16*, 683-692.

Tyler, L.K. (1981). Serial and Interactive Theories of Sentence Processing. *Theoretical Linguistics 7,*(1).

Tyler, L.K. and Marslen-Wilson, W.D. (1978a). Some developmental aspects of sentence processing and memory. *Journal
of Child Language 5*, 113-129.

Tyler, L.K. and Marslen-Wilson, W.D. (1978b). Understanding
sentences in contexts: some developmental studies. *Proceedings of the Tenth Stanford Child Language Research
Forum,* Stanford.

Weil, J. and Stenning, K. (1978). A comparison of young
children's comprehension and memory for statements of
temporal relations. *In* "Recent Advances in the Psychology

of Language" (R.N. Campbell and P.T. Smith, eds). New
  York: Plenum Press.
Wetstone, H.S. and Friedlander, B.Z. (1973). The effect of
  word order on young children's responses to simple questions and commands. *Child Development* 44, 734-740.

PART III: UTTERANCES

THE ORIGINS OF GRAMMATICAL ENCODING OF EVENTS

DAN I. SLOBIN

Department of Psychology, University of California, Berkeley, USA.

1. INTRODUCTION

Some time after the child begins to combine words, he or she begins to mark these combinations grammatically, through the use of word order regularities and grammatical particles. I suggest that the range of notions encoded simply by word combination is broader than the range of notions which first receive grammatical expression. That is, while two- and three-word utterances may express a number of conceptual relations, only some of those relations are candidates for grammaticization at the earliest phase of structured speech. Those notions that are first marked grammatically are in some sense *salient* to the child, and I shall refer to them as prototypical. Furthermore, I suggest that prototypical situations are encoded in the most basic grammatical forms available in a language, and I shall refer to such basic forms as *canonical*.

The way into grammar involves attention to both prototypical situations in the world of reference and canonical forms in the world of language. I will develop this point by examining one intersection of meaning and form: the encoding of transitive events. The same argument could be made for various semantic domains — e.g. locative relations, situations which involve beneficiaries, and many others. The general picture I wish to elaborate is the following: the child is anchored to a narrow meaning-form correspondence in the earliest phase. The meaning can be characterized as a highly salient, "prototypical" event type, such as object transfer, physical manipulation, voluntary movement, and the like. I will not attempt to explain why such events have special status for the child, but take such general cognitive representations as given for purposes of the present discussion. Their special status is to be found in an intersection

of factors involving basic perceptual categories, emotion,
and habitual activities and interactions. The input language
encodes such prototypical event types in a canonical way —
say, the encoding of transitive events by means of a basic
SVO declarative sentence in English, or the use of an accusative inflection and variable word order in Turkish. Growth
proceeds from this initial pairing of prototypical event and
canonical form.[1]† I propose that the meaning of the form is
gradually extended — through metaphorical and semantic extension of the sort discussed by Schlesinger (this volume) —
while the form is held constant. Later in development the
form changes as well, and other variants are mastered.

2. PROTOTYPICAL EVENTS

These ideas can be explored through a close examination of
transitive events — first looking at the prototypical transitive situation, and then at the canonical forms used to encode
this situation in various types of languages. In a recent
paper on transitivity, Paul Hopper and Sandra Thompson
(1980) argue that transitivity can be seen as a continuum,
in which clauses highest in transitivity involve nouns that
are: proper, human, animate, concrete, singular, count,
referential, and definite; and in which actions are willful,
punctate, and concrete. They demonstrate a number of linguistic consequences of high transitivity in various types of
languages. For example, in Spanish direct objects are marked
by a particle, *a*, only if they are human or human-like and
referential. In many languages, including Turkish, Hebrew,
Amharic, and Persian, objects are morphologically marked only
if definite. On the side of the agent and action, in many
languages special means are employed to mark clauses which
encode a high degree of "directed physical activity" — what
Hopper and Thompson call the kinetic quality of the event,
and the degree of deliberateness or spontaneity of the agent
— the *volitional* quality of the event. I will not review
the many linguistic arguments, embracing such forms as accusative and ergative markers, passives and antipassives, per-
fectives, and so forth. The important point is that Hopper
and Thompson have, on linguistic grounds, identified a "highly transitive clause type" characterized by a human-like agent
"behaving actively, volitionally, and totally to a definite
or referential object". The languages of the world have
chosen — in one way or another — to give special status to
such clauses in their grammars.

---

† The superscript numeral refers to the note which is to be
found at the end of the chapter.

I suggest that children, also, give special status to such
clauses in the earliest phases of grammatical development.
On the basis of evidence from both linguistics and child
language, we can define the prototypical transitive event
as one in which an animate agent willfully brings about a
physical and perceptible change of state or location in a
patient by means of direct body contact. Such events are
encoded in consistent grammatical fashion by about age two,
whether the means of encoding be regular word order, accusative case marking, or ergative case marking.

Let us begin with ergative case marking, for here the situation is clearest. The input language clearly distinguishes
transitive events in grammatical terms. The only ergative
language for which we have clear acquisition data, thus far,
is Kaluli — a language of Papua New Guinea, studied extensively by Bambi Schieffelin (1979a, b). In Kaluli there is
a special grammatical marker — an ergative noun suffix —
that indicates the agent of action. This suffix is typically
used in situations where someone does something with an
effect, as when an agent acts on some object or person to
change its state or location. The ergative suffix would thus
be attached to agent nouns in sentences such as the following:

    Mother is cooking food.
    Father is cutting wood.
    The pig knocked over the bucket.

But if someone acts without effect on another entity, the
ergative suffix is not allowed. Thus it would be lacking in
sentences such as:

    Mother is sleeping.
    Father is thinking.
    The pig is running.

That is, the ergative suffix marks only the subjects of
transitive verbs. The subjects of intransitive verbs (and
the objects of transitive verbs) are unmarked or marked with
a neutral particle (absolutive or nominative).

The acquisition of this marker reveals the special status
of high transitive situations. It is acquired early: in
all of Schieffelin's samples it is present by age 26 months
in two-word utterances. It commonly appears on the agents
of verbs such as "give", "grab", "take", and "hit" — that is,
highly kinetic, direct actions. It tends to be lacking in
utterances of lower transitivity, with verbs such as "say",
"call-out", and "see". Additional evidence for the importance of high transitivity is provided when we ask about the
extension of the ergative suffix to the subjects of *intransi*-
tive verbs.

On the basis of what has been written about the acquisition
of non-ergative languages (such as English) and the cognitive
bases of grammar, we might expect the ergative suffix to be
overextended at first to all actors, whether they are causal
agents or not. In almost all semantic characterizations of
early child speech in the American psycholinguistic literature,
it is assumed that "human actor" is a basic prelinguistic
category. On these grounds it would not be surprising if
Kaluli children incorrectly applied the suffix to the subjects
of intransitive sentences, such as "Mother is sleeping",
"Father is thinking", and "The pig is running". However, this
sort of error *never* occurs in Schieffelin's extensive data.
  I suggest that this lack of overextension is due to the
fact that the Kaluli child has begun with what Martin Braine
(1976) has called a "limited scope formula". I find this
notion more useful than an approach based on semantic case
categories or *a priori* categories of infant cognition. It
seems that the child does not begin with categories, such as
"actor" or "agent", looking for the linguistic expressions
of such notions in his or her native language. What the child
may begin with is much more limited and childlike ways of
conceiving of basic events and situations, at first matching
grammatical expression to primary or basic event schemata.
Many psycholinguistic accounts have depicted the child on
the threshold of structured language already equipped with a
prelinguistic analysis of events into the categories required
for linguistic expression. Perhaps it is not the categories
which are primitive, however, but the basic events and parameters out of which the linguistic categories will be built.
The fact that Kaluli children limit their use of the ergative
suffix to the encoding of prototypical transitive events is
consistent with the suggestion that the basic notion is not
something like "human actor", but "causal agent". "Causal
agent", however, is not an isolated notion in itself; it is
part of an entire scene or event in which the agent is embedded. It is such prototypical events, rather than case
categories, that seem to provide the initial conceptual
framework for grammatical marking.
  Now consider the opposite sort of language from Kaluli —
the sort of language in which the object, rather than the
agent, receives grammatical marking. In such languages —
accusative languages — the input does not provide a clear
guide to the marking of objects involved in prototypical
transitive events. Accusative inflections or placement of
direct objects in sentence frames apply to the objects of all
types of verbs. In Russian, for example, the direct object
(in an affirmative sentence) is marked by an accusative

inflection regardless of the type of action involved. The
word for "book" would receive the accusative suffix in all
of the following sentences:

I read the book.
I saw the book.
I picked up the book.
I tore the book.
I threw away the book.

If the suffix corresponds to some underlying semantic notion
of "patient", it should be applied in all such utterances by
children. In the case of the child studied by Gvozdev (1949),
however, the accusative was at first limited to a particular
subset of events — namely those of high transitivity. The
suffix emerged when the child was 23 months old, and was only
applied to the objects of verbs involving direct, physical
action on things — such as "give", "carry", "put", and
"throw". Thus the child would say things like "I picked up
the book", "I tore the book", and "I threw away the book" —
all with an accusative suffix on the word "book"; but he
would not use this suffix when saying things like "I read
the book" and "I saw the book".

The Russian *under*extension makes the same point as the
Kaluli lack of *over*extension, although in one language we
are concerned with object marking and in the other with agent
marking. In both cases the child seems to be using grammar
to encode a prototypical event of physical object manipulation.

It is hard to find additional data, since most child language
studies do not subcategorize grammatical devices on the basis
of the semantics of the lexical items in utterances. The most
useful data come from Martin Braine's (1976) reanalyses of
two-word combinations in various languages, arguing for
limited range semantic categories. At this stage one would
look for limited-scope formulae which reflect a saliency of
prototypical transitive events. The clearest example comes
from Braine's analysis of two-word utterances in the Samoan
child, Tofi, studied by Keith Kernan (1969). This analysis
suggests an early word-order pattern for talking about moving
or holding objects — a pattern apparently not immediately
generalized to all events involving action on objects. In
examining the Finnish speech of Seppo, studied by Bowerman
(1973), Braine suggests "that Seppo is groping for the means
of expressing movement in a way that permits both the object
that moves and the agent of movement". A similar analysis is
presented for the Swedish child, Embla, studied by Lange and
Larsson (1973). Braine concludes (1976, p. 67) that an early
limited-scope formula may be described as: "act + object-
moved-or-manipulated-during-the-act". So even in the case of

early word order regularities, there seems to be some evidence that limitation of grammatical patterning may reflect a sensitivity to events of high transitivity.

Evidence from historical linguistics is also strikingly consistent with these notions. In some cases it has been possible to trace the origins of grammatical case markers back to meaningful words. Both in Chinese and in a number of West African languages direct object markers have been developed from verbs which originally meant "take" or "hold" (Givón, 1975; Li and Thompson, 1973; Lord, 1973, 1979). These verbs, of course, are drawn from the prototypical transitive event, and are the same verbs which first received accusative marking in child Russian and ergative marking in child Kaluli. And, like child Russian and child Kaluli, in Mandarin the use of "take" to mark direct object cannot be used with verbs such as "see", "hear", "read", and others in which the object is not a patient which is acted upon in a more directly manipulable manner.

Both in historical language change and in child language development such semantically transparent applications of grammatical forms are gradually extended, at first metaphorically, and ultimately becoming more or less opaque. Accusative inflections, for example, are eventually extended to mark the direct objects of verbs which are not part of the prototypical event of physical object manipulation, as in the examples from adult Russian cited above. That is to say, in learning such a language the child must extend his prototypical event category to include events of lower transitivity, until the notion of transitivity has become fully grammaticized.

3. CANONICAL SENTENCE FORMS

While carrying out such semantic extensions, the child at first remains syntactically anchored in the canonical sentence form used to encode the prototypical notion. This is perhaps clearest in the case of English transitive sentences, where the active sentence form is predominant in both child and adult speech. Non-canonical forms, such as passives and clefts, are later acquisitions, in both speech and comprehension. A large and familiar body of research data shows that English-speaking children at first respond randomly to passive sentences, apparently not even treating them as interpretable, and later impose the canonical SVO order, leading to misinterpretation of passives (Bever, 1970; de Villiers and de Villiers, 1973; Maratsos, 1974; and others).

In inflectional languages the definition of canonical sentence form is more complex. In Indo-European, where inflectional systems are no longer fully functional, both inflectional and word order information are necessary components in the sentence processing system, although some sentences can be interpreted with only inflectional or only word order cues. In such languages, children appear to define the canonical sentence as one in which both sorts of information are consistently present. For example, when the Serbo-Croatian-speaking children studied by Radulović (1975) began to apply the accusative inflection regularly in their speech, they adhered to standard SVO word order for several months, only later employing the variability in word order allowed by the input language. In Serbo-Croatian not all nouns have a distinctive accusative inflection. In sentences which have a clearly marked direct object, variation in word order is possible; lacking such marking, SVO order is generally required. Thus both devices — word order and inflection — are necessary for the interpretation of transitive sentences in general throughout the language. What these children have done is to take the canonical transitive sentence to be one with two syntactic features: fixed SVO word order and direct object inflection.

By contrast, consider a language such as Turkish, in which nominal inflections are regularly and consistently applied. Here word order is free to function pragmatically while case inflections signal semantic relations. In such languages children, early on, define the canonical transitive sentence form as one with two nouns and a verb — in any order — provided one of the nouns is inflected for direct object and the other is in the unmarked, or nominative form.

The issue of sensitivity to canonical sentence forms is most easily explored in comprehension studies, rather than in the exploration of corpora of speech production. It is, of course, suggestive that English-speaking children use many active sentences; that Serbo-Croatian children go through a phase of using fixed SVO order with inflected objects; that Turkish children freely vary word order while maintaining inflected objects in all positions; and so on. In comprehension studies, however, it is possible to probe the limits of a child's sentence processing strategies, revealing the range of forms that children are willing to entertain as possible sentences in their language. In the remainder of the chapter I explore several such comprehension studies — from our research at Berkeley and several other projects — indicating that at an early stage of development children respond consistently to transitive sentences in experimental situations only if those sentences are presented in canonical form. Canonical form always includes the requisite finite inflection on the verb, and some indication of

the semantic roles of the participants — word order and/or
case inflections, depending on the language. (For details,
see Slobin and Bever, 1980; Slobin, 1981).

3.1 *Empirical Evidence from Several Languages*

The basic experimental setting in all of these studies is one
in which the child is presented with a reversible sentence
comprised of two animate nouns and a verb, such that either
noun could be agent or patient of the scene; and the child
is given referent objects for the two nouns and asked to act
out the sentence. For example, when given a toy cow and a
toy horse, the child is asked to show: *The cow kicks the
horse*.

Let us consider first the role of word order in languages
which lack nominal case inflections, such as English, Italian, and French. As a part of our Berkeley cross-linguistic
studies, we presented American and Italian children with
strings in the three possible orders, NVN, NNV, and VNN,
using the appropriate articles and subject verb agreement
(e.g. *The dog scratches the cat, Il gatto graffia il cane*).
Overall, children between the ages of 2;0 and 4;8 responded
consistently only to sentences in NVN order, corresponding
to the standard SVO order of those languages. Apparently,
strings in nonstandard order, such as *The dog the cat
scratches* and *Scratches the dog the cat*, were simply not
heard as sentences. That is, they were not treated as
stimuli capable of linguistic analysis. Note that this finding is different from the usual finding in regard to passive
sentences in English. Passives correspond to canonical NVN
order, but the inflectional morphology is non-canonical —
both in regard to the verb and the second noun. A stimulus
such as *The cat is scratched by the dog* is, at first, simply
not heard as a possible English sentence, since the canonical
definition of a sentence is limited to the two noun phrases
and an appropriately inflected verb. At a later stage, when
the additional morphology of a passive sentence can be assimilated as within the bounds of interpretable English, it
falls prey to the canonical SVO interpretation.

The French findings of Sinclair and Bronckart (1972) can
be understood from this point of view. In their studies,
children were also presented with sentences in the three
possible orders, NVN, NNV, and VNN, but, unlike the Berkeley
studies, the stimuli lacked all morphological markers. Nouns
were presented without articles, and the verb was in the
infinitive (e.g. *garçon pousser fille*). Whereas we found
consistent response to NVN stimuli by about age three in

English and Italian, Sinclair and Bronckart did not find
consistent response to their corresponding French stimuli
until later than age five. I suggest that their younger
subjects simply did not hear three-word strings lacking in
standard morphology as sentences, just as English-speaking
children at first do not apply consistent sentence interpretation strategies to passives. The canonical sentence form
requires that the verb be inflected in standard form (probably third person singular), thus excluding the French infinitive and the English auxiliary-participle construction.

The French stimuli also lacked articles, but it is not
clear what role this omission played, since the verb morphology was also non-canonical, and since proper nouns can occur
without articles. In languages with inflectional nominal
morphology, however, it is clear that the canonical sentence
form requires that the appropriate morphology be present.
Relevant evidence comes from our experiments on Turkish. In
those studies we presented children with all six orders of
S, V, and O, with appropriate accusative inflection on the
object noun. Children as young as 2 years performed consistently and appropriately in response to all six sentence
types. We also presented them with ungrammatical strings in
which neither noun was inflected: NVN, NNV, and VNN. Children's response to such stimuli was random, reflecting the
fact that word order does not play a significant role in
identifying semantic relations in Turkish, but that case
inflections are essential. For these children a canonical
transitive sentence must have inflectional marking of the
patient, but may be in any order.

Similar evidence, though not as clear, is also available
for Japanese. Hakuta (1976) presented children with three-
word strings in which both nouns lacked the postposed inflectional particles and the verb was in the infinitive,
using the three possible orders of two nouns and a verb.
Four-year-olds performed inconsistently to these non-canonical strings, though three-and-a-half-year-olds correctly
responded to SOV sentences with the accusative particle.
However, we cannot separate the results of the deviance in
verb and noun morphology in this study. At any rate, the
canonical Japanese sentence form must have grammatical
markers.

In Serbo-Croatian, as in other inflectional Indo-European
languages, it is possible to consider the contributions of
both word order and nominal inflection to the child's definition of canonical sentence form. We have already seen that
in early production Serbo-Croatian children adhere to standard
word order when first acquiring the accusative inflection.

Our comprehension studies reinforce this impression. In
Serbo-Croatian many nouns no longer have a distinctive form
in the accusative. That is, in some instances nominative
and accusative are morphologically distinct (generally true
of masculine animate and feminine nouns), while in other
instances there is no distinction (masculine inanimate and
neuter nouns). Thus, depending on the nouns involved, in
any particular transitive sentence distinctive case inflection
may appear on either subject or object, or both, or neither.
When there is no clear surface marking of case roles, an SVO
word order rule generally applies. We presented children with
most of the major possibilities for transitive, reversible
sentences: Using the three orders of NVN, NNV, and VNN,
there were five possibilities for each of the three word
orders. For example, considering NVN order: (1) SVO with
subject marked; (2) SVO with object marked; (3) OVS with
subject marked; (4) OVS with object marked, and (5) NVN, with
neither subject nor object distinctively marked. Accordingly,
there were 15 different sentence types, as shown in Table 1.

TABLE 1 *Serbo-Croatian Stimuli*[a]

SVO	SOV	VSO
SVO	SOV	VSO
OVS	OSV	VOS
OVS	OSV	VOS
NVN	NNV	VNN

[a] In sentences containing S and O, the underlined element represents a feminine noun, thus distinctively marked morphologically as either subject or object, while the other
noun is neuter, with no morphological distinction of subject
and object. Sentences with two Ns have two neuter nouns,
and can only be interpreted on the basis of word order.

The youngest children, 2;0-2;8, responded consistently to
only one of these 15 types — namely, the most canonical in
their language: SVO with object marked. This sentence con-
forms to standard order, and has inflectional marking on
the salient case in this accusative-type language. Apparently none of the other sentence forms is, at first, heard as an
interpretable string.
    As Serbo-Croatian development continues, it becomes clear
that the accusative inflection plays a salient role. In a
later phase of development, reversed object-subject orders

are only comprehended if it is the object that is morphologically marked. That is, an accusative inflection on the
first noun can indicate to the child that the first noun is
not the agent, resulting in an appropriate object-subject
order interpretation. However, if the first noun is unmarked
and the second noun has a distinctive subject inflection, a
word order strategy overrides inflectional information, and
the first noun is incorrectly chosen as agent. Thus later
developmental reveals that the canonical sentence form includes a more salient status of object marking, in relation
to subject marking.

Further development also reveals a special status for the
canonical word order, NVN. The development of patient-first
strategies for sentences in which the first noun is in the
accusative is most rapid for sentences in standard word
order. Thus, in a language with mixed word-order and inflectional marking of semantic relations, the definition of
canonical sentence form relies on both sorts of information.
As children move beyond the canonical pattern, they remain
anchored in the crucial features of that pattern — in this
case, NVN order and accusative inflection. They thus include
verb medial position in their definition of canonical sentence
form.

A similar developmental pattern has been recently documented in Hebrew development by Daniel Frankel and co-workers
(Frankel, Amir, Frenkel, and Arbel, 1980; Frankel and Arbel,
1979). In Hebrew the direct object is a preposed particle,
preceding the object nounphrase. The verb agrees with the
subject in number and gender. Children's responses to reversible transitive sentences is most consistent when all of
the grammatical cues are present and in agreement — that is,
SVO order with the object particle and with appropriate
subject-verb agreement by gender. (This was tested by having
masculine and feminine participants in the sentences.)
Response was most consistent if all three types of grammatical information were present: word order, object marking,
and gender agreement. By systematically varying these features, however, Frankel and co-workers were able to show that
word order is the most salient feature of the canonical sentence form for Hebrew children, followed by object marking,
with subject-verb gender agreement the least central feature
of the basic sentence form.

This is exactly the same pattern we found in Serbo-Croatian.
The two languages are unrelated, and the grammatical expressions are quite different. Object marking is by suffix in
Serbo-Croatian; by preposed particle in Hebrew. Subject
marking is based on the nominative form of the noun in Serbo-

Croatian; on subject-verb gender agreement in Hebrew. But
both languages are accusative in type, and allow varying word
order while adhering to a predominant standard order. In
both cases, children's canonical sentence form includes both
order and inflectional features, weighting order most heavily,
object marking next, and subject marking least. A similar
weighting of inflectional cues has been found for German by
Mills (1977), who also found that the tendency to pick first
noun as agent was more readily blocked by an initial object
inflection (in this case a masculine accusative article) than
by subject marking on the second noun (a masculine nominative
article) in sentences where the first noun was neutral in
regard to subject or object marking. The roles of subject
and object inflection on nouns is the same in both Indo-
European languages, Serbo-Croatian and German, although the
sentential position of these inflections differs. These
cross-linguistic similarities suggest that there may be some
very general principles on which children come to form expectancies, or Gestalten, in regard to the basic sentence
forms of their language. Table 2 summarizes the canonical
sentence forms which emerge from these studies. Presumably
there are other canonical sentence forms for other prototypical events in early experience.

TABLE 2 *Children's Canonical Sentence Forms for Transitive
Events*[a]

English, Italian

   Article   Noun   Verb$_{person}$ Article   Noun

Turkish

   any order of Noun, Noun, and Verb$_{person}$, provided
   one Noun is Noun$_{accusative}$

Serbo-Croatian

   Noun$_{nominative}$ Verb$_{person}$ Noun$_{accusative}$

German

   Article$_{nominative}$ Noun   Verb$_{person}$ Article$_{accusative}$
   Noun

Hebrew

   Article   Noun   Verb$_{person, gender}$ Accusative Particle
   Article Noun

---

[a] In these sentence schemas, the verb always agrees with the
first noun.

In conclusion — although the data are still scanty — I hope to have shown that there is some commonality in the ways in which children conceive of basic events; and that, in each type of language, children initially isolate and generalize basic sentence forms. Furthermore, I believe there are some important links, however shadowy, between these two processes of pattern formation, such that proto-typical events and canonical sentence forms constitute a nucleus for the growth of language.

NOTE

1 What I refer to as a "pairing of prototypical event and canonical form" is a special instance of what Fillmore (1975, 1977) refers to as the association of *scenes* with linguistic *frames*. Prototypical events are scenes involving high perceptual salience and kinetic-emotional loading for the child. They are, in Fillmore's terms, "familiar kinds of interpersonal transactions" and "standard scenarios de-fined by the culture" (1975, p. 124). Canonical sentence forms are privileged linguistic frames — namely, those frames that most reliably embody the language-specific syntactic and morphological means of encoding salient scenes. Such forms are probably also those used most fre-quently and reliably by adults to encode prototypical events. Thus, in Fillmorean terms, this essay can be under-stood as an elaboration of the claim that the association of scenes with frames has its origins in the association of prototypical scenes with prototypical frames.

REFERENCES

Bever, T.G. (1970). The cognitive basis for linguistic structures. *In* "Cognition and the Development of Language" (J.R. Hayes, ed.), pp. 279-352. New York: Wiley.
Bowerman, M. (1973). "Early Syntactic Development: A cross-linguistic Study with Special Reference to Finnish". Cambridge: Cambridge University Press.
Braine, M.D.S. (1976). Children's first word combinations. *Monographs of the Society for Research in Child Development* 41.
de Villiers, J.G. and de Villiers, P.A. (1973). A cross-sectional study of the development of grammatical morphemes in child speech. *Journal of Psycholinguistic Research* 2, 267-278.
Fillmore, C.J. (1975). An alternative to checklist theories of meaning. *In* "Proceedings of the First Annual Meeting

of the Berkeley Linguistics Society" (C. Cogen, H. Thompson,
G. Thurgood, K. Whistler and J. Wright, eds), pp. 123-131.
Berkeley: Berkeley Linguistics Society, Institute of Human
Learning, University of California.
Fillmore, C.J. (1977). Topics in lexical semantics. *In*
"Current Issues in Linguistic Theory" (R.W. Cole, ed.),
pp. 76-138. Bloomington: Indiana University Press.
Frankel, D.G., Amir, M. Frenkel, E. and Arbel, T. (1980).
A developmental study of the role of word order in compre-
hending Hebrew. *Journal of Experimental Child Psychology*
29, 23-35.
Frankel, D.G. and Arbel, T. (1979). A developmental study
of children's assignments of sentence relations on the
basis of conflicting and complementary strategies. Unpublished paper, Hebrew University, Jerusalem.
Givón, T. (1975). Serial verbs and syntactic change: Niger-
Congo. *In* "Word Order and Word Order Change" (C.N. Li, ed.),
pp. 47-113. Austin: University of Texas Press.
Givón, T. (1979). "On Understanding Grammar". New York: Academic Press.
Gvozdev, A.N. (1949). "Formirovaniye u rebenka grammatiches-
kogo stroya russkogo yazyka. Moscow: Izd-vo Akademii
Pedagogicheskikh Nauk RSFSR.
Hakuta, K. (1977). Word order and particles in the acquisition
of Japanese. *Papers and Reports on Child Language Development* (Department of Linguistics, Stanford University) 13,
110-117.
Hopper, P.J. and Thompson, S. (1980). Transitivity. *Language*
56, 251-299.
Kernan, K.T. (1969). The acquisition of language by Samoan
children. Unpublished doctoral dissertation, University
of California, Berkeley (Working Paper No. 21 (1969),
Language-Behavior Research Laboratory, University of
California, Berkeley.)
Lange, S. and Larsson, K. (1973). Syntactical development
of a Swedish girl Embla, between 20 and 42 months of age, I:
Age 20-25 months. Report No. 1, Project Child Language
Syntax, Institutionem for nordiska sprak, Stockholms
Universitet.
Li, C. and Thompson, S. (1973). Serial verb constuctions
in Mandarin Chinese: subordination or coordination.
Parasession Volume, Chicago Linguistic Society No. 9,
University of Chicago.
Lord, C. (1973). Serial verbs in transition. *Studies in
African Linguistics* 4(3).
Lord, C. (1979). The evolution of object markers in Benue-Kwa.
Paper presented to Internation Conference on Historical

Linguistics IV, Stanford University.

Maratsos, M.P. (1974). Children who get worse at understanding the passive: a replication of Bever. *Journal of Psycholinguistic Research* <u>3</u>, 65-74.

Mills, A.E. (1977). First and second language acquisition in
German: a parallel study. *Ludwigsburg Studies in Language
and Linguistics* <u>2</u>.

Radulovic, L. (1975). Acquisition of language: studies of
Dubrovnik children. Unpublished doctoral dissertation,
University of California, Berkeley.

Schieffelin, B.S. (1979a). A developmental study of word
order and casemarking in an ergative language. *Papers and
Reports on Child Language Development* (Department of Linguistics, Stanford University) <u>17</u>(a).

Schieffelin, B.S. (1979b). How Kaluli children learn what
to say, what to do, and how to feel: an ethnographic study
of the development of communicative competence. Unpublished doctoral dissertation, Columbia University, Teachers'
College.

Schlesinger, I.M. (1979). Semantic assimilation and the
development of rational categories. Paper presented to
Symposium "Beyond Description in Child Language", Max-
Planck-Gesellschaft Projektgruppe für Psycholinguistik,
Nijmegen, The Netherlands, June 1979.

Sinclair, H. and Bronckart, J.P. (1972). S.V.O. A linguistic universal? A study in developmental psycholinguistics.
Journal of Experimental Child Psychology <u>14</u>, 329-348.

Slobin, D.I. (1981). Universal and particular in the acquisition of language. *In* "Language Acquisition: State of
the Art" (L. Gleitman and E. Wanner, eds). Cambridge:
Cambridge University Press. (In press.)

Slobin, D.I. and Bever, T.G. (1980). Children use canonical
sentence schemas: A cross-linguistic study of word order
and inflection. Unpublished paper, Departments of Psychology, University of California at Berkeley and Columbia
University.

CATEGORIES THAT BRIDGE BETWEEN MEANING AND SYNTAX IN FIVE-YEAR-OLDS

JUDITH ATKINSON HARDY and MARTIN D.S. BRAINE

Department of Psychology, New York University, New York, USA.

1. INTRODUCTION: SEMANTICS AND GRAMMAR

One of the persistent puzzles that confronts students of
language is that of the relationship between semantics and
grammar. Since the publication of Noam Chomsky's revolu-
tionary book in linguistics twenty-two years ago (Chomsky,
1957), language has come to be broadly viewed as a system of
rules for translating some inner understandings into sentences.
But exactly how the linguistic rules perform this task is
unclear.

We assume that speech begins as an idea in the speaker's
mind. Suppose that the speaker wishes to assert that some
particular entity is performing a certain activity that
affects another entity (e.g. a horse and a farmer — one of
whom is kicking the other). The event is a Gestalt, a constellation of components that are simultaneously present.
Speech, however, unfolds in time and is necessarily linear.
Thus the syntactic rules must translate this constellation
into a string of words. Furthermore, the rules must specify
how the words are to be organized in relation to each other,
so that there is no confusion about which entity is playing
which role. In this particular example, the sentence structure must make clear which entity is performing the activity,
and which is affected by it (is the horse kicking the farmer,
or vice versa?).

A reasonable and economical linguistic system would accomplish this task by cataloging words and phrases into some
general categories such as "noun phrase" and "verb phrase",
or "subject", "verb", and "object", or "actor", "action",
and "object-of-action". The syntactic rules would then
specify how these categories are to be combined to form
sentences.

While the syntactic rules that exist in people's minds undoubtedly work along these general lines, it turns out to be very difficult to determine exactly which categories are actually employed in the sentence construction process. We certainly need some abstract categories like "noun phrase" and "verb phrase", but these do not seem to be sufficient. In our example, both the entity performing the activity and the entity affected will be represented by noun phrases; presumably we must invoke some semantic concept, like "actor", in order to know which to put as sentence subject.

Aside from this theoretical argument, there are some good empirical reasons for assuming that some semantic concepts play an important role in the grammatical organization of sentences. The empirical evidence comes from two sources: linguists' analyses of adult speech across a variety of languages; and developmental psychologists' observations of language development in children.

Over the years, linguists have repeatedly noted that nouns and noun phrases in sentences often play roles like Agent, Patient (the term often given to an entity that incurs or suffers the action of the verb), Instrument, Location, and so forth. It is easy to spot these roles in a sentence like "Mary captured the horse with a lasso down in the canyon." We will follow Fillmore (1968a) in referring to such roles as "cases" or "case" categories. The interesting thing is that every language has some grammatical devices for coding these roles. In English, noun roles are coded primarily by prepositions, and by word order — "Mary tickled John" means something different from "John tickled Mary". There are also vestiges of a morphological ending code on some of our pronouns: "she", "her", and "hers", and "he", "him", and "his". Other languages, like Latin and Russian, rely almost entirely on morphological endings to identify the roles being played by the nouns. (These are, of course, the cases that many of us learned to decline in high school.)

Both the fact that every language has a way of coding noun roles, and that there is great similarity across languages in the roles that nouns play, have led linguists to theorize about a universal set of cases, and to develop case grammars (e.g. Fillmore, 1968a, 1971; Chafe, 1970). These case grammars have been particularly attractive to those of us who study language development because the general outlines are in accord with our observations on the language of young children, although they differ considerably in particulars.

When two-year-olds begin to combine two words into a single utterance, there appear to be perhaps a dozen relationships that they talk about universally, although there are great

individual differences in which ones will be talked about
most, or first (Bloom, 1971; Bowerman, 1973; Braine, 1976;
Brown, 1978; Schaerlaekens, 1973). The children talk about
the disappearance of things, saying "Allgone lettuce",
"Allgone sticky", and "Allgone outside". They talk about
possession (e.g. "Mommy purse", and "Kendall rocking chair"),
states and attributes (e.g. "dry pants", "big boat"), and
class membership (e.g. "that a dog", "Mommy lady"). They
locate entities and actions (e.g. "raisin cup", "walk street").
And they talk about actors and actions, as in "Melissa bounce",
"cow moo", and "Kimmy bite". Besides making assertions, the
children negate them ("no wet"), ask questions ("where ball"),
and make requests ("more juice", "more walk").

   These utterances are not truncated imitations of adult
sentences. Instead, they seem to have been produced from
rules that specify how certain semantic roles should be combined. For example, the children might have rules like
"possessor first, followed by possessed", "actor and action",
"*allgone* plus object that has disappeared", "object and location". The children apparently have a set of role-like
concepts into which the ideas they wish to express can be
analysed, and in English and in most language studies so
far, they are using word order systematically to reflect
relationships among the roles. Thus, the earliest syntactic
rules seem to be applied to some semantic role-like concepts.

   There is then rather wide empirical support for the suggestion that the syntactic rules that actually exist in people's
minds do indeed utilize some semantic role concepts. However,
the exact definition of these concepts, or cases, and their
function in the grammar, remains a matter of controversy.

   The concepts that two-year-olds employ are probably not
the concepts that are important for mature language. The
evidence indicates that they are narrower and more concrete
than the case categories proposed by linguists (Braine, 1976).
But we cannot actually watch the development of these concepts, since this is an internal process. We cannot even be
sure whether the concepts become broader, or more differentiated, or both, during development.

   When we analyse adult sentences carefully, we find that
each syntactic category — like subject and direct object —
seems to be associated with a number of distinguishable roles
or concepts. For example, when we say "John felt the baby's
forehead" we perceive the subject, John, to be actively exe-
cuting some action. But if we say "John felt the baby's
head resting against his shoulder" John seems to be more
passive — he is having an experience, and not acting. For
this reason, linguists have tended to distinguish "Agent"

and "Experiencer" roles (e.g. Fillmore, 1968a, 1971; Chafe, 1970), although they have not all drawn the distinction the same way. Or, to take another example, when we say "John kicked the ball" the object is playing the role of the thing affected by the action, or "Patient". When we say "John painted the picture" the object is, instead, created by the action. Thus, Fillmore (1968a, 1971) has differentiated "Patient" from "Factitive" (Fillmore's term for an object created during an action). We could go on and on making finer and finer distinctions, since the exact role played by the nouns differs somewhat for each verb (i.e. the actor in "John hit ball" is doing something different from the actor in "John kicked the ball"). The question is where to stop. Is it these particular roles, or some broader concepts, that the syntactic rules must take into account in order to construct sentences?

To further complicate matters, many roles seem to be associated with several syntactic categories. The sentence subject and indirect object seem to have reversed roles in "Mary sent a letter to Joe" and "Joe received a letter from Mary". The noun "door" is subject in "The door is open" and object in "John opened the door", yet it seems to play much the same semantic role in both sentences (that being in or put in the state of being "open"). Almost all linguistic theories have assigned such nouns the same role in both sentences, usually labelling the role "Patient" (e.g. Fillmore, 1968a; Chafe, 1970; Jackendoff, 1972). Again, the subject and indirect object "Mary" in "Mary sees the picture", and "John showed the picture to Mary", have been regarded as playing similar roles: Mary is the one that sees the picture in both sentences. Is the underlying role or concept played by these nouns really the same in each of these pairs of sentences? Have different syntactic rules simply translated the same underlying role into different sentence forms?

2.   GENERAL APPROACH

By employing a new method of investigation we have begun to find answers to such questions. Our evidence strongly suggests that the system of semantic concepts that is relevant to the syntax is organized along different principles than most linguists have supposed.

It seemed to us, together with Robin Wells, that four- and five-year-old children might help us solve some of these puzzles. Their language is sufficiently developed so that they might well use many, if not all, of the same concepts for sentence construction as adults. At the same time,

since the children's judgments are not influenced by any
formal teaching of grammar, they might perform more naively
on certain tasks than adults would.

Martin Braine and Robin Wells developed a method for exploring the semantic concepts that four- and five-year-old
children associate with the subjects, objects and prepositional phrases of various sentence types. We begin by showing the children pictures of scenes accompanied by simple
descriptive sentences such as "The big bear is washing the
little bear with a washcloth", and "The blue jeans are being
sewn with a needle by the gorilla". During a training
phase, the children learn to place tokens of different shapes
on the objects in the pictures according to the role they
play in the scene. For instance, each picture is accompanied
by an instruction like "We're going to put the star on the
big bear because it's the big bear who is washing the little
bear. The circle goes on the little bear because it is the
little bear that she is washing. We'll put the triangle on
the washcloth because she's washing the little bear with the
washcloth". (See the top part of Fig. 1.) Our reasoning is
the following. If four-year-olds actually possess concepts
like Actor or Agent, Patient, and Instrument, then we should
be able to lead them to associate the tokens with the roles
that they perceive the objects to be playing in the pictured
scene. That is, if they have some general semantic concepts
into which they naturally and automatically analyse the components of a sentence, and if our proposed categories mesh
with theirs, then they should learn to perform the token
placing task rather quickly. On the other hand, our knowledge of four-year-olds suggests that, if they do not possess
these concepts then, with this training procedure, they
should find it difficult if not impossible to learn our concepts and perform the task. It is, of course, important to
control artifactual bases for learning the correct response —
the experimenter must not give vocal cues which emphasize one
sentence component more than another, the concepts must not
appear in the same order in each sentence or picture, and
so forth.

We have performed a number of experiments exploring several
different role concepts like Actor, Patient, Instrument, and
Location, and have found that children catch on very quickly
indeed to associating the tokens with these sorts of concepts.
Only a few demonstration pictures and sentences are usually
required. When we present the children with new pictures and
sentences after the training session, and let them choose
the tokens, they have no trouble placing the appropriate
token on the new role exemplars. And they ignore irrelevant

cues like word order.   The Actor token will be placed on the
boy whether we say "The boy is stroking the rabbit" or "The
rabbit is being stroked by the boy".   Rapid learning and
easy transfer to new role exemplars suggest that we are, in
fact, tapping concepts which the children already possess
before they come to our experiment.

FIG. 1 *(a) The big bear is washing the little bear with a
washcloth. (b) The blue jeans are being sewn with a needle
by the gorilla. Four- and five-year-old children listened
as an experimenter described a set of pictures with sentences
in which the nouns played the roles of Actor, Object, and
Instrument. The children quickly learned to place particular tokens on the items (e.g. a star on the Actor, a circle
on the Object, and a triangle on the Instrument — the particular tokens varied from child to child). (a) and (b) provide samples of the training pictures and sentences (redrawn —
the originals were coloured). After this training, the children were given a new series of pictures and sentences, and
told that now they were to place the tokens without help.*

   Once we have tapped the concept, there are two ways in
which we explore the children's definitions of the concept
and the association of the concept with various sentence
structures. First, some of the new role exemplars have attributes that differ from those in the training. For example,
suppose the children have been trained on animate Actors
and Patients (e.g. "The horse is kicking the farmer", "The
mouse is being lifted by the turtle"). Later, they may be
presented with pictures and sentences like "The fan is blowing the curtains". If the children think that Actors can
be inanimate, as well as animate, they should not hesitate
to put the Actor token on the fan. But if they think that
Actors are necessarily animate then they will become confused when they are presented with the inanimate "Actors" and
their token placement will be either random of based on
irrelevant strategies.

The second method for querying definitions is one of forcing children to choose between tokens. For example, suppose they have been trained with Actor, Object, and Instrument tokens on sentences like "The big bear is washing the little bear with a washcloth". Will they choose the Actor or the Instrument token for the fan, when presented with "The fan is blowing the curtains?"

3. THE ACTOR

The initial studies (Braine and Wells, 1978) explored the children's Actor concept. In an early study, two groups of children, each composed of 16 three-, four-, or five-year-olds, were trained with two tokens, one for the actor, and the other for the object acted on. The first group was trained with pictures where both role exemplars were predominantly animate (e.g. "The horse is kicking the farmer"). The second group was trained with inanimates (e.g. "The saw is cutting the log"). After training, both groups of children were given the same new pictures and sentences. These contained all combinations of animacy in subject and object (e.g. "The cat is drinking the milk", "The boy is stroking the rabbit", "The ice is cooling the soda", and "The hydrant is spraying the children".) Both groups of children transferred the appropriate token to 80% of the actors and objects acted upon, regardless of animacy. However, the children were slightly more consistent on sentences with animate subjects (87%) than those with inanimate subjects (73%), although they selected the Actor to a statistically significant extent on all sentences. The result suggests that while it is not essential for Actors to be animate, animate Actors may be prototypical. Another study showed that the same response pattern occurred regardless of whether the generalization sentences used the active or passive voice.

In a separate study, another group of 20 five-year-olds learned to use Actor, Object and Instrument tokens (Braine and Wells, 1978). When the new pictures and sentences included exemplars of all three roles, the children had no problem distinguishing between the roles. However, when the new pictures were described by sentences like "The fan is blowing the curtains", or "The bricks are being lifted with a rope", the children put either the Actor or the Instrument token on the more active entity (i.e. the fan or the rope), but they preferred the Actor token. This was true even when the active entity was not in sentence subject position, and was marked by the preposition "by" or "with". Table 1 summarizes the main pattern of choices. Note that chance is 33%, for an arbitrarily chosen token on an arbitrarily picked item.

TABLE 1 *Results of the studies on the children's Actor concept*

Ten test sentences with three nouns (e.g. The rabbit is cutting
  the log with the saw; The rug is being cleaned by the bear
  with the vacuum cleaner; The elephant is lifting an Indian
  with his trunk; The cat is using a screwdriver to open the
  can)

Actor token on actor	95%
Object token on object	92%
Instrument token on instrument	92%

Two test sentences with two nouns, actor animate (e.g. The
  banana is being eaten by the monkey)

Actor token on actor	95%
Object token on other item	68%

Six test sentences with two nouns, actor or instrument inanimate (e.g. The fan is blowing the curtains; The bricks are
  being lifted with a rope; The soda is being cooled by the
  ice)

Actor or Instrument token on actor	89%
(55% Actor and 34% Instrument)	
Object token on other item	66%

Taken altogether, the results of these studies indicate that
one important case category of these young children is an
Actor concept that is broadly defined as anyone or anything
that is performing the action. In their own words, the Actor
token went on "The thing that was doing the work", or "The
thing that is doing the thing to the thing that isn't doing
anything". Animacy is not an essential feature. The data
suggested that the children saw users and instruments as kinds
of Actors. They did not make the distinction unless they had
to, but they were perfectly capable of making it, and brought
the finer distinction into play whenever both subcategories
of the Actor appeared in the same sentence. Although Actors
can be either animate or inanimate, it seems that Instruments
have to be inanimate, since the Instrument token was almost
never placed on an animate actor. When asked, they often
said the Instrument token went on "The thing they're doing it
with", or "The thing that helped do it". The data also suggested that the children had a category, which we may call the
Object-of-Action, for the thing that is *not* the Actor. They
described this token as going on "The things not doing anything", or "The things that were getting it done to".

4. THE SUBJECT OF ATTRIBUTION

The broadly defined Actor concept appears to be associated
with the sentence subject in English. There are, however,
sentence subjects that cannot be viewed as Actors, no matter
how broadly the concept is defined. These are the subjects
of predicate adjectives — the grass in "The grass is green",
and the vase in "The vase is broken".
What role, or semantic concept, could possibly be associated
with these sentence subjects? There are actually several
possibilities. As noted earlier, Fillmore and Chafe have both
suggested that these subjects play the same role as the direct
object of many transitive verbs. Their reasoning is based,
in part, on the fact that for many action verbs like "open",
the same word can also indicate the state that is the result
of the action (e.g. "John opened the door", "The door is open").
For Fillmore and Chafe "the door" would be the "Patient" in
both sentences. Our own intuitions suggested another possibility; the subjects of sentences like "The grass is green"
and "The door is open" might play the role of the thing to
which something is being attributed, a role distinct from
both the Actor and the Object of Action. We therefore named
this proposed role "The Subject of Attribution". We felt
that the role of the Subject of Attribution might not be
the same thing as the role of sentence subject. For instance,
the role of the Subject of Attribution might be invoked when
a property of condition is being attributed to something,
but it might not be invoked when an action is being attributed
to an actor.
To investigate how children view these new kinds of sentence
subjects, we decided to see if we could train the children to
place a token on someone or something in a picture that was
the subject of a predicate adjective (e.g. "is hot", "is
messy", etc.) in the accompanying sentence, and distinguish
it from some other object that was mentioned in the sentence.
For example, the children would need to choose the pig, not
the sofa, in "The pig is all curled up on the sofa", and the
vase rather than the ball in "Because the ball hit it, the
vase is broken". We found, in fact, that four- and five-
year-olds could quickly learn the task.
This time we wanted to reassure ourselves that the children were influenced by the language, and that their responses
were not based primarily on some pictorial analysis. Therefore, after the training session, we divided the children
into two groups for the new pictures and sentences. Each saw
the same picture but heard a different description. For
example, all children saw a picture of a cat in a large hat.

However, one group got the description "The cat is all dressed up in a hat", while the other got "The hat is too big for the cat". Almost all our four- and five-year-olds learned quickly. They placed the token on the thing mentioned as sentence subject — either the cat or the hat — depending upon which sentence they were given. They were clearly responding to the sentences, not just the pictures.

The crucial question, of course, is what concept the children have associated with the token: a concept that embraces the object noun in many transitive verb sentences as Fillmore and Chafe have suggested; the thing to which something is being attributed, as we hypothesized; or simply the notion of sentence subject. To find the answer we conducted three studies involving a total of 64 four- and five-year-olds (Braine and Hardy, in press). In each study the children first learned to put a token on the subject of a predicate adjective, as just described above. After they had learned this, they saw new sentences and pictures, including both new predicate-adjective sentences and several other new types of sentences and pictures. The latter included sentences with instransi- tive verbs whose subjects seemed to be somewhat inert (e.g. "In front of the airplane, the cloud is floating"), and sen- tences with intransitive verbs and active animate subjects (e.g. "The cat is jumping towards the boy"). We also included transitive verb sentences, both active and passive (e.g. "The pig is washing the mirror", "The frog is being kicked by the rabbit"). The three studies all used the same training (always sentences with predicate adjectives), but differ slightly in the set of test sentences (see Fig. 2).

If Fillmore and Chafe are correct in assuming that subjects of predicate adjectives belong to the same category as ob- jects of transitive verbs, then the children should transfer the token to objects of transitive verbs. Their performance on the sentences with intransitives should be less consistent. If, instead, the children simply acquire the concept of a sentence subject during the training phase, then they should transfer the token to all pictured objects mentioned as sentence subjects regardless of their semantic role in the sentence. Alternatively, if our hypothesis is correct, and the children possess a concept like the Subject of Attribu- tion, they might transfer the token to the subjects of in- transitive verbs, but they should certainly not include either subjects or objects of transitive verbs.

Table 2 shows the item on which the children chose to put the star, for various kinds of test sentence. Results of three studies are combined. The children responded by trans- ferring the token to the subjects of both predicate adjectives

and intransitive verbs, even when the subject of the intransitive verb was an animate actor. On these stimuli, they picked
the subject with a consistency enormously above chance. However, they were confused by the sentences with transitive
verbs, their choices being close to the chance level of 50%.
On these sentences, most individual children did not consistently choose the thing mentioned as sentence subject, the
thing playing the role of Actor, or the thing acted upon.
Choices often fluctuated from sentence to sentence. Some of
the children remarked "That's a hard one".

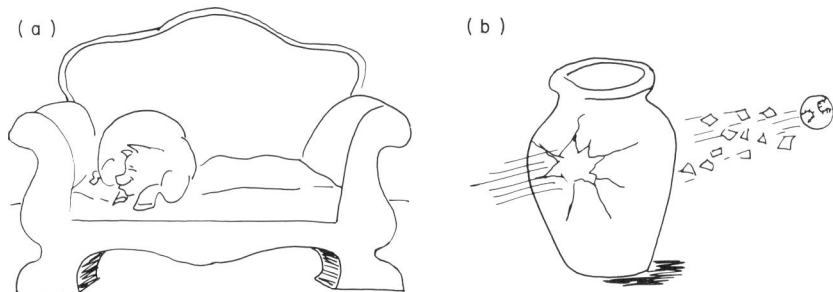

FIG. 2 (a) The pig is all curled up on the sofa. (b) Because
the ball hit it, the vase is broken. The children first
learned to place a star on the thing in a picture that was
described by a predicate adjective as being in some state
or condition. (a) and (b) provide samples of the kind of
training pictures and sentences (redrawn — the originals
were coloured). We assumed that the children would associate
the star with the role they perceived the subject nouns to
be playing. After this training the children were tested
with new pictures, described by various kinds of sentences.
All the sentences contained two nouns but differed in the
type of predicate. For each picture, half the children received the description with one noun as subject and half the
description with the other noun. The child's task was to
decide which of the two things in the picture should get the
star.

Thus, the children seem to have a concept like our proposed
Subject of Attribution. The concept apparently includes subjects of intransitive verb sentences, but not those of transitive verb sentences. Since the children's performances were
random on the transitive verb sentences, the Subject of
Attribution is not equivalent to the concept of a sentence
subject. At this point, it is unclear whether four- and
five-year-olds possess the concept of a sentence subject.
The children's performances do seem to indicate rather clearly

that they do not have a concept that embraces the subject of predicate adjectives and the objects of transitive verbs as Fillmore and Chafe predict. They did not transfer the token to the objects of transitive verbs.

TABLE 2 *Results of the studies on the children's Subject of Attribution concept*

Test sentences with predicate adjectives (e.g. The cat is all dressed up in the hat/The hat is too big for the cat)	
40 children, 3 sentences each; Token on subject:	83%
24 children, 4 sentences each; Token on subject:	86%

Test sentences with intransitive verbs and inanimate subjects (e.g. Under the pot the fire is burning/Over the fire the pot is boiling)	
40 children, 3 sentences each; Token on subject:	78%

Test sentences with intransitive verbs and animate subjects (e.g. Snoopy is running with Woodstock on his head/Woodstock is yoyoing on Snoopy's head)	
20 children, 3 sentences each; Token on subject:	78%
24 children, 4 sentences each; Token on subject:	86%

Test sentences with transitive verbs (e.g. The pig is washing the mirror/The mirror is being washed by the pig; The turtle is lifting the mouse/The mouse is being lifted by the turtle)

40 children, 2 active and 2 passive sentences each;

Token on subject:	50%
Token on Actor:	56%
Token on Object of Action:	44%

Thus, the data showed that children have a concept that groups the subjects of predicate adjectives and intransitive verbs into one category. But what do these subjects have in common? As a preliminary to answering this question, let us note that predicates can be classified according to the number of nouns that must occur with them. (By "predicate", we mean the state, category, or action that is attributed to the nouns — almost always a predicate adjective or verb; we do not mean the entire verb phrase of a complete sentence.) Some predicates, like "is hot", "is here", "is a lady", and "is running", require only one noun. (*John* is running, etc.)

We call these one-noun predicates. "Hit" and "is larger than" are two-noun predicates because they must refer to two entities. (*Mary* hit *John*, etc.) "Give" and "put" are three-noun predicates. (*He* gave *it* to *her*.)

The children seem to have a category that embraces the subjects of all one-noun predicates regardless of the particular role the subject is playing. This Subject of Attribution category might be described as "the one thing I'm telling about". As such it is not a role that can be applied to nouns of two- and three-noun predicates.

This conclusion suggested the interesting possibility that the case roles that are necessary for constructing a sentence depend upon the number of nouns that are required by the predicate. Suppose that the propositional core underlying the sentence is composed of the predicate and its nouns. If the predicate requires two or three nouns, their roles must be differentiated. For example, one may be an Actor, and the other acted upon. If two things are acted upon as with a verb like "give", one may be a gift, the other the recipient of the gift. In order to avoid confusion about which entity is playing which role, the syntactic rules must take note of these specific roles and assign each role to a syntactic category like sentence subject or object, or mark the role with a case ending or preposition. How any case role is signaled (i.e. word order, preposition, morphological ending on noun, etc.) is not relevant to our discussion; what is important is that the rules must mark the roles distinctively in some fashion.

However, when the predicate requires only a single noun, as in the case of predicate adjectives and intransitive verbs, there is no other main noun that its role must be differentiated from. In this instance, the noun's role in the proposition can be ignored by the syntactic rules. Regardless of its contribution to the meaning of the sentence, the noun will simply become the sentence subject. It is of interest that a system of this sort, in which the categories depend on the number of nouns required by the verb, was proposed many years ago by Diver (1964) as appropriate for Latin.

5. THE OBJECT OF ACTION

Is this analysis correct? It carries certain implications for the category "Object of Action", and we decided to test these. The analysis implies that the case roles depend upon the number of nouns whose roles have to be distinguished. For two-noun transitive verbs, only two roles have to be distinguished and for most such verbs these will be the Actor and the Object of Action. One should expect the latter to be defined primarily by exclusion: the Object of Action should be the noun that is not Actor. The category should ignore the differences among the specific roles played by the object in sentences like "Mary bumped Joe", "John painted a picture", "Dante loves Beatrice", etc. It should not matter whether the object is affected by the action ("Mary bumped Joe"), or created by the action ("John painted a picture"), or neither of these ("Dante loves Beatrice"). As long as we mark one noun as the Actor, this is all that is necessary for avoiding ambiguity.

But simply marking the Actor noun is not sufficient in the case of three noun predicates like "give". Since there are two nouns that are non-Actors, the receiver needs to be distinguished from the gift. In this instance, in order to create an unambiguous sentence, the syntactic rules must also take note of the specific role of each non-Actor noun.

Thus, we predicted that, in our token-playing test, children would see all grammatical objects of two-noun verbs as playing a similar role (Objects of Action, or non-Actor). However, this Object of Action would not correspond directly to either of the non-Actors of the three-noun verbs like "give"; given a single Object token, the children should not know whether to place it on the recipient or the gift. Conversely, if we trained the children on three-noun verbs like "give", with one token for the Actor, one for the Recipient, and one for the object given, they should learn readily; however, if later presented with sentences containing two-noun verbs like "hit" or "paint", they should be confused as to which token to put on the object noun: Neither the Recipient token nor the Transferred-Object token should seem to them entirely appropriate.

We carried out both these tests. Our first study involved 20 children whose average age was five and a half. We began by training them to use Actor and Object tokens on pictures containing three things. The describing sentences all used two-noun verbs, and the third noun in the sentences was never a grammatical object or indirect object; it was usually an instrument or the location of the action. The objects were always "Patients", i.e. they incurred the action. The children's task was to distinguish the Actor and the Object from the third constituent, and to place the tokens accordingly. Thus, in "The paper is being cut with the scissors by the Lady", the children learned to place the Actor token on the lady, the Object token on the paper, and to ignore the scissors as being neither Actor nor Object. In "The fan is blowing the curtains in the window", the Actor and Object

tokens went on the fan and the curtains, and the window had
to be ignored. There were 12 such stimuli.
  After this training, we gave them eight new sentences containing two-noun verbs with a third constituent. Some of
the objects were Patients, as in the training; others had a
different relation to the verb's action (e.g. "The mouse is
drawing a cheese on the easel", where the object would be
classified as "Factitive" by linguists like Fillmore (1968b)
because it is created by the action of the verb, and "The
magazine is being read in the chair by the elephant").
The children always placed the Actor token correctly; they
put the object token on the object 87% of the time, and about
equally for the various kinds of objects. Thus, they successfully distinguished the object from the third constituent,
and showed that they had a general Object-of-Action category
opposed to Actor, for two-noun verbs.
  We also included four sentences with the three-noun verb
"give": "The big bird is giving the little bird a worm", "The
man is giving a new tire to the car", "The mother is giving
the Christmas tree a decoration", and "Santa is giving the
little girl a rabbit". Here we predicted that the children
would not know which non-Actor the Object token should go on.
A few of the children chose the transferred object regardless of the sentence form. A few others preferred the recipient. Others sometimes put the token on one and sometimes
on the other. When shown the picture of Santa, the rabbit,
and the little girl, a child who chose to put the Object
token on the recipient explained, "It's the girl that's getting the rabbit, the rabbit isn't getting anything". Another
child, who consistently put the Object token on transferred
objects said the rabbit should get the token because, "the
rabbit's getting gived away".
  Thus, the children were clearly responding according to
meaning. They did not base their choices on strategies like
"put the token on the thing mentioned by the noun that comes
directly after the verb", or "avoid the constituent mentioned
in the prepositional phrase". They distinguished the grammatical object from the third constituent for two-noun verbs,
but were confused between the direct and indirect objects for
three-noun verbs.
  Afterwards, we held up each of the tokens and asked the
children what they went on. Again the Actor was for "the
thing that was doing it". The children explained that the
Object token was meant for "the one that's doing nothing",
"the one that's not doing the stuff", "the things he's doing
it to", etc.
  The children do indeed seem to have a broad definition of
the role of the object noun in propositions that are based on

two-noun verbs. Perhaps we could describe it as something like "The thing which is an integral part of the action, but which is not the Actor". As predicted, this very general Object concept does not seem to have provided the children with a basis for choosing between the two object nouns in sentences containing three-noun verbs like "give". In these instances most of the children adopted the strategy of focusing on what was happening to one of the objects while ignoring the other. Some focused on the transferred object and chose it consistently. Some others focused on the recipient. The fact that most individual children did not perform randomly on these sentences suggests that there are indeed specific concepts associated with both object nouns of three-noun verbs, and that these concepts are highly distinguishable for the children. Neither of these more specific concepts seems to be identical to the role of the object noun in two-noun verbs.

It seemed to us then that Transferred Object and Recipient might be subcategories of the general Object concept that are brought into play only when both must appear in the same sentence. This kind of organization parallels the User-Instrument distinction which appears to be invoked only when both of these subcategories of the Actor appear in the same sentence.

Would this analysis be supported if we worked backwards? What would happen if we trained the children with three-noun verbs, and then asked them to choose two of the tokens to use on sentences like "The fireman is washing the firetruck"?

In our next study (Hardy and Braine, 1979) 20 five- and six-year-olds were trained with tokens on sentences with three-noun verbs like "The hunter is bringing the elephant to the zookeeper", "Snoopy is giving the plant some water", and so forth. In a few of the sentences (e.g. "The mother is handing the baby to someone", "The zookeeper is bringing a load of something to the monkeys", "The ball is being thrown to the baseball player by someone") the picture lacked one of the objects, and only two tokens had to be placed. Three-quarters of the children reached our rather strict learning criterion. After the training session they were given six new sentences with both direct and indirect objects, and six other sentences using two-noun verbs and only one object.

When the new pictures and sentences contained an Actor and two objects, the children placed the tokens appropriately, regardless of sentence form: The Actor token was placed correctly 100% of the time, and the Transferred Object and Recipient tokens 96%. Thus, the children clearly associated a particular role with each token. Afterwards, we again asked the children to tell us what each of the tokens went on. The Actor token was for "the one who's doing it", or "the one who's giving it". The Transferred Object token was for "the gifts", "the thing that was given to someone", "the thing the person was giving to the other one", etc. The Recipient token was for "the getters or the keepers", "the person who's gonna be given to", and so forth.

On the sentences that contained a single object, the Actor token again went on the actor 100% of the time. For the object, most of the children were consistent, rather than random, in their choices. But some children used the Transferred Object token on these objects, while others used the Recipient token most, if not all, of the time. Some of the children were also able to explain their choice of tokens. One child, who chose the Recipient token consistently, commented "I knew this (the Transferred Object token) didn't belong because he's not bringing anything". Later, the same child said, "The boy's giving the building a wall, so this (Recipient) token goes on". The sentence we actually gave the child was "The boy is building a wall". When we used a picture of a bear breaking a clock, we were told "It's like when the kangaroo is giving the snowman a hat. The bear is giving the clock a bang". Other children, who chose the Transferred Object token in these situations, rationalized·like this: "The horse is kicking the farmer to *somebody*, so the farmer gets this (Transferred Object token)", and "The little girl is drawing the picture *for her papa*". The phrases in italics were not in the sentences given to the children and were not indicated in the pictures.

We take these results as evidence that our analysis is along the right lines. Each token was associated with a limited role, both of which are subcategories of the more general Object of Action category that is associated with the role of the object noun in two-noun verbs. When the children were given the sentences that contained a single object, they had no basis for choosing between the two object tokens. The children coped by trying to restructure the general situation in various ingenious ways so that it would fit the more specific one.

6. CONCLUSION: THE CHILDREN'S CASE SYSTEM

There are many conceivable ways in which a set of syntactic rules might accomplish the task of translating a predicate and its nouns into sentences. Each predicate is stored in memory with a great deal of specific information about the role of the nouns that can be involved in the predication.

For example, the predicates "sleep" and "kick" are stored
with the information that one noun, or one of the nouns,
involved in the predication must refer to an animate being,
while "hit" makes no such requirement. (Thus, we can't say
"The rock slept", but we can say "The rock hit the window".)
We know that "sleep" requires a single noun while "hit" and
"kick" require two nouns, one referring to something capable
of being physically acted upon. (Thus, "The dream hit the
faith" is nonsense.) "Draw" like "hit" and "kick" also requires two nouns, but, unlike "hit" and "kick", one of the
nouns must refer to something that is capable of being created
by a tool that is dragged across a surface. We can envisage
an elaborate system of syntactic rules that employs all of
this specific information for the purpose of marking the nouns
and placing them around the verb in sentences.

However, by the time children have reached the age of four,
it looks as though they have made some broad generalizations
about the roles nouns play. The system of syntactically relevant semantic concepts (i.e. case categories) that appears to
exist in the minds of our four- and five-year-olds is a simple
but elegant one. The children's concepts are broadly defined
so that the essential function of distinguishing between the
nouns' roles is accomplished with a minimum number of concepts.
Thus, the syntax distinguishes the Actor from the Object, but
fails to mark the created object differently from the affected
object. Such syntactic marking would serve no distinguishing
function, and is unnecessary for conveying the meaning of the
proposition because the exact role played by the object is
part of the verb's meaning anyway. Specific markings of
these object roles would simply be redundant, and the system,
by and large, seems to avoid such cumbersome redundancy when
no distinguishing function is being served.

Figure 3 summarizes the system indicated by the research
so far. There are other potential categories that we have
not yet investigated, e.g. the "Experiencer" subjects mentioned earlier and various kinds of locatives and other
oblique cases. However, we doubt that further work will
change the general picture of the way the system distinguishes
the roles of nouns with a minimum number of categories.

Within the children's system there is no absolute one-to-
one correspondence between the relevant concepts and the syntactic positions in the sentence. However, the system seems
to be more constrained than we might originally have thought.
For example, while the syntactic category of sentence subject
(of active sentences) is associated with more than one role
or concept, it is, in fact, *primarily* associated with only

two concepts: The Subject of Attribution and the Actor.
When we say, "The door is open", "the door" is not playing
the same role as "the door" in "John opened the door". The
syntactic rules can place "the door" in sentence subject
position in the first sentence because it is a *Subject* of
Attribution: it is simply the one thing being talked about.
The rules need not take note of the fact that doors can at
other times be acted upon. Likewise, when we say, "The
garden is swarming with bees", "the garden" is not playing
the same role as "the garden" in "The bees are swarming in
the garden", as Fillmore (1968b) has claimed. In the first
sentence "the garden" is playing the role of the Subject
of Attribution *as far as the syntactic rules are concerned.*
It is not playing the role of Location that it plays in the
second sentence.

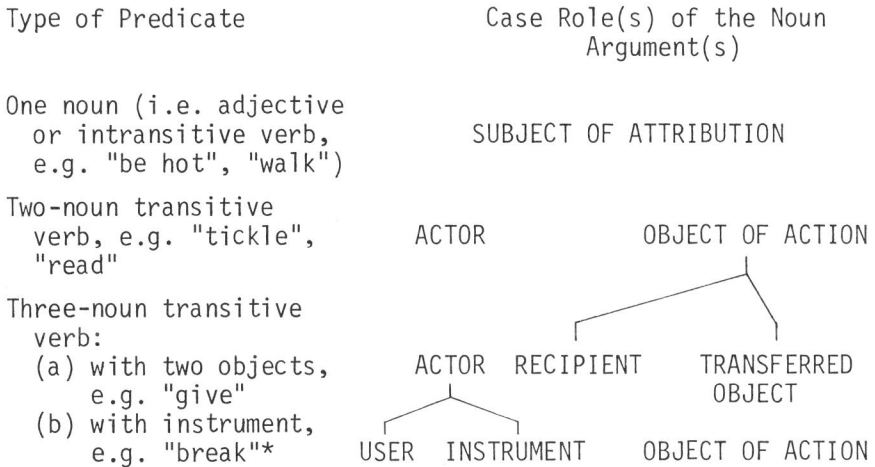

Type of Predicate	Case Role(s) of the Noun Argument(s)

One noun (i.e. adjective or intransitive verb, e.g. "be hot", "walk")   SUBJECT OF ATTRIBUTION

Two-noun transitive verb, e.g. "tickle", "read"   ACTOR   OBJECT OF ACTION

Three-noun transitive verb:
(a) with two objects, e.g. "give"   ACTOR RECIPIENT   TRANSFERRED OBJECT
(b) with instrument, e.g. "break"*   USER INSTRUMENT   OBJECT OF ACTION

* If the Instrument is not explicit, we have a two-noun
transitive verb with cases of Actor and Object of action.

FIG. 3 *Schema of the organization of the case roles that
the studies indicate have psychological reality. The cases
depend on the number of noun arguments that a predicate
(i.e. verb or predicate adjective) has.*

While Subject of Attribution and Actor are the concepts
primarily associated with the sentence subject in English,
they are clearly not the only ones, at least not in adult
speech. When we say, "Joe received a letter from Mary", the
subject noun "Joe" is playing the role of Recipient. It
seems to us that the children must learn that there can be
exceptions to general principles. Predicates like "receive"

assign noun roles to syntactic categories in an unusual way.
Note, however, that neither the definition of the roles,
nor the way in which they are organized in relation to each
other has changed. What is unusual is the way in which
these roles are associated with the sentence subject and
prepositional phrase. The reassignment of noun roles for
exceptional verbs like "receive" is probably learned individually for each such verb.

In English, children must also learn a rule for constructing passive sentences. They must learn that for most transitive verbs the object noun can become sentence subject, and
the Actor can be represented with a "by" phrase. "The rabbit
kicked the frog", can always be rephrased as "The frog was
kicked by the rabbit". It is well known that children at a
certain age have a difficult time interpreting passives —
especially if both nouns are animate so that the action
could conceivably have occurred in either direction. In
these situations, if children do not have a picture or an
event to refer to, they are likely to interpret the sentence
subject as the Actor, and reverse the chain of events. Even
some four-year-olds do not seem to have a complete grasp of
the passive construction.

Clearly, the four- and five-year-olds' system is not completely developed. What then can it tell us about how these
syntactically relevant semantic concepts are organized in
adult speech? It seems to us very likely that the adults'
case system is remarkably similar to the children's. There
may be developments within purely syntactic categories: that
is, categories like sentence subject probably gain in salience
and psychological reality during later childhood. However,
within the case system, the definition of the case roles,
and the way in which they are organized, probably remain unchanged. We suspect that the adults' syntactic rules also
employ a Subject of Attribution concept for placing and marking the noun in a sentence that is based on a one-noun predicate. Actor and Object concepts are used for two-noun
predicates, and Actor, Transferred Object, and Recipient are
used for three-noun predicates. What changes during development after five years is the knowledge that these roles can
at times be reassigned to the syntactic categories of sentence
subject, object, and prepositional phrase. However, even after
such exceptions are learned, we adults are still inclined to
interpret the sentence subject as an Actor in ambiguous situations. For example, if we hear "Joe received John" we are
much more likely to picture Joe opening a door, or in a receiving line, than to assume that John was sent to Joe. We
also interpret nonsense verbs the same way. If we tell you
that "Joe spizzled Jack" you may not know what "spizzle"

means, but you'll probably guess that it is an action of some kind, that Joe as Actor did to Jack. Thus, while we learn more about exceptions during development, and the basic system may become amplified and refined, it is probably not fundamentally reorganized.

ACKNOWLEDGEMENT

The research reported was partially supported by a grant (HD-08090) from the National Institute of Child Health and Human Development, Martin Braine, Principal Investigator.

REFERENCES

Bloom, L. (1971). Why not pivot grammar? *Journal of Speech and Hearing Disorders* 36, 40-50.
Bowerman, M. (1973). "Early Syntactic Development: A Cross-Linguistic Study with Specific Reference to Finnish". Cambridge: Cambridge University Press.
Braine, M.D.S. (1976). Children's first word combinations. *Monographs of the Society for Research in Child Development* 41, No. 1 (Serial No. 164).
Braine, M.D.S. and Hardy, J.A. (In press). On what case categories there are, why they are, and how they develop: an amalgam of *a priori* considerations, speculations, and evidence from children. *In* "Language Acquisition: The State of the Art" (L. Gleitman and W. Wanner, eds). Cambridge: Cambridge University Press.
Braine, M.D.S. and Wells, R.S. (1978). Case-like categories in children: the actor and some related categories. *Cognitive Psychology* 10, 100-122.
Brown, R. (1973). "A first Language: The early Stages". Cambridge, Mass.: Harvard University Press.
Chafe, E.L. (1970). "Meaning and the Structure of Language". Chicago: University of Chicago Press.
Chomsky, N. (1957). "Syntactic Structures". The Hague: Mouton.
Diver, W. (1964). The system of agency in the Latin noun. *Word* 20, 178-196.
Fillmore, C.J. (1968a). The case for case. *In* "Universals in Linguistic theory" (E. Bach and R.T. Harms, eds), pp. 1-87. New York: Holt, Rinehart and Winston.
Fillmore, C.J. (1968b). Lexical entries for verbs. *Foundations of Language* 4, 373-393.
Fillmore, C.J. (1971). Some problems for case grammar. *In* "Report on the Twenty-Second Annual Round Table Meeting on Linguistics and Language Studies" (R.J. O'Brien, ed). Washington, D.C.: Georgetown University Press.

Hardy, J.A. and Braine, M.D.S. (1979). Semantic concepts that five-year-olds associate with direct and indirect objects. Paper presented to the Eastern Psychological Association, April 1979.

Jackendoff, R.S. (1972). "Semantic Interpretation in Generative Grammar". Cambridge, Mass: MIT Press.

Schaerlaekens, A.M. (1973). "The Two-Word Sentence in Child Language Development". The Hague: Mouton.

SEMANTIC ASSIMILATION IN THE DEVELOPMENT
OF RELATIONAL CATEGORIES

IZCHAK M. SCHLESINGER

The Hebrew University Jerusalem and The Israel Institute of Applied Social Research, Jerusalem, Israel.

1. INTRODUCTION

There seems to be fairly general agreement about the central role of semantic relations in the earliest stages of language development.[1]* The child must discover how to express in speech certain semantic relations in terms of which he perceives his environment. Analyses of the child's two-word utterances (e.g. Bowerman, 1973) showed no evidence for the operation of the syntactic relations proposed by linguists for adult grammar. The latter are much broader than the semantic relations now widely held to function in early child language. For instance, the syntactic category subject of sentence (or noun phrase dominated directly by S) is more comprehensive than the agent category expressed in the child's two-word utterances; there are many sentence subjects that do not appear to be agents, as for example in:

1) People heard the bell ringing.
2) The concert hall seats 500 people.
3) White wine goes with fish.
4) Hamlet disliked the human race.
5) Man delights not me.

On the other hand, it has been argued that a given semantic relation may be encoded by different syntactic structures, as exemplified by the following pairs of sentences (Maratsos, 1979):

---

* Superscript numbers refer to notes which are to be found at the end of the chapter.

6) a. John sold a car to Mary.
   b. Mary bought a car from John.
7) a. Forty marbles were in this box.
   b. This box contained forty marbles.

A parsimonious statement of the rules of grammar seems to
be possible only in terms of the more comprehensive syntactic
categories, which is why these have been adopted by linguists.
The task of a theory of language acquisition is therefore
to show how the child, who starts out with semantic relations,
arrives at these syntactic relations figuring in adult grammar.
Presumably, the requirements of parsimony that led the linguist to describe adult grammar in terms of these syntactic
relations will impel the child towards gradually reorganizing
his system of rules operating on semantic structures into the
mature system of rules operating on syntactic structures.
But what is the process responsible for this reorganization?
A solution to this question is proposed in the present chapter. Implications of this solution will also be discussed
and one of these concerns the origin of the child's early
semantic relations.

2. THE SEMANTIC ASSIMILATION HYPOTHESIS

It has been proposed that the child reorganizes semantic
relations into syntactic ones by observing that two semantic
relations are expressed by similar linguistic structures
(Bowerman, 1973). He may note, for instance, that the agent
and the so-called "experiencer" (or "person affected") are
treated alike, as in (8) and (9):

8) John eats apples.
9) John sees apples.

Since the two relations function in the same way, they are
subsumed under one broader category: the subject. Essentially, this would be an instance of acquiring a stimulus
equivalence class (Jenkins and Palermo, 1964).
Now such linguistic similarities undoubtedly provide the
motivating force in the formation of the broader, syntactic
categories figuring in adult grammar; note that it is precisely these similarities that constitute the rationale for
linguistic descriptions in terms of syntactic categories.
However, I propose that often the subsumption of two semantic
categories under a more comprehensive one proceeds by noting
not merely similarities in *form* but also similarities in
content. On observing a formal similarity between the
linguistic expressions of semantic relations A and B, the
child's attention is directed toward the similarity between

these semantic relations, and eventually the situation originally conceived by the child in terms of A may come to be construed by him in terms of B, that is, A is *assimilated* into B.

To illustrate, suppose the child has had ample experience with utterances having a structure like (8) — which involves the agent-action relation (between *John* and *eat*) and the patient-action relation (between *apple* and *eat*) — and has learned the rules mapping these relations into utterances like (8). He then may encounter utterances like (9), which on the usual account involve different relations (*John* is the experiencer and *apple* the source of *see*). On hearing (9), he may try to apply the rules in his repertoire for dealing with the agent-action and patient-action relations and he will do so to his satisfaction, because a construal of *see* as an action of sorts performed by John does make sense. True, seeing is much less of an action than the prototypical ones of eating, pushing, kicking and kissing, but there is sufficient similarity between all these situations to permit conceiving of John seeing apples as a kind of action (much like looking at apples, which involves directing one's gaze at them). Similar experiences with words like *see*, *hear*, *feel*, *like*, etc., eventually leads to instances of the so-called experiencer being assimilated into the agent category, and the source of the experience — into the patient category.

Eventually, still other semantic notions will be assimilated into the agent category. The subjects of (1)-(5) stand for notions that, in the mature system, have been assimilated into agents. The adult often also has available to him alternative ways of construing a given situation. Thus in (6)a *John* is the agent, but in (6)b the same situation is described with *Mary* as agent, and whereas *the box* is a locative in (7)a, it is the agent in (7)b. Now this should not be taken to mean that the speaker (or hearer) will always be aware of the agentive character of sentence subjects like those in (1)-(5) and in (6)b and (7)b. But it does imply that the subject retains some of the flavour of the agent, a fact that may have significant linguistic consequences, as will be seen in the following section.

The semantic assimilation hypothesis, then, pertains both to the process by which syntactic categories, like subject, develop out of earlier semantic ones and to the way in which these extended categories function in the adult system. The subject, according to this hypothesis, is really an extended agent. In the preceding account, I have described only one of the ways semantic assimilation proceeds. Other variants of the process will be discussed later on.

   When the hypothesis was first propounded (Schlesinger, 1974),
it was objected that it required too much stretching and
straining of the agent concept. The agent has been defined
as the "typically animate perceived instigator of the
action..." (Fillmore, 1968, p. 24), and, so the argument
went, one can hardly accommodate all sentence subjects under
this definition. However, not too much store should be set
by the definition of a concept. "Instigator of the action"
is a good description of prototypical agents, viz. those of
actions, denoted by *pull, eat, kiss* and *kill*.[2] But, like
many concepts, the agent concept permits of different degrees
of membership, and agents of "actions" like seeing, liking,
containing and justifying are peripheral members of the concept, to which the definition cannot be applied stringently.

   Elsewhere (Schlesinger, 1977a, Section 2B; in press, Section
9.4) I have dealt with some putative counter-examples to the
claim that subjects are really agents come of age. It should
be noted, however, that the semantic assimilation hypothesis
does not require that everything expressible by a given syntactic relation has come to belong there through semantic
assimilation. There may be instances of subsumption under a
syntactic category which are not affected by this process,
but instead are prompted merely by formal similarity of
linguistic surface structures. For instance, I don't see
how the subjects of most sentences with *be* as connector (e.g.
Brutus is an honourable man) can have resulted from semantic
assimilation into the agent. What the hypothesis does claim
is that semantic assimilation is prevalent in the formation
of adult syntactic categories, not that it is invariably
responsible for it.

   The semantic assimilation hypothesis accounts not only for
the ontogenesis of relational categories, but also for their
phylogenesis. That a certain language should have chosen
the same manner of expression for different semantic notions
can be explained by assuming that these notions were perceived as being somehow similar to each other. The child
learning language retraces the way of his ancestors, avail-
ing himself of the same semantic similarities in reorganizing
his relational concepts.

3. EVIDENCE FOR SEMANTIC ASSIMILATION

There are two lines of evidence for the semantic assimilation
hypothesis. The one that will be considered here first is
based on certain linguistic phenomena. It can be shown that
in some instances semantic assimilation breaks down, and this
can only be explained on the assumption that when a semantic

relation is assimilated into another one, the latter imparts to it its flavour. This is what occurs in the assimilation of the instrument into the agent, the manner into the instrument, and the patient into the agent, as will be shown in the following.

Assimilation of Instrument into Agent

The instrument of an action can be expressed as the sentence subject, as for instance in:

10) The broom was sweeping the floor.
11) This detergent cleans aluminium pots instantly.

Here, I propose, the instrument has been assimilated into the agent.   When it comes to language, we all are sorcerers' apprentices, and for the purpose of talking about it, a broom can be brought to life. This interpretation of the subjectivization of the instrument is supported by the constraint on subjectivization exhibited by the following examples:

12) *An ivory baton conducted the symphony.
13) *The new brush was painting a still-life.
14) *The pencil was scribbling a proof of the theorem.
15) *The knife was cutting sandalwood into a statuette.

What makes these sentences sound odd is obvious. Batons, brushes, pencils, knives, and other instruments cannot be entrusted with tasks requiring deliberation, planning, or creativity. It takes a human agent to cope with such tasks, whereas inanimate tools can only be agents of menial jobs, like those in (10) and (11). You may assimilate, but you must discriminate.
     This explanation hinges on the claim that the subject has developed out of the pristine agent concept and hence retains the flavour of agentivity. If the subject were, instead, a semantically neutral category, the unacceptability of (12)-(15) would be left unaccounted for. Formal constraints on the transformations involved do not explain the phenomena. It is not the case that subjectivization is simply blocked for some verbs and not for others (which in itself would stand in need of an explanation), for while it may be true that with some verbs, like *conduct*, subjectivization of the instrument is inadmissible, there is no such formal constraint on the verbs of (13)-(15). Compare:

13') The brush was painting the surface a bright red.
14') The pencil was scribbling fast.
15') The knife was cutting sandalwood.

There is no longer any spark of creativity here, and thus
defused, the sentences no longer strike us as odd, although
they involve the same verbs as (13)-(15).
  Naturally, there is no clear boundary between "low-level"
tasks permitting instruments as agents, and those that are
considered to require deliberation. Among the above sentences
there are some that sound better than others. The fuzziness
of this distinction may be part of the explanation for the
acceptability of (16), which has been proposed by Martin
Braine (pers. comm.) as a counterexample:

16) The theory was developed by a curious accident.

Here the accident seems to be credited with performing a
high-level task. (Note also that abstract entities - like
fortune and chance - seem in general to be more eligible to
agent-hood than concrete inanimate tools.) Significantly,
however, the active-voice counterpart of (16) seems odd:

16') *A curious accident developed the theory.

This difference may be explained on the assumption that the
passive has an underlying structure differing from that of
the corresponding active, and that the *by*-phrase therefore
does not express the agent (a proposal that has been made
on independent grounds in Schlesinger, in press, Section
8.4). The acceptability of (16) therefore does not argue
against our explanation.
  On the present account, subjectivization of the instrument
is not a surface phenomenon, as case grammarians would have
it (e.g. Fillmore, 1968): instead of "subjectivization" one
might call this "agentivization". Further evidence for the
explanation advanced here has been presented elsewhere
(Schlesinger, 1974; 1977a, Section 2B).
  Note now that assimilation into the agent is only one way
of expressing the instrument. The instrument can also remain
unassimilated, as when it is expressed by a *with*-phrase (e.g.
with an ivory baton). According to current analyses of
transformational grammarians, these *with*-phrases belong to a
more comprehensive syntactic category: the prepositional
phrase. However, the following observations indicate that
the instrument category retains some autonomy and other relations can be assimilated into it.

Assimilation of Manner into Instrument

The manner in which an action is performed can be expressed
either by an adverb or else, like the instrument, by a *with*-
phrase:

17) a. The floor was swept fast.
    b. The floor was swept with great speed.
18) a. He prepared for the exam assiduously.
    b. He prepared for the exam with assiduity.

According to our hypothesis, manner is assimilated into the instrument in (17)b and (18)b. Support for this interpretation is provided by a constraint on realizing manner by a *with*-phrase exemplified in the following (Schlesinger, 1979):

17') *The floor was swept with slowness.
18') *He prepared for the exam with laziness.

While great speed and assiduity may be viewed, for the purpose of speaking, as instruments, slowness and laziness cannot. To become acceptable (17') and (18') will therefore have to be reformulated, with the adverbs *slowly* and *lazily* expressing manner.[3]

Assimilation of Patient into Agent

Certain verbs permit assimilation of the patient into the agent:

19) a. The butler closed the door on the salesman.
    b. The door closed on the salesman.
20) a. One can put up a good tent in about two minutes.
    b. The tent puts up in about two minutes.
21) a. She washed the wash-and-dry shirt with no trouble.
    b. The wash-and-dry shirt washes with no trouble.

But assimilation into the agent is blocked in the following:

20') *The tent puts up in my backyard.
21') *The wash-and-dry shirt washes with no trouble, because
     I have lots of time.

The reason for the unacceptability of (20') and (21') is, according to Van Oosten (1977), that the sentence subject is invested with some responsibility, and no responsibility can be ascribed to the events related in the latter sentences: There is nothing in the nature of the tent that makes it put up in the backyard, whereas there is something in its nature which makes it put up fast; and similarly for (21') and (21)b.
    Another example given by Van Oosten is (22) versus (22'):

22) The book is selling like hot cakes.
22') *The book is buying like hot cakes.

The book — normally the patient of *sell* and *buy* — can be

agentivized in (22) but not in (22'), because in talking
about buying it, one ascribes all the responsibility to the
buyer.

4. SEMANTIC ASSIMILATION AND THE CHILD

It has been argued above that the child's earliest semantic
categories are narrowly circumscribed and that he extends
them gradually into the broader categories of adult grammar
through semantic assimilation. Note now that the semantic
assimilation process can take two forms. The child may
learn that an entire semantic category may be assimilated
into another one, as for instance that of the instrument,
which may be viewed as an agent. He also may find out that
semantic assimilation of a category is possible for certain
words; the patient of *put up* and of *wash*, for example, (but
not that of *put* and of *kick*) may function as an agent, and
the same is true of the experiencer of *see*, *hear*, and *feel*
(but not of those of certain other verbs, as will be seen
below).
    Further, we have seen that semantic assimilation does not
result in a semantically neutral, "abstract" category.
Rather, the child considers the assimilated instrument and
patient as metaphorical agents and credits them with a modi-
cum of responsibility and participation in the planning of
deliberate, intentional actions. The constraints discussed
in the foregoing are therefore presumably not something the
child has to learn, but are abided by as a consequence of the
way he conceives of the extended category. The agent metaphor in (10)-(11) and (19)-(22) is never quite dead, and
hence he has no tendency to overgeneralize and err by saying
things like (12)-(15) or (2o'), (21') and (22').[4]
    But not only the assimilating category, the assimilated
category, too, retains some of its semantic flavour. As
noted earlier, the experiencer may be assimilated into the
agent and the experience (see, like, know, forget, etc.) into
the action. However, the experience will not be treated completely like an action: its origin makes itself felt in
ruling out the progressive, for instance. Children, in fact,
do not overgeneralize the progressive form to stative verbs
like *know* (Brown, 1973). For all its being viewed as an
action, then, *know* is at the same time felt to be an experience
which, unlike more prototypical actions, does not involve a
process having well-defined duration (cf. de Villiers, 1979).
    That the child starts out with relatively homogeneous
semantic categories which are much narrower than those figuring in case grammar has been shown in detailed studies of his

early utterances (e.g. Braine, 1976). Bowerman (1973) cites the case of a Russian-speaking boy whose patient category (marked by the accusative ending) comprised only patients that changed location in space. Eventually he must of course have extended this category to all patients that receive an accusative ending in Russian, and presumably he did so by noting resemblances between his original patient and other instances of the adult category that were linguistically expressed in the same way, i.e. by semantic assimilation.

Similarly, the child may start out with a very narrow agent concept (perhaps partly due to the nature of adult linguistic input, as Bowerman, 1973, suspects). At any rate, at the preschool age, the instrument has already become assimilated into the agent, as has been shown in an ingenious experiment by Braine and Wells (1978). In this connection it is of interest that already the 11-month-old child, according to a suggestion made by Greenfield, Nelson and Saltzman (1972), who holds a cup conceives of it as an extension of his own hand, and somewhat later "by connection with the child's hand a cup becomes 'animate' and therefore an actor..." (pp. 305-306). The child's animistic tendencies may also be a contributing factor in the assimilation of the instrument into the agent.

As for the experiencer, Maratsos, Kuczaj and Fox (1979) found that children in their third year of life over-regularize the past tense ending -*ed* to experiencer verbs like *see* and *think* just as much as to action verbs like *run*, and this suggests that at that age the experiencer has already been assimilated into the agent. One might argue that all this shows is that the child has a rule inflecting verbs for past tense. But this is not necessarily an alternative explanation. For consider where the verb category comes from. The best theory seems to be that for the child the verb is initially the action term of an agent-action construction (Schlesinger, in press, Section 8.1). If this is so, my explanation in terms of the experiencer being assimilated into the agent (and the "experience" into the action) and one in terms of verb inflection come to the same thing. Other findings of Maratsos et al. that might appear to conflict with this interpretation have been discussed in Schlesinger (in press, Section 9.3). The possibility that the experiencer is a peripheral member of the agent category has also been discussed by de Villiers (1979), who obtained experimental evidence consonant with this notion.

The data on child language available to date therefore fit in well with the semantic assimilation hypothesis. It should be noted, however, that the above studies do not bear on the

question of whether in extending his categories the child
avails himself of semantic similarities in addition to formal ones. The role played by these semantic similarities
is highlighted by the constraints on semantic assimilation
discussed previously, but these are phenomena pertaining
to adult language and so far there are no data on similar
constraints in child language. The available evidence
therefore does not rule out the possibility (suggested to
me by Michael Maratsos, pers. comm.) that the child extends
his categories solely on the basis of similarities between
linguistic constructions, and that only later he comes to
notice the semantic flavour of the assimilating categories
that is responsible for the constraints described above.
This alternative to the semantic assimilation hypothesis,
however, has very little plausibility on its side. Once
the child notices linguistic similarities between constructions
he comprehends, he can hardly avoid noticing resemblances between the notions expressed by these constructions. As pointed
out by Slobin (1973), the child is out for "semantic sense", and
rules that are semantically consistent are acquired before
those that are not. It is therefore extremely unlikely that
he should evince a dogged determination to bypass semantics
in the process of extending his categories, instead of striv-
ing for semantically coherent categories.

5. THE COGNITIVE AND THE SEMANTIC LEVEL

It has been argued above that not only the assimilating but
also the assimilated category retains some of its semantic
flavour. Although the subject in *The broom is sweeping the
floor*, (10), partakes of the character of an agent, it does
not cease thereby to be regarded at the same time as an
instrument. (To claim otherwise would be to embrace an extreme version of the Whorfian hypothesis.) We begin by thinking of the broom as of an instrument and choose one of two
options: to realize it linguistically as an instrument (*with
a broom*) or as an agent. Similarly, we may resort to a figure
of speech and "agentivize" *the box*, in (7)b, but there can be
no doubt that before, during, and after uttering this sentence
we do not cease to regard the box as the location of the
marbles.

   These considerations lead up to a view of a performance
model comprising (at least) three levels:

1) *The cognitive level*, constituted of those concepts and
   relations in terms of which we perceive the world. At
   this level the broom in (10) is an instrument and the box
   in (7)b a location.

2) *The semantic level*, into which the relations of the cognitive level are funneled, at times through semantic assimilation. At this level the broom and the box in (10)
   and (7)b function as agents. The formalizations of the
   relational structures at this level have been called *I-
   markers* (Schlesinger, 1971, 1974, 1977).

3) *The surface level*, at which one out of several stylistic
   variants are realized for each structure at the semantic
   level. For instance:
   23) a. This box contained forty marbles.
       b. It is this box that contained forty marbles.
       c. What this box contained was forty marbles.
   For a *different* I-marker corresponding to the *same* structure at the cognitive level, we have a choice of, among
   others, the following variants at the surface level:
   24) a. Forty marbles were in this box.
       b. In this box there were forty marbles.
       c. It is forty marbles that were in this box.

The distinction between the cognitive and the semantic
level is thus a corollary of the semantic assimilation hypothesis. When the distinction was first proposed in Schlesinger
(1974), it met with some opposition. Understandably, for it
might seem, at the first blush, so much simpler to collapse
these two levels into one. We would then be left with a
neat partition into relations in terms of which we conceive
of reality on the one hand, and linguistic structures expressing these relations, on the other. In fact, this is the way
I originally thought of I-markers, namely, as "...just the
way the child views the world" and as determined by the innate cognitive capacity of the child (Schlesinger, 1971, p.
70). But I have long since been compelled to abandon this
seemingly parsimonious approach, because of the overwhelming
weight of linguistic evidence against it. The evidence, to
be discussed presently, shows that very similar notions, and
sometimes even one and the same notion, can be assimilated
into different semantic relations.

6. THE VAGARIES OF THE EXPERIENCER

When one experiences a sensation, emotion, pain or indis-
position, there will be several determinants for the type of
linguistic structure appropriate for talking about it. The
experiencer may, oddly enough, consider himself to be an
agent:

25) I hear (see, enjoy, detest, etc.) the stupid commercial.

Or else he may attribute to himself a property, as in

26) a. I am disgusted with (delighted with, depressed by, angry at, etc.) the stupid commercial.
    b. I am glad (sorry, hungry, enthusiastic, etc.).

Besides agent and attributee, the experiencer may also be a possessor; to wit:

27) a. I have a headache (an allergy, the flu, a feeling that something is wrong, etc.).
    b. My headache (allergy, etc.) is getting worse.

All these situations have this in common that there is an experiencer (person affected) and an experience. At the *cognitive* level very similar relations must therefore be involved. Why should the experience of a headache, for instance, be so much more of a "possession" than that of disgust with a commercial? And why should a headache and disgust with a commercial involve less agency than hearing a commercial or detesting it? Furthermore, there are cases of a description of the same situation permitting of different semantic assimilations, as in

28) a. I like the commercial.
    b. The commercial pleases me.

(See also (4) and (5) above.) Sometimes there are even alternative semantic assimilations for one and the same word (Sidney Greenbaum, pers. comm.):

29) a. I have worries.
    b. I worry.
    c. Something worries me.

There seems to be no other way to account for these phenomena but to postulate a level between our cognitions and their linguistic expressions through which the former are funnelled. At this intermediate, semantic level the experiencer of *like* is assimilated into the agent, that of *please* into the patient, headaches are "had", and hunger is an attribute. (Other cognitive notions beside the experiencer may also be assimilated at this level, as shown in Schlesinger, 1977a, Section 2B). As stated, there is nothing inherent in the various experiencers that might actuate their assimilation in one way rather than in another. The specific uses of *like*, *please*, and *worry*, and the way of talking about headaches, hunger, and delight must therefore have been learned by the child through observing adult usage.

This brings us to another claim running counter to a current assumption, namely, that structures at the semantic level are language specific. Speakers of English may *be thirsty*, but they do not **have thirst*. This seems quite natural to us (and

to speakers of Hebrew, Polish, and Hungarian, among others),
but not to the French, who say *J'ai soif*, and concur on this
point with the Germans and Dutch, who all "have" thirst
(Germans can opt between the possessive and the attributive).
In a language called More the roles are reversed (Nida, 1964,
p. 214): there it is the thirst who is possessor and the
speaker of that language is "possessed" by it (which is
after all quite a sensible way of looking at it).

Thirst is experienced in the same way everywhere (it
would take an extremely dogmatic Whorfian to deny this), but
the languages of the world differ in regard to the possible
ways this experience — or others, for that matter — are
categorized at the semantic level. There are many more examples of cross-linguistic differences in semantic assimilation. For instance, the instrumental in English and several
other languages can be assimilated into the agent, whereas in
Hebrew, Arabic, Japanese, and Finnish it is assimilated into
the locative.[5] To what extent, if at all, these differences
at the semantic level then permeate the cognitive level and
colour our perception of the world, as claimed by Linguistic
Relativism, is a question on which we have unfortunately
little empirical evidence; the semantic assimilation hypothesis is neutral on this issue.

7. PARSIMONY RECONSIDERED

An intermediate, semantic level might appear to be extra
conceptual baggage, an infringement of the principle of parsimony. But, aside from the foregoing arguments to the effect
that this level really is indispensible, such invocations of
parsimony should be viewed with caution. In a given system,
parsimony may be achieved in different ways. In the present
case, it can easily be shown that by postulating only two
levels, the rules mapping meanings into sounds would become
hopelessly complicated.

Take, for instance, the above analysis of the experiencer.
Suppose that the semantic level were abolished, and (25)-(27)
were viewed as alternative surface manifestations of a single
cognitive category. But note now that for each of these
structures there exist several stylistic variants. For (25),
for instance, we have, among others

30) a. It is the stupid commercial that I hear.
    b. It is I who hear the stupid commercial.
    c. What I hear is the stupid commercial.

These and other variants have to be taken care of by transformational rules, some of which are inapplicable to other

realizations of the experiencer, as in (26) and (27). In
other words, the differences between (25), (26), and (27)
would after all not be represented at the most superficial
level, but at an intermediate level, which is precisely the
kind of construct we intended to get rid of.

Or, perhaps, this does not follow. Perhaps, it might be
argued, we can do without any intermediate level after all,
by devising rules mapping cognitive structures directly into
surface structures. Some rules would take as their input the
experiencer, for instance, and each would specify one of its
stylistic variants in (30); and other rules would specify
the various variants possible for (26) and for (27).

However, this proposal of direct mapping rules making no
local stops at an intermediate level would entail a very
serious infringement of parsimony. Only the introduction of
an intermediate level will permit the parsimonious formulation of
rules. By relegating the relation in (25) to the semantic level,
for instance, all those rules that are applicable to the prototypical agent will be applicable to these structures. And
the same rules will also be applicable to other agents,
whether these resulted from the assimilation of the location category, as in (23), the instrument, as in (10), or
the patient, as in (22). This intermediate level can therefore be abolished and direct rules be formulated only at the
price of restating the rules several times over. The "saving"
attained by abrogating the semantic level would entail a
multiplication of rules — a poor bargain, indeed. Especially so, since we would have no way of dealing with the
constraints on semantic assimilation — see (12)-(16) — once
the semantic level is pulled out from under our feet.

Finally (and at the risk of being accused of indulging in
an overkill), I invite you to look at the two-levels-with-
direct-rules proposal from the vantage point of the child who
has to master the grammar of his language. After having
learned one of the stylistic variants in (30) for the experiencer, he would be ignorant of the existence of a quite
similar variant for other notions (assimilated, on our
account, into the agent), such as the location and the agent.
Thus, while understanding, say, (30)b he would be at a complete loss to deal with the structurally similar (23)b, since
the latter involves a rule for a different cognitive notion.
This is clearly not the way things happen, and if they did,
the child would be badly off indeed.

To conclude, the facts of language are such that a parsimonious description of the rule system requires the postulation of a semantic level in addition to the cognitive level.
But, one might continue to ask, why should the facts of

language be such? Why should language not be so constructed
that it maps those categories in terms of which we perceive
the world around us directly into speech, instead of funnel-
ing them through language-specific semantic categories? One
might be tempted to dismiss this as an idle question, but in
fact there is a perfectly satisfactory answer to it, as will
be seen presently.

8. THE NATURE OF COGNITIVE STRUCTURES

Many discussions of language acquisition are based on the
tacit assumption that the child comes into the world having
certain semantic categories in terms of which he organizes
his perceptions of the environment. On this view, the categories that eventually emerge in his language — like agent,
action, patient — reflect his innate propensities for organizing experience, and in learning language he merely dis-
covers the way these categories have to be expressed. This
approach derives its apparent plausibility from a confusion
between the *interpretation* of experience and its *categorization* (Schlesinger, 1977b). The distinction here is a subtle
one, but one that it is crucial to make, as I now try to show.
    There can be no doubt that the way we interpret our exper-
iences is to a large extent innate. We cannot help but
conceive of actions being carried out by actors on objects
at certain locations; and while various cultural influences
may bring about certain ramifications of our conceptions,
the world is interpreted in the same way, basically, by all
human beings (and presumably by many other species, too).
Now, in *talking about* this common way of interpreting, one
has to resort to categories, and the handy terms "agent",
"action", "patient", and so on, seem to be appropriate here.
However, there is no basis at all for claiming that interpretation of the environment, when divorced from language, goes
on in terms of these categories, or any other categories
for that matter. There is no evidence, and no need to assume,
that experience is proffered to the child in neat little
packages of agents, patients, and so forth. That the child
discerns *instances* of these does not imply that he lumps all
the relevant instances together into one category.
    For why should he? Having a category is useful for making
a distinction between instances and non-instances of that
category. It is hard to see what purpose could be served
by the child's categorizing the events and states in his
environment into agents, patients and attributes (see
Schlesinger, 1977b, where this argument is spelled out in
detail). One may be said to "have" a certain category if, in

some respect, all instances of the category function in the
same way; otherwise such talk about categories becomes empirically meaningless. But what could conceivably be the
common function of all patients or of all attributes for the
prelinguistic child?

For the purpose of speaking about the world, of course, the
child will have to impose a categorization on it, because
there is no way for a limited number of syntactic rules to
operate but by applying to a limited number of categories.
This answers the above question of why there are no direct
mapping rules. However, as far as the cognitive structures
that antedate language are concerned, the existence of such
categories remains to be proven, and no such proof is likely
to be forthcoming unless it is shown what function they might
fulfill in coping with the environment. So far, all we have
to postulate for the cognitive level is the perception of
events, states, and relations constituting them that are more
or less similar to each other.   There is an innate multi-
dimensional similarity space, and interpretation of the world
surrounding us involves locating the goings-on in this space.
With the advent of language, and with the help of language,
the child then partitions this space into semantic categories.

Support for this approach comes from observations on the
relationships holding between semantic structures and the
cognitive structures that presumably underlie them. Take
the experiencer, for instance. We have noted in the foregoing that there appears to be no such category at the semantic
level, at least in English; instead, the experiencer is represented at that level by the agent, by the attributee, or by
the possessor, as in (25)-(27). The so-called experiencer
therefore seems to exist only at the cognitive level. But is
it a *category* at that level? This appears rather doubtful,
to say the least, when we observe how what one might call by
that name may merge gradually into what one might call an
agent. Consider the following sentences, all of which exhibit
the agent category at the *semantic* level (in part through
semantic assimilation):

31) a. Tom knows the date of Tito's birth.
    b. Tom remembers the date of Tito's birth.
    c. Tom recalls the date of Tito's birth.
    d. Tom guesses the date of Tito's birth.
    e. Tom figures out the date of Tito's birth.
    f. Tom writes down the date of Tito's birth.

Where precisely in this series does Tom stop being an experiencer and start being an agent? Rather than trying to answer
this question (different people will be likely to propose

different cut-off points), I would submit that it is an inappropriate one. At the cognitive level each of the above sentences has a different relation underlying it. These relations are all more or less similar to each other. But no hard-and-fast dividing lines can be drawn between them, because there are no categories at this level to begin with, but a continuum on which (31)a-f represent a number of points.

Such continua seem to be the rule rather than the exception. To give one more example, the *with*-phrase in English may express what is usually called the instrumental and the comitative, as in (32) and (33):

32) Tom went to town with his wife.
33) Tom solved the problem with a slide-rule.

But, as shown by ratings of English sentences as well as by crosslinguistic data, these are really points, perhaps extreme points, lying on a continuum (Schlesinger, 1979). A sentence expressing a point on this continuum lying between (32) and (33) is, for instance,

34) Tom won the appeal with a highly-skilled lawyer.

A further example of continua at the cognitive level and a discussion of the multi-dimensional nature of this level is to be found in Schlesinger (1979). Haas (1973) provides further observations concerning the variegated constitution of relations expressed in speech.[6] All this should help to demolish the belief in a straight-laced system of categories at the cognitive level.

It is time to point out a lack of precision in the way of talking adopted in preceding sections. For the purpose of exposition it has been convenient to lapse into talk about categories — experiencers, agents, instruments, etc. — at the cognitive level which may then be assimilated into others at the semantic level. In view of the foregoing discussion, each such reference to a category at the cognitive level should be regarded as a label for a variety of cognitive notions more or less aptly described by the term in question.

To learn language, the child must find out how the multi-dimensional cognitive space is mapped into language-specific semantic categories. The next and last section discusses how the child masters this mapping.

9. FORMING SEMANTIC CATEGORIES

The child, it has been argued above, does not approach the task of language learning with a system of ready-made categories. Instead, he has to discover the nature of the system into which his native language maps various cognitive notions.

Now, one might wonder how the child manages to create such a
categorization out of thin air, with nothing but language to
guide him.

   This problem would indeed loom portentuously so that one
might despair of a solution, *if* the linguistic system of
categories were arbitrary. But, in fact, it is far from that.
There are many constraints on the categorizations that a
language can impose. These constraints are due to our cognitive apparatus, to which the world appears as anything but
amorphous. We are so built that we cannot but organize our
experience in a multidimensional similarity space, to which
any system of categorization has to accommodate itself. Like
has to go with like. The world as perceived by us has what
may be called *texture* (Schlesinger, in press, Section 5.6),
and while there are various ways of carving up experience,
language does not carve against the grain: it respects the
world's texture. Differences between languages are great,
but the similarities are perhaps even greater. In this
chapter only the differences have been concentrated on, because they have a bearing on the proposals made. The points
of agreement between languages have not been emphasized,
nor do they appear to deserve emphasizing: they seem to be
unavoidable, rooted, as they are, in the texture of the world.
There is some leeway for language to impose its order on
experience, but not much leeway.

   The child capitalizes on the world's texture in learning
language. His task is to find out which of the several
possible categorizations that are consonant with this texture
has been adopted by his language, and he goes about it by
noting similarities between linguistic structures and between
the corresponding cognitive notions. His mother bringing
him food, his father bringing him food, his mother moving
away, and his father opening the door are all, cognitively,
occurrences initially not conceived of as belonging to a
single agent category. But since all agents are typically
treated similarly in the language addressed to the child
(that the agent may be expressed in different ways in *adult*
language is immaterial here), the agent concept gradually
crystallizes around its linguistic expression. There is a
certain problem with this proposal, a solution of which has
been attempted in Schlesinger (in press, chapter 7). The
only alternative to this proposal now in sight would be to
decide by fiat that the cognitive level is endowed at the
outset with just those categories encountered subsequently
in language. This does not solve the problem; it just be-
heads it.

   The above account of how the child forms a semantic category by noting both formal and conceptual similarities permits

us to view the semantic assimilation process from a new perspective. At the beginning of this chapter, semantic assimilation was described as an extension of already existing
semantic categories (as when the agent assimilates the instrument or the various experiencer notions). It now appears that
the same process occurs, perhaps on a smaller scale, in the
formation of these categories: various cognitive notions are
assembled into one semantic category. Semantic assimilation,
then, is the clue not only to the *recategorization* of semantic relational concepts into the broader syntactic concepts
of the adult system, but also at the original process of
category formation.

NOTES

1 Preparation of this paper and some of the research reported
   here have been supported by the Human Development Center,
   Hebrew University. I have benefited from stimulating
   discussions with the participants of Roger Brown's depart-
   mental seminar at Harvard University before which I presented an earlier draft of part of this paper in 1978.
2 The qualification "typically animate" which Fillmore (1968)
   included in the definition above was dropped by him subsequently (Fillmore, 1971, p. 376). Presumably he saw the
   need to assimilate robots and other machines into the agent
   concept.
3 After this was written, Professor Dwight Bolinger has
   pointed out to me that the unacceptability of (17') and
   (18') may be due to the affix -*ness*, which does not seem to
   fit well into a *with*-phrase (cf. *She spoke with clearness/
   gracefulness/sensitiveness). He also has adduced various
   counterexamples to my explanation. I believe that in the
   absence of an alternative explanation my proposal may still
   be upheld, but ultimately the story will turn out to be
   a vastly more complicated one.
4 One would also expect these constraints not to be
   language dependent. In fact, speakers of Korean, Finnish
   and Swedish have informed me that, while the instrument
   can be subjectivized in their languages, sentences like
   (12)-(15) are unacceptable. It remains to be seen whether
   the semantic flavour of agency can account completely for
   the rules governing the subjectivization of the patient
   or whether additional restrictions apply, admitting subjectivization of patients of certain verbs only.
5 Incidentally, the English proposition *with*, used today for
   expression of the instrumental, originally had "in proxi-
   mity to" as one of its meanings.

242   I.M. SCHLESINGER

6   What, for Haas, are semantic aspects of a relation, I
    would assign to the cognitive level, thus leaving the
    semantic level with more homogeneous categories —
    cf. (31) — and, incidentally, closer to the surface
    (Schlesinger, 1977a, Sections 2B and 5B).

REFERENCES

Bowerman, M. (1973). Structural relationships in children's
    utterances: syntactic or semantic? *In* "Cognitive Develop-
    ment and the Acquisition of Language" (T.E. Moore, ed.),
    pp. 197-214. New York: Academic Press.
Braine, M.D.S. (1976). "Children's First Word Combinations".
    Monographs of the Society for Research in Child Development,
    41 (1, Serial No. 164).
Braine, M.D.S. and Wells, R.S. (1978). Case-like categories
    in children: The Actor and some related categories. *Cogni-
    tive Psychology* 10, 100-122.
Brown, R. (1973). "A First Language: The Early Stages".
    Cambridge, Mass.: Harvard University Press.
de Villiers, J. (1979). The process of rule learning in
    child speech: A new look. *In* "Children's Language" (K.E.
    Nelson, ed.), Vol. 2. New York: Gardner Press.
Fillmore, C.J. (1968). The case for case. *In* "Universals
    in Linguistic Theory" (E. Bach and R.T. Harms, eds), pp.
    1-90. New York: Holt, Rinehart and Winston.
Fillmore, C.F. (1971). Types of lexical information. *In*
    "Semantics: An Interdisciplinary Reader in Philosophy,
    Linguistics and Psychology" (D.D. Steinberg and L.A.
    Jakobovits, eds), pp. 370-392. Cambridge: Cambridge
    University Press.
Greenfield, P.M., Nelson, K. and Saltzman, E. (1972). The
    development of rulebound strategies for manipulating serialed
    cups: A parallel between action and grammar. *Cognitive
    Psychology* 3, 291-310.
Haas, W. (1973). Rivalry among deep structures. *Language*
    49, 282-293.
Jenkins, J.H. and Palermo, D.S. (1964). Mediation processes
    and the acquisition of linguistic structure. *In* "The
    Acquisition of Language" (U. Bellugi and R. Brown, eds).
    Monographs of the Society for Research in Child Development
    29 (1, Serial No. 92).
Maratsos, M. (1979). How to get from words to sentences? *In*
    "Perspectives in Psycholinguistics" (D. Aaronson and R.
    Rieber, eds). Hillsdale, N.J.: Erlbaum.
Maratsos, M., Kuczaj, S.A. and Fox, D.M.C. (1979). Some
    empirical studies in the acquisition of transformational

relations: Passives, negatives, and the past tense. *In*
"Children's Language. The Minnesota Symposia on Child
Psychology" (W.A. Collins, ed.), Vol. 12. Hillsdale, N.J.:
Lawrence Erlbaum.
Nida, E. (1964). "Toward a Science of Translating". Leiden:
Brill.
Schlesinger, I.M. (1971). Production of utterances and
language acquisition. *In* "The Ontogenesis of Grammar"
(D.I. Slobin, ed.). New York: Academic Press.
Schlesinger, I.M. (1974). Relational concepts underlying
language. *In* "Language Perspectives - Acquisition, Retarda-
tion and Intervention" (R.L. Schiefelbusch and L.L. Lloyd,
eds), pp. 129-151. Baltimore, Maryland: University Park
Press.
Schlesinger, I.M. (1977a). "Production and Comprehension
of Utterances". Hillsdale, N.J.: Lawrence Erlbaum.
Schlesinger, I.M. (1977b). The role of cognitive development
and linguistic input in language acquisition. *Journal of
Child Language* 4, 153-169.
Schlesinger, I.M. (1979). Cognitive and linguistic structures:
The case of the Instrumental. *Journal of Linguistics* 15,
307-324.
Schlesinger, I.M. (In press). "Steps to Language: Toward a
Theory of Language Acquisition. New York: Lawrence
Erlbaum.
Van Oosten, J. (1977). Subjects and agenthood in English. *In*
"Chicago Linguistic Society: Papers from the Thirteenth
Regional Meeting" (W.A. Beach, C.E. Fox and S. Philosoph,
eds), pp. 459-479. Chicago, Ill.: University of Chicago
Press.

PROBLEMS IN CATEGORIAL EVOLUTION: CAN FORMAL CATEGORIES ARISE FROM SEMANTIC ONES?

MICHAEL MARATSOS

Institute of Child Development, University of Minnesota, Minneapolis, Minnesota, USA.

1. INTRODUCTION

One of the central problems of language acquisition lies in the child's construction of categories such as noun and verb, categories which cannot be readily identified with semantic notions such as object and action term, despite their semantic tendencies in these directions. Present evidence does not justify the use of such formal categories as noun and verb, or subject and object, to describe children's early speech (Braine, 1976). Thus, somehow the years after the early stages must see the child's construction of such categories.

The purpose of the present chapter is to investigate analytically one of the general possibilities for describing this process: that later formal categories evolve from earlier semantic-based grammatical categories. The appeal of this account lies in the fact that formal categories often seem to have some kind of notional (Lyons, 1968) or semantic core even in adult speech, and such semantic categories seem present in many children's early speech. In the present chapter, some preliminary remarks will be made on the general analytic and empirical constraints upon our formulation of the problem of formal category growth (especially for form classes). Then an outline will be made of a fairly simple inductive mechanism for the change of categories over time. This mechanism will be illustrated initially by application to the derivation of early semantic-structural rules such as mover-movement. Then a tentative hypothesis about how such a mechanism might operate to transform early semantic categories into later formal ones will be outlined. Finally, one or two general aspects and problems of such transforma-

tion-over-time models of formal category formation will be
discussed. At the present very much preliminary stages of
theoretical and empirical examination of these problems, it
is impossible to judge what theories or models will be best
to apply to particular problems, though various constraints
under which such models have to operate may be identified.
Nor is it a purpose of the present chapter to compare transformation-over-time theories with other available models.
Rather, the purpose is to consolidate the relevant problems
by examining a particular proposal and its attendant characteristics, in an initial brief formulation.

2. ANALYTIC AND EMPIRICAL CONSIDERATIONS

First, what do we mean by saying something is a formal category? In grammar, it seems to mean that groups of terms are
members of a category which follows one or more grammatical
regularities, but membership in the category cannot be predicted for a term on the basis of its semantic denotation *per
se*. The clearest examples are to be found in systems such as
arbitrary gender systems in languages such as German and Russian, where the endings on adjective modifiers or the set of
pronouns used to refer to a noun, or determiner or noun endings, are assigned to terms on the basis of arbitrary gender.
Categories such as noun, verb, and adjective, are less clear.
For verbs tend to denote actions, nouns to denote concrete objects, and adjectives to denote states or physical properties
or evaluative qualities.
  Nevertheless, in adult language, groups of terms share grammatical regularities of behaviour, which terms cannot be grouped
together on the basis of such semantic denotations reliably.
For example, verbs include not just actional meanings such as
hit, kick and *run,* but also nonactional meanings such as *like,
consist, belong, feel (good)* and *know.* Nouns include both concrete object terms such as *boy, girl* and *table* and abstract
terms such as *idea, game* and *verb.* Adjectives include clear
stative terms such as *big, tall* and *happy,* but also more actional terms such as *quick, fast, nasty (he is being nasty to
someone)* and *busy.* The semantic overlap among members of different grammatical classes may be considerable. For example,
the verb *like* clearly resembles the adjective *fond (of)* in
meaning more than it does the term *kick.* Yet *like* and *kick*
are verbs, while *fond* is an adjective.
  In adult grammar, we group the terms this way because members of a formal category share, or tend to share, various
reasonably distinctive ways of combining with other morphemes.
For example, despite their semantic dissimilarities, the terms

idea, action, girl, and *table* can all be marked for plural
reference with *-s* (*ideas, actions, girls, tables*), be preceded by members of the determiner class (*that idea, that
girl, the action, the girl*), take adjectives as prenominal
modifiers (*that good idea, a good girl*), and take other grammatical combinations in similar fashion. The terms *like* and
kick, despite their dissimilarities of meaning, can comprise,
without any helping auxiliary verb, the sole predicate term
of a clause (*they like it, they kick*), take preceding *do*-forms
to mark tense and negation (*they don't like it, he didn't
kick it*), or be marked directly for tense (*he likes it, they
kicked it*). The adjective *fond*, despite its semantic similarity to *like*, cannot do any of these. It must take a sup-
porting form of *be* when it is the main predicate of a main
clause (**he fond of it, he is fond of it*), cannot be marked
directly for tense (**he fonded of it, *they fonded of it*),
and takes preceding forms of *be* (*he is fond of it, he isn't
fond of it*). Most adjectives can be prenominal modifiers of
nouns (*the nice boy, the quick girl*), which verbs can generally not do (**the go boy, *the sing girl*), except as parti-
ciples (*the singing girl*) or as part of rather idiomatic expressions (*a go-cart*).
  It should be noted that members of major grammatical classes
are not completely distinctive in their grammatical behaviours.
For example, either verbs or adjectives may constitute the
major predicate of a sentence, requiring an initial noun
phrase argument (*he - came; he - (is) nice*). Both adjectives
and verbs may take initial agentive arguments, and take
agentive arguments initially with great reliability if they
are semantically of a nature to do so (*he made noise - he was
noisy*) (Fillmore, 1968). Fillmore (1968) found adjectives
and verbs to be similar enough in many grammatical behaviours
to propose that they were members, or subclasses, of a larger
predicate class. Thus, distinctions among the major form
class categories are frequently tied up with finer detail of
grammatical behaviour than it might initially seem.
  Empirically, as mentioned above, there is presently little
evidence that children initially employ grammatical descriptions that require the use of categories such as noun, verb,
or adjective as part of their categorial repertoire. On the
other hand, they seem to form such organizations with considerable accuracy, considering the possible pitfalls of their
task. They generally do not, for example, make errors such
as **he nastied to me*, treating highly actional terms as though
they were verbs, despite the fact that a majority of terms
which take verb operations such as *-ed* past tensing denote
actional qualities. On the other hand, they extend *-ed* past

tensing appropriately to non-actional terms such as *think*, *feel*, *know*, *see*, and *hear*, producing over-regularizations such as *thinked*, *knowed*, *feeled*, *thoughted*, *seed*, *sawed*, and *heared*, even as they also produced over-regularizations such as *runned* and *breaked* (Maratsos, Kuczaj, Fox and Chalkley, 1979; Maratsos and Chalkley, 1980; Maratsos, in press).

The question is how children proceed from early semantic-based categories such as actor and action, to the later appropriate formal categories. Do the former comprise developmental ancestors of the latter? Or do later formal categories arise largely independently of the early categories? How can early semantic categories be transformed into later formal ones?

As discussed above, this question really cannot be answered at present. Instead, the present goal in this chapter is to examine an inductive mechanism which might be capable of transforming early semantic-based categories into later formal ones, and to see what advantages and disadvantages such an account might have. To do this, I shall begin with a brief outline of the general characteristics of such a mechanism, applied initially to the semantic-structural rules of early grammar, then applied to formal problems such as those of deriving noun and verb.

3. AN INDUCTIVE MECHANISM

The basic idea here is that the mechanism of grammatical categorial growth is the establishment of sequential loci, to which individual terms are individually linked. Such loci are implicitly defined by the properties of the terms linked to them. Over time, semantic-structural sequences similar enough in nature are also linked to the original loci, resulting in the development and growth of the category.

This is clearer in illustration than in statement. Illustration will be made initially with the growth of a scheme approximating mover-movement (Bowerman, 1976). Consider hypothetically a child who initially analyzes and remembers the combination *daddy walk*. By hypothesis, the child describes this combination with a rule for ordering two sequential nodes, X and Y, each of which is defined by just the properties of the terms defining them, here *daddy* and *walk*. Any such statement of the rule must be quite tentative, but suppose it to be something like the following:

$$X \quad + \quad Y$$

properties of *daddy*   properties of *walk*

="movement of X initiated by X, including manner of movement described by Y"

Now suppose the child hears another utterance, *mommy walk*.
Let us suppose that already stored semantic-structural patterns, like Piagetian assimilatory scheme, scan incoming
stimulation to see if similar examples are heard which can
be assimilated to the already existing schema. *Mommy walk*
upon being analysed, will activate many properties already
encoded by the *daddy walk* pattern. The individual parts are
clearly similar, and their sequence and relations are also
similar. The result of this is that the initial X-locus
assimilates *mommy* as another example of itself, resulting
in a new schema something like the following:

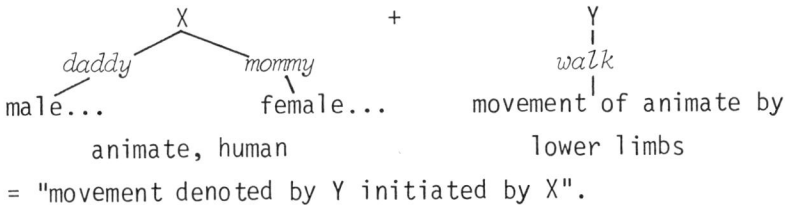

```
              X                +                Y
         ╱‾‾‾‾╲                                 |
    daddy       mommy                          walk
    ╱                ╲                           |
male...              female...        movement of animate by

        animate, human                      lower limbs
```

= "movement denoted by Y initiated by X".

The properties of animacy and humanness gain more influence
in the representation of X because of their double linkage,
compared to the properties of male and female and other properties peculiar to *daddy* and *mommy*. Over time, this schema
will be on its way to becoming something like animate+*walk* = "movement of animate by lower limbs, controlled by animate", or
roughly X+*walk* = "walking by X". This is of course very much
like the kind of single-word centred rule found to be common
in children's early speech by investigators such as Bloom
(1970) and Braine (1976). Clearly, of course, what examples
are attracted to grammatical nodes depends on judged similarity to the properties already present under the node, and
the power of various properties in attracting other examples.
It is quite likely that some properties such as animacy or
movement are more salient or easily activated by input than
others; animacy and movement constitute two such highly
likely properties, quite possibly because of their salience
in prior cognitive development, or because the organism is
generally biased towards looking for them and incorporating
them into analyses of phenomena.

Of course, such schemata are capable of assimilatory expansion in the other locus as well. Hearing utterances
such as *daddy go* and *doggy run*, the sequential-semantic similarity of these utterances to the schema animate+*walk* will
readily result in the expansion of the Y-locus as well, thus
giving:

$$\begin{array}{cc}
X & Y \\
| & \\
\text{animate} & go\ walk\ come\ fly\ run\ away \\
& \text{movement}
\end{array}$$

= "movement of X as described by Y"

What happens when the child hears other sequences beginning with animates? This will depend upon their semantic-
structural similarity to the available schemata. For example,
the child might hear *daddy chair*, which begins with an animate. The semantic relation of the parts, however, and the
nature of the second term, are too dissimilar to the evolving
movement schema. Thus, *daddy chair* will not be assimilated
to the already present schema, and will form instead the
basis for a new analysis that will eventually result in the
formation of a possessor + possessed object schema.

It should be evident that a semantic-structural sequence
need not be exactly alike those already present to be assimilated to an old schema. For example, suppose the child to
be building a schema that might be summarized roughly as
"cause of activity + activity", a wider schema than the
above, which would include examples such as *daddy sing*, *daddy
tickle*, *mommy eat*, and others, and hears *Sally drop vase*. In
the case of *drop*, *Sally* need not be an intentional agentive
causer of the activity; often dropping is a matter of let-
ting something happen, and so being a responsible animate
force, but not an intentional one. This use will nevertheless be assimilated by virtue of sufficient similarity, thus
making fuzzier the sense of "causative force" characteristic
of the initial position locus. In short, the grammatical
schemata are becoming prototypical schemata, in which some
examples are better examples (have properties characteristic
of more examples of the schema) than others. As Schlesinger
(1977) has noted, notions such as "agent" and "patient" (recipient of force of action) are often somewhat vague in just
this fashion:

Consider first that a concept has been acquired only to
the extent that one knows what belongs to it and what
does not. Now, what are the boundaries of the agent
concept? Mummy handing the bottle to the child is no
doubt an event where an agent is performing some action,
but what about mummy just holding the bottle? To take
one further step, can the bottle be said to be an agent
"containing" the milk in the same way that mother is an
agent holding the bottle? Clearly there are gradations
here of "agentiveness". In our adult judgment of what

does and does not fall under the agent concept, we are
very much influenced by what our language expresses as
an agent (Schlesinger, 1977, pp. 6-7).

Similarly, regarding the notion of patient, Schlesinger writes:

Suppose you hit a wall with your head — is the wall
"affected" without showing it? And when you sit on a bed
which has been made and the bed shows it very much, should
it be considered a patient (and hence *sit* as a transitive verb), contrary to what is suggested by the sentence
I sit on the bed? Cognitive development will not furnish
the clue to this problem of where the boundaries are to
be drawn (Schlesinger, 1977, pp. 7-8).

What Schlesinger seems to be saying is that a grammatical
category is codefined both by semantic and structural similarity. This seems to be correct. The foregoing model (or
sketch of one) captures this, in that both semantic properties, and semantic-sequential resemblance to examples already present, determine whether or not an incoming example
will be taken as an example of the already extant schema.
At the same time, since exact similarity is not required for
assimilation, over time, the grammatical locus will come to
be defined by a set of properties clustering around a central
set, but imperfectly. These all seem to be plausible characteristics of the process of grammatical category formation.

4. INDUCTION OF FORM CLASS CATEGORIES

If in fact categorial nodes may assimilate new members if
they bear sufficient similarity to those already present, this
allows for the possibility of gradual change in the nature of
the category over time. First, the new members which are
assimilated may be slightly different in nature from those
already present. This will result in a gradual change in
the nature of the properties linked to the node. Second,
the already present members may acquire new properties
themselves over time. This will alter the configuration
of properties which characterize the members of the category. Thus, the basis for assimilation of new members may
change over time, as the nature of the category members
changes by the second process.

It is in fact theoretically possible to view early categories such as action-term and concrete object-term changing
over time gradually into the major constituent categories
verb and noun by such processes. The basic proposition is
that over time, terms originally described for major constituent purposes as action-terms and object-terms acquire

linkages to smaller-scale grammatical operations. When non-action and non-object terms are used in grammatical configurations similar to the new operations, they become similar enough in nature for assimilation to the already existing categorial nodes to take place. This process results in adult verb and noun classes. These hypothetical processes will be sketched for the verb and noun classes in turn.

Developmentally, for verbs, the possible originative class is a class of action terms. Early grammars seem to show achievement of some kind of actor-action schema sometime in Stage I for many, though probably not all, children (Braine, 1976). Such early action categories seem to include some terms which will not be adult verbs, such as *away* or *back* (Bloom *et al.*, 1975a,b; Braine, 1976), which have actional denotation for the child. They also apparently fail to include some terms which will be verbs in adult grammars, such as *want* or *see*. These often appear initially to be the foci of single-word rules such as *want*+X = "desire or demand for X", *see*+X = "indication of X".

Generically, let us refer to all terms which state some relation or property of referents as *predicates*, and terms used to denote described or related entities as *arguments* of the predicates. (This usage extends beyond traditional predicate-argument description, since by it, a formula such as *more* + X has *more* as a predicate, and whatever fills the X-slot, as an argument.) An early rule is thus one for placing animate arguments before action terms, to denote an activity carried out by the animate, roughly

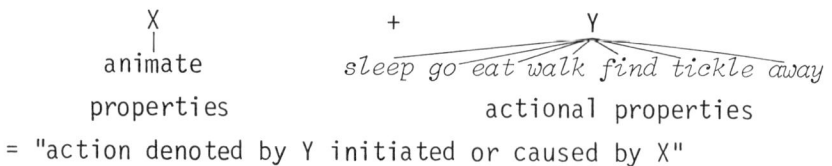

$$
\begin{array}{ccc}
\text{X} & + & \text{Y} \\
| & & \\
\text{animate} & & \textit{sleep go eat walk find tickle away} \\
\text{properties} & & \text{actional properties}
\end{array}
$$

= "action denoted by Y initiated or caused by X"

At this point then, terms are grouped into major predicate-argument categories presumably on the basis of a combination of major structural position and semantic denotation. The question is what causes action terms such as *sleep, go,* and *walk,* members of an actional predicate category, to somehow be grouped with non-actional terms such as *want, need, see, hear, like,* and *know,* but not with other predicates such as *happy, sad, quick,* or *fast.* Mechanisms relying only upon major predicate-argument orders and semantic denotations of the terms *per se* appear inadequate. For *happy, sad, quick, fast,* and *nice,* also take initial arguments (*he - go*; he - *quick*; *he-want-soup*; *he-happy-*(*about*) *it*). *Want, need,* and *like*, for example, all denote emotional states, and take initial arguments denoting the feeler. But so do *happy* and *sad*. Thus, it appears that inductive mechanisms depending only upon major predicate-argument configurations and semantic denotations would be likely to result in incorrect groupings.

But in fact, as noted above, children seem to be adept at avoiding such incorrect groupings. For the different major constituent categories have different other grammatical markings characteristic of them. For example, terms such as *kick* and *go* take -*s* to denote present tense (*he kicks it, the boy goes*). Terms such as *happy* and *sad* take a form of *be* (*he is happy; the boy is sad*). If children thought that actional terms such as *kick* and *go* and *quick* and *noisy* were members of the same major constituent class, and applied morphological operations according to membership in this major class, errors such as **he noisies* should be common, which they are not. Similarly, terms such as *want* and *need*, which denote emotional states, might be expected to take markings characteristic of terms such as *sad* and *happy*, if these were all grouped together. Errors such as **he is want it* might result, which they do not do (Maratsos, in press). Therefore, we must assume that some other properties are acting to draw terms together past the early period.

In English, as well as many other languages, members of the verb category share certain grammatical properties more reliably than they share semantic denotations. Among such properties are ways of indicating tense and aspect of the predicate. For example, as noted above, *like* and *kick* are semantically less similar than *like* and *fond*. Yet *like* and *kick* behave similarly in operations such as past tensing (*he liked it, he kicked it*), negation (*I don't like it, I don't kick those*), and present tensing with third person initial arguments (*he likes it, he kicks it*). Eventually, there are a number of other properties they share in common, such as infinitival form (*he ought to like it, he ought to kick it*), and participle uses (*liking this is a good idea; kicking this is a good idea*). Some of these seem likely to appear later than others, developmentally, though the empirical facts are not well-known.

One hypothesis, then, is that over time, members of the original actional predicate class come to be linked to grammatical loci for smaller-scale grammatical patterns such as use of *do*-forms, *can't, will,* and various tensing operations. There is some evidence (see Maratsos and Chalkley, 1980; Maratsos, in press) that initially such operations are linked to the relevant terms in a one-by-one fashion, and that the

operation is not governed productively by the major predicate-
argument class of the relevant terms. For example, *-ing*
progressive is always linked to actional predicates, such
as in *singing, kicking, going*. For some time, children seem
to treat terms such as *back* as members of the major actional
predicate class (Bloom *et al.*, 1975a,b), and this time includes the period when *-ing* progressive aspect is being
acquired. Yet the children do not produce errors such as
*I backing it. Another such piece of evidence is the well-
known fact that *-ed* past tense is always applied accurately
initially; over-regularizations such as *I breaked it* are
initially not present. Bellugi (1967) also discusses evidence that *don't* and *can't* are linked individually to the
relevant terms in early development.

It is not clear what the best representations are for such
small-scale operations. But it is clear that children are
not simply encoding them only according to the major predicate-argument class of the term. Let us assume that they
have some independence of encoding, and are linked to terms
individually. Then at some intermediate time, members of
both the actional predicate class, and also members of the
non-actional predicate classes or terms are becoming linked
to such operations. (Empirically, it is *not* the case that
children learn verb operations first for action verbs, then
for non-action verbs. Examples from Bellugi (1967) and
Braine (1976), for example, make it clear that early uses of
don't and *can't* include uses such as *I don't want it, I don't
like it*, and *I can't see it*; Bloom, Lifter, and Haifiz,
(1980) find that *-s* tensing tends to be applied first to
less actional terms.) We might posit a representation something like the following at this intermediate time, symbolizing lexical items by W_1, W_2, $W_3...W_n$, and symbolizing
individual small-scale operations by O_1, O_2, O_3, O_4, and so
forth, where O_1 might be, for example,

Argument + *don't* + X... = "present negation of X":
[1 person]

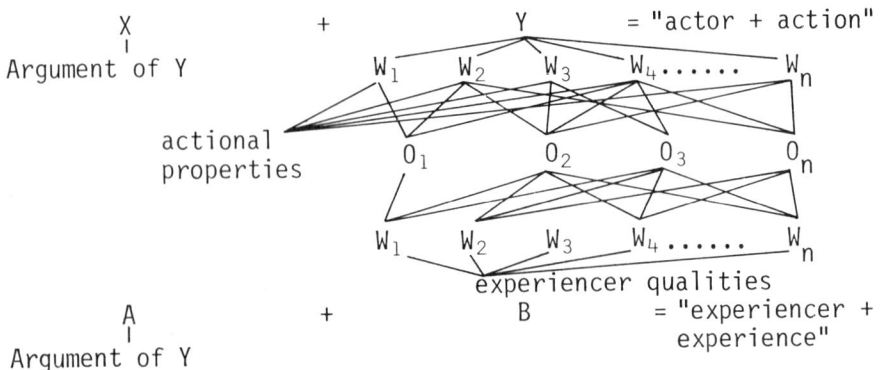

The above representation simply says that there is a major
constituent rule actor + action, and another major constituent rule experiencer + experience. Many of the terms connected to the action predicate node, are also connected to
various small operations. The latter are in turn connected
to terms connected to the predicate node initially organized
upon experience properties, such as *like, want, need.*

What has happened over time, compared to an earlier point,
is that the members of the Y-predicate class and members of
the B-predicate class are becoming more similar because of
shared properties such as taking *do*-forms, tensing morphemes,
and other auxiliary forms. As posited above, grammatical
schema are actively assimilatory, and seeking to see if new
sequences can be interpreted as examples of themselves. In
particular, suppose at this intermediate time the child hears
a sequence such as *he wants some cereal. Want* is appearing
in a sequence characteristic of the actional predicate class.
It has also become more generally similar over time, through
linkage to various operations which also characterize the
actional predicate class. The result may be the assimilation
of *want* to the Y-predicate class, despite its lacking actional
denotation. Over time, the original Y-predicate class comes
to absorb other terms such as *need, like, know, see,* and *hear,*
as they appear in grammatical configurations characteristic
of the members of its class. The result is that the original
actional predicate class, is becoming less unifiedly actional
in semantics, and transforming over time slowly into the adult
verb class. It is assumed here that the original Y-class is
the class likely to absorb members more actively, probably
because of the higher general use of actional predicates,
making this category more available for active assimilation.

This kind of account has even more appeal for nouns as a
major predicate-argument class. For while small-marker operations or other operations can provide a basis for unifying
terms such as *dog* and *chair* with non-concrete terms such as
idea and *action* they do not provide much basis for unifying
with the former terms, proper names and pronouns such as *Mary,
Paris, you,* and *me.* The difficulty is that while *dog* and
idea take various common operations such as pluralization with
-s (*dogs, ideas*), and various markings for definiteness and
indefiniteness (*the dog, the idea, a dog, an idea, some dogs,
some ideas*), and other properties, they do not share these
with proper names and pronouns. For the latter usually cannot
take pluralization or definiteness and indefiniteness markings
(**the Paris, *some Marys*) except under special referential
circumstances which are atypical of the use of these terms.

This suggests that at some early time, a major argument

class is somehow unified on the basis of making concrete
reference to objects or object classes, and providing arguments for major predicate classes. Over time, some of these
terms (ones denoting classes rather than individuals or
deictically specified pronominal references) also begin to be
linked to operations such as a + X = "indefinite reference to
X", X + s + "plural of X", modifier + X = "property of X",
= part of argument phrase. Thus, terms such as *dog*, *chair*,
and *table* are characterized by reference to concrete classes,
uses as argument heads, and uses in small-scale operations.
When terms such as *idea* and *trip* are heard in utterances such
as *I've got an idea* or *that was a good trip*, they can be
assimilated into the early major argument class by similarity
to terms such as *chair* and *dog*, even though they do not share
concrete object denotation with those terms. The class of
nouns thus contains terms assimilated because they refer to
concrete argument heads (*you*, *Paris*), terms which are assimilated because they are argument heads which take appropriate
small-scale operations (*idea*, *chair*), and terms which are
members for all these reasons (*dog*, *chair*).

   Although applied here to nouns and verbs, a model of an
originally semantically-based (or largely semantically based)
grammatical node evolving into one defined at least partly
in terms of operations characteristic of the class, could be
applied plausibly to a number of other problems. For example,
grammatical case markings such as nominative and accusative
might plausibly begin organized around role qualities such
as agentiveness, patienthood, described entity, and other
relations. Over time, the node unifying the uses might
come to absorb new uses on the basis of sufficient similarity
of form and meaning (sometimes mostly form), in a way such that
the semantic denotations characteristic of the original organization become diluted or transformed or even largely irrelevant.

5. DISCUSSION

The general appeal of a transformation theory of formal category evolution is that it uses semantic-structural categories
both characteristic of early speech, and modally characteristic
of the formal categories, to serve as a kind of originative
point for later more formally-based categories. The theory
is perhaps especially well-suited to nouns, for which properties such as denoting a concrete object argument appear to
play a partial unifying role even in the organization of the
adult category. It is not at all well-suited for treatments
of arbitrary gender categories such as those of German gender
and Russian gender for noun operations (Maratsos and Chalkley,

1980). The fact that children learn such arbitrary classes
with considerable skill (Maratsos and Chalkley, 1980),
points up the fact that alternative formulations of the evolution of formal classes are indeed available. Detailed
comparison of the utility of a transformation-over time theory
to other theories of formal category formation, however, is
not the purpose of the present chapter.[1]†
What I would like to do is make a few observations on
necessary assumptions, and possible problems with a transformation-over-time account. (These criticisms are meant to
apply fairly generally to a theory of the type outlined
here, rather than to the exact detailed form presented here,
which has many problems of detail not necessarily characteristic of the general type of formulation.)
One of the first aspects of such models that should be
immediately apparent is that they are not well-defined, and
would depend upon considerable auxiliary assumptions about
what the child considers salient or important organizing
properties, in their application to a particular domain. For
example, in the preceding pages, it is implicitly assumed that
reference to concrete object arguments is a powerful organizing property, because this property is sufficient to unify
a subdomain of the noun category. Conversely, it is implicitly assumed that properties such as having some actional denotation, or taking agentive arguments, do not lead to a unifying of, or confusion of, what will become adjective vs. verb
predicate categories. It is explicitly assumed that small-
marker operations must be capable of becoming powerful organizational properties. Thus, in the end, considerable particular hypotheses about important organizing properties are
necessary. This is only reasonable, because the basic mechanism is the judgment of sufficient and insufficient similarity for absorption into an already existing category.
What is similar or dissimilar depends upon the analytic
capacities and predispositions of the organism, whether these
come from general cognitive development or innate biases,
or particular linguistic biases or experience.
A problem (as opposed to a consideration or assumption)
for such theories, in which an earlier semantic-grammatical
category truly becomes a later formal one, is whether information characteristic of the old category would not be lost
or diluted in transformation to the new one. Let me illustrate this with two examples, the first in the transformation of the action-term category into the verb category, the

---

† The superscript numerals refer to notes which are to be
found at the end of the chapter.

second in a possible transformation of agentivity into sub-
jecthood, both of these developments either suggested or
implied in various writings. In the present account, an
early property of action terms (or at least a major class of
them) is that if they have an argument denoting a doer or
initiator of the action, this argument appears initially.
Now suppose the former action node changes into a later verb
node. The question is what happens to the original actor-
action rule as the action node becomes the verb node. In
particular, it is true that verbs take initial arguments
obligatorily in various circumstances. But it is not true
that for the whole class of verbs, this initial argument is
an actor, or particularly actor-like. For example, we have
pairs such as *John owns this house* — *this house belongs to
John*; *John likes this table* — *this table pleases John*;
two precedes three — *three follows two*; and so forth. So
overall, the semantic value of the initial argument rule
apparently must become quite diffuse. But for terms denoting actional verbs, there are in fact some fairly rigorous,
applicable, and complex rules about which kinds of arguments
can appear in what positions. If a predicate use has a
true agentive argument, that argument reliably appears in
subject position (for non-passives), for example. So in
fact, the original semantic subclass has ordering rules
which are clearer than the overall evolved more formal class;
that is, action predicates have clearer rules for the ordering
of semantic roles than non-action predicates. If one wishes
to expand "agent" into "subject" in general, this problem
becomes even worse. For subjects include arguments of non-
verbs, including the initial arguments of sentences such as
John — *is big, John* — *is in the yard, this glass* — *is
visible to Harry* (compare to *Harry can see this glass*), *This
is annoying to John, John is annoyed at this*. The semantic
range of subject arguments is essentially every available
semantic role. Thus, expanding "agent" into subject loses
considerable sharpness of grammatical definition, when in
fact there is every reason to suspect that the semantic ordering regularities characteristic of the semantic subclass are
not lost, either permanently, or temporarily during development.
The general difficulty is that transformation-over-time theories (at least if they fall into the general type outlined
here, in which the later category truly descends directly
from the earlier) seem to assume that the later formal category has all the desirable characteristics of the early
semantic one, when this is not clearly true. It seems likely
that often one wants to have generalizations characteristic
of both, rather than transform one completely into the other.

This last problem strikes me as the most serious difficulty
of such theories.[2]

6. CONCLUSIONS

In the present chapter, an inductive mechanism was proposed,
in which categorial nodes established by the analysis of
individual examples, absorb new examples(with their properties), on the basis of sufficient similarity, where both
structural and semantic properties may be used to define
similarity. This mechanism was applied to the derivation
of early semantic-structural rules such as mover-movement or
actor-action, and shown to result in the formation of prototypical grammatical categories in which both semantic and
structural factors play some role. It was then outlined how
with certain assumptions, originally semantic-based categories such as action-term might evolve into categories such
as verb, by a mechanism in which individual members of the
category acquired new properties, including properties of
grammatical combination, thus changing both the nature of the
category, and the basis for assimilation of new members. It
was discussed that the model of necessity has many *post hoc*
assumptions about basis of similarity, and also has a possible
difficulty that early categories may have certain regularities
associated with them not sharply evident in many members of
the later expanded class. The more the early class is expanded, the more this may be the case. It may be concluded that
such models are interesting and plausible, but will require
important analytic supplementation to become applicable to
the relevant problems.

ACKNOWLEDGEMENTS

This paper was written while the author was a fellow at the
Center for Advanced Study in the Behavioral Sciences, on
sabbatical from the University of Minnesota. I wish to express gratitude to both institutions for their support, and
to acknowledge the support of National Institute of Mental
Health grant No. 5-T32-MH14851-05, and the Andrew W. Mellon
Foundation during this time.

NOTES

1 This is not meant to imply that a transformation account or
  the account in Maratsos and Chalkley (1980) are the only
  available alternatives. For example, Pinker (in press)
  offers a nativist account in which the child inspects the

behaviour of "good" action terms to see what the grammatical behaviour of verbs is in the particular language he is
exposed to. Schlesinger (1974) offers an account in which
major grammatical categories are always essentially semantic-
based, as do Bates and McWhinney (in press). For criticisms
of the latter kinds of accounts, see Maratsos and Chalkley
(1980) and Maratsos (in press).

2 These remarks are not meant to preclude the use of theories
in which early semantic-based categories somehow "help" or
catalyse the formation of more nearly formal ones. For
example, suppose the child formed two early rules actor-
action and experiencer-experience, and many action and
and experience terms began to take on many similarities of
grammatical behaviour. We could posit an "abstraction"
process in which a higher node forms under these conditions
which "abstracts" the common properties of the two lower
nodes, but also leaves them in place. This would give us
action verbs and experiencer verbs. The former would re-
tain considerable regularities of grammatical behaviour
(e.g. agentive arguments, if present, going first) while
the latter would not. Such differing behaviours would be
left to the lower nodes, while the characteristics common
to the appropriate groups of terms would be left to the
higher (e.g. verbs take certain tense markings, obligatory
initial arguments under various conditions, and so on).
If some argument could be worked out that the initial presence of certain types of lower nodes facilitated the formation of higher ones, then the earlier semantic-based
categories could be said to play an important role. This
kind of process, however, is considerably different from a
true transformation-over-time theory, in which the later
category is directly descended from the same category node
as the earlier one.

REFERENCES

Bates, E. and MacWhinney, B. (in press). A functionalist
   approach to grammatical development. *In* "Language Acquisition: The State of the Art" (L. Gleitman and H.E. Wanner,
   eds). Cambridge: Cambridge University Press.
Bellugi, U. (1967). "The acquisition of negation". Unpublished
   doctoral dissertation, Harvard University.
Bloom, L. (1970). "Language Development: Form and Function
   in Emerging Grammars". Cambridge, Mass.: MIT Press.
Bloom, L. Lightbown, P. and Hood, L. (1975). Structure and
   variation in child language. *Monographs of the Society for
   Research in Child Development* <u>40</u> (Serial No. 160).

Bloom, L., Miller, P. and Hood, L. (1975). Variation and reduction as aspects of competence in language development. *In* "The Minnesota Symposium on Child Psychology" (A.D. Pick, ed.), Vol. 9. Minneapolis: University of Minnesota Press.

Bloom, L., Haifiz, E. and Lifter, K. (1980). Semantic organization of verbs in child language and the acquisition of grammatical morphemes. *Language* 56, 386-412.

Bowerman, M. (1976). Semantic factors in the acquisition of rules for word use and sentence construction. *In* "Normal and Deficient Child Language" (D.M. Morehead and A.E. Morehead, eds). Baltimore: University Park Press.

Braine, M.D.S. (1976). Children's first word combinations. *Monographs of the Society for Research in Child Development* 41 (Serial No. 164).

Brown, R. (1958). "Words and Things". Glencoe, Ill.: The Free Press.

Fillmore, C. (1968). The case for case. *In* "Universals in Linguistic Theory" (E. Bach and R. Harms, eds). New York: Holt.

Maratsos, M. (In press). The child's construction of grammatical categories. *In* "Language Acquisition: The State of the Art" (L. Gleitman and H.E. Wanner, eds). Cambridge: Cambridge University Press.

Maratsos, M. and Chalkley, M.A. (1980). The internal language of children's syntax: The nature and ontogenesis of syntactic categories. *In* "Children's Language, Vol. 2" (K. Nelson, ed.). New York: Gardner Press.

Maratsos, M., Kuczaj, S.A., Fox, D.E.C. and Chalkley, M.A. (1979). Some empirical findings in the acquisition of transformational relations. *In* "The Minnesota Symposium on Child Psychology" (W.A. Colling, ed.), Vol. 12. Minneapolis: University of Minnesota Press.

Pinker, S. (In press). A theory of the acquisition of lexical-interpretive grammars. *In* "The Mental Representation of Grammatical Relations" (J. Bresnan, ed.). Cambridge, MA: MIT Press.

Schlesinger, I.M. (1974). Relational concepts underlying language. *In* "Language Perspectives - Acquisition, Retardation, and Intervention" (R. Schiefelbusch and L. Lloyd, eds). Baltimore: University Park Press.

Schlesinger, I.M. (1977). The role of cognitive development and linguistic input in linguistic development. *Journal of Child Language* 4, 153-169.

PART IV: WORDS

THE ACQUISITION OF MEANING OF THE CONNECTIVES

GIOVANNI B. FLORES D'ARCAIS

*Department of Psychology, University of Leiden and
Max-Planck-Institute for Psycholinguistics, Nijmegen,
The Netherlands.*

1. INTRODUCTION

This chapter deals with children's acquisition of a class
of words used to connect a subordinate clause to a main clause
or to bind two subordinate clauses to each other. Their
function is to connect the clauses with a specific meaning:
the event expressed is the *cause, reason* or *result* or the
other, indicates a relation of *time* between the events expressed in the two clauses, etc. The words which will be
considered can be roughly divided into the following subclasses: (a) *causal*: e.g. *because*; (b) *temporal*: e.g. *before,
after, while*; (c) *consecutive*: e.g. *so that*; (d) *final*: e.g.
in order to; (e) *conditional*: e.g. *if, unless*; and (f) *concessive*: e.g. *although*.

Function words such as the connectives have some typical
characteristics very different from those of content words.
They have a relational character, and normally are not used
in isolation. Their common sense meaning is difficult to
define even for the literate adult. Often, aphasic patients
have particularly great difficulties with function words:
they may be able to read nouns and adjectives, but not function words and have a clear resistance against these
("Small words are the worst" and "One of them horrid words
again", as G.R., a patient studied by Marshall and Newcombe,
1966, expressed himself.) Still, *knowledge* of these words'
meaning is part of the lexical semantic knowledge of an adult
speaker, and to trace its acquisition and development is an
interesting problem.

Within linguistics, systematic attempts to deal with the
domain of the connectives as a whole are still lacking.
Several studies have dealt with the syntax and the semantics

of the most common conjunctions such as *and* and *but*, and
the "logical" connectives *if/then*; *either/or*, have also
received considerable attention. As for the subordinators,
one finds studies in contemporary literature about the structure and function of single words (such as *before*, or *because*),
and of the syntax of the clauses they subordinate.

Within psycholinguistics, studies exist on several types of
relational words. For example, Clark (1968) for English,
and Grimm and Schöler (1972) for German have studied the
structure of *prepositions*. Prepositions have also been the
object of classification studies by Deese (1965). One of
the studies reported by Fillenbaum and Rapoport (1971)
dealt with the psychological representations English speakers
have about some connectives, mostly coordinating conjunctions.

At the developmental level, there have been some studies on
the acquisition of the meaning of certain prepositions and
of adverbs, such as spatial and temporal prepositions and
spatial and temporal adverbs. The attention of researchers
for this area has recently increased (see e.g. Bloom, Lahey,
Hood, Lifter and Fiess, 1980).

Both at the adult and at the developmental level, most of
these studies have involved comprehension and use of the connectives in a *sentence*, and the conclusions reached have been
made about the knowledge of these words as they function in
utterances.

This brings us to an important distinction. In talking
about knowledge of the connectives we need to distinguish
different kinds of knowledge. One kind is that which is
required to understand a sentence which contains a connective. A second is the knowledge of the word "in isolation",
which is normally not required in language use, but which
still characterizes part of the lexical competence of both
adults and children: after all, every child knows what it is
to ask "what is the meaning of a word", for he often asks
for definitions about the meaning of a word, and even at
early stages may be capable of giving to his peer or to an
adult an appropriate definition of single words, or at least
a good example.

In the study of the acquisition of the connectives an important problem concerns the relation of the acquisition of
their meaning to the development of notions of the conceptual relations which are expressed through these words. For
example, to what extent does full knowledge of the meaning of
the word *because* require full development of the notion of
causality? This issue is certainly important for a comprehensive theory of language and cognitive development. In
the present framework, however, I will deal only with the

child's increasing knowledge of the meaning of these *words*, not with the full conceptual notions which is related to the possession of these words in the adult. Most children in some contexts correctly use the word *why* or *because* very early in their development, say, even before 3 years of age. However, all evidence we have indicates that at that age the child does not yet possess a mature notion of causality, as much Genevan work has shown.

2. CHILDREN'S COMPREHENSION OF COMPLEX SENTENCES

In a series of studies (Flores d'Arcais, 1978a,b) I have tried to investigate how children understand different types of complex sentences: temporal, causal, final, etc. Frequently I have used some form of an "acting out" task, and obtained evidence pointing to principles underlying children's performance with complex sentences. For example, when they are given sentences with temporal or causal clauses, in the absence of other cues, children will tend to rely on an order-of-mention strategy. By the age of eight or nine years, however, most children seem capable of correctly performing an acting out task when given most sentences made up of two clauses joined by a connective. This was not the case for "difficult" connectives such as *unless*.

In the 1978 study (Flores d'Arcais, 1978b) I have reported on several experiments involving different tasks, ranging from judgments of appropriateness of paraphrases, to choice of one out of two structures having a particular meaning, to judgments of correspondence of meaning between two complex sentences. In these experiments I have obtained some indication on the order of acquisition of the connectives. Also, it became clear that the capacity to differentiate the meaning of connectives presented in isolation develops much more slowly than one would predict on the basis of the results of "acting out" experiments using complex sentences.

It also became clear in this work that children often do not have to know the full meaning of the connectives in order to correctly perform in acting out tasks. Let us take the sentence

1) The cup is broken because it fell off the table.

The child can understand what the sentence means even if he doesn't yet know the meaning of the word *because*, simply on the basis of other information provided in the sentence and his knowledge of the world. This brings us to the simple conclusion that we cannot make strong inferences about the semantic knowledge children have at a given age just on the basis of the performance with complex sentences in "acting out" or other comprehension tasks. We have found in a series of experiments that the performance is impaired when the relation between the events described in the two clauses is arbitrary, as in sentence (2)

2) The boy washes the dog before the mother cooks the soup

as compared to situations in which the relation is inferrable or pragmatically obvious, as in (1).

Even when a child's performance in any task with two clause sentences indicates correct comprehension of the sentences, we can ask whether at that particular age the child also fully possesses the meaning of the connectives. Is complete mastery of such a meaning necessary for the correct performance observed?

Consider the following three possibilities.

a) The child's comprehension of the sentences indicates full knowledge of the connectives. The semantic knowledge of the child corresponds to that of the adult. The child correctly understands the connectives in isolation.
b) The child comprehends the sentence correctly but its comprehension is based on the sum of the linguistic information provided by the two clauses. The connectives as such are not understood and used by the child.
c) The child has only partial knowledge of the meaning of the connectives, which allows him to process them in context but not in isolation.

As we have suggested and our data strongly emphasize, from the fact that a child at a certain age correctly performs an acting out task with complex sentences which include a connective, we cannot immediately infer that his semantic knowledge includes full mastery of the meaning of sentence parts, including the connectives. When we find that at 7-8 years children are able to understand causal sentences which include the word *because*, we cannot conclude that the children necessarily possesses the full meaning of the word *because*. Correct performance may be based on something else about the information given. The child might process the sentence without computing the meaning of the connective, and even should he grasp some aspect of this meaning in context, his semantic knowledge may still be very limited and different from the knowledge of the adult.

3. THE ACQUISITION OF THE MEANING OF CONNECTIVES

As a kind of continuation of this work on the comprehension of complex sentences, I started a series of studies specifically aimed at obtaining some knowledge on the course of acquisition of the meaning of the connectives. I had observed in a series of pilot studies that the same children who perform correctly in an "acting out" task with a complex sentence which includes a connective such as *before* or *unless*, may be incapable of correctly performing a task which requires, for example, judgments of equivalence of meaning of one connective with another.

I came to the conclusion that there are different types and levels of semantic knowledge. The knowledge of the connectives needed to perform in tasks such as acting sentences out is different from the knowledge needed to give judgments of equivalence of the meaning of pairs of sentences identical in every detail except for a given connective, or to sort words on the basis of similarity of meaning. Children at a given age may perform well on one task, and less well on another task making somewhat different linguistic demands. When we talk about semantic development, we have to keep this very clearly in mind.

These conclusions bring one to a perspective on the ontogeny and development of meaning which is different from the positions implicit in most available theories on semantic development.

Several such theories have been proposed during the last years. Each emphasizes a different aspect of development (see Clark, 1979, for a summary of some of the most interesting ones). A very elegant theory supported by a series of ingenious experiments has been proposed by Clark (1979). According to this position, two factors determine the order of acquisition of word meaning. One factor is a principle of semantic complexity: within a given semantic field, children acquire the meaning of simple words before they acquire the meaning of more complex ones. The second factor is the use of non-linguistic strategies: non-linguistic knowledge leads the children to the "right" meaning. Semantic complexity and non-linguistic knowledge jointly constrain children's acquisition of meaning.

A characteristic aspect in Clark's theory is the attention for the semantic distinction the child learns to operate within a given semantic domain, until he reaches the state of differentiation which characterizes the adult's knowledge. This differentiation is reached through the progressive acquisition of knowledge along several semantic dimensions.

Consider, for example. the acquisition of the meaning of the words pair *before* and *after* (Clark, 1971). According to the observations of Clark, the child first learns that both words refer to *time*. At a further stage, the child learns to distinguish within the words the aspect of *simultaneity*, but while he correctly interprets the meaning of *before*, he misunderstands the word *after* and attributes the same meaning to it as *before*. Finally, the child reaches the full adult level of understanding and uses the two words correctly. This theory, as other positions on the development of word meaning, implicitly or explicitly assumes that development takes place on a single dimension. Initially the child does not possess the meaning of some word, and through a series of stages he progressively learns to make semantic distinctions through which he eventually acquires the meaning known to the adult.

The results of series of experiments on children's comprehension of complex sentences (Flores d'Arcais, 1978a) and on the use of connectives (Flores d'Arcais, 1978b) quoted above have shown that the picture is probably not so simple. The view taken in this paper will be that the acquisition of the meaning of a word is not all-or-none, or even a gradual progress along a single dimension. Acquisition of the meaning of a word is rather seen as an extended process and not as a simple transition from a state of "no-knowledge" to a state of "knowledge". What a child knows about a word becomes differentiated progressively on several dimensions. This development coincides with the use of different strategies and procedures the child adopts in dealing with the word in different linguistic "tasks" to which he is exposed. Laboratory experiments are only special cases of such linguistic tasks. The availability of these strategies and procedures will constitute part of the semantic knowledge the child possesses about a word, a given semantic domain or a lexical class.

4. THE PRESENT STUDY

The present chapter will illustrate the results of three different studies, carried out to give some answer to a series of questions concerning two topics, namely (a) the process of meaning differentiation within the domain of the connectives, and (b) the process through which the child acquires a notion of the structure and of the function of words in the class in isolation.

The problems which I have tried to face in the studies reported can be summarized by the following groups of questions.

a) How does acquisition of the meaning of the connectives take place? How are different connectives differentiated? Which are the semantic distinctions which the child learns to make first, and which ones come later?
b) What kind of notions does the child have about the function and the meaning of the connectives when they are presented in isolation? What kind of metalinguistic knowledge does the child have about these words, and how is the course of acquisition of this knowledge compared, for example, with other word classes?
c) What kind of strategies and procedures does the child acquire for dealing with different linguistic tasks?

The experiments carried out within the present study include the following:

i) Choices of a connective as the appropriate word for joining two clauses to form an adequate description of a picture.
ii) Sorting connectives and nouns on the basis of their respective similarity in meaning.
iii) Lexical decision tasks with connectives.

The experiments were conducted with variety of stimulus sentences and connectives, and were carried out with Italian and Dutch children.

5. STUDY 1. CHOICES OF CONNECTIVES TO JOIN TWO CLAUSES

The first two experiments reported here used a task in which the subjects chose one of two connectives to join two clauses which were given separately, with the aim of constructing a sentence as a description of a picture. In both experiments the children were given (a) the picture, (b) two cards with one clause typed on each, and (c) two cards with one connective each, and the request to make a choice among the two connectives by picking up the card considered appropriate to join the two clauses to make a two-clause sentence which would be a good description of the picture.

In such a task the child is confronted with each connective separately, more or less in isolation. However, by "trying out" either connective in the frame, the material presented might become equivalent for the child to a coherent sentence, as in previous experiments (Flores d'Arcais, 1978a), and in this sense the child would be confronted not with a "frame" and two connectives in isolation, but with whole sentences. But to the extent to which the child has to "try out" the two connectives, he will have to use his knowledge of the meaning of the individual words.

The two experiments differed only in one substantial aspect. In the first, one of the two connectives was *appropriate* and the other clearly *wrong*: choice of the first would give an appropriate description of the picture while choice of the second would give a sentence which would be an inappropriate description of it. In the second experiment, *both* connectives were inappropriate, so that no matter which one the child chose, the sentence obtained was not an appropriate description of the picture.

Experiment 1

In this experiment, the children had to choose one connective out of two, to join two clauses and make a sentence which would be a good description of a picture. I assumed that the patterns of responses would give some indication on the differentiation of the meaning of the connectives given to the children: errors made could be used as evidence about how differentiated in meaning the words may be for a child at a given age.

Material, Subjects and Procedure The following six Dutch connectives were used: *voordat* (before); *nadat* (after); *omdat* (because); *tenzij* (unless); *zodat* (so that); *hoewel* (although). Short clauses were used, with canonical SOV (or S complement V in the subordinate clause) order. Not all possible pairs of connectives were used. For example, *because* and *after* are almost always both acceptable in a given context, as in the following example:

3) The glass is broken *because* the glass fell off the table

   and

4) The glass is broken *after* the glass fell off the table.

Both (3) and (4) can be acceptable descriptions of the same picture, and there would be no easy way of telling whether the child does not know the meaning of the one connective or the other.

The subjects were 20 Dutch children in the *second, fourth* and *sixth* grade. The child was first familiarized with the task with a series of eight pairs of clauses which included four examples with simple coordinating conjunctions. Then the child was given the experimental material, namely on each trial (a) *first the picture* (which remained available on a table in front of him, (b) then the *two cards* with the clauses, and finally (c) *the two cards with the connectives*. The data consisted simply of the proportion of times each of the two connectives was chosen.

Results The proportion of times a "wrong" connective was chosen is plotted for each age level by the *appropriate* connective in Fig. 1. Among the results, let us point out to the following: *before* and *after* are differentiated earlier than the other connectives. *Because* is confused with *although* only at the second grade level, and *although* and *unless* are still rather frequently confused even at the sixth grade level.

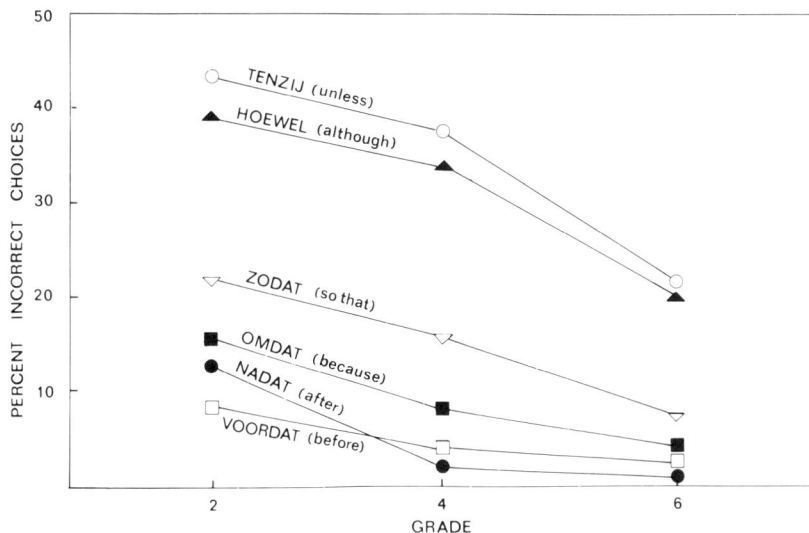

FIG. 1 *Study 1, Experiment 1. Proportion of incorrect choices of the connectives over all possible pairs used.*

The pattern of progressive differentiation of the meaning of these connectives is clear. The *temporal before/after* and the *causal because* differentiate earlier, followed by the connective *so that* and finally *unless* and *although*. The latter pair is still confused in its meaning even for the oldest children in our sample.

Experiment 2

The subjects of this experiment, Italian children, were given *pictures* and *two clauses* on separate cards, accompanied by *two connectives*, which were both *inappropriate* in the context of the picture, as possible words to join the clauses.

The assumption underlying this experiment was as follows. If a child does not know the meaning of the connectives, he will either not answer or chooses at random; as a result, a fifty-fifty distribution of the responses for the two connectives should be expected. If the child has fully developed knowledge of the meaning of the connectives, on the other hand, he should refuse to choose either word, on the ground of both being inappropriate for the resulting complex sentence.

If the results show a preference for one of the two connectives given, however, this can be interpreted in different ways. The proportion of choices for one of the two connectives might indicate any of the following:

a) The word chosen has the same meaning, or some similarity in meaning to another, more appropriate connective.
b) The child chooses the word it is more familiar with independently of its appropriateness in meaning.
c) The child chooses the connective, the meaning of which is *not* known, as a way of avoiding choosing that which he knows to be inappropriate.

These alternatives will guide the interpretation of the results.

Material, method and subjects   The connectives used were the Italian equivalent of the Dutch connectives of Experiment 1, with one addition: *prima che* (before); *dopo che* (after); *perché* (because); *a meno che* (unless); *cosicché* (so that); *nonostante che* (although); and *affinché* (in order to). The clauses were simple Italian sentences with the subjunctive form of the verb in the subordinate clause, to ensure the appropriate syntactic structure. Again not all pairs of connectives were used, for in several cases one or both would have been appropriate for a given picture, and in other cases no clear differentiation of two inappropriate items could have been made. To ensure that the task would be acceptable even to children who had considerable knowledge of the connectives, the material included dummy sentences with two appropriate coordinating conjunctions, or one appropriate and one inappropriate.

The subjects were Italian children in the first, third and fifth grade, with a total of 16 each in the three groups. Ss were given first a series of six trials with "appropriate" connectives. The task was administered as in Experiment 1. Only in few cases did some of the older children refuse to fill in the "slots" and instead provided an appropriate word. The children were requested, whenever possible, to give a reason for their choice. This material was subsequently used for the analysis of individual data.

Results   The data obtained consisted of proportion of choices of each connective as compared with the other ones with which

the connective had been paired. These data were treated in
two different ways. First, separately for each connective
which — although not given — would have been appropriate
in the context of the picture, the proportion of choices of
all connectives used was computed. Second, again for each
appropriate, but not given, connective, the proportion of
choices of each connective against the other ones has been
computed. For example, if the contextually appropriate
connective was *before*, how many times was *unless* chosen
against the other connectives? How many times *so that*, etc.?
The data available in this way for each age group were these:

a) Six arrays of proportions of choices of each connective;
b) an overall matrix (based on incomplete entries because
   not all pairs of connectives have been used for the different situations).

Only elaboration on the last set of data will be presented
here, for the detailed picture obtained by the choices of
the different "correct" connectives is rather consistent with
the latter and the results of the first analysis will be,
when appropriate, simply illustrated in the text.
   The matrix of proportion of choices can be interpreted as
a "confusion" matrix: the higher the proportion of choices
of a given connective, the less that connective has been
"distinguished" from the appropriate one. Under the assumption of Thurstone (1927) Case V of Comparative Judgment, the
proportions were transformed in normal deviates, and the means
of these values yielded normal deviate scale values. The
scale obtained represents an overall "confusion" scale: the
higher the value of the connective on the scale, the more is
the connective confused with the appropriate ones. This can
be interpreted as indicating that the meaning of the connectives higher on the scale is still less differentiated from
the other ones. The scale values obtained for the three
groups of subjects studied are presented in Fig. 2. The
most clear result is the *differentiation* of the confusion
values with increasing age: the connectives *before, because*
and *after*, for example, tend to become much less often "confused" with the correct ones; this results in a lower proportion of choices and this makes the scale values more dis-
tant on the scale.
   From these data, as well as from inspections of the pre-
ferences of the specific connectives as related to each of
the correct ones, the following pictures emerge.
   Typically *before* and *after* on the one hand, and *because* on
the other, differentiate first. At a later level the children
also differentiate *so that* and *in order to*, and finally *although*

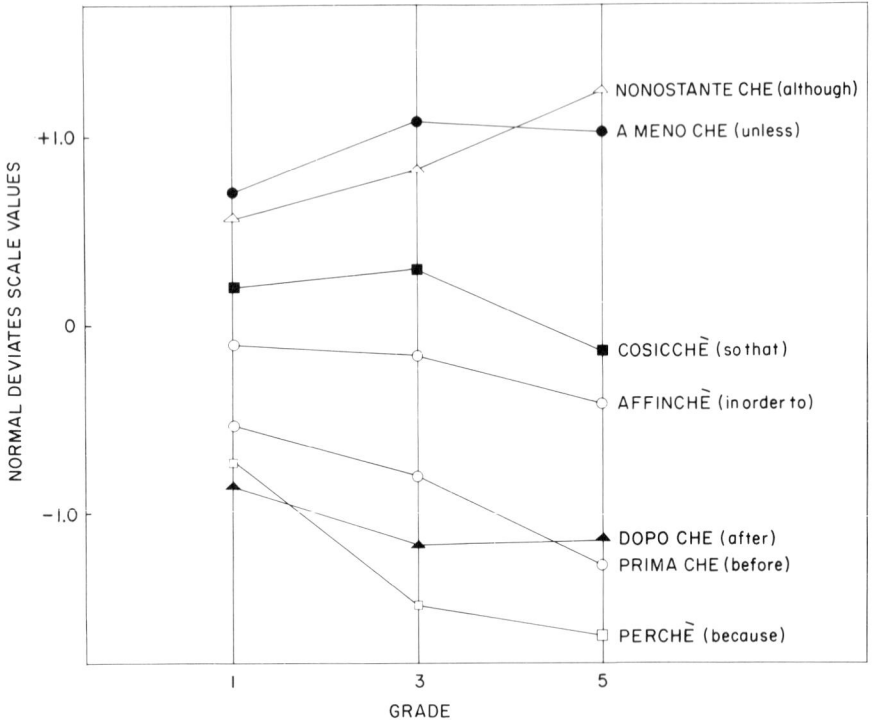

FIG. 2 *Study 1, Experiment 2. Scale values indicating pre-ferences for the different connectives as compared to the contextually appropriate ones (which were not given). The higher the value on the scale the more often a connective has been inappropriately chosen.*

and *unless*. Notice, however, that when some confusion is present, the children still do not seem to choose at random. They use their knowledge to infer something about the meaning of the connectives they don't know, and they also seem to have "some" knowledge of the connectives they don't know to perfection. For example, in the concessive *although* there is a causal element — in a negative form, and children do frequently choose *because* and *although*, but much more rarely a temporal connective. Or, they seem to have a notion that the causal typically has a temporal component involved. Final connectives (*in order to*) also have a temporal aspect involved, and this is also reflected in the developmental errors.

Analysis of individual response patterns   The individual responses and the comments and reasons for choices provided

by the children also allowed a more detailed analysis to be
undertaken. The following analysis is based on two data
sets, namely (a) inspection of individual protocols, and (b)
examination of the arguments or comments provided by the
children after the choice was made, at the request of the
experimenter. These two data sets were analysed and scored
by two independent judges on the basis of the categories
presented in Table 1, which were chosen on the basis of a
preliminary analysis of all data available. Whenever dis-
agreement among the two judges emerged, the response was
classified in the "rest" category, which also included all
cases in which either no clear criterion could be used for
classification, or in which it seemed likely that the child
had chosen at random.

TABLE 1 *Proportions of choices made on the basis of various
criteria. The values are based on unequal N. (Multiple coding
has been made in several cases; proportions do not sum to
unity.)*

Criterion for choosing	Grade		
	2	4	6
Random choice or no evident criterion found	0.31	0.18	0.11
Physical similarity with appropriate connective	0.07	0.20	0.06
Familiarity with a connective	0.28	0.15	0.08
Physical similarity with a familiar connective	0.25	0.12	0.06
Selection of not known word as a "rest choice" with exclusion of the inappropriate, known word	0.10	0.21	0.29
Partial meaning overlap with the appropriate connective	0.02	0.16	0.35
Refusal to choose	0.00	0.04	0.09

Multiple coding of a response was possible and was done in
some cases. For example, the same response could be classified as determined by similarity of the word selected with
the appropriate response (e.g. *cosicché* for *affinché*) and
depending on "partial" meaning overlap.

In the analysis, careful consideration of the possible
effects of pragmatic type on the choice of a connective was

made. Within each subject, the consistency across responses
was examined. The main source for classifying the response,
however, was the child's own comments. The relevant information is given by the differences in *each* category in Table 1
for the three age levels.

The proportions reported in Table 1 suggest several interesting differences. At a lower age level the child seems to be
more readily guided by criteria such as *familiarity* with a
given connective, or *physical similarity* with a familiar one.
At this stage the child does not seem capable of using much
semantic knowledge in order to make his choice. At a second
level of this development, on the other hand, the child seems
to use already some semantic knowledge: he chooses more frequently the connective physically similar with an appropriate
one and begins to select the connectives; a "negative choice",
excluding the one whose meaning he knows and which is then
clearly inappropriate. Overlap of features of meaning seems
to begin to be used as a criterion for choice. Finally, at
the most advanced stage in our sample, "negative" choices
and overlaps of meaning seem the most frequently used to
guide selection of the connectives.

Discussion

The results of these two experiments carried out with two
different languages and with different materials show a very
similar trend regarding progressive differentiation of the
meaning of the words studied. Underlying the choice of the
connectives made by the subjects of the two experiments, there
seems to be a regular and consistent pattern of meaning differentiation.

The order in which the connectives differentiate in both
languages is the following. First the causal and the temporal, then the final and the consecutive, and finally conditional and concessive.

The results of the second experiment suggest the following
developmental trand regarding response strategies a subject
uses in dealing with this kind of material.

At the earliest stage observed the child tends to rely,
more than everything else, on the following strategies

    (Strategy 1a) "From the two connectives choose the
                      one with which you are more familiar."
    (Strategy 1b) "Choose the connective which is physi-
                      cally more similar to one you know."

Then at a further stage, the following two strategies become more dominant.

(Strategy 2a) "Choose the connective which is physi-
              cally more similar to one you consider
              appropriate but is not presented."
(Strategy 2b) "Knowing one of the two connectives,
              and that it is not appropriate, choose
              the other one, less or not at all known,
              as likely to be correct."

At a third stage, together with strategy (2b), children tend
to rely on a fifth principle:

(Strategy 3a) "Select the word which shares some fea-
              tures of meaning with the appropriate
              one."

These strategies or operating principles are presented here
only tentatively. To verify them, direct experimental work
with appropriate stimulus material designed to correspond to
a particular critical difference suggested by each of these
proposed strategies will be necessary. (For example, it will
be important to establish the familiarity of the connectives
for each individual child, and *then* check for the reality of
Strategy (1a).)

6. STUDY 2. JUDGMENTS OF SIMILARITY OF WORD MEANING BY SORTING

The task of "sorting" words on the basis of their meaning,
putting together those words which are judged similar in meaning into the same class or category, has been widely used
with adults and children (e.g. Miller, 1971; Anglin, 1973;
Fillenbaum and Rapoport, 1971) as a method for obtaining
some indication on the structure of the "mental lexicon" of
the subjects observed. Such data typically yield a similarity matrix which can be analysed by a multidimensional
scaling algorithm or by a clustering procedure such as
Johnson's clustering schema. The task can be easily understood even by rather young children (e.g. seven-year-olds,
as in the experiments by Anglin, 1973).
In a previous study (Flores d'Arcais, 1978b) I let the most
frequent 20 connectives of Dutch be sorted by children in
the second, fourth and sixth grades and by adults. The main
result of that study was that children tended to group connectives simply on the basis of physical similarity (word
length, phonetic similarity, identical initial or final syllable, etc.). This criterion was still used by the oldest
children studied, even when they already had begun to use
appropriate semantic criteria. One possible source of this
tendency for children to tend to sort connectives mainly on

the basis of phonetic or graphic similarity rather than their
meaning, could have been in a particular interpretation made
of the instructions. The children may have understood that
they should discover certain similarities among the written
words, in which case word length, word contour, identical
initial letter or identical syllables and the like would be
obvious and simple criteria for sorting the words. As test
of this hypothesis I have replicated the first sorting experiment but using an additional word sorting task, namely
adding lexical items for which, on the basis of the results
obtained by Anglin (1973) and other researchers, we might
expect to find a clear differentiation on the basis of meaning and not other properties. This was done by asking children to separately sort out (a) a group of connectives and (b)
a group of concrete nouns.

Material, subjects and method Twenty-one connectives and 21
concrete nouns were used. The connectives were the 20 words
used in the older study (Flores d'Arcais, 1978b), plus an
additional word. I have tried to obtain a good *match* between
the connectives and the nouns using criteria such as length,
word contour, initial and final syllables and number of subclasses with similar meaning. For example, six connectives
ended in *-dat*, so as matching material, six words were chosen
ending in *-bloem*, some indicating a *flower*, other a type of
flour. Similarly *boter* (butter) and *bodem* (ground) were
matched to *terwijl* (while) and *tenzij* (unless). Of course,
simultaneous use of the different criteria listed above
required several compromises on the matching procedure, which
can be observed in the actual words used, presented in Figs 3
and 4.

The subjects were 20 Dutch children for each of the second,
fourth and sixth grades. Each child was tested separately
in a room provided by the school.

Nouns and connectives were given separately in two different test sessions. Approximately one half of the Ss were
given the task of sorting the nouns followed by the task of
sorting the connectives, the other half the task of sorting
the connectives first. Each word was presented typed on a
card. The children were invited to place the cards into as
many groups as they wanted, on the basis of which words they
thought would "belong" together. Each pair of words placed
together in the same cluster was given a score of 1, all
other pairs were given a score of 0. The similarity matrices
obtained by summing over the individual scores were analysed
using the hierarchical clustering schema by S.C. Johnson
(1967).

GRADE 2

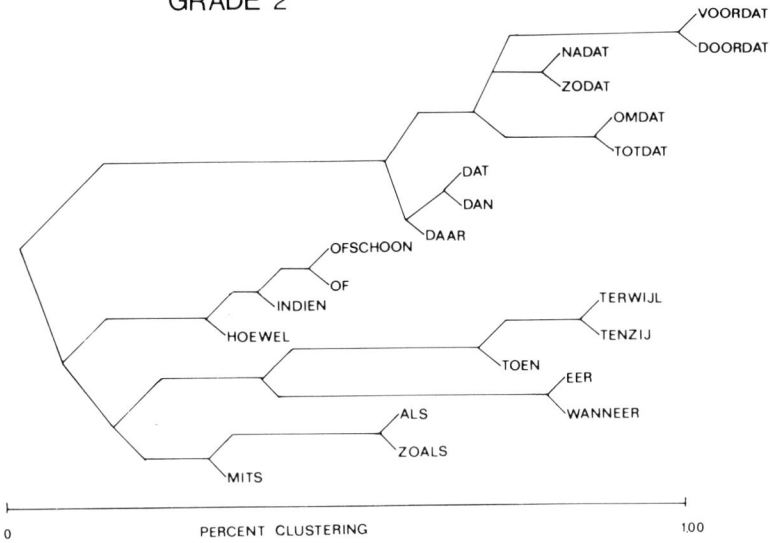

FIG. 3a *Hierarchical clustering structure for 21 Dutch connectives sorted by meaning similarity by second grade children.*

GRADE 4

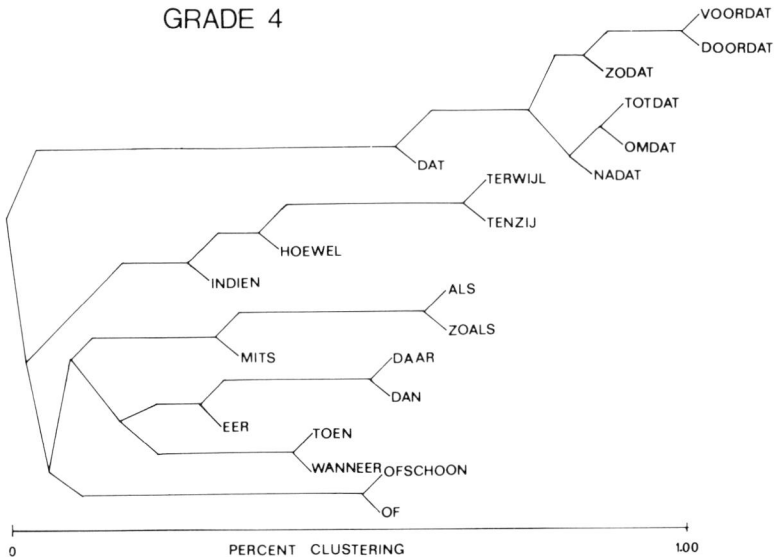

FIG. 3b *Hierarchical clustering structure for 21 Dutch connectives sorted by meaning similarity by fourth grade children.*

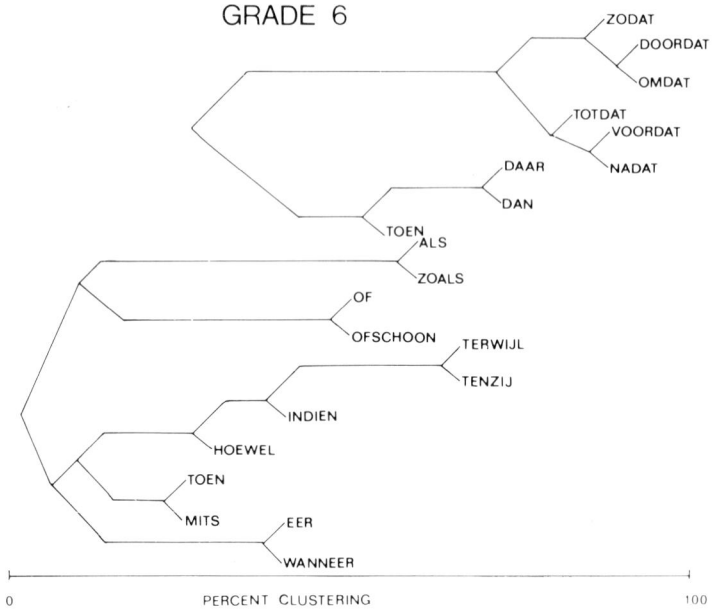

FIG. 3c *Hierarchical clustering structure for 21 Dutch connectives sorted by meaning similarity by sixth grade children.*

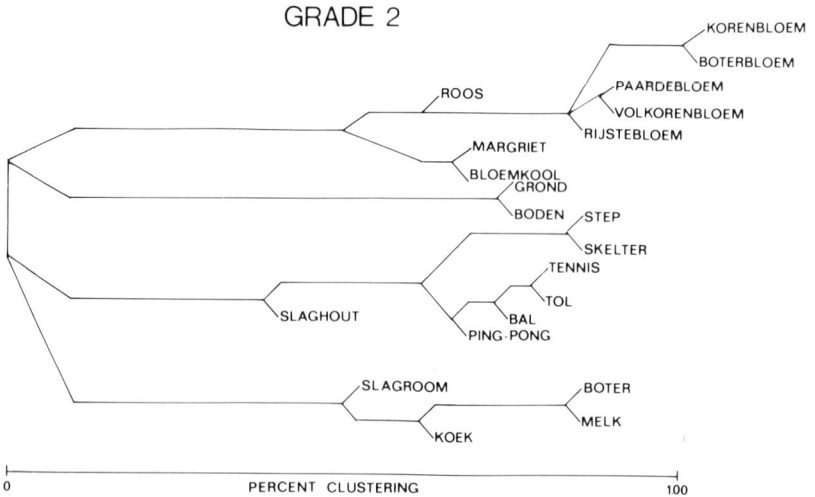

FIG. 4a *Hierarchical clustering structures for 21 Dutch nouns sorted from meaning similarity by second grade children.*

GRADE 4

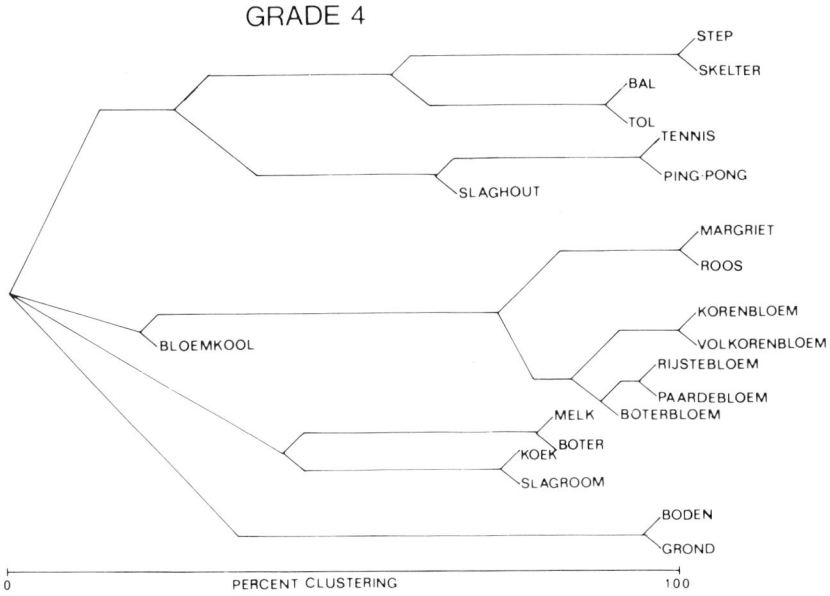

FIG. 4b *Hierarchical clustering structures for 21 Dutch nouns sorted from meaning similarity by fourth grade children.*

GRADE 6

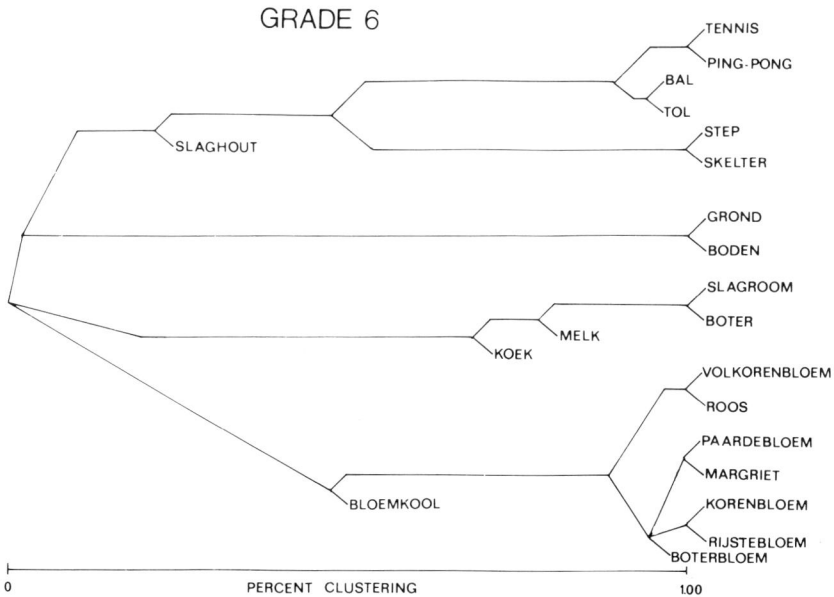

FIG. 4c *Hierarchical clustering structure for 21 Dutch nouns sorted from meaning similarity by sixth grade children.*

Results

The results are presented in Figs 3 and 4. As far as the
connectives are concerned, the results neatly correspond to
those reported in Flores d'Arcais (1978b). As in the 1978
study, the children tended to sort these words almost exclusively on the basis of phonetic and graphic similarity,
and semantic distinction emerged only gradually, going up
to the sixth grade.

At the second grade level, the placing of the words seems
entirely based on phonetic and graphic similarity. All words
ending in -*dat* are clustered together. *Terwijl* and *tenzij*
show up in another cluster, and *wanneer* and *eer* form a third
cluster, presumably because of the similarity of their last
syllables, as *als* and *zoals*.

At the fourth grade, the structure obtained is still very
similar to the one for the second graders. All connectives
ending in -*dat* again fall in the same cluster, and so are
the short words beginning with *a*, words ending in *als*, etc.
The clusters, however, are also beginning to reflect another
classification criterion. The temporal connectives *wanneer*
(when) and *toen* (when, then) appear now in the same cluster.

At the sixth grade level, the structure still remains much
the same, but several other distinctions are made. For
example, within the larger cluster of the words ending in
-*dat*, the temporal connectives *voordat* and *nadat* now are
closely related. Similarly the causal connectives *omdat* and
doordat cluster together. *Terwijl* and *tenzij* also appear in
the same cluster, and are associated with *indien*.

As far as the nouns are concerned (Fig. 4), the children
from the sixth grade seem capable of clearly sorting these
words on the basis of "natural" semantic criteria. This is
also the case for the younger children, except for a few
words ending in -*bloem*, which are clustered together with
other words ending with the same morpheme and belonging to
a different semantic domain.

If we look further at the individual data, we find that
some Ss used criteria of physical similarity while others
were using semantic criteria. The overall picture obtained
however, cannot be explained only as the result of a combination of the responses of Ss using different criteria to put
together some words, but seemed attracted by physical similarity in putting together other words.

Discussion

We find a clear difference in performance, up to the sixth
grade, for the two types of material. For the *connectives*

two types of principles seem to underlie the classification.
The first is physical similarity of the stimulus words, including both phonetic similarity (initial syllable, final
syllable, initial or final sound) and graphic similarity
(spelling, word contour and word length). The second principle underlying the classification is knowledge of the meaning of the connectives.

The children at the lowest age level seem to take into
account only physical similarity. Developmentally, this
principle gradually combines with the principle of semantic
similarity, but grade six children still seem strongly influenced by it. The first semantic distinction which seems
to emerge, at the fourth grade level, concerns temporal conjunctions. By the sixth grade, there seem to be certain distinctions within the class of conditionals as well. The
general picture is of a mixed strategy. On the one hand,
the words ending in -dat are clustered together. But within
this cluster some semantic principles seem to operate. Results from my earlier experiments (Flores d'Arcais, 1978b)
suggest that this mixed picture reflects the fact that some
sixth grade children sort the words exclusively on the basis
of physical similarity, others do so only on the basis of
semantic criteria, and a third group is guided by both principles at the same time.

For the concrete nouns, on the other hand, even at the
lowest age level studied the children use clear semantic
and pragmatic criteria for classifying the words. It therefore cannot be difficulty in understanding the instructions
or in comprehending the task which explains the difference
found. The same children who are capable of sorting out
nouns on the basis of semantic criteria use criteria of
physical similarity when given connectives.

7. STUDY 3. TWO LEXICAL DECISION EXPERIMENTS

In this section I will report on two different lexical decision tasks with children of different ages. The first is a
replication of a pilot study reported in Flores d'Arcais
(1979), in which children were asked to decide whether a
string of letters printed on a card was a word in Dutch or
not, without time limits. In the second experiment, latencies of the decisions were measured. In both experiments,
a control comparison was made with the knowledge children
have about the "wordness" of nouns and adjectives.

In the pilot study (Flores d'Arcais, 1979), connectives
were judged to be words by second grade children much less
often than nouns and adjectives. In fact, they were judged

as words about as often as strings of letters which were
possible ("legal") but non-existing words in Dutch.

On the basis of these results a simple hypothesis became
apparent, namely that content words (nouns, adjectives and
verbs) would be considered by the child as "words" much
earlier than function words (such as connectives, prepositions
and perhaps adverbs). The knowledge or recognition that function words are, in isolation, also "words" of the language
would develop later. The two experiments reported here are
a contribution towards testing this hypothesis.

Lexical decision tasks have become a very popular technique to obtain information about the organization of the
internal lexicon. Almost all studies carried out so far made
use of *written* material, meaning that subjects must already
have acquired a reasonable level of literacy. However, a
few studies have been carried out with children of different
ages, and rather good results have been obtained even with
ones as young as seven years of age (Schvaneveld, Ackermann
and Semlear, 1977). These results open the possibility of
using the technique to obtain information about the structure
of the developing internal lexicon.

In most lexical decision experiments, latencies are taken
as an indication of processing complexity. An hypothesis
compatible with this assumption is that differences in latencies indicate something about the "strength" or "depth" with
which a word is already known. It is well known, for example,
that lexical decision latencies for words in a non-native
language are usually longer than latencies for words of one's
first language, even when the second language seems, even by
strong criteria, mastered rather perfectly. In a similar
way, lexical decisions about words which are mastered relatively late and whose meaning may not yet be well established
could also be longer.

It is known from lexical decision studies that latencies
for more frequent content words are shorter than those for
ones of low frequency. But one could not explain greater
decision latencies for function words as compared to content
words as due to differences in frequency of use. On the one
side, in general, function words are among the most frequent
lexical items in a language, but probably the connectives
used in this experiment are not so frequently used in language
spoken to children. The only thing one could do in this complicated issue was to try to match for frequency the content
words and the function words used.

I will report on two lexical decision experiments. In both
studies, the children were presented with strings of letters
which were non-words, nouns, adjectives or connectives in

Dutch. In both experiments the children had to decide whether the string was a word in Dutch or not. In the first
experiment the subjects were given the stimuli printed on
cards, and had as much time as they wanted to decide whether
the items were Dutch words or not. The dependent variable
was simply the number of correct decisions, or errors, deciding
(a) that the word was a non-word, and (b) that a non-word was
a word. In the second experiment, as in most lexical decision
experiments, the stimulus words were presented on a visual display and latencies were measured.

The two independent variables, number of errors and decision
latencies, chosen for our experiments, provide two different
indications of the developmental course of the metalinguistic
notion of "word" for connectives, nouns and adjectives.

Experiment 1

Method, subjects and material The subjects, children in the
second, fourth and sixth grades, were presented with written
strings of letters (words and non-words, and had to decide,
without any time limit, whether these were words of Dutch
or not. The dependent variable was the frequency of correct
(or false) decisions about each word. The child was handed one
word at a time, printed on a card, and had to tell the experimenter whether it was a "good" word of Dutch or not. The subjects were 20 children of grade two, 19 of grade four and 20
of grade six, with the respective mean ages 7;6, 9;6 and 11;6.

Eight nouns, eight adjectives and eight connectives were
used as material, together with sixteen "legal" non-words and
eight "illegal" non-words. The eight connectives were chosen
among the 20 most frequent connectives in written and spoken
Dutch (Uit den Bogaart, 1973, De Jong, 1979) with an attempt
to cover a variety of semantic types (temporal, causal, consecutive).[1] The nouns and the adjectives were chosen with
the following two constraints: (a) their frequency in the
language should match the frequency of the connectives; (b)
they should very roughly match the connectives in length,
word contour and number of syllables. This last constraint
also guided the preparation of the non-words: for each of the
eight connectives, for example, we constructed a matched non-
word, similar in length, initial or final syllable and approximate phonological structure (for example, the word TERWIJL was
"matched" with the non-word TROVAAL).

[†] Superscript numerals refer to notes which are to be found
at the end of the chapter.

288 G. FLORES D'ARCAIS

It is clear that frequency norms obtained from adult
language are not the best basis for selecting verbal material
for an experiment with children. On the other hand, in the
absence of specific norms based on child language, one can
assume that adult norms, especially those for spoken language,
might to some extent approximate the relative frequency of
exposure of the child to his linguistic environment.

The experiment was carried out on an individual basis, and
in the school. The experimental words were preceded by a few
examples, to familiarize the child with the task and to allow
him to more fully comprehend what he was being requested to do.

For each subject we counted the number of errors (a) saying
that a word was not a word, and (b) that a non-word was a word.

Results The proportion of errors (deciding that a word is
not a word and that a non-word is a word) is reported in
Fig. 5. A very clear result is that by the fourth grade the
performance of the children is already almost perfect. The
most interesting differences are present at the second grade:
a not small proportion of children do not yet consider the

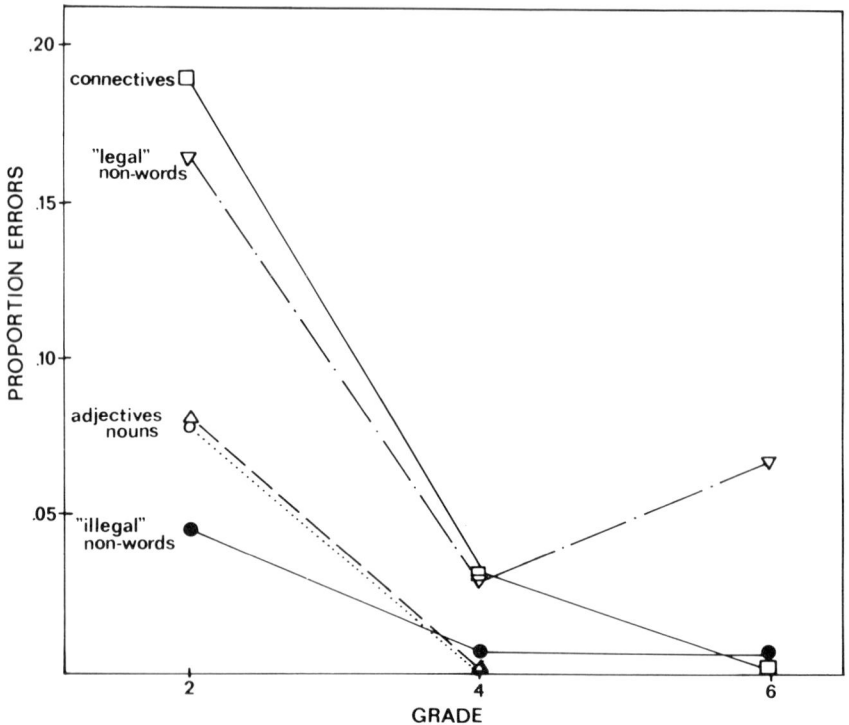

FIG. 5 *Experiment 1. Proportion of errors in the lexical
decisions for the different classes of words (or non-words).*

connectives as words. Notice that at this age level the proportion of errors for the non-words is almost the same as
the proportion of errors for the connectives. Perhaps we
could comment on this result by saying that a child at this
age has the same probability of accepting a non-word as a
"good" word as he has of refusing a connective as being a
non-word. The proportion of errors for the "illegal" non-
words is very low at all age groups tested.

Discussion At the second grade, the lower age level at which
I have obtained data, the children already seem to have very
clear notions of the difference between a word and an illegal
non-word. By the age of 7 or so, then, they must already
possess some specific metalinguistic knowledge about the
phonological and the morphological constraints within the
language. At this age, on the other hand, for some children
the connectives do not yet seem to have the property of being
"words".
   A more detailed discussion will follow the presentation of
Experiment 2.

Experiment 2

Material, subjects and method This experiment differed from
the previous one only in one important feature: the time
necessary to take the decision about the words was measured.
In this way, two dependent variables were obtained, namely
(a) the type of response (correct/wrong) and (b) the latencies.
The same stimuli were used as in Experiment 1.
   The subjects were children of two age groups, 7 and 9 years
(19 and 23 children respectively) and 20 adults, mostly university students.
   The experiment was carried out with a Vector General Display
controlled by a PDP 11/20 configuration. The subject sat in
front of the display, with his hands on two response buttons,
one for "*word*" and one for "*non-word*". A series of trials
with examples of well known and common words and obvious non-
words was given as a learning phase at the beginning of the
experiment to familiarize the subject with the situation.
The experiment was described to the child as a game in which
he had to play "against" the computer. All children enjoyed
the game, and none seemed to have problems in understanding
the instructions or the type of performance required. No
difficulty was anticipated with the task by adult subjects,
nor was any found.

Results The results consisted of the frequencies of word/non-word decisions and the corresponding latencies. The proportion of errors made was rather low. The average latencies for the two groups of Ss and the different classes of stimulus words (correct responses) are shown in Fig. 6. An analysis of variance on these latencies showed a significant overall effect of age (F: 26.73; 2,59 d.f.; $p < 0.001$) and for class of words (min F': 12.21; 4,43 d.f.; $p < 0.001$).

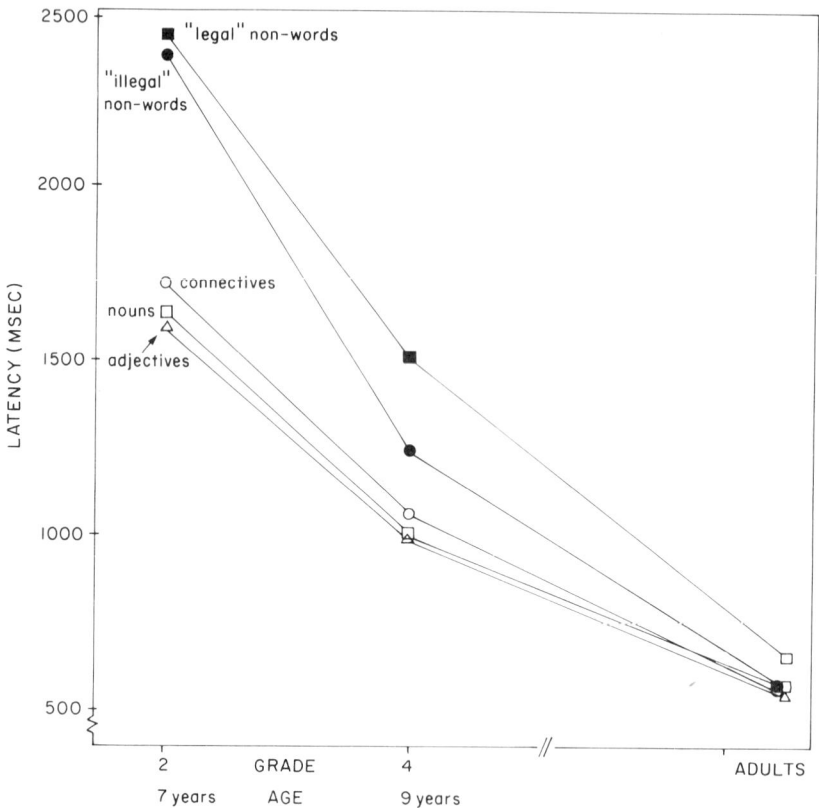

FIG. 6 *Experiment 2. Latencies (msec) in lexical decisions for the different classes of words (or non-words).*

Let us first look at the data for the children. The main results are the following. First, there is a clear overall difference in the latencies between the 7- and 9-year-olds. This might be explained both in terms of a longer time needed to reach the decision about the words and longer reading times. Second, the variance of the distribution of latencies for the 7-year-olds is larger than for the 9-year-olds and this could indicate both larger individual differences in the level of metalinguistic competence and in reading ability. Third, non-words at both age levels require a much longer time for decision than words. Fourth, connectives are slower to be decided upon than nouns and adjectives, which themselves require approximately the same decision time within each age level. Comparisons between pairs of classes of words show that nouns and adjectives do not differ in decision latencies, that connectives take significantly longer than these first two classes of words, and that non-words take at both age levels significantly longer than the words. Age interacts significantly with the latencies for the connectives and for the illegal non-words: connectives take always longer than nouns and adjectives, but more so for the lower age group, and illegal non-words are decided upon faster than legal non-words, but more so for the older children.

As for the adults, the latencies are of the order of magnitude we know from the literature on lexical decision. Adjectives, nouns and connectives take approximately the same time. Illegal non-words are faster than legal non-words, again a rather established result, and legal non-words are significantly slower than all classes of actual words.

Discussion   The results of both experiments can now be discussed. For the "words" in general, the results of the two experiments are consistent with each other.

Let us consider an interesting difference which emerges for the non-words. While in Experiment 1 the proportion of errors for the illegal non-words is very low, and the proportion of errors for legal non-words is at any rate no higher than that of the connectives, the latencies for the non-words in Experiment 2 are much longer than those for the words. On the other hand, illegal non-words require a shorter latency than legal non-words, and this trend corresponds to the proportion of errors on illegal non-words in Experiment 1.

In the two experiments, adjectives and nouns obtained about the same amount of errors and very similar latencies. The error curves from Experiment 1 show a characteristic "break" from monotonic decrease for the legal non-words for the sixth graders. When tested for significance as a deviation from a linear trend this break does barely not reach the significance level: however, if we want to take this result as a possible indication of a non-random effect, we could make the hypothesis that while at a lower age level the child "checks" the input strings with the words he knows, and then he decides that it does not belong to the existing words, at an older age the child would be more aware of the fact that a given

string, being a "possible" word of the language, could potentially be in the dictionary, and therefore he would be more
uncertain and possibly make more errors.

   In the second experiment, the difference in latencies between legal and illegal non-words increased with increasing
age: older children were faster on both classes of stimuli
as compared to the younger ones, but were relatively more so
for the illegal non-words. This could be interpreted in two
ways, either as due to increased reading ability, which would
allow the older child to take in the word — or the "part"
of it which is necessary to decide — faster, or as due to
more advanced internalization of the structure of the possible
words — and therefore to a better knowledge about "possible"
words and impossible ones. Both the effect of Experiment 1
and the interaction of Experiment 2 are, of course, extremely
interesting if seen in the theoretical framework of the search
process through which the child reaches a decision about the
strings presented. In both experiments, the connectives
turned out to be the class of real words with which the child
had the most difficulties. This result is evident at both age
levels studied in Experiment 2 (and in the first two levels
studied in Experiment 1). This supports the hypothesis that
for relational words the kind of knowledge which is necessary
to perform in a lexical decision task, namely the explicit
notion that these words are part of the language, may develop
more slowly. Beside this simple conclusion, the present
study shows that children can produce reliable and interpretable data in a lexical decision task even with classes of
words which are usually disregarded in most such studies.

8. CONCLUSIONS

The studies presented in this chapter offer different types
of evidence about the acquisition and development of the meaning of the connectives. The results obtained allow one to
reach some conclusions about the following points.

a) The progressive differentiation of meaning of the connectives, and of semantic distinctions the child acquires to
   make among different subclasses of these words.
b) The development of the notion of "wordness" the child has
   about connectives.
c) Some of the strategies the child uses in dealing with these
   words in different linguistic tasks.

   I will briefly present these conclusions, which are based
both on the results of the experiments discussed in this
chapter and on several clear indications obtained by a care-

ful examination of individual data such as the error pattern
for single subjects.

The Differentiation of Meaning of the Connectives

The main evidence comes from the results of Study 1: the two
experiments reported here, carried out with different populations of children and in two different languages, Dutch
and Italian, have provided results which are consistent with
each other, and which can be used as a basis to make some
inferences about the similarity and differentiation in meaning of the connectives, and about patterns of meaning overlap and meaning differentiation with increasing ages. This
evidence has been supplemented by the results obtained in the
sorting experiment of Study 2. The following conclusions are
based on both studies, although more directly on Study 1.

At a first stage, *because* is most readily differentiated
from the other connectives, while almost at the same time
before and *after* also are being differentiated from the other
connectives. *So that* and *in order to* are the next to differentiate, although they are sometimes still confused with *because* or with *before/after*. *Unless* and *although* are the last
to become available to the child with their own meaning.
Briefly, *causal* and *temporal* connectives seem the first to be
differentiated, *final* and *consecutive* come last. The patterns
of confusion of the connectives are quite intriguing. Temporal connectives are the least confused with others. However, when, especially early in development, they are confused with other connectives they tend to be confused with
causal and *final*. The causal connectives are sometimes confused with the consecutive and the concessive ones, the final
can be confused with the consecutive, and the concessive with
the consecutive. These patterns of confusion suggest that
the differentiation of the meaning of these words does not
take place at random, but along dimensions which are clearly
interpretable: for example, the causal and the final connectives possess a temporal component which is reflected in the
confusion among connectives.

On the basis of the results we can propose the following
stages of development in knowledge about the connectives.
At a first stage, probably earlier than at the lowest age
level explored in our studies, only few connectives, such as
because, are normally used by the child correctly in sentences. Most connectives still may not have any specific
meaning for the child. These words gradually become recognized and perhaps repeated by the child, but the specific
meaning of most of them still remains unknown. Most of the

connectives would probably be mutually substitutable in a
context without any problem for the child.

At this level the child may understand that the connective
has a given relational function within a complex sentence,
but he tends to rely on other syntactic, semantic and especially pragmatic cues to construct the meaning of the
sentence as a whole and probably even to infer the meaning
of the connective. The specific meanings of the single words
differentiate then gradually along the above mentioned lines
and the child becomes able to make clear distinctions of the
meaning of these words, first only of some, then of the most
ones, within appropriate contexts. Gradually, the child
reaches the lexical competence of the adult speaker, and is
capable of correctly performing with these linguistic units
in tasks which rely on a complex and "sophisticated" mastery
of the meaning of these words.

Children's Strategies in Processing Connectives

The analysis of the individual responses of Experiment 2 of
Study 1 have shown that when a child does not know the meaning of some connectives and is requested to perform in a
task in which the "unknown" words have to be used, he does
not seem to operate at random. Instead, the children of our
Study 1 seemed to rely on several alternative ways of dealing with the material, which can be regarded as strategies
which guided the children's performance. I have briefly
summarized these strategies at the end of the discussion of
Study 1.

While familiarity with a connective, or physical similarity
with a familiar connective, seem the two strongest operating
principles at a first stage of development, exclusion of a
known word as inappropriate is possibly a strong principle at
a second stage, and partial overlap in meaning is a principle
operating at a further stage.

The Notion of "Wordness" about the Connectives

The knowledge that a given string of letters or a sequence
of speech sounds is a word of a language is a part of the
linguistic competence a speaker has about the language in
question. This notion develops in the child more slowly than
the comprehension and use of words (see e.g. Papandropoulou
and Sinclair, 1974). How important this metalinguistic notion
is for language acquisition and language use is not of central
concern here. I have tried to trace the course of the development of this notion for the connectives — as an instance of

function words — in the attempt to explain why relational and function words are so "different" for the child.

The data obtained in the lexical decision experiments here presented are very clear. The knowledge that connectives are "words" of Dutch develops more slowly than the corresponding knowledge about nouns and adjectives. At an early stage (around 7 years) connectives are considered as non-words about as often as legal non-words are considered words. At the same age, on the other hand, nouns and adjectives are considered by the child to be words almost all of the time.

Notice that this notion is not to be confounded with the "concreteness" of the referent. The child does not confuse the notion of wordness with the notion of "being a real or a concrete thing". The data, as well as observations in pilot studies, show that the child of 7 years can decide that a noun is a word, whether it be a concrete or an abstract noun. Moreover, in the case of the adjectives this distinction does not apply, and the child seems to do with adjectives as well as with nouns. Even when the child correctly decides that a connective is a word, the decision latency is longer than the lexical decision latencies for nouns and adjectives. There is clearly a different rate of development of the notion of wordness about the connectives and other classes of words. This difference has disappeared by adulthood.

Differentiation of Meaning of the Connectives: The Sorting Task

With the sorting experiment, as in the Flores d'Arcais(1978b) study, I have tried to obtain some evidence about the structure of the internal lexicon of the child for the class of the connectives. The data obtained have to be interpreted at two levels. First, they give us another indication about the development of metalinguistic notions about these words: while children use clear semantic criteria to sort nouns, they tend to sort the connectives on the basis of physical similarity. Performance on the connectives, therefore, does not seem to depend on miscomprehension of the task, for in such cases they should adopt the same criterion for sorting out nouns. Instead, the children seem to use different criteria for the two different classes of words. Meaning seems to become attached to the two classes of words in a different way, and at different stages of linguistic development. Nouns seem to acquire a meaning even in isolation much earlier than connectives.

Second, the data obtained tell us something about the process of gradual acquisition of meaning of some of the connectives, and of the progressive differentiation of the different classes of connectives.

With respect to the ways in which, through the age levels, the different connectives gradually emerge with a clear meaning and the different semantic classes take shape within the class of the connectives, the data provide a picture which is consistent with the data obtained in the experiments of Study 1. In this sense they add to the reliability of the conclusions drawn on the basis of Study 1, and already discussed.

Children's Knowledge and Use of the Connectives

Acquisition of the connectives seems to develop much later and more slowly than that of content words. The conclusions about the knowledge of the meaning of the connectives which we can reach on the basis of comprehension tasks using full sentences, such as "acting out" tasks with toys, give us only a somewhat deceptive picture of the semantic competence of the child. The full knowledge of the meaning of the words we have studied develops more slowly than the available data on understanding of complex sentences have led us to think, and is characterized by different aspects.

There is a clear difference between the performance in one type of task and in other tasks. At a given age the child might be capable of performing correctly in one task, but not yet in another one. The knowledge necessary to understand one word in a context is different from the knowledge required to distinguish a word from another, to judge equivalence of meaning, to decide that a connective is a word, or to perform at a very abstract level necessary to sort out words according to meaning. The process of acquisition of the meaning of words is probably not uncomplicated, and different levels of meaning and of knowledge are likely to be involved. For words like the connectives, the process seems to be very long, and the last level, which includes some meta-linguistic knowledge about these words, is probably not completed even at the end of the first school cycle.

ACKNOWLEDGEMENTS

Part of the experiments reported in this study have been supported by a Z.W.O. Research Grant through the Dutch Psychonomic Foundation.

The two experiments of Study 3, Lexical Decision, have been carried out by I.E. de Vos and C. Verduin, both supported by a special grant of the Faculty of Social Science of Leiden University (Knelpuntenreserve). The data for Study 2 have

been collected by I.E. de Vos. Dr R. Schreuder has prepared
for Study 3 one of his elegant programs: his contribution is
here gratefully acknowledged.

The paper has been entirely written at the Max Planck
Institute for Psycholinguistics in Nijmegen.

For the partial relief of teaching and administration duties
during the execution of the work here reported and writing
of this chapter I am grateful to my colleagues of the Vakgroep
Psychologische Funktieleer in Leiden.

I wish to thank Dr R. Jarvella for insightful comments and
for several substantial suggestions regarding style and read-
ability of the manuscript, Professor W. Klein for comments on
an earlier version of it, and Dr M. Bierwisch for a friendly
and helpful discussion on the structure and content of the
chapter.

NOTE

1 The words have been chosen when the frequency values of
the spoken language (de Jong, 1979) had not yet been published. Of the 20 connectives chosen for the sorting
experiments — and for the 1978b study (Flores d'Arcais,
1978b) 5 do not show up in the frequency count. These were
words lowest in frequency in the count of the 20 chosen
on the basis of the written language frequency counts (Uit
den Boogaard, 1973). The relative frequencies of the remaining 15 connectives do correspond very closely in the
two frequency counts: the rank correlation between the two
frequency distributions is Spearman's ρ = 0.85.

REFERENCES

Anglin, J. (1973). "The Growth of Word Meaning". Cambridge,
Mass.: MIT Press.
Bloom, L., Lahey, M., Hood, L., Lifter, K. and Fiess, K. (1980).
Complex sentences: Acquisition of syntactic connectives and
the semantic relations they encode. *Journal of Child
Language* 7, 235-261.
Bogaard, Uit den, P.C. (1973). "Woord Frequenties". Utrecht:
Oosthoek, Scheltema en Holkema.
Clark, E.V. (1971). On the acquisition of the meaning of
before and *after*. *Journal of Verbal Learning and Verbal
Behavior* 10, 266-275.
Clark, E.V. (1979). "The Ontogenesis of Meaning". Wiesbaden:
Athenaion.
Clark, H.H. (1968). On the use and meaning of prepositions.
Journal of Verbal Learning and Verbal Behavior 7, 421-431.

Deese, J. (1965). "The Structure of Associations in Language and Thought". Baltimore: The John Hopkins Press.

Fillenbaum, S. and Rapoport, A. (1971). "Structures in the Subjective Lexicon". New York: Academic Press.

Flores d'Arcais, G.B. (1978a). The acquisition of subordinating constructions in child language. *In* "Language Development and Mother-Child Interaction" (R.N. Campbell and P.T. Smith, eds). New York: Plenum Press.

Flores d'Arcais, G.B. (1978b). Levels of semantic knowledge in children's use of connectives. *In* "The Child's Conception of Language" (A. Sinclair, R.J. Jarvella and W.J.M. Levelt, eds). Berlin-Heidelberg: Springer.

Flores d'Arcais, G.B. (1979). The acquisition of connectives. Paper presented at the Conference on "Beyond Description in Child Language". Nijmegen, June 1979.

Grimm, H. and Schöler, H. (1972). Semantic organization of German spatial prepositions. Mimeo-Psychologisches Institut, University of Heidelberg.

Johnson, S.C. (1967). Hierarchical clustering schemes. *Psychometrika* 32, 241-254.

Jong, S. de. (1979). "Spreektaalfrequenties". Utrecht: Oosthoek, Scheltema en Holkema.

Marshall, J.C. and Newcombe, F. (1966). Syntactic and semantic errors in paralexia. *Neuropsychologia* 4, 169-176.

Miller, G.A. (1971). Empirical methods in the study of semantics. *In* "Semantics: An Interdisciplinary Reader in Philosophy, Linguistics and Psychology" (D.D. Steinberg and L.A. Jakobovits, eds). Cambridge: Cambridge University Press.

Papandropoulou, I. and Sinclair, H. (1974). What is a word? Experimental study of children's ideas on grammar. *Human Development*, 241-258.

Schvaneveldt, R., Ackermann, B.P. and Semlear, T. (1977). The effect of semantic context on children's word recognition. *Child Development* 48, 612-616.

Thurstone, L.L. (1927). A law of comparative judgment. *Psychological Review* 34, 273-286.

LEXICAL INNOVATIONS: HOW CHILDREN LEARN TO CREATE NEW WORDS

EVE V. CLARK

*Department of Linguistics, Stanford University,
Stanford, California, USA.*

1. INTRODUCTION

As speakers, we often find ourselves in situations where
there appears to be no word that is quite appropriate for the
entity or event we wish to convey to a listener. At such
times we have recourse to coinage and create new lexical items
from the lexical resources available in our language. And we
create these new lexical items in just such a way that our
listeners will be able to compute the intended meanings,
readily and uniquely, on each occasion of use. Although it
often goes unnoticed, the process of coining new words — new
meanings expressed with forms that fit the word-formation
paradigms of the language — is widespread in adult speech
(e.g. Brekle, 1977; Clark and Clark, 1979; Downing, 1977;
Gleitman and Gleitman, 1970). It is no less widespread in
children's speech and, I will argue, serves the same function —
that of filling lexical gaps. Moreover, in children's speech
coinages provide a window on the developmental process whereby
children acquire both the adult conventions governing the
creation of new meanings and the conventions on uses of the
word-forms that carry those meanings. In the present chapter,
I shall consider both sides of this coin: the kinds of *meanings* young children create and the *forms* they employ for their
expression.

To keep the two sides of the coin distinct, the chapter is
divided into two parts. In the first, I take up the *why* of
children's lexical creativity — why they create new meanings and the circumstances under which they do this. Under
this heading I will consider the evidence that children's
lexical innovations play the same role, communicatively, as
the adults', and I will draw on illustrations from a variety
of sources: diaries, vocabulary studies, and my own

observational and experimental data, mainly from children
aged between two and six. In the second part of the chapter,
I take up the *how* of children's lexical innovations — the
forms they pick to express their new meanings during the
early stages of acquisition. Under this heading I will look
at the available evidence for a developmental sequence in the
word-formational devices children rely on, and will back the
observational data with some experimental data on the comprehension and elicitation of those word-forms acquired early
in acquisition. Although I shall discuss meanings and forms
separately, they clearly go hand-in-hand for both child and
adult speakers of a language. However, the child's knowledge
of the possibilities is limited on both sides and it is therefore worthwhile considering them, for the moment, as if they
were acquired separately.

2. LEXICAL INNOVATIONS

2.1 *Lexical Gaps*

The lexical inventories of languages differ and no language
has words for every possible concept its speakers might want
to talk about. The result is that the stock of vocabulary is
constantly renewed through the acceptance of those newly
coined meanings that are useful enough for large groups of
speakers to take up and add to the idiomatic or well-established meanings already in the lexicon. Many innovations,
of course, remain nonce uses — coinages that were quite
interpretable on the occasion of their use but failed to re-
tain a permanent place in the lexicon. But even the nonce
uses of lexical innovations *fill lexical gaps*. They supply
a meaning not otherwise expressed by any lexical items available to the speaker in question (cf. Lehrer, 1970; Lyons,
1977).

   Lexical gaps may be *momentary* — as when someone has difficulty retrieving the right word form from memory — or
chronic — where there is no word form that is conventionally
used to express that particular meaning. In order to fill
chronic gaps, there are three general conditions that must
pertain. First, the exact meaning to be expressed must not
be expressed by any other lexeme already in the lexicon.
(This condition is violated in the case of momentary gaps,
where the gap results from loss of memory or some retrieval
difficulty that prevents the speaker from coming up with the
form conventionally used for a particular meaning. Fromkin
(1973) cites a number of speech errors where speakers constructed new word forms in lieu of those conventionally used.)

Secondly, the new meaning has to be carried by an appropriate form, one that fits the word-formation rules of the language in question. And thirdly, the speaker and listener must jointly observe whatever conventions govern the use of such innovative meanings in such a way that the innovation will be readily understood as the speaker intends it on the occasion of its use.

These three general conditions on chronic gaps are so frequently met on an everyday basis that most of us do not even notice how often we process lexical innovations in the course of understanding utterances. As long as the utterance containing an innovation is interpretable in context, we tend to take it for granted. Only when we pause to reflect might we notice that we have just heard a new verb formed from a noun ("I've got to *launderette* those sheets", meaning "take those sheets to be washed at the launderette"), a new noun compound ("Why don't you sit in the *apple-juice-chair*?", meaning "the chair nearest the glass of apple-juice on the table"), or a new derived agentive noun ("Dare to be a *juicer*!", meaning "a drinker of juice", from an advertisement on a bottle of apple juice). These meanings are all novel in that they are not expressed by any well-established expressions already in the English lexicon. Despite their innovative status, each of them is easily interpreted in context.

Both adults and children, I claim, fill lexical gaps, but the process of filling gaps is in one case the same and in the other different for the two populations. Like adults, children may experience momentary gaps: when they have difficulty retrieving a known word form, they may construct a new one on the spot. Two examples from my data are the construction of *sleeper* (in lieu of *bed*) by a three-year-old, and the construction of *pourer* (in lieu of *cup*) by a four-year-old. These children knew the correct terms, but because of a passing difficulty in retrieving the "right" words, constructed alternatives. (These momentary forms are often corrected seconds later when the right word comes through.)

The process is different, however, for chronic gaps. Adults fill what are gaps in the adult lexicon: ideally, they work from what is already *in* the well-established vocabulary and only coin new words where there are discernible gaps that require filling on particular occasions, e.g. the verb *to charcoal* (meaning, make into charcoal, said of potatoes that boiled dry). Children, though, have not yet mastered the adult lexicon. What they know about it is not only fragmentary; it can change from day to day as they acquire additional well-established lexical items. As a result, they may fill many chronic gaps that are *not* gaps for adult

speakers (e.g. *to needle* in lieu of *mend*, *to nipple* in lieu of
nurse, *a fixer* in lieu of *tool*, *a plant-man* in lieu of *gardener*) in addition to those that are gaps for adults. One
way to differentiate these two situations is to characterize
the innovations adults produce as *legitimate innovations*:
these fill true gaps in the (adult) lexicon where there are
meanings to be expressed that lack any conventional (well-
established) means for doing so. Children, in contrast, produce both *legitimate* and *illegitimate* innovations. Their
legitimate innovations fill true chronic gaps and could as
well have been produced by adults, while their illegitimate
ones fill what are currently gaps in the child's but not in
the adult's lexicon.
    Illegitimate innovations are illegitimate precisely because
they are pre-empted for adult speakers by the existence of
well-established lexical items with the requisite meanings.
Illegitimate innovations, such as the verbs *to needle* and *to
broom*, should therefore give way to the appropriate well-
established terms, here *to mend* and *to sweep*, as soon as
children acquire them. The criterion for legitimacy for
children's innovations is simply the existence of a gap in
the adult lexicon. For a child innovation to be illegitimate,
then, it must coincide in meaning with some well-established
lexical item that takes precedence or pre-empts that innovation.
    Lexical innovations in adult speech are relatively easy to
detect, although what's an innovation for one speaker may not
be for another (Clark and Clark, 1979). In children's speech,
detection should be rather more of a problem. First, their
legitimate innovations may be underestimated by the observer
just because they conform or appear to conform to the adult
conventions on innovation and will thus be less noticeable
than illegitimate innovations. The latter by their very
nature will be more noticeable and more likely to be noted in
diary and vocabulary studies. Second, children's lexical
creativity may be further underestimated wherever their innovations happen to coincide with actual well-established forms.
For example, a child might coin the agentive noun *gardener*
from *garden*, meaning "the person who usually works in the
garden". Such innovations will generally be indistinguishable from all the other well-established terms that children
have picked up wholesale from the adult speakers around them.
Re-creations, like *gardener*, coincident with well-established
or conventional adult forms, will be virtually undetectable
as innovations.
    The hypothesis I am putting forward is that filling chronic
lexical gaps provides the major motivation for both adult and

child innovations in the lexicon. Adults have little reason
to duplicate exactly meanings that are already expressed by
well-established lexical items and indeed avoid doing so
(e.g. Motsch, 1965; Bolinger, 1977). But filling a lexical
gap, for adults, has an obvious communicative function: it
allows a speaker to be more precise in conveying his intended
meaning on a particular occasion where no well-established
term is entirely adequate to the task.

What would constitute evidence for or against this hypothesis in the case of children's innovations? Evidence for
such an hypothesis would be children's making up new words —
new meanings — where they lacked other words to express
their meanings, e.g. the agentive noun *fix-man* in the absence
of *mechanic*. Such innovations should be more likely to occur
in domains where children's vocabulary of available terms is
relatively small, and the innovations they produce should
contrast in meaning with the vocabulary items they have already acquired. On the other hand, it would be evidence
against the hypothesis if children coined synonyms for meanings they had already acquired, and simply used innovations
and well-established terms interchangeably with no contrast
in meaning.

In fact, there is considerable evidence *for* the hypothesis.
First, even very young children treat words as if they contrast in meaning. Upon learning a new animal term like *horse*,
for example, they will narrow the domain of a previously
over-extended term, *dog*, in order to contrast it with the
new term just acquired (e.g. Clark, 1978). Moreover, there
is evidence from the language acquisition of bilingual children that at one stage they will reject having two separate
labels (from different languages) for the same entity and,
for instance, will accept only one of *dog* and *perro* or of
water and *agua* (e.g. Fantini, 1976). Children also seem to
assume that any new words introduced to them by adults contrast with the known set they co-occur with. Thus, children
introduced to the term *chromium* in the context of other colour
terms, took it to be a colour term that contrasted with the
ones they already knew (Carey, 1978); and, introduced to a
novel (nonsense) word in the physical context of objects
differing in either colour or shape, children took it to encode a colour in the one case, a shape in the other (Dockrell,
1979).[1][†]

[†] Superscript numerals refer to notes which are to be found
at the end of the chapter.

Secondly, more direct evidence for the hypothesis comes from children's lexical innovations. I will present illustrations from three domains: (1) children's coining of innovative denominal verbs, (2) their coining of names for subcategories, and (3) their coining of new agent and instrument nouns. In all three domains, as in most adult innovations, precision of communication appears to be what is at stake (e.g. Downing, 1977; Clark and Clark, 1979). To take the first domain of examples, why do children coin new verbs? Children are much slower in mastering well-established verb-meanings than they are in mastering noun-meanings (e.g. Clark, 1978; Gentner, 1978; Huttenlocher, 1979). As a result, they have few verbs available early on for talking about a large range of actions. To communicate about particular actions, many children take up the option of coining new verbs from nouns where the noun in question designates one of the objects involved in the particular action being talked about. Some typical examples of such denominal verbs from English-speaking children are listed in Table 1. Such verbs are also coined by young children acquiring other languages (see Clark, in press). The importance of such innovative verbs is that they allow small children — as young as two — to be very precise, in context, about the actions they are talking about.

TABLE 1 *Some typical examples of innovative denominal verbs (based on Clark, in press).*

1.	S	(2;4, wanting to have some cheese weighed): *You have to scale it.*
2.	EB	(2;8, after roaring with "claws" outstretched at a towel): *I monstered that towel.*
3.	S	(3;0, watching a truck pass): *It's trucking.*
4.	S	(3;2, putting on a cowboy hat, fastened with a bead-and-string): *String me up, mommy.*
5.	CB	(3;11, putting crackers in her soup): *I'm crackering my soup.*
6.	JA	(4;0, playing the role of a doctor dealing with a broken arm): *We're gonna cast it.*
7.	ME	(4;11, talking about Christmas trees): *We already decorationed our tree.*
8.	JW	(5;7, hitting a ball with a stick): *I'm sticking it and that makes it go really fast.*

Secondly, in labelling things, even very young children set up contrasts and will divide up known categories into subcategories. But since they lack well-established terms for each subcategory (and these may be lacking altogether in the language), they may opt to coin new compound nouns — combining two (or more) nouns with the appropriate stress pattern and modifier-head word order.[2] One child, for example, at 1;11 contrasted *baby-bottle* (a bottle used when she was a baby) with *bottle* alone (Leopold, 1949). Another, aged 2;0, distinguished fried from boiled eggs (her breakfast fare) with the expressions *plate-egg* and *cup-egg*. The same child distinguished dogs in general, *dog*, from a particular yellow dog found at the site of a local fire and subsequently given to a neighbouring child, by use of the compound *fire-dog*, which she used frequently in requests for a similar pet (Pelsma, 1910). Other two-year-olds I have observed consistently contrasted subcategories by means of such compounds: one distinguished kinds of smoke such as *house-smoke* (from a chimney) versus *car-smoke* (exhaust), and another kept his T-shirts apart with the same device, with *butterfly-shirt*, for instance, for the one with a butterfly design on it. While I have listed only a few examples here, they are widespread both in the vocabulary and diary literature and in my own longitudinal records.

The third domain of innovations illustrated here is that of agent and instrument nouns. Young children will construct new compound nouns for these categories, e.g. the spontaneous *fix-man* (for a car mechanic), *garden-man* (for a gardener), or *rat-man* (for a man who worked with rats in a psychology laboratory, a colleague of the child's father) — all from two-year-olds. Moreover, children as young as two-and-a-half or three will coin such terms on demand. In an elicitation study, Barbara Hecht and I specified meanings — describing what the agent or instrument did — and asked young children for a way of conveying those meanings. Examples typical of the agentive forms we elicited are shown in the top half of Table 2. The commonest type of compound noun children produced combined a noun or verb base as the first element with the noun *-man* in second place, as in *fire-man* and *sweep-man*. This type fits a common adult pattern for constructing agent nominals. These children sometimes marked the agent redundantly, adding an *-er* to the verb base in addition to combining it with the noun *-man*, as in *hitter-man*. This pattern is comparatively rare in adult English, and the occasional well-established form like *fisherman* seems an unlikely model for children this age to work from. Since the derivational ending *-er* marks instruments as well as agents in English,

it could be that the children add *-man* to a *verb + er* form
just to make quite clear they are designating an agent and not
an instrument. (The older children tended to opt simply for
the forms composed of a *base + er* to mark agents.) Some
typical instrument nouns coined by the same children are
shown in the bottom half of Table 2. The head nouns (in second place) were usually *-thing* or *-machine*, and they followed a verb base, a verb + *ing*, a verb + *er*, or a noun base.[3]
Again, older children tended to opt for forms combining a
noun or verb base with the derivational *-er* ending, just as
for the agent nouns.

TABLE 2   *Typical agent and instrument nominals elicited from
young children (based on Clark and Hecht, in prep.).*

A. Agent nominals: some compound forms produced by three-
                     year-olds

  1. *fire-man* = someone who burns things[a]

  2. *sweep-man* = someone who sweeps things

  3. *smile-person* = someone who smiles at people

  4. *hitter-man* = someone who hits things

  5. *kicker-man* = someone who kicks things

  6. *reader-man* = someone who reads things

  7. *hider-man* = someone who hides things

B. Instrument nominals: some compound forms produced by
                        three- to five-year-olds

  1. *jumping-thing* = thing for jumping with[a]

  2. *hugging-machine* = thing for hugging people

  3. *eating-thing* = thing for eating with

  4. *knock-thing* = thing for knocking with

  5. *blow-machine* = machine for blowing with

  6. *package-machine* = machine for pushing things

  7. *rock-machine* = machine for throwing things

  8. *kicker-machine* = machine for kicking things

---

[a]The glosses represent the meanings given to the child for
which the pertinent form was elicited.

What is important, for all three domains illustrated here, is that these children lacked other words to express these innovative meanings. This is particularly clear in the case of diary and vocabulary records, but it was also the case for our experimentally elicited innovations. The children did not have other terms to express the meanings we offered since we deliberately chose meanings for which there was not any obvious English word. These data, then, offer strong preliminary support to the hypothesis that children, like adults, innovate in order to fill lexical gaps.

2.2 *Contextual Innovations*

Do children's innovations have any particular properties, apart from the variety of forms they draw on in their coinages? As the glosses in Table 2 suggest, the context is often, and maybe always, critical to the meaning being expressed. Without the gloss — here the meaning offered to the child for expression — there is no way to tell that the combination of *fire* and *man* in the compound *fire-man* on this occasion designated not someone who puts out fires (the well-established adult meaning of this form) but someone who sets fire to things. Equally, the meaning of *rock-machine* is not a transparent composition of the two constituent nouns, *rock* and *machine*. One has to know that on this occasion, the machine so designated was one that could throw rocks rather than grind them up, arrange them in lines, polish them, or the myriad other activities that could link rocks and machines. Without the context, utterances containing innovations like these are often uninterpretable. Although we supplied the meanings in these instances, this dependence on context is just as typical of children's spontaneous coinages as of those we elicited.

Elsewhere, I have characterized innovations like these — dependent on context on the occasion of their use for proper interpretation — as *contextuals* (Clark and Clark, 1979). They contrast with innovations whose interpretation can be computed from the composition of the constituent elements of the innovative expression alone. For instance, adjectives plus the ending *-ness* all have the meaning "quality of being X", as in *smoothness, quickness, flashiness,* etc., while most verb stems plus *-able* have the interpretation "possible to be X-ed", as in *houseable, rideable,* etc.[4] (see Aronoff, 1976). The combination of ending plus base in such cases makes for a predictable meaning, a composition of the parts.

Contextuals, as a type of innovation, have the following properties:

1) They have an indefinitely large number of potential senses. An innovative denominal verb (like *launderette*), a compound noun (like *apple-juice chair*) or a derived noun (like *juicer*) could be used with one sense on occasion, another on another, and so on. This, I would argue, also appears typical of many child innovations. For example, one two-year-old I have been recording used the noun *broom* as a verb on one occasion to mean "hit with a broom" and on another to mean "sweep with a broom" (an illegitimate coinage given the existence of adult *sweep*).

2) Contextuals depend for their interpretation on the context in which they are produced. As a result, they bear a strong resemblance in many ways to indexicals or deictic terms such as *he* or *there*. This dependence on context is especially obvious when it comes to interpreting children's innovations: without contextual information, they are usually just as opaque as children's uses of deictics like *that* or general purpose verbs like *do*.

3) Contextuals demand cooperation between the speaker and the listener in the following way: the speaker has to assess what the listener knows or could infer from the context, and the listener has to use clues from the context plus any other facts he could assume the speaker would expect him to use in arriving at the speaker's intended interpretation of the innovation. With children, such deliberate cooperation is usually lacking, but the fact that young children restrict much of their conversation to the here-and-how allows it by default. The adult listener can nearly always rely on the context to provide clues to the child-speaker's meaning for an innovative term.

Among adults, speakers and listeners rely on conventions governing such innovations in order to arrive at the intended interpretations. These conventions spell out the conditions under which the speaker can expect the listener to arrive at a readily computable, unique interpretation on each particular occasion of use. This is done essentially by considering both the expression itself — in the examples given above: a denominal verb, a compound noun, or a derived noun — and the speaker's and listener's mutual knowledge in a particular context of use.

The adult convention on innovative denominal verbs takes the following form, where the first five conditions seem to be conditions that would apply to any contextual:

The Innovative Denominal Verb Convention In using an innovative denominal verb, the speaker means to denote:

1) the kind of situation
2) he has good reason to believe
3) that on this occasion the listener can readily compute
4) uniquely
5) on the basis of their mutual knowledge
6) such that the parent noun denotes one role in the situation and the remaining surface arguments of the denominal
   verb denote other roles in the situation (Clark and Clark,
   1979, p. 787).

The sixth condition applies specifically to innovative denominal verbs, and the form of this condition would clearly
change for each type of contextual — denominal adjectives,
compound nouns, derived agent and instrument nouns, and so
on, to name just a few such categories in English. However,
the first five conditions specify the general circumstances
required for the appropriate interpretation of contextuals,
specifying their dependence on mutual knowledge and context
for ready computation of a unique meaning by the listener.

A convention of this type places constraints on what can be
used as an innovation — in this instance, which nouns can be
used as innovative denominal verbs. However, children do
not yet observe these constraints and therefore produce a
number of illegitimate innovations alongside their legitimate
ones. A major constraint imposed by the denominal verb convention can be called the principle of pre-emption by synonymy.
Innovations are pre-empted or accounted illegitimate if there
is a common term already in the language with just the meaning
the innovation was intended to have. For denominal verbs there
are several subtypes of such pre-emption.

First, there is pre-emption by suppletion, where there already exists some other verb (morphologically unrelated to the
parent noun of the (potential) innovation) with just the meaning the innovation would have supplied. For example, among
vehicle terms in English, noun/verb pairs form a highly productive paradigm (*taxi/to taxi, canoe/to canoe, helicopter/to
helicopter*, etc.) but there are some striking exceptions.
Neither *car* nor *aeroplane* fits the verb paradigm since, for
adult speakers, the verbs *drive* and *fly* fill the respective
meaning slots for these two vehicles. The verb *drive* is in a
suppletive relation to the noun *car* since it pre-empts use of
to car for the meaning "go by vehicle".

Suppletion accounts for the illegitimacy of one child example mentioned earlier, the verb *broom*. For adults, the
noun *broom* is not a member of the noun/verb paradigm of instruments that can be exemplified by pairs like *saw/to saw, ham-
mer/to hammer*, and so on. *Broom* is paired with *to sweep*,
which pre-empts the use of *broom* as a verb with the meaning,

"clean with a broom". Other examples of where children fail
to use the adult suppletive forms are *scale* for *weigh*, *nipple*
for *nurse*, *gun* for *shoot*, and *axe* for *chop*. Failure to use
suppletion is a common source of illegitimate child innovations among denominal verbs (Clark, in press).

A second type of pre-emption by synonymy is pre-emption by
entrenchment. Although one can form the verb *to jail* from
the noun *jail*, one cannot use *to prison*, from *prison*, meaning "to put into prison", because of the existence in the
language of the verb *imprison* with just that meaning. And one
can *house* someone (from the parent noun *house*) but not *hospital* someone ("put into a hospital") because of the prior existence of *hospitalize*. In all cases of entrenchment there is
already in use a verb derived ultimately from the same parent
noun, with just the meaning that would be carried by the proposed innovation. The verbs already entrenched in language,
like *imprison*, *enthrone*, or *hospitalize*, take precedence over
the innovations. Because children often lack the necessary
adult knowledge of the lexicon, they produce illegitimate
innovations of this type.

A third type of pre-emption by synonymy is pre-emption by
ancestry. If the potential parent noun the speaker uses is
itself derived from another noun or verb base, then that
noun cannot normally become the parent of an innovative denominal verb. Consider the noun *baker*. This noun cannot give
rise to a verb *baker* with the meaning "do what a baker would
do professionally" in the way *butcher* can give rise to *to
butcher*, because the noun *baker* itself was originally derived
from the verb *to bake* which has just the meaning in question.
Equally, the noun *farmer* does not provide for *to farmer* because the meaning ("to do what a farmer would do professionally") is itself carried by the (denominal) verb *to farm* from
which the noun *farmer* derives.[5] The morphological relations
in cases of ancestry are usually transparent so it is normally
clear that a particular noun is related by both meaning and
form to a particular source. Children also produce illegitimate innovations of this type; for instance, they use a
noun like *decoration* as the parent noun of a verb, *to decoration* — presumably because they do not know *to decorate* or
fail to recognize the synonymy of *to decorate* and *to decoration*.

A second principle that seems to place constraints on innovations, although it does not seem to have such force as the
avoidance of synonymy, is the principle of pre-emption by
homonymy. This constraint covers coincidence of forms with
difference of meanings. If a potential innovation coincides
in form with a common verb, say, that has a quite different

meaning, the innovation tends to be avoided. For example, although one can use all sorts of car names as verbs where that level of specificity is required ("He didn't VW to New York, he Chevied"), one would avoid saying *He Forded to New York* (meaning "go by Ford car") because of the presence of the common verb *to ford*, meaning "to cross by a ford". Equally, *to Dodge*, meaning "go by Dodge car", is avoided because of *to dodge*, "to evade pursuit". And while season names like *winter* and *summer* occur as verbs, the potential verbs *spring* and *fall* are pre-empted by the common verbs *fall* ("let drop") and *to spring* ("to jump"). There seem to be relatively few instances of children's using illegitimate innovations of this type. However, one could perhaps consider here such uses as *button* ("turn on by pressing a button") pre-empted by adult *button*, "fasten by means of a button"; *key* ("open with a key"), pre-empted by adult "make a key for"; *needle* ("mend with a needle"), pre-empted by adult "irritate"; and *cement* ("make cement"), pre-empted by adult "put cement on".

Since children produce numerous illegitimate innovations, both among their denominal verbs and in other categories of innovations, it is clear that, for them as for adult speakers, filling gaps is relative to what vocabulary one knows. The difference is that adults normally know a great deal more vocabulary — and hence the meanings conventionally available — in their language. This knowledge, in combination with the conventions on innovations, is what constrains the process of innovation. Young children, however, at first have only a limited vocabulary, and while they add to it steadily, both through the acquisition of well-established lexical items and through coinages, it takes them a long time to acquire the vocabulary that limits innovations. As a result, they produce both illegitimate and legitimate innovations, with the former only lessening in number as they acquire more vocabulary. This finding, observed first for children's denominal verbs (Clark, in press), also seems to hold for innovative nominals, both in the diary and vocabulary study data and in our experiments (Clark and Hecht, in prep.). Children produce a number of illegitimate innovations in lieu of the terms adult speakers would normally use. They also, of course, produce many quite legitimate innovative nominals - innovations that fill true gaps in the adult lexicon.

In summary, innovations drawn from three areas of the lexicon — denominal verbs, object nominals, and agent and instrument nominals — strongly suggest that children, like adults, coin new words in order to communicate more precisely what they mean. They are engaged in filling chronic lexical gaps.

But innovations are constrained by the well-established lexicon, so the elimination of illegitimate innovations depends on children's acquisition of the pertinent well-established vocabulary, an acquisition that takes considerable time.

3. CONSTRUCTING LEXICAL FORMS

Once children have decided what meaning they want to express, they have to select a form appropriate to convey it. With well-established or idiomatic lexical items, meaning and form are already joined, in that knowing the one is inextricably linked to knowing the other. But with innovative meanings, children have to learn to select appropriate word forms for their expression from whatever stock they have available. The choice and construction of these word forms, and some of the principles that guide children's choices, are my second concern in this chapter.

3.1 *Three Principles*

The first of the principles to be considered here — the one I shall focus on most — is what I will call the *principle of productivity*. This principle states that those word formation devices that are the most productive, relatively speaking, should be the most available to children, and should therefore be acquired earlier and used in preference to less productive devices. By productivity, I mean the degree to which a particular pattern of word formation may be used as a model for new lexical items (Adams, 1972; Aronoff, 1976). For example, in forming new agent nouns in English, the suffix *-er* is more productive than either *-ist* or *-ian*, so *-er* should be acquired earlier than the other two suffixes. The principle of productivity has as its corollary the following strategy for children forming new words:

  S1: Look for the commonest device that expresses the desired meaning

Reliance on this strategy predicts that the forms children will acquire earliest will be those most readily available to them, namely those that are more productive. Children acquiring the same language will presumably pick up the same forms: initially these will probably be few in number, depending on the domains in which children coin new words. This prediction will be considered in light of some of the more productive word formation devices for coining certain types of new verbs and nouns in English, and in light of the types of word forms used by adults speaking to young children.

The second principle to be considered here, which interacts
with productivity, is the *principle of semantic transparency*.
This principle states that those word formation devices that
mark their meaning clearly (i.e. with one-to-one matches of
meaning and form) are easier to acquire than those where multiple meanings are expressed by one form, or vice versa (see
Slobin, 1973, 1977). This principle enjoins children to use
as transparent a device as possible in constructing new word
forms. This suggests that the principle has two attendant
strategies:

S2: Look for devices that mark only one meaning.

and

S3: Look for devices that are words in their own right.

Reliance on the first strategy predicts, for instance, that
in forming new agent nouns, suffixes like *-ist* and *-ian*
should be acquired before *-er* because the *-er* form serves to
express instrumental as well as agentive meaning. But this prediction goes counter to the one based on productivity. Which
principle takes precedence? I will argue that productivity
does. In fact, it is not clear that the prediction from S2
is testable in English since the elements that mark only one
meaning, one could argue, are likely in English to be words in
their own right. For example, the noun *-man* added to a noun
or verb base marks agentive meaning and thus should be simpler
to acquire than the suffix *-er*. But *man* is a word in its own
right while *-er* isn't. So S3 really makes a more general prediction, that in acquisition, compounding, where the constituent elements are words, should be used before affixation.
This prediction is quite compatible with the prediction based
on productivity provided one assumes that children attend more
to productivity as they acquire more vocabulary and see which
lexical paradigms in the language express particular meanings.

A third principle that should play a role in word formation
is the *principle of regularization*. This principle asserts
that paradigms in language — the subsystems found in inflection and word formation — are regular in form (Clark and
Clark, 1977). The attendant strategy here in forming new words is:

S4: Use the same device everywhere to mark the same meaning.

This strategy is essentially equivalent to Slobin's (1973)
operating principle "Avoid exceptions" and is amply supported
by the data on children's acquisition of inflectional systems.   Reliance on this strategy, then, predicts that children will pick up on one device to mark a particular meaning and over-use it, much as they over-use *-ed* to mark

past tense in English or -*om* to mark the instrumental case in Russian. This regularization of lexical paradigms will give way to a more diverse set of options only when children find out more about the word formation devices available in the language.

The predictions, then, can be summarized as follows: first, children should pick the more productive devices initially and use them in preference to less productive devices in the language. Second, in order to mark their meaning for new lexical items clearly, as far as possible, they should pick devices that are words in their own right. Thirdly, the devices they pick up first should be over-used and therefore result in over-regular lexical paradigms.

Critical to testing these predictions is the presence of innovative lexical items in children's speech. Idiomatic or well-established word forms could have been picked up wholesale from adult speakers, without any analysis of the structure, and thus cannot yield any insight into children's knowledge of word formation. It is only when children construct new forms for new meanings that one can impute to them knowledge of the word formation devices being utilized. Children's innovations have been recorded in numerous diary and vocabulary studies, and they can also be elicited in experimental settings. I will draw on both types of data in assessing the predictions that follow from the principles of productivity, semantic transparency, and regularization.

The data considered here are mainly production data — lexical innovations produced spontaneously or on demand from children aged between two and six. First, I draw on seven vocabulary studies of children up to age three (Bateman, 1915; Bohn, 1914; Boyd, 1915; Brandenburg, 1915; Grant, 1916; Nice, 1915; Pelsma, 1910). All their complex word forms were extracted and divided into two categories: (a) idiomatic (well-established) items that could have been acquired directly from adults, and (b) innovative terms constructed by the children. The latter were normally flagged by the authors as having special or idiosyncratic meanings and identified as child coinages. I also cite example innovations from some recent diary studies and articles such as Bowerman (1974), Lord (1979), and my own longitudinal observations. Second, I rely on some data from elicitation studies where we created a situation in which children had to come up with a form for an agent or instrument that performed a specified action (Clark and Hecht, in prep.; Clark, Hecht and Mulford, in prep.). The third type of data cited is some comprehension data where we looked at when children were able to understand some of the linguistic properties of compounding in English (Clark and Morse, in prep.)

Together these data allow for a preliminary sketch of what
forms children acquire when, which forms they rely on initially to carry new meanings, and how productivity, semantic
transparency, and regularization affect the course of acquisition. Lastly, I draw on some unpublished data from Berko
Gleason[6] on the kinds of complex word forms adults use in
their speech to three-year-olds.

3.2. *Productivity*

Where do children get their word forms? The simple answer
to this question is, from the adults around them. But this
answer does not, by itself, provide any clue to which forms
children opt for when they first coin new words. The hypothesis put forward here is that contained in the principle
of productivity, that children acquire first the more productive word formation devices of the language. These devices are the ones used more frequently by adults and hence
should be more available to children than less productive
ones. I will take up two lines of evidence pertinent to
this hypothesis. First, I will consider the availability of
complex word forms as represented (a) in adult speech to
young children, and (b) in the well-established forms in the
three-year-old repertoire. After looking at the productivity
of some of these devices, I shall then consider their use
through a comparison of well-established and innovative forms
in children's spontaneous speech.
   Is there any evidence that adults use complex word forms in
talking to young children? One reason for even asking this
question is that there is growing evidence that adults "edit"
their syntax to some extent, select their vocabulary, and
clarify their phonology when talking to young children (Snow
and Ferguson, 1977). *A priori*, it wouldn't be surprising if
parents tried not to use complex forms at least to very
young children. However, when one considers items in the
well-established lexicon, such a possibility becomes rather
more remote: one does not stop and analyse the structure of
forms like *something, exactly, handful, supermarket,* or *screwdriver*. They are simply treated as lexical items on a par
with any others. To do an editing job on one's words on the
basis of their forms would probably be very difficult, especially with common, everyday expressions. Indeed, Berko
Gleason found that parents talking to their three-year-olds
in three different settings (playing shop, talking about pictures in a book, and taking a toy car to pieces) used a
variety of derivational affixes[7] as well as a number of compound nouns. The parents in these situations also coined

some new terms (e.g. *store-man*) and even used innovations
coined by their child (e.g. *fixer* or *fixer-thing* for one of
the tools used in taking the car apart). In other words,
these adults freely used many, if not all, of the word formation processes at their disposal even when talking to
children as young as three. They used some innovations
themselves in the settings studied, and they freely picked
up and used innovations produced by their children. Productive word formation devices, then, should be available
to children as models for constructing new words very early
in the process of acquisition.

The other source of information about the complex word
forms children have been exposed to is the forms found in
their well-established vocabulary. For example, the well-
established complex forms of agent nominals in the vocabulary of seven three-year-olds were split almost equally
between noun + noun compounds and noun or verb base + *er*
forms. Their complex instrument nominals fell into three
groups: noun + noun compounds, noun or verb base + *er*, and
verb + noun or noun + verb compounds. These forms are shown
in the left-hand column of Table 3. When all their complex
nominals were considered, 89% of the complex well-established
items had the form of noun + noun compounds.

TABLE 3 *Forms used for agent and instrument nominals in the
spontaneous speech of three-year-olds*

	Idiomatic (n=42)		Innovative (n=14)	
(i) Agents	$\left\{\begin{matrix}V\\N\end{matrix}\right\}$ + *er*	50%	$\left\{\begin{matrix}V\\N\end{matrix}\right\}$ + *er*	50%
	N + N[a]	45%	N + N	50%
	Idiomatic (n=141)		Innovative (n=20)	
	V + *er*	31%	V + *er*	25%
ii) Instruments	N + N	33%	N + N	35%
	$\left\{\begin{matrix}V + N\\N + V\end{matrix}\right\}$	27%	V + ∅	25%

[a] The second noun in agent nominals was nearly always *-man*
for both idiomatic and innovative forms.

The predominance of such compounds in children's well-
established vocabulary should not be surprising. Compounding is a productive process in English for constructing new

nominal forms such as *the canary-boy*, meaning "the boy who owns a prize-winning canary", *the umbrella-man*, meaning "the man who walks around with his head concealed by an umbrella", or *the Ferrari-woman*, meaning "the woman who specified in her will that she was to be buried in her Ferrari", (all adult examples). Innovative compounds are very common in adult speech (Gleitman and Gleitman, 1970; Meys, 1975; Kay and Zimmer, 1976; Downing, 1977; Bauer, 1978).

To take a second example, among the well-established verbs that children use by age three are many denominal verbs, verbs originally derived by conversion from nouns. In the same seven vocabulary studies, such verbs were common. Although the relation between verb and noun may not have been analysed by the children, in most cases they also had the relevant noun in their repertoires. A major pattern in conversion, then, is well represented in children's well-established lexical items at an early age.

The process of conversion, like compounding, is very productive in English and has been so for several centuries, particularly for the formation of new verbs from nouns (Jespersen, 1942; Marchand, 1969; Adams, 1973). Denominal verbs are rife in the English lexicon, and adults continue to coin such verbs very frequently (see Clark and Clark, 1979, for numerous examples).

Do compounding and conversion predominate in children's lexical innovations? The principle of productivity would predict that the more productive devices — here, the use of noun + noun forms in compounding, and of denominal verbs in conversion — should be acquired early. The evidence available supports the prediction in both cases.

Even very young children construct new compound noun forms for their innovative meanings. And they mainly use the highly productive noun + noun form, like *rat-man* (for someone who worked with rats in a psychology lab), *fire-dog* (for a yellow dog found at the site of a local fire), or *matchbox-flag* (for a matchbox stuck on the end of a pencil and waved), all from two-year-olds. If one takes the innovative nominals coined by the seven children considered earlier, there are clear parallels between their well-established and innovative forms. Consider the data in Table 3. The proportions of two highly productive forms for agent nominals, noun + noun nominals and derived forms with the *-er* suffix among the innovations, match those found for well-established forms. The parallel is not quite as striking for the instrument nominals, but again the two most frequently used forms among the well-established items were also the most frequent among the innovations.

The most productive devices children used in coining agent
and instrument nominals, then, are compounds formed from two
(or more) nouns, and derived forms with -*er* added to a noun
or verb base. When all the innovative complex nominals
the children coined were counted in, some 80% consisted of
noun + noun compounds. (This compares with 89% of their well-
established complex nominal forms.) The most productive device for constructing new nominal forms among three-year-olds,
then, is compounding, with two or more noun bases.

The main criterion in identifying children's compounds is
the stress pattern used — heavier stress on the first, modi-
fying element, and lighter stress on the second, head element.[8] Although few vocabulary studies mentioned the criteria they relied on in identifying certain innovations as
noun + noun compounds, diarists like Leopold (1949) discussed
stress patterns explicitly and used them as the main criterion
for compounds. In my own longitudinal and experimental data
as well as in more casual observations of a larger number of
children, I have found consistent use of the appropriate
stress pattern on all noun + noun compounds.

But does the correct assignment of stress in the production
of innovative compounds connote understanding of the modifier-
head relation marked by this stress pattern? Robert Morse
and I set out to answer this question by asking children to
select the appropriate pictures from sets of four as referents of innovative compounds. For example, given the instruction "Show me the mouse-hat", children had to choose one from
the following set of four: a hat decorated with a mouse, a
hat, a mouse, and a hat decorated with a fish. Erroneous
choices allowed us to see whether children were choosing the
referent on the basis of word stress (choice of the mouse because of the heavier stress on *mouse*) or word order (choice
of the hat because *hat* was the last word heard), and whether
they understood the modifier relation of *mouse*- to -*hat*. If
not, they could choose the hat alone or the hat decorated
with a fish. Other picture sets were used to distinguish
further between the latter possibilities.

Half the children we tested between the ages of 2;0 and
2;9 consistently chose the appropriate picture (the hat with
a mouse on it), and, in another task where the modifier was
not pictured together with the head noun referent, the same
children consistently opted for the picture designated by
the head noun alone, -*hat*. The other children under three
usually chose the referent of the noun carrying the heavier
stress, and this was in fact the commonest error at all ages.
By the age of three, children chose the appropriate referent
to fit the modifier-head relations in compounds over 80% of

the time, and by four made virtually no errors. The children
in this study also produced a number of noun + noun compounds
spontaneously to name the pictures not chosen on each trial.
All these compounds carried the appropriate stress pattern.
The answer to our question, then, is that young children not
only produce compounds with the appropriate stress pattern,
but also understand the modifier-head relations exemplified
by the word order and primary-tertiary stress. Compounding
with noun bases is truly productive for children acquiring
English as young as age two.

Young children also rely on conversion. And, just as
adults do, they use it most commonly in the coining of new
verbs from nouns. Some typical examples of this were listed
in Table 1 (see also Clark, in press). And young children
rarely, if ever, use such suffixes as *-ize*, *-ify*, or *-ate* —
suffixes that are all less productive than conversion. Moreover, although children mainly use conversion to form new
verbs from nouns, they also rely on it to form new verbs
from adjectives and prepositions, as in the following examples:

a) Adjective to verb:

Child aged 2;6, scribbling on a piece of paper: *I'm
darking the sky.*

Child aged 2;11, trying to smooth some paper: *How would
you flat it?*

Child aged 3;0, holding up a pencil: *How do you sharp this?*

b) Preposition to verb:

Child aged 3;0, watching her mother use the eggbeater:
I wanta...wanta...round it.

Child aged 3;3, pushing on her sister's flexed knee: *Down
your little knee!*

These examples, like those in Table 1, of the construction
of new verb forms by conversion are typical (Bowerman, 1974;
Lord, 1979; Clark, in press). Lastly, as Table 3 indicated,
children also use conversion to form nouns from verbs, as in
a rub (meaning "an eraser") or *a stir* (meaning "a spoon").
But, like adults, children rely on conversion mainly to
form new verbs. So here too children conform to the principle of productivity.

3.3 Semantic Transparency and Regularization

Productivity is not the only factor that affects children's
acquisition of word formation. At least two other principles
also play a role: semantic transparency and regularization.

Children first look for a device that conveys their meaning
clearly and then rely on that device (until they learn otherwise) to convey that meaning wherever needed. This reliance
on semantic transparency in turn allows children to organize
their lexicon into paradigms of words with like structure
and meaning, akin to paradigms based on inflectional patterns.

   How do productivity, semantic transparency and regularization interact? Since the most productive device may not be
the most transparent, during certain stages of acquisition,
semantic transparency may take precedence over productivity.
For example, the -*er* suffix for agency is less transparent
than a compound with -*man* in second position, since the noun
man clearly denotes the kind of individual carrying out some
action. *Garden-man* or *plant-man*, for the three-year-old, are
more transparent than *gardener*. The priority of productivity,
then, will depend on how much children already know. Where
they know relatively little, semantic transparency will play
a more important role than where they have already acquired
the conventional adult device for forming new words with a
particular meaning. In the case of agent nouns, younger
children might therefore rely rather more on compounding
than older ones who have correctly analysed the -*er* suffix
as the conventional (and most productive) device for forming
new agent nouns.

   These predictions were supported by the kinds of agent
nouns children coin in an elicitation task. Barbara Hecht
and I solicited innovative "names" from children aged 3;0 to
6;0 by means of a word game with a deck of cards. The cards
were visible initially only to the experimenter, who described each card and asked for a name for the agent pictured.
The descriptions all contained·verbs familiar to children
this age. The percentages of different agent noun forms produced by different age groups are shown in Table 4.

   As predicted, the youngest children produced a fair number
of compound forms while the oldest produced hardly any. Overall, the terms children coined for agents showed a steady
increase with age in the use of the -*er* suffix added to the
verb that had been used to describe the actions of the agent
in question (from 55% for the youngest up to 91% for the
oldest). At the same time, the number of compounds used decreased, with the youngest group using them 21% of the time,
versus the three older groups using them only 4% of the time.
Both these trends conform to the predictions about the relative status of semantic transparency and productivity during
the earliest stages of acquiring knowledge about word formation. While semantic transparency is important at first — all
the compounds children coined had -*man*, -*woman*, -*person*, or

TABLE 4 *Percentage of each agent form elicited by age (based on Clark and Hecht, in prep.)*

		Word form	
Age	V + *er*	Compound[a]	Suppletive[b]
3;0-3;8	55	21	3
3;9-4;5	90	5	2
4;6-5;2	76	5	10
5;3-6;0	91	2	3

[a] Most of the compounds elicited in this study combined a verb and noun stem, but some children also constructed a few noun + noun forms.
[b] We called "suppletive" those responses that were labels for some other category known to the children, e.g. *clown* given in response to "someone who smiles" instead of *smile-man* or *smiler*.

-people as the second element — productivity takes over once children acquire the conventional device for expressing a meaning like agency.

Another small category of responses was suppletive, where children would supply the label for a familiar category that they appeared to equate with the description of the agent given by the experimenter. For example, "a person who gives things" would sometimes elicit *Santa Claus* from the younger children rather than *give-man*, *present-man*, or *giver* — the forms offered otherwise, or "a person who smiles at people" would sometimes elicit *clown* rather than *smile-man* or *smiler*. This type of response was fairly rare for agents, averaging only 3% overall. Lastly, there were a number of "Don't knows" or no response at all, ranging from 18% for the youngest children to a mere 2% for the oldest.

Using the same technique, we also looked at the kinds of nouns children coined for instruments. The pattern of word forms used, as shown in Table 5, differed in certain respects from that found for innovative agent nouns. Instead of constructing compound forms, the younger children used a large number of suppletive responses. Terms like *shovel* or *spade* were offered for "a thing used to dig with" instead of *dig-thing* or *digger*. The latter was the commonest response for older children and adults. Or terms like *scissors* or *knife* were offered for "a thing used to cut with" instead of *cut-thing*, *cut-machine*, or *cutter*. Again, the latter was the

commonest response among the older children and adults, an
indication that productivity by then took precedence over
semantic coherence. Although the number of suppletive responses decreased with age, the oldest children still used
them 6% of the time. One possible reason for this reliance
on suppletive responses for instruments is that children's
vocabulary for instruments is much more elaborated, by age
three even, than their vocabulary for agents.[9] And if available words take precedence over innovations, children should
use what we have called suppletive responses.

TABLE 5 *Percentage of each instrument form elicited by age
(based on Clark and Hecht, in prep.)*

| Age | V + *er* | Word form | |
		Compound	Suppletive
3;0-3;8	42	6	28
3;9-4;5	71	2	8
4;6-5;2	70	3	10
5;3-6;0	72	10	6

One consequence of children's looking for devices that express their intended meanings clearly is that they use those
devices wherever those particular meanings are in question.
This leads them to regularize their lexicon much as they regularize inflections. Until they learn otherwise, when they
form new words, they rely on one particular device to convey
a particular meaning, e.g. the noun -*man* in compounds like
plant-man, fire-man, sweep-man, and *hit-man.* In other words,
children set up lexical paradigms, acting as if the lexicon
were much more regular than it is in fact. Even when they
reach the stage of identifying the most productive device for
a particular meaning, the -*er* suffix for agency, say, they
still have to learn many exceptions in the well-established
vocabulary that do not fall into tidy paradigms, e.g.
bicyclist rather than "bicycler", or *librarian* rather than
"librarier" alongside *farmer, teacher, trucker,* etc.
In our elicitations of agent and instrument forms from
young children, we have found considerable consistency in
the choices of device to convey agency or instrumentality.
Among the younger children, agency was usually indicated by
a noun like -*man* or by the -*er* suffix, and each child tended
to stick with a single device for all his innovations. A
few of the younger children used a double marking for agency,

adding the -*er* suffix to the verb base and then forming a
compound with -*man* as in *hitter-man* or *kicker-man* (see Table
2). These children were also very consistent in the forms
they constructed. Older children always used the most productive device, the -*er* suffix. The coining of instrument
terms showed a similar consistency in the reliance on various
devices. Some of the younger children used compound forms
with -*thing* or -*machine* as the second element; a few used
conversion or zero derivation, taking the verb base and
making it into a noun with a preceding article, and one or
two used the -*er* suffix. As in the case of agents, more of
the older children relied on the productive device, the suffix -*er*, and used it consistently in constructing new instrument noun forms (Clark and Hecht, in prep.; Clark, Hecht and
Mulford, in prep.).

Some children may start out by picking on the productive
device to convey such notions as agency, while others may
pick up some alternative that to them appears more transparent, or at least offers a straightforward meaning-to-form
match. Until they learn otherwise, they will use that device
when constructing new word forms for meanings that belong
in the same set or paradigm — here, other agent terms.
Semantic transparency, then, has to be considered from the
child's perspective and not all children will necessarily
pick on the same device to express the same meaning. Once
chosen, though, that device will be the one used in constructing further, related terms. Regularization of forms in the
lexicon follows from identification of a consistent meaning
with some word formation device. Both semantic transparency
and regularization, therefore, play important roles in the
child's acquisition of knowledge about forming new words.

4. CONCLUSION

In this brief chapter, I have sketched some hypotheses and
issues that arise in the study of children's knowledge of
word formation. I have distinguished the meanings of their
lexical innovations from the forms they rely on to convey
these meanings, even though, in fact, the two — meaning and
form — are tightly linked. Children's innovative meanings
are often contextual. They require knowledge of the context,
and what mutual knowledge that would entail, for the addressee
to arrive at the child-speaker's intended meaning. This is
often achieved by default, since children tend to limit
their early conversations to the here-and-now, thus making it
possible for the addressee to use the context even when the
speaker is not taking it explicitly into account. Learning

to assess what the addressee does and doesn't know is only
one of the factors children must eventually attend to as
they acquire the conventions on innovation.

Lexical innovations require word forms for their expression.
These seem to be acquired in a predictable order, with forms
that are productive in the language — and hence more readily
available — being mastered earlier. In addition to the
principle of productivity, children also attend to the semantic transparency of the new forms they are constructing, and
they regularize the lexical paradigms that result, for instance, choosing a single form for all agent nouns. But the
three principles outlined here — productivity, semantic
transparency, and regularization — are only some of those
that operate in the acquisition of the word formation rules
for a language.

To study word formation, and children's acquisition of
word formation rules, one has to take into account both the
meanings of lexical innovations and the forms used to convey them. The present chapter represents a preliminary
step towards that goal.

ACKNOWLEDGEMENTS

This chapter was completed while at the Center for Advanced
Study in the Behavioral Sciences, and partially supported
by a grant from the Spencer Foundation. The research des-
cribed here was supported in part by the National Science
Foundation (BNS 75-17126), and is being carried out in colla-
boration with Barbara F. Hecht, Robert M. Morse, and Randa C.
Mulford. I am greatly indebted to Manfred Bierwisch, Melissa
Bowerman, Herbert H. Clark, Barbara F. Hecht and Randa C.
Mulford for their comments and suggestions on an earlier
version of this chapter.

NOTES

1 Even where children are apparently using synonyms, it seems
   unwise to assume sameness of meaning. For example, there
   is a difference, for adults, between such "synonymous" expressions as *sweep the dust into the pan* and *make the dust
   go into the pan*. The first expression clearly implicates
   the use of a particular instrument in the action while
   the second doesn't. Such contrasts between lexicalized
   causatives (like *sweep*) and periphrastic causatives, to
   take but one example, are the rule rather than the exception (cf. Shibatani, 1976; McCawley, 1978). But when
   children produce lexicalized and periphrastic verb forms

side by side, investigators like Bowerman (1974) have
assumed synonymy. However, the assumption of contrast
by children in such studies as Carey's (1978) and Dockrell's
(1979) suggests that careful checking to make sure children
really do think two expressions are synonymous is needed
first. An alternative interpretation of children's uses
of apparent synonyms is that they are actually contrasting
the meanings of different expressions, and the second of
the two uttered is a repair to the initial communication.
The norm, for children and adults alike, seems to be one
of contrast in meaning.

2 The hyphen between two nouns or a verb and noun indicates
use of compound stress by the child, i.e. primary stress
on the first element and tertiary stress on the second.
I will take up the question of the correct assignment of
compound stress and word-order in the second part of this
paper (see also Clark and Morse, in prep.).

3 The stress patterns for both agent and instrument compounds
were always correct. In the nominals containing a verb
base, however, the younger children made many mistakes on
the order of the elements, failing, for instance, to in-
vert verb and direct object, as in *puller-wagon* for "wagon-
puller", or *cut-grass* for "grass-cut" or "grass-cutter"
(see Clark, Hecht and Mulford, in prep.).

4 Even in such compositional cases, the interpretation is
not always as simple as these examples would suggest. A
tourist advertisement, for example, talks of a particular
lake in California being "boatable", meaning that it is
possible to use a motor- or sail-boat on it. And a recent
newspaper article talked about different types of people
being "labelable" meaning "easily pigeonholed". Both
these innovations, of course, combine a *noun* base with
-able, rather than an adjective or verb base.

5 *To farmer*, with a sense that contrasts with *to farm*,
namely "to play at being a farmer" or "to act the (gentle-
man) farmer", is, of course, quite a legitimate innovation.
This is because the meanings in question do contrast with
each other.

6 Jean Berko Gleason, pers. comm., 6/78 (unpub. data).

7 Among them were adverbial *-ly*, diminutive *-y* (*-ie*), agentive
and instrumental *-er*, comparative *-er*, nominal *-ness*, and
the negative verb prefix *un-*.

8 Even at the two word stage, use of this stress pattern would
distinguish compounds used to name an entity from two word
utterances used to predicate a property of something. In
the latter, the heavier stress normally falls on the
second, not the first, element. Once beyond the two word

stage, other criteria can also be applied: use of an
article preceding the compound, placement of the compound
immediately before the verb (the subject), or immediately
after the verb (the direct object), and so on.

9 One possible explanation for the difference in the number
of suppletive forms offered for instrument nouns compared
to agents is the following: Any particular human being can
do a large number of different actions, with the particular
action specified by the verb used in the utterance describing agent and action. Most instruments, however, are tied
to a single action in which their role as instrument is
very specific. Instruments therefore tend to have more
precise labels that are often unrelated morphologically to
the verb denoting the usual action the instrument is
connected with. The generality of nouns for agents (man,
woman, child, human being, or proper names of individuals)
therefore contrasts with the specificity of nouns for instruments (a spade is normally only used for digging, scissors
only for cutting, and so on). Children, then, may have a
larger stock of ready-made terms for instruments and rely
on that, where for agents they look earlier for some conventional device that will single out an agent as the
agent of a particular action.

REFERENCES

Adams, V. (1973). "An Introduction to Modern English Word-
   Formation". London: Longman.
Aronoff, M. (1976). "Word Formation in Generative Grammar".
   (Linguistic Inquiry, Monograph Supplement No. 1). Cambridge,
   MA: M.I.T. Press.
Bateman, W.G. (1915). Two children's progress in speech.
   Journal of Educational Psychology 6, 475-493.
Bauer, L. (1979). On the need for pragmatics in the study
   of nominal compounding. *Journal of Pragmatics* 3, 45-50.
Bohn, W.C. (1914). First steps in verbal expression. *Peda-
   gogical Seminary* 21, 578-595.
Bolinger, D.L. (1977). "Meaning and Form". London: Longman.
Bowerman, M. (1974). Learning the structure of causative
   verbs: A study in the relationship of cognitive, semantic
   and syntactic development. *Papers and Reports on Child
   Language Development* (Stanford University) 8, 142-178.
Boyd, W. (1914). The development of a child's vocabulary.
   Pedagogical Seminary 21, 95-124.
Brandenburg, G.C. (1915). The language of a three-year-old
   child. *Pedagogical Seminary* 22, 89-120.
Brekle, H.E. (1977).   Reflections on the conditions for the
   coining, use and understanding of nominal compounds   Paper

presented at the XIIth International Congress of Linguists,
Vienna, 28 August/2 September 1977.
Carey, S. (1978). The child as word learner. *In* "Linguistic
Theory and Psychological Reality" (M. Halle, J. Bresnan and
G.A. Miller, eds), pp. 264-293. Cambridge, MA; MIT Press.
Clark, E.V. (1978). Discovering what words can do. "Papers
from the Parasession on the Lexicon", pp. 34-57. Chicago,
IL: Chicago Linguistic Society.
Clark, E.V. (In press). The young word-maker: A case study of
innovation in the child's lexicon. *In* "Language Acquisi-
tion: The State of the Art" (L.R. Gleitman and E. Wanner, eds).
Clark, E.V. and Clark, H.H. (1979). When nouns surface as
verbs. *Language* 55, 767-811.
Clark, E.V. and Hecht, B.F. (In prep.) Learning to coin agent
and instrument nouns.
Clark, E.V., Hecht, B.F. and Mulford, R.C. (In prep.) A cut-
grass, a grass-cut, or a grass-cutter? The acquisition of
verbal compound forms by young children.
Clark, E.V. and Morse, R.M. (In prep.) "Show me the 'mouse-
hat'": Young children's understanding of compound stress.
Dockrell, J.E. (1979). "Acquiring new words in two contexts".
Unpublished paper, University of Stirling.
Downing, P. (1977). On the creation and use of English com-
pound nouns. *Language* 53, 810-842.
Fantini, A.E. (1976). "Language Acquisition of a Bilingual
Child". Brattleboro, VT: The Experiment Press.
Fromkin, V. (ed.). (1973). "Speech errors as linguistic
evidence". The Hague: Mouton.
Gentner, D. (1978). Testing the psychological reality of a
representational model. *In* "Theoretical Issues in Natural
Language Processing - 2" (D.L. Waltz, ed.), pp. 1-7. New
York: Association of Computing Machinery.
Gleitman, L.R. and Gleitman, H. (1970). "Phrase and Para-
phrase". New York: Norton.
Grant, J.R. (1915). A child's vocabulary and its growth.
Pedagogical Seminary 22, 183-203.
Huttenlocher, J. (1979). "The development of verb meaning".
Paper presented at the Conference on "Beyond Description
in Child Language". Nijmegen, June 1979.
Jespersen, O. (1942). "A Modern English Grammar on Historical
Principles. Part VI: Morphology". Copenhagen: Munksgaard.
Kay, P. and Zimmer, K. (1977). On the semantics of compounds
and genitives in English. "Sixth California Linguistics As-
sociation: Conference Proceedings - 1976", pp. 29-35.
Lehrer, A. (1970). Notes on lexical gaps. *Journal of Linguis-
tics* 6, 257-261.
Leopold, W.F. (1939-1949). "Speech Development of a Bilingual
Child", 4 vols. Evanston, IL: Northwestern University Press.

328 E.V. CLARK

Levi, J. (1978). "Syntax and Semantics of Complex Nominals".
New York: Academic Press.
Lord, C. (1979). "Don't you fall me down": Children's gene-
ralizations regarding cause and transitivity. *Papers and
Reports on Child Language Development* (Stanford University)
17, 81-89.
Lyons, J. (1977). "Semantics". Cambridge: Cambridge Univer-
sity Press.
McCawley, J.D. (1978). Conversational implicature and the
lexicon. *In* "Syntax and Semantics, Vol. 9: Pragmatics"
(P. Cole, ed.), pp. 245-259. New York: Academic Press.
Marchand, H. (1969). "The Categories and Types of Present-
Day English Word-Formation", (2nd revised ed.). München:
C.H. Beck.
Meys, W.J. (1975). "Compound Adjectives in English and the
Ideal Speaker-Listener" (North-Holland Linguistic Series
18). Amsterdam: North-Holland.
Motsch, W. (1962). Zur Stellung der "Wortbildung" in einem
formalen Sprachmodell. *Studia Grammatica* 1, 31-50.
Nice, M.M. (1915). The development of a child's vocabulary
in relation to environment. *Pedagogical Seminary* 22, 35-64.
Pelsma, R. (1910). A child's vocabulary and its development.
Pedagogical Seminary 17, 328-369.
Roeper, T. and Siegel, M.E.A. (1978). A lexical transforma-
tion for verbal compounds. *Linguistic Inquiry* 9, 199-240.
Shibatani, M. (1976). The grammar of causative expressions:
A conspectus. *In* "Syntax and Semantics, Vol. 6: The Grammar
of Causative Constructions" (M. Shibatani, ed.), pp. 1-40.
New York: Academic Press.
Slobin, D.I. (1973). Cognitive prerequisites for the develop-
ment of grammar. *In* "Studies of Child Language Development"
(C.A. Ferguson and D.I. Slobin, eds), pp. 175-208. New
York: Holt, Rinehart and Winston.
Snow, C.E. and Ferguson, C.A. (eds). (1977). "Talking to
Children: Language Input and Acquisition". Cambridge:
Cambridge University Press.

ON THE DEVELOPMENT OF SEMANTIC RELATIONS BETWEEN NOUNS

HANS-DIETER SCHMIDT and HUBERT SYDOW

Department of Psychology, Humboldt University, Berlin, GDR.

1. INTRODUCTION

Conceptual cognitive structures are presumably represented
on various levels in human long-term memory. As *single* concepts they might be stored as sets of semantic features or
as procedures enabling their appropriate use in special situations. With respect to *other concepts* they are probably
stored as a set of relations between two or more concepts.
These relations might be of a more or less general nature:
they connect either concepts referring to concrete objects
or concepts corresponding to classes of objects. In the
latter case they are not only constituents of elements in
memory structure but cognitive operations that may be used
in searching for relevant concepts, in learning new concepts,
and in defining their intended meaning.

Our experimental investigations are embedded in this frame
defined by general cognitive psychology and to be specified
with respect to *developmental* psychology. This has been
realized on the basis of experimental studies which presuppose
that the lexicon acquired between 2 and 5 years of age is already highly organized. They were performed to identify the
age-dependent ability *to use semantic knowledge* in analysing
relations between nouns. Our results refer to the age group
from 4 to 8 years, a developmental phase supposed to be
characterized by important structural changes of cognitive
functioning. The theoretical and methodological assumptions
of our approach are the following:

a) The organization of knowledge in human long-term memory
   is characterized by *semantic relations* which enable the
   comprehension of semantic information. They mediate between the sensory input and the mental or motor output.
   This is brought about by means of cognitive and evaluative

operations and the cognitive structures produced in this
way, which enable an adapted control of elements, events,
and rules within our environment, such as the recognition
of the value of objects and persons, the localization of
objects within spatio-temporal frames of reference, the
logical and causal relations between objects, actions,
and events (A.A. Leontjew, 1971; Klix, 1976; Klix and
Sydow, 1977; Bierwisch, 1977, 1979; Geier *et al.*, 1977).
b) Concerning the classification of semantic relations, our
starting point is the distinction between *inter-* and
intraconceptual ones as defined by Klix (1976). Interconceptual relations refer to situations which are represented in memory to form its "semantic kernels" (Klix,
1976), representing our knowledge about experienced
events. Their components are elements of the categories
actor, action, object, instrument, location, etc. (cf.
the case relations defined by Fillmore, 1968). Intraconceptual relations refer to logical relations between
featural codes of concepts (e.g. coordinations, sub- and
superordination, comparation).
c) Findings obtained by numerous child psychologists during
the last fifty years prove the significance of *actions*
and *action references* for the development of cognition
and language.

Analysing the development of word knowledge, C. and W. Stern
(1922) defined an "actional phase" preceding "relational" and
"featural" phases. Furthermore, the reader is referred to
the "action principle" elaborated by Werner (1953), Piaget
(1975), A.N. Leontjew (1964), and Bruner (1977). This principle suggests that semantic kernels with their action-oriented
interconceptual relations are the *origin* of the development
of word meaning and that intraconceptual relations are derived
from semantic kernels during language development. We do
not intend to verify this hypothesis. We are rather concerned
with the question, whether the above mentioned classification
of semantic relations may be used to explain the *development
of semantic relations and their use* in various cognitive tasks,
both closely connected to the development of metalinguistic
abilities (Sinclair *et al.*, 1978). Starting from these
general assumptions (and considering this latter question)
we derived the hypotheses given in the following section.

2. HYPOTHESES AND METHODS

In formulating our hypotheses we took into account the following facts and arguments (Przybilski, Schmidt and Sydow, 1980).
Children older than 3 years, having finished their elementary

"lessons" of language acquisition, should be able to perform a rough semantic analysis of noun patterns. They should be able to identify the existence of intra- and interconceptual relations between nouns if they are requested to choose between related and unrelated noun pairs. Concerning this task, the two classes of semantic relations defined by Klix must not be understood as a too strict distinction. Intra-conceptual relations between nouns may be recognized by the child as location or action relations (e.g. the coordination cup-plate or the subordination plate-dishes).

Furthermore, the child himself has identified numerous features of objects in his perceptive and exploratory activity since birth, which may well have been represented in semantic kernels as well as in conceptual structures (the latter defined by means of intraconceptual relations). This follows from the fact that actions accentuate, use, and refer to features of objects. Considering these arguments, we specified the above-mentioned questions and tried to substantiate the following hypotheses:

a) Even the youngest children (at the age of 4 years) perform a *rough semantic analysis* of noun pairs and distinguish between related and unrelated noun pairs in a noun pair comparison test (NPC test).

b) The nouns in two noun pairs presented in an NPC test may be connected by either an intra- or an interconceptual relation. If Ss are asked to choose the noun pair realizing the *stronger* relation, younger children prefer *action oriented* interconceptual relations rather than intraconceptual ones. This tendency decreases with increasing age.

c) If (within a sequence of pairs of noun pairs), the choice of one semantic relation (e.g. the instrument relation) is consistently reinforced, Ss will learn to use a *general decision rule*, i.e. to choose consistently the reinforced relation. That is to say, we assume that there exists a general concept, e.g. "instrument relation", and that special noun pairs connected by an instrument relation are special instances of this general "instrument relation".

d) Two *intra*conceptually related nouns at the same time can be connected by a more or less familiar *action*. Younger children will prefer noun pairs connected by more familiar actions. In our experimental paradigm we used a cognitive task similar to the CST-technique (Kagan, 1964). Ss were presented two noun pairs. They were asked to choose that one which contained the nouns "belonging together", "fitting together", being "best matched". The noun pairs were presented as triplets or as two pairs, e.g.:

Triple technique   *Pair technique*

apple   apple - knife

knife —— fruit   apple - fruit

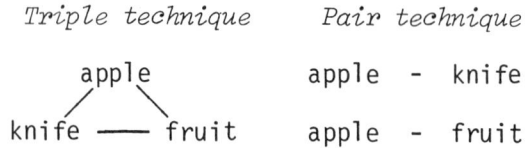

In the triple technique, two noun pairs were connected by the instrument relation (knife-apple, knife-fruit) and one noun pair by subordination (apple-fruit). In our data analysis this fact had to be considered. It implied special difficulties in testing statistical hypotheses. Therefore we switched over to the pair technique in our later experiments.

We only used those nouns which were well known to all children in the age range considered. Noun pairs were instances of four semantic relations:

Interconceptual: instrument relation (I; e.g. knife-apple)

Intraconceptual: subordination (S; e.g. apple-fruit)

coordination (C; e.g. apple-pear)

part-whole relation (P; e.g. finger-hand)

Our Ss were about 200 normally developed preschool and school children. The NPC-test instrumentation was explained by means of noun patterns containing one related and one unrelated pair (e.g., nose-eye, nose-car). The test was performed with a list of 24 items comprising pairs of related nouns. The items were orally presented, the S having to repeat the pair chosen. In order to avoid sequential and position effects (with respect to the position of noun pairs within the whole list and within pairs of noun pairs) appropriate item lists were used. Ss received a feedback concerning the "correctness" of decision only in the third experiment.

3. RESULTS

As a first step of data analysis we tested the *consistency* of decisions. Ss could have preferred the first or the second pair of an item above change due to short-term memory effects. Of course, Ss should choose noun pairs *independent* of their position in an item. That means: given n items of the I-S type (e.g. apple-knife (I), apple-fruit (S)), Ss could have preferred the I-pair and the S-pair with about the same frequency.

In opposition to this case, Ss should choose one of the two competing semantic relations with a frequency above chance. About 63 per cent of our 5-to 8-year old Ss met these two criteria of consistency in our experiments. Thus we should not overestimate the ability of Ss in the considered age range to execute a consistent semantic analysis of noun patterns with respect to a hypothesized prevalence ordering of semantic relations as an organizing principle of long-term memory structure.

Consistent preschool-children preferred the instrument and part-whole relations to coordination and subordination (I-P-C-S). About 50 per cent of the consistent school children (second grade) showed the same preference ordering, but the remaining 50 per cent preferred coordination and subordination to instrument and part-whole relations (C-S-I-P). These data may indicate the existence of different *cognitive styles*, an action-oriented one in the first case, a logically oriented (categorical) one in the second case.

With reference to the four hypotheses and not taking account of possible subgroups of consistent Ss, the following results were found.

The youngest children (4 years, 18 Ss) were able to select related noun pairs in the NPC test (e.g. saw-tree v. saw-cloud). Table 1 presents the percentages of correct choices.

TABLE 1 *Identification of related noun pairs*

Semantic relation	Percentage
I	100
P	97
C	92
S	85

The four semantic relations are identified by almost all Ss. Only subordinated noun pairs proved to be less well developed (the difference between P and S was significant at the 5% level). Thus, if we present items comprising two related noun pairs the Ss should be able to identify both relations. In the following experiments only noun pairs with *competing* semantic relations were presented. Ss had to choose the sub-jectively stronger related pair.

In the second experiment 24 items were used, four instances of each of the two pairs of semantic relations (I-C, I-S, I-P, S-C, S-P, and C-P). Items were presented to two experi-

mental groups (age: 5 to 6 years, 29 Ss each) with the
triple and pair technique respectively, and to a third group
(age: 8 years, 16 Ss) with the pair technique. Table 2
shows choice frequencies. A data comparison in the first two
rows reveals a strong *effect of the method* used. The triple
technique gives, as mentioned above, an advantage to one of
the two relations (cf. finger-soap-hand v. finger-soap,
finger-hand). The differences observed for the pairs I-C,
I-S, I-P, and S-P could be explained by this fact, but differences for S-C and C-P are in the opposite direction. Some
Ss may choose their answer from two, some from three alternatives.

TABLE 2 *Decision between competing semantic relations.*
Relative frequencies of decisions in favour of the first
relation

Age	Technique	*I*-C	*I*-S	*I*-P	*S*-C	*S*-P	*C*-P
5-6	triple	0.73	0.71	0.64	0.33	0.23	0.64
5-6	pair	0.63	0.67	0.41	0.45	0.37	0.41
8	pair	0.60	0.54	0.41	0.28	0.31	0.42

The second and third row show that the relations I and P
are preferred to the relations C and S. This action-oriented
preference gives support to our second hypothesis. This
preference of action-oriented v. categorical relations decreases with age only with respect to instrument relation,
subordination and coordination receiving a higher position.
But this decrease of (average) frequencies, calculated for the
whole experimental group, may be explained partly by the individual differences between consistent Ss mentioned above.

The third hypothesis refers to the level of generality of
semantic relations. Adults are able to solve analogy problems (e.g. dog: animal = tulip: ?). They identify the semantic relation connecting dog-animal as subordination, apply
this relation to the argument tulip, and produce answers like
flower or plant. The solution of such problems presupposes
the existence of a general concept of subordination. Dog
and animal are not only connected by a very special relation,
but the pair dog-animal is an instance of this general concept "subordination", i.e. "subordination" functions as a
generalized *cognitive operation* enabling the retrieval and
identification of nouns in demand.

Confronted with the item saw-tree, saw-cloud, children are
able to select the related noun pair. Do they identify a

special relation between saw and tree, or is the output
"instrumental relation" the result of a *semantic analysis*
performed with the item?

Using a learning task, we tried to answer the question of
whether there exist generalized semantic relations such as
"instrument relation", "subordination", and "coordination".
Presenting a list of items of the same type (C-S. e.g.
elephant-lion, elephant-animal) we can consistently reinforce
the choice of one of the two relations (e.g. C). If Ss have
acquired a general concept "coordination", they should be
able to use it as a general decision rule in order to receive
solely positive feedbacks. If not, they should be incapable
of meeting consistently the reinforcement schedule. Two
lists of 24 items each were prepared, the first of the C-I
type (e.g. nail-hook, nail-hammer) and the second one of the
C-S type (e.g., elephant-lion, elephant-animal). Two groups
of preschool children (age: 5 to 6 years, 10 Ss either)
performed the NPC test without feedback. In the C-I condition 62 per cent of the 240 decisions were in favour of the
instrument relation. The result in the C-S condition was
45 per cent for subordination.

80 Ss performed the NPC test as a learning task: 40 preschool children (age: 5-6 years) and 40 second graders (age:
8 years). 20 Ss of each group were tested with the C-I list,
20 Ss with the C-S list. These groups were split once more;
10 Ss received C-reinforcement, the other 10 Ss I (S)-re-
inforcement.

The feedback given was effective. Absolute frequencies
calculated for the last 8 decisions (out of 24 totally) are
given in Table 3. Significant differences between feedback
conditions were received for the younger group already in
the *second* block of 8 items, for second-graders even in the
first block.

TABLE 3 *Absolute frequencies (last 8 items) for the 8 experimental groups and Chi² values*

Age	Feedback	I	C	Chi^2	C	S	Chi^2
5-6	I (S)	58	22		16	64	
	C	35	45	13.6	55	25	43.4
8	I (S)	63	17		1	79	
	C	26	54	34.7	69	11	117.4

Table 4 presents the absolute frequencies for the 8 groups
compared with the data received without feedback for the

younger Ss (last 8 items). Differences between the first two
rows are significant at the 5% level except for the S-C condition (I reinforced). Differences between the second and the
third row are significant for S-C and S-C conditions. The
second-graders increase their choice frequencies for the reinforced relation earlier and to a higher degree, especially
if the items contain coordination and subordination as competing semantic relations.

TABLE 4 *Absolute frequencies for the experimental groups
(the first row refers to the two groups I-C and S-C without
feedback).*

Age	Feedback	S-C		I-C		S-C		S-C	
5-6	(-)	50	30	50	30	39	41	39	41
	(+)	58	22	34	45	64	16	25	55
8	(+)	63	17	26	54	79	1	11	69

The last 8 items were consistently correctly answered by
varying numbers of Ss (Table 5). Although instrument-related
nouns are earlier and to a higher degree identified by preschool children (cf. first experiment), subordination and
coordination seem to attain a higher degree of generality.

TABLE 5 *Numbers of Ss (out of 10) with consistently correct
answers throughout the last 8 items*

Age	S-C	S-C	I-C	I-C
5-6	4	1	1	3
8	9	5	3	2

Table 6 presents items with particularly high error frequencies. They contain noun pairs that are *less typical* instances of the reinforced semantic relations. Ss answering
these items correctly with respect to the reinforcement
schedule, have acquired the corresponding semantic relations
at a generality level of high degree.

If two nouns, connected by an intraconceptual relation
(part-whole, coordination), correspond to objects which are
moreover involved in everyday action sequences, they should
be preferred (according to the fourth hypothesis) to noun
pairs without such an additional connection. In this sense,
cup and can are more closely connected coordinated concepts

than plate and dish. Jacket and zip-fastener are more closely
connected by the part-whole relation than jacket and collar.

TABLE 6 *Items with high error frequencies*

Age	Condition	Reinforced pair	Preferred pair
5-6	*C*-S	banana-apple	banana-fruit
	C-*S*	table-furniture	table-cupboard
	I-C	hands-brush	hands-feet
	I-*C*	soup-sauce	soup-spoon
8	*C*-S	carrot-spinach	carrot-vegetable
	I-C	skirt-washing-powder	skirt-blouse
	I-*C*	wood-plastic	wood-drill

Two groups of Ss (19 five-year-olds and 17 six-year-olds)
took part in the fourth NPC-test experiment. Three types of
items were used: C-S, C-P, and P-S. Items of the C-S type
(and of the C-P type) contained coordinated noun pairs which
were more or less actionally related. Two similarly varied
sets of items of the P-S type were constructed containing
part-whole related nouns with a different degree of action-
relatedness. The relative frequencies of decisions in favour
of the more or less action-related noun pair are presented in
Table 7.

TABLE 7 *Relative frequencies of decisions in favour of*
strong/weak action-relatedness

Age group	C-S		C-P		P-S	
	C strong	C weak	C strong	C weak	P strong	C weak
5	0.72	0.34	0.62	0.21	0.62	0.32
6	0.64	0.30	0.53	0.17	0.77	0.46

The data show that decisions between competing intraconceptual relations are strongly influenced by the degree of
action-relatedness. All differences between relative frequencies corresponding to the two subsets of items of the
same item-type are highly significant. Variation of age did
not produce significant differences.

4. DISCUSSION

The ability of our youngest Ss to identify semantically related noun pairs is a result of semantic, cognitive, and
metalinguistic development. Almost all binary *inter*conceptual relations (Klix, 1976) can be found already in early two-
word utterances (Slobin, 1972). The identification of *intra*-
conceptual relations presupposes cognitive abilities acquired
very early in life, too. Experimental data gained by Meltzow,
Bower, Leslie (cf. Leslie, 1979) shows that 6- to 8-month-old
infants not only recognize many perceptual features of objects,
but have at their disposal abstract concepts (as "angular"),
too, generated on the basis of as yet unknown mechanisms of
discursive representation (proved, e.g. in cross-modal matching experiments). Association experiments by Ciechanowicz
(1978) demonstrate the production of a great number of types
of semantic relations by preschool children. In summary, we
can assume that almost all semantic relations involved in
spatio-temporal meaning structures representing objects,
events, and situations are recognized and comprehended in
the late preschool age. However, our learning experiments
show that this ability relies on specific conditions. Semantic relations are recognized and comprehended only with respect to object-specific conditions. In preschool and early
school age the recognition of semantic relations must not be
understood as the application of a strategy-like instrument
of cognitive analysis on the basis of generalized semantic
relations. Only if the child is able to perform this generalization, he can be said to master semantic relations in a proper sense.
   Different semantic relations attain this level of generality
at different points of development. In this context, subordination is of special interest. Our data show (experiments 1
and 2) that subordination is not as well developed in preschool age as, e.g. the instrument relation. This fact, however, is not very surprising if we consider numerous similar
results gained by child psychologists since about 1920.
   As soon as the child is able to apply the necessary cognitive abilities (identification of features, recognition of
feature dimensions, comparison of objects) in an integrative
manner, subordination seems to be well established whereas
the interconceptual instrument relation leaves behind. Thus
the question arises whether the dichotomization between intra-
and inter-conceptual relations is as useful for cognitive
developmental psychology as for *general* cognitive psychology.
It is evidently necessary, first to study the age-specific
task requirements given by each semantic relation, and then

to try the classification of semantic relations — but under developmental aspects.

Considering the low level of generality of semantic relations, the preference of action-related noun pairs was to be expected in the second and fourth experiment. This result can be explained by the above-mentioned "action principle". On the other hand we have to consider the fact that even adults in association experiments produce with a relative frequency of about 30%, e.g. the word chair given the word table (Ciechanowicz, 1978).

Also adults tend to reproduce situational context information. This result draws the attention to the following essential problem: until now we do not know what is really going on in the internal system of cognitive structures and operations if the child is confronted with our noun patterns. Do they analyse feature sets? Do they try to construct sentences on the basis of noun pairs? Do the noun patterns generate internal images? Further experiments are necessary to explain the *nature of representational cognitive processes* in the child that are suppositions of comprehension and application of semantic relations.

ACKNOWLEDGEMENTS

We are indebted to A. Przybilski and D. Ruskova for their assistance in carrying out the experiments. The research has been supported by the medical research project "The Defective Child", granted by the Ministry of Health of the GDR.

REFERENCES

Bierwisch, M. (1977). Sprache und Gedächtnis: Ergebnisse und Probleme. *In* "Zur Psychologie des Gedächtnisses" (F. Klix and H. Sydow, eds). Berlin: Dtsch. Verl. Wiss.

Bierwisch, M. (1979). Three psychological aspects of meaning. *Z. Psychol.* <u>187</u>, H. 3, 295-309.

Bruner, J.S. (1977). Early social interaction and language acquisition. *In* "Studies in Mother-Infant Interaction" (H.R. Schaffer, ed.). London, New York: Academic Press.

Ciechanowicz, A. (1978). Changes in the associative structure of the semantic field between ages 2 and 15. *Polish Psychol. Bull.* <u>9</u> (4), 215-222.

Fillmore, C.J. (1968). The case for case. *In* "Universals in Linguistic Theory" (E. Bach and R.G. Harms, eds). New York: Wiley.

Geier, M. *et al.* (1977). Bedeutung als Bindeglied zwischen Bewusstsein und Praxis. *In* "Ber. I. Kongr. Kritische

Psychologie" (K.H. Braun and M. Holzkamp, eds), Bd. 2.
Köln: Pahl-Rugenstein.

Kagan, J. (1964). Information processing in the child.
Psychol. Monogr. 78.

Klix, J. (1976). "Psychologische Beiträge zur Analyse
Kognitiver Prozesse". Berlin: Dtsch. Verl. Wiss.

Klix, F. and Sydow, H. (eds). (1977). "Zur Psychologie des
Gedächtnisses". Berlin: Dtsch. Verl. Wiss.

Leontjew, A.N. (1971). "The Semantic Structure of Words".
Moscow: Nauka.

Leontjew, A.N. (1964). "Probleme der Entwicklung des Psy-
chischen". Berlin: Volk. u. Wissen.

Leslie, A.W. (1979). The discursive representation of perceived causal connection in infancy. Conference on knowledge and representation, Netherlands Inst. Advanced
Studies, March 8-10, 1979.

Piaget, J. (1975). "Der Aufbau der Wirklichkeit beim Kinde".
Stuttgart: Klett.

Przybilski, A., Schmidt, H.D. and Sydow, H. (1980). The
development of semantic relations in childhood. *In* "Cognition and Memory" (J. Hoffman and F. Klix, eds). Berlin:
Dtsch. Verl. Wiss.

Sinclair, A., Jarvella, R.J. and Levelt, W.J.M. (eds) (1978).
"The Child's Conception of Language". Berlin, Heidelberg,
New York: Springer.

Slobin, D.I. (1972). Seven questions about language development. *In* "New Horizons in Psychology" (P.C. Dodwell, ed.),
No. 2. Baltimore: Penguin.

Stern, W. and Stern, C. (1922). "Die Kindersprache", 3rd
edn. Leipzig: Barth.

Werner, H. (1952). "Einführung in die Entwicklungsphychologie",
3rd edn. München: Barth.

BASIC ISSUES IN THE DEVELOPMENT OF WORD MEANING

MANFRED BIERWISCH

*Akademie der Wissenschaften, Zentralinstitut
für Sprachwissenschaft, Berlin, GDR.*

1. AIMS AND POSITIONS

The following considerations are centered around two rather
general and vague questions that might help, though, in
organizing the perspective in which language acquisition is
to be placed. The two questions are:

I) What is to be acquired?
II) How is it acquired?

These questions will be pursued with respect to word meaning,
which requires, however, some side-glances at areas beyond
both word and meaning, as the development of word meaning can
only be understood if placed in the appropriate context.
  As to (I), I will argue that the answer is by far less
obvious than most approaches are aware of, as the notion of
word meaning is much more complicated than it might appear
even at the second or third glance. More specifically, I
will claim that (at least) two aspects of meaning are to be
distinguished that are organized according to independent,
though interacting principles: *Semantic Structure*, determined
by the rules of language and thus pertaining to the realm of
tacit linguistic knowledge; *Conceptual Structure*, based on
rules in terms of which mental representations of the world
are built up.
  As to (II), I will argue that the answer depends in part on
the answer to (I), and in part to independent notions of a
rather different sort. I will distinguish between three
conceptions provisionally characterized as follows:

A 1) *Association:* Word meanings are acquired by establishing
       associative links between word forms and their meanings.
A 2) *Accretion:* Word meanings are acquired by integrating
       one specification after the other until the eventual

meanings are built up.

A 3) *Projection:* Word meanings are acquired by determining
particular projections between independently developing
levels of structure.

2. LEXICAL ENTRIES

Any answer to the first question should certainly start with
considering the linguistic account of the notion of word. For
obvious reasons, no simple definition can be given independently from a more general conception of phonological, morphological, syntactic, and semantic structure of natural languages.
As a first approximation, the following will do:

D 1) A word $w = (p, syn, sem)$ is a specification of the phonetic, syntactic, and semantic information that w contri-
butes to the expressions it may occur in.

This leaves open a large number of questions. Without further
ado, we cannot solve on the basis of (D 1) such well known
puzzles as:

1) Is *cat* the same word as *cats*? If so, what about *child* and
children, bring and *brought, large* and *larger*, or even *he*
and *his, go* and *went, long* and *length*? Where is the
boundary?
2) Is *bank* one word, or two, or three? And what about transitive and intransitive *melt, break, eat*?
3) Does *typewriter* consist of one word or two? And what about
items like *bold-face, baseball, armchair, on-line* and so on?

Problems can easily be multiplied. In order to answer (1),
we may introduce a distinction between word and wordform to
the effect that e.g. *cat* and *cats* or *bring* and *brought* are
different forms of the same word. More specifically, we must
distinguish between the information a lexical item *can* contribute to that of an expression it may occur in, and the information that actually *is* contained in an expression because
of the occurrence of a particular word form, where the latter
is determined by the former together with various grammatical
rules. To capture this distinction, I will introduce the
notion of a lexical entry in the following way:

D 2) A lexical entry $le = (p^{le}, syn^{le}, sem^{le})$ is a specification of the phonetic, syntactic, and semantic information
that, depending on the pertinent rules of the grammar ,
determines the contribution of le to the expression it
may occur in.

We may assume now that there is one lexical entry that determines both *cat* and *cats*, the differences being due to syntactic

semantic, phonological and morphological rules. This still
does not provide a complete answer to the problems in (1),
though it indicates the direction in which further clarification is to be sought. Without going into any of the necessary details,[1]* the following point is to be made.

The notion of word cannot be specified without fixing at
the same time the various rules and their interaction determining the way in which lexical information functions within
the set of linguistic expressions of a given language. It is
only with respect to this division of labour that the boundary
asked for in (1) can be drawn.

This immediately turns into a crucial point with respect
to question (I) above: What is to be acquired, is the joint
system of lexical entries and rules determining their role in
the language.

Returning briefly to the problems in (2) and (3), they are
now to be turned into questions about lexical entries. (2)
concerns ambiguity and its treatment in the lexicon. One
might argue that there are no ambiguous lexical entries, i.e.
that there are for example two lexical entries for *bank*
which happen to have identical phonological information, just
as synonyms happen to have identical semantic information.
A strict position in this respect would lead to rather im-
plausible and empirically unwarranted assumptions. I will
therefore assume that *le* can be semantically and syntactically
ambiguous. Question (3) concerns compounding (and more
generally word formation). As I will touch this highly intricate area only marginally, it will be sufficient for the time
being to acknowledge the fact that lexical entries might be
morphologically complex and that the rules or patterns of
word formation are a powerful means to enrich systematically
the set of lexical entries of a language.

With this clarification in mind, I will continue to use the
term "word" in the provisional sense of (D 1), covering both
fully specified word forms and underlying lexical entries,
as long as the distinction in question is not specifically at
issue.

Turning next to some remarks concerning the components p,
syn, and *sem*, I shall have to say little about the phonetic
information p. Suffice it to say that p is to be characterized
in terms of a matrix of universally defined phonetic features
determining at the same time the articulatory and perceptual
patterns according to which a word is produced and identified,
and the systematic relations among words like contrast, simi-

---

* Superscript numerals refer to notes which are to be found
at the end of the chapter.

larity, rhyme, etc.

The semantic information *sem* is supposed to determine the contribution of a word *w* to the meaning of complex expressions relative to the context in which the expressions are interpreted. This involves three distinct, though interlacing aspects. First, *sem* must determine the way it combines with the semantic information of other words in order to yield the semantic representation of complex expressions. That amounts to assigning *sem* to appropriate semantic categories. Sentential connectives for example are of a different semantic category as nouns or transitive verbs. Secondly, *sem* must determine the range of possible denotations of the word in various contexts. This aspect is related to semantic categorization by the fact, that the combinatorial category determines in part the type of denotation to which the particular instance of denotation belongs. Third, *sem* must determine the relations that connect and differentiate the various words within the vocabulary. Thus *father* must be related to *male* in the same way as *mother* to *female*, *long* to *short* in the same way as *high* to *low*, etc. This aspect is related to the second by the fact that semantic relations reflect in a non-trivial manner the relations between possible denotata. And it is related to the first by the fact that semantic relations are governed by categorization, i.e. they hold only within or between certain categories.

As to the third aspect, there are presently two conceptions under debate: advocates of *Componential Analysis* claim that word meanings are composed of more primitive elements, such that their compositional structure determines the semantic relations. Advocates of *Meaning Postulates* take word meanings as primitive elements, whose interconnection is fixed by a particular type of axioms called meaning postulates. Componential analysis is underlying most work in the linguistic tradition of semantic analysis and has recently brought to a fairly high degree of sophistication by Miller and Johnson-Laird (1976). Meaning postulates are currently argued for by Fodor *et al.* (1980). In principle, I take some version of componential analysis to be the right approach to semantic structure. More specifically, I will assume that something like (4) and (5) might be a first approximation to the semantic representation of transitive and intransitive *melt*, respectively:

4) $\hat{X}[\hat{Y} \; [\exists Z \; [[DO \; Y \; Z] \; \wedge \; [CAUSE \; Z \; [GO \; [RIGID \; X] \; [LIQUID \; X]]]]]]$

5) $\hat{X} \; [GO \; [RIGID \; X] \; [LIQUID \; X]]$

Two remarks should be made with respect to the otherwise self-explanatory notational conventions. First, the tentative

semantic primes DO, CAUSE, GO, RIGID and LIQUID as well as
the variables X, Y, and Z must all be categorized in the
sense discussed above. This categorization can be taken as
an inherent property of the universal specification of semantic primes. Thus CAUSE should be a functor turning two propositions into a complex proposition, the same holds for GO,
while DO takes a name and a proposition turning it into a
proposition, and LIQUID and RIGID are one-place predicates.
Second, $\hat{X}$ is to be understood as an abstractor binding the
variable X in its domain. If X is of category α, then $\hat{X}$
turns a formula of category β into a functor that combines
with an argument of category α to yield a formula of category
β.[2]

As can be seen immediately, (4) and (5) can be combined
into a single representation with an optional part capturing
the causative ingredient of transitive *melt*. See (9) below
for an explicit exploitation of this possibility. This then
illustrates the way along which systematic generalizations
for lexical entries can be captured by appropriate semantic
decomposition.

Turning finally to the syntactic information *syn*, we might
say that it somehow mediates between *p* and *sem*. More specifically, *syn* determines the way in which a word can combine
with other words to form complex structures to the meaning
of which it makes its semantic contribution. As we have
claimed a combinatorial categorization already for *sem*, one
might wonder whether *syn* cannot be abandoned altogether
(except for features determining irregular plural or tense
formation etc., which are, however, morphological rather
than syntactic). To sharpen the discussion, consider the
following two positions:

P 1) Autonomy of *syn* (Formalism): *syn* specifies information
     that is independent of *sem* and belongs to an autonomous
     system of syntactic organization.
P 2) Dependency of *syn* (Functionalism): *syn* is a function of
     sem and hence need not be specified as independent in-
     formation.

Between these two positions, there are several intermediate
positions claiming partial dependence between *syn* and *sem*.
On the one hand, there are obvious correspondences between
syn and *sem*, both for words and complex linguistic expressions. The parallelism between syntactic and semantic categorization of transitive and intransitive *melt* noted above
would be an almost trivial case in point. More interesting
generalizations going across syntactic and semantic structure
are pointed out e.g. by Jackendoff (1978).

On the other hand, it is equally obvious that there are syntactic properties that cannot reasonably be derived from or reduced to semantic ones. To give a simple example, in German there are three causal sentential connectives *denn, da,* and *weil,* as in:

6) Er kommt nicht, denn er ist krank.
   (He doesn't come, since he is sick.)
7) Er kommt nicht, da er krank ist.
   (He doesn't come, as he is sick.)
8) Er kommt nicht, weil er krank ist.
   (He doesn't come, because he is sick.)
   Er kommt nicht, weil er ist krank. (Substandard)

Whatever slight semantic differences there are, they cannot account for the fact that *denn* introduces a main clause, *da* introduces a subordinate clause, and *weil* introduces a subordinate clause in standard German, but a main clause in some versions of colloquial speech.

The decision between (P 1) and (P 2) is not a matter of various syntactic idiosyncracies, but rather a matter of the underlying principles determining the framework of *syn* and *sem,* respectively. In other words, *syn* and *sem* relate to different systems of structure governed by different principles. Thus syntactic and semantic categories are crucially different things, whatever interesting and relevant correspondences might be revealed. *John, he, who* and *everybody* for instance are all syntactically categorized as NP in accordance with essential properties of their syntactic behavior, whereas semantically *John* is a constant name, *he* is a variable name, and *who* and *everybody* are quantifier-like phrases of different kinds. In general I will take (P 2) to be correct, which leaves us with the interesting task to account for whatever systematic correspondences might obtain between syntactic and semantic properties. I suppose this to be the right perspective, the generalizations to be captured by systematic interaction of modular systems rather than by reducing syntax to the combinatorial aspect of semantics.

To summarize, with respect to our initial question (I), I will assume that a lexical entry (and hence a word form based on it) is a relation between mutually accessible structured entities belonging to the phonological, syntactic, and semantic system, respectively. Viewed in this perspective, the problem of word acquisition has two rather different aspects:

I') (a) The specification of *p, syn, sem,* respectively.
    (b) The connection between *p, syn,* and *sem.*

It should be obvious that this partial answer to (I) has important consequences for the question (II).

For the sake of illustration, (9) could be considered as a tentative lexical entry for *melt*.

9) /melt/

V, [___ (NP$_X$)]

$\hat{X}$ ([$\hat{Y}$ [∃Z [[DO Y Z] ∧ [CAUSE Z) [GO[RIGID X][LIQUID X]]]]]]

The parentheses enclose corresponding optional parts in *syn* and *sem*, the index of the object NP indicates by which variable its semantic representation is bound.

3. SEMANTIC AND CONCEPTUAL STRUCTURE

Most linguists and psychologists seem to be inclined to consider the semantic representation *sem* of a given word to be the conceptual unit represented or expressed by the word at least in its normal or literal uses. More specifically, I will argue that the notion of meaning refers in part to the semantic structure of a word, and in part to the conceptual unit expressed by the word in a given utterance, and that these two things — although closely related and sometimes almost indistinguishable — are to be carefully distinguished in a very principled way. Since this point plays a crucial role in the following considerations, I will illustrate it briefly by a number of fairly different examples, which can easily be multiplied.

Before turning to the illustrations, let me introduce a distinction between *ambiguity*, *vagueness* (or *fuzzyness*), *indeterminateness*. All three have to do with a lack of specification, though on rather different levels. Although there are borderline cases, the differences are fairly clear in principle. Ambiguity relates to alternative possibilities on the semantic (and possibly also the syntactic) level. (10) and (11) are familiar illustrations:

10) The visitors enjoyed the old port.
11) What did you expect to melt?

Vagueness relates to a range of possibilities on a continuous domain of interpretation, often, but not necessarily, at the perceptual level. (12) is vague with respect to the interpretation of *many*, *young*, and *dark*:

12) Many young people have dark hair.

What I am after is indeterminateness. It does not turn on syntactic or semantic ambiguity, nor on vagueness on a continuous domain. It rather relates to discrete conceptual

distinctions which do not correspond to different semantic
structures.
    Consider the following examples:

13) (a) On Friday morning, Bill came out of the university
        and took a cab.
    (b) For two years, Bill has been teaching at the Univer-
        sity of Appletown.
    (c) The university by now covers the whole area around
        the house you lived at.
    (d) The university is a typically European institution
        that developed during the Middle Ages.

    Here *university* denotates conceptually different entities —
a building in (a), an institution in (b), a campus in (c),
and something like an educational principle in (d) — which
are related in systematic ways and cannot be considered as
instantiating a semantic ambiguity in the sense of say *bank*
or *port*.
    The same is true in a slightly different respect for the verb
find in the following examples:

14) (a) Max found an elegant proof for the theorem.
    (b) John finally found the book he had looked for in
        various book stores.
    (c) John found the book in the mess on his desk.

The type of activity involved in constructing a proof, searching for a book, and retrieving a particular copy leads to
accordingly different types of finding, although there is no
lexical ambiguity involved.
    The conclusion to be drawn from these and many other examples
is this: The semantic structure *sem* of a word determines a
conceptual unit denoted by the word relative to a given context. To put it the other way round: *sem* determines a family
of related conceptual units the differentiation of which depends on the context within which the word is interpreted.
We are thus dealing with the second aspect of semantic structures mentioned in Section 2, namely that of how *sem* determines the denotation. Formally, the conclusion arrived at
can be made precise in two ways:

D 3) The semantic information *sem* of a word w is a function
     from a context c_i into a conceptual unit con_j, i.e.
     $sem(c_i) = con_j$, where con_j is the denotation of w rela-
     tive to c_i.

    If we were to take *con* as the extension of an expression,
(D 3) would roughly amount to the explication of meaning
proposed in model theoretic semantics: *sem* would have to be

construed as the intension, which is a function from a context (more precisely: from a possible world) to the extension.
It would take us too far afield to pursue the parallels and
the differences of the two approaches. (For a discussion see
Johnson-Laird (1979) and Bierwisch (1980a).) Some of the
problems involved will become obvious by the further discussion
of *con*.

The second way to construe the relation between *sem* and
con can be formulated as follows:

D 3') The semantic information *sem* of a word w is evaluated
relative to a context c_i by a function V determining the
conceptual unit con_j denoted by w in context c_i, i.e.
$V(sem, c_i) = con_j$.

Here *sem* is not interpreted directly as a function, but rather
as a parameter of a general evaluation that provides the required mapping. Substantially, the difference between (D 3)
and (D 3') is relevant only if there are specific rules and
principles defining the mapping V such that V captures relevant
generalizations concerning the conceptual interpretation of
semantic structures. I take this to be the case and will thus
adopt (D 3'), although nothing in what follows crucially depends on that decision. To give at least a vague hint, it
seems to me that V is based on a system of principles and
rules comprising among others the following:

15) (a) Variable assignment, interpreting non-anaphoric pronouns, determiners, time variables etc.
(b) Rules of conceptual shift, accounting for cases like
(13).
(c) Rules of conceptual differentiation, accounting for
cases like (14).

(15) (a) must in part be based on principles of deictic orientation. The formal principles possibly underlying (15) (b)
and (15) (c) are discussed in Bierwisch (1981). (See
also Nunberg (1979) for a revealing discussion of phenomena
turning on conceptual shift.) Further rules and underlying
principles are most likely to be added, such as Jackendoff's
(1978) representational principle capturing a large variety of
quid-pro-quo phenomena, but I will leave it at that. It should
go without saying that the above illustrations are not meant
to suggest that c_i is to be verbalized context.

To summarize, we have arrived at the notion that a word relates p, *syn* and *sem* as a grammatically determined unit of
the language, and that its meaning consists of *sem* and *con*
(corresponding to some extent to the logician's intension and
extension) where the latter varies according to the context c.

Acquisition of word meaning hence also comprises the ability
to appropriately relate *sem* and *con*.

4. CONCEPTUAL STRUCTURE AND MENTAL WORLD

So far I have introduced conceptual units from the point of
view of interpreting semantic structures. Let me now briefly
put them in their own right. Two notions might be useful
in that endeavour, namely that of *mental world* and of *mental
model*.

Human beings organize their experience of, and interaction
with, their environment on the basis of internal, mental
representations, that extract and project the relevant information from and to the environment according to a complex
system of underlying principles. Let me call the realm of
those representations, the elements, rules, and structures
on which they are based the mental world MW. Suppose in
particular that MW comprises representations of what is often
called systems of belief and common sense theories. Although
it would be pointless to make any particular claims with
respect to the structure of MW at the present state of knowledge, it is certainly warranted to suppose that MW is not
an amorphous agglomeration of piecemeal reflections of reality, but rather a highly organized complex structure developing according to specific organizing principles.

Suppose furthermore that MW interacts in a systematic way
with a system of representations that integrates sensory information into structures of the perceptual world PW. Just
as MW, PW must be thought of as organized according to specific principles, this time those of visual, auditory and
other modes of perception. I leave it open whether PW is
to be construed as a particular sub-system MW determining
particular aspects of representations pertaining to MW, or
whether PW constitutes a system of representations of its own,
interacting in a systematic way with MW. For the time being,
it is sufficient to make the following two assumptions. First,
not all entities and representations of MW are related to
(or have an aspect determined by) PW, i.e. MW might contain
non-perceptual, "abstract" entities and structures. Second,
for entities and structures of MW that are related to (or have
an aspect determined by) structures of PW, the perceptual
level of structure is determined by the specific rules and
principles of PW and thus forms a level of representation of
its own. For further discussion of the notion of the perceptual world and its relation to the conceptual structures of
MW, see Miller and Johnson-Laird (1976).

Turning next to the notion of mental model, which I have
adopted from Johnson-Laird (1979; 1980), it attempts to cap-

ture the fact that we deal with particular situations of
whatever complexity in terms of representations built up
according to whatever bears on them within the mental world.
The resulting representation is a mental model M. If M concerns
a veridical situation, it is related to (projected on) it at
least in part by actual representations pertaining to PW. In
other words, a mental model represents our experience of an
actual or possible (real, fictitious, hypothesized, concrete
or abstract, past or future) situation.

It is based on the structures of the mental world as well
as the sensory, linguistic and inferentially gained information eventually to be integrated. It is the mental models in
terms of which we experience, interpret, think and also speak
about the various aspects of reality. Hence understanding a
connected discourse involves among others the construction
of a mental model M that satisfies the sentences of the discourse.

I will now suggest that conceptual units and the structures
in terms of which they are interrelated, provide the building
blocks, relations, and patterns by means of which both MW and
the different models M_i are organized. The context c_i in
particular is to be construed as a (maybe partial) mental
model plus whatever further specifications of the mental
world might be adduced as relevant in interpreting a given
expression. And the conceptual unit con_j denoted by a word
w is the entity that w identifies within or adds to the mental
model to be made up in order to interpret the expression in
which w occurs.

The conceptual structure is organized according to its own
characteristic principles and not just as a derivative of
linguistic expressions that are interpreted in terms of structures of the mental world. (If one went into evolutionary
speculations, one should assume that the principles underlying the conceptual structure of the mental world are at
least in part phylogenetically prior to those of linguistic
structures.)

Before turning to some comments on the properties of conceptual structure, I will add a few terminological remarks.
As I said initially, terminology and viewpoints are varied
and somewhat confusing. I have adopted the notion of mental
world from Wexler and Culicover (1980), who use it in considerations of learnability in roughly the same way that I
have proposed. Jackendoff (1978) talks about conceptual
structure in much the same way as I would, but as he is
interested primarily in the relevant correspondences between
semantic and conceptual structure, he does not distinguish
the two systems. Similarly Miller and Johnson-Laird (1976)
in discussing conceptual structures do not provide the dis-

tinction in question, although the later work of Johnson-
Laird on mental models clearly relies on the distinction between linguistic (i.e. semantic) and model representations.
I cannot decide whether Fodor's (1976) "Language of Thought"
is closer to semantic or conceptual structure; it does not
provide, in any case, a distinction to that effect. Chomsky
(1980) on the other hand distinguishes between Logical Form
and "fuller semantic representation" which might come close
to the distinction between semantic and conceptual structure
in the sense envisaged here. Finally Searle (1980) talks
about the "background of meaning" which seems to be a notion
rather similar to that of the mental world. These hints by
no means exhaust the list of pertinent proposals, they are
just a selection from the more recent writings on the subject.

5. SOME REMARKS ON CONCEPTUAL STRUCTURE

It would, of course, go far beyond the limits of the present
paper to even provisionally characterize the principles of
conceptual structure. The following remarks shall thus be
limited to the aspect of word meaning. To make the discussion handy, let me introduce the following provisional notions:
    Let SEM be the set of all semantic structures and CON the
set of all conceptual structures a person might ideally be
able to come up with. Thus SEM must be determined by the
rules of the grammar, among them the combinatorial principles
inherent in the categorization of semantic units. Similarly
CON must be determined by rules and principles governing the
combinatorial structure within the mental world — whatever
these may be.
    Among SEM the set LSEM of lexicalized semantic structures
might be distinguished, i.e. those structures that are related
to the pertinent syntactic and phonetic information by lexical entries. On this basis we can distinguish among CON the
set LCON of lexically determined structures, where each element of LSEM determines a subset of LCON, depending on the
pertinent contexts. In other words, if sem is an element of
LSEM, it determines a family of concepts, where the elements
of this family are differentiated according to the (classes
of) contexts c_i with respect to which sem can be interpreted.
These families of concepts are (not necessarily disjoint)
subsets of LCON.
    Although we have sorted out by LCON those conceptual units
that are relevant with respect to word meaning and its acquisition, it should be clear by now that they cannot be divorced
from the structure underlying the encompassing set CON. That
means that they cannot develop piecemeal and in isolation,
but are rather to be embedded in the development of the mental

world. Bearing this in mind, we might consider some of the
properties that are particularly relevant for LCON.
Let me call for short the elements of LCON "concepts".
Clearly, concepts must be of different types. Thus, the various concepts interpreting *and* are relations that connect particular states of affair in a mental model with respect to
time, causality or other dimensions. The different classificatory concepts denoted by *university* sort out particular
types of entities, and so on. In short, concepts are ordered
into types derived from what might be called the ontology of
the mental world. These conceptual types correspond to the
categories of semantic structure. This correspondence must
not be thought of as a simple one-to-one mapping, but it
channels the interpretation of semantic items in terms of
concepts.
A closer look at the structure of LCON and its underlying
principles must therefore recognize the differentiation
according to different types of concepts. One of the different subsystems of LCON that has been subject to closer
study is that of classificatory concepts and its organization
according to principles of class inclusion, part-whole
relation, or mutual predicability. Let me briefly take up
the latter point for the sake of illustration. In a recent
paper, Osherson (1978) discusses three conditions on conceptual naturalness determining the organization of natural conceptual systems. One of these conditions is based on the
notion of predicability (which amounts to the exclusion of
type crossing or category mistake). Thus, *heavy* is predicable
of *stone*, but not of *theory*. Predicability relations can be
represented in the following way, where a concept labelling a
non-terminal node can be an attribute of all terminal node
concepts dominated by it.

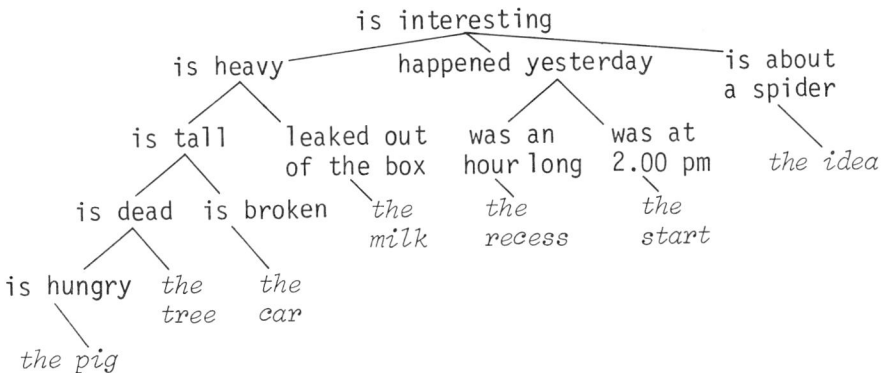

FIG. 1   *A predicability tree*

Osherson proposes the following condition: A set of concepts
comprises a natural conceptual system only if they can be
organized as a predicability tree, without violation of the
M principle.

The "M principle" prevents subordination of a terminal node
under different branches. Osherson demonstrates that conceptual structures develop ontogenetically according to his
above mentioned condition by gradually expanding the tree
structure with occasional confusion with respect to the rank-
ing on a branch, but never violating to the branching structure.

Without going into the network-feature controversy of conceptual structures, I would merely point out that the notion
of predicability tree is by no means incompatible with a
characterization of terminal node concepts in terms of whatever "features" or rather systematic parameters are relevant
for further specification. Notice in particular, that the
notion of prototypes that has been developed in order to deal
with a "family resemblance" type of structure makes sense
only if viewed as marking out certain categorial points in a
conceptual subdomain that is organized according to certain
underlying dimensions along which resemblances can be assessed.

Let me conclude this provisional illustration of one aspect
of the structure of LCON by three more general remarks. First,
it should be obvious, that rather different principles of
organization are necessary to account for other types of concepts. Sentential connectives for one denote concepts that
cannot be captured at all by predicability relations. (See
the third condition of Osherson (1978) for an interesting
proposal in this respect.) Individual concepts denoted by
proper names, or the complex relations between correlated
states of affairs denoted by particles like *also, even, only*
are just hints to rather different types of conceptual organization.

A second crucial point is that the range of conceptual
structures must be based on specific innate principles of
various kinds, but can be developed in certain respects
according to individual experience, social needs, particular
tasks and requirements with varying degrees of refinement.
Thus a biologist's concepts not only of taxonomies of animals,
but also of abstract notions like *life, environment, nature*
etc. might considerably differ from those of the average man
on the street.

Finally, I suppose that logical operations (or rules of
thinking for that matter) are defined primarily for conceptual
structures, i.e. representations pertaining to the mental
world. (See Johnson-Laird (1979) for interesting suggestions
to that effect.) More specifically, I suppose that language-

bound reasoning is in a sense derivative from inferential
operations in mental world. This does not only concern the
highly regimented way of operating in half or fully formalized
languages, but also inferential operations in non-regimented
natural language. Once language starts interacting with conceptual representations, it provides, of course, a powerful
means to enrich the capacity for controlled reasoning. But
in a sufficiently clear sense, inferential abilities are im-
ported into language from the mental world.

6. FURTHER REMARKS ON SEMANTICS AND CONCEPTS

Turning to the structure of LSEM, I will add three remarks
to what has already been said. First, LSEM is certainly not
a mere list of semantic representations. Although the lexicon of a language must contain all the idiosyncrasies of the
individual entries, LSEM is still an organized system integrating the sem^{le} according to general principles (just as
the p^{le} and syn^{le} are determined by the principles of phonology and syntax, respectively). The notion of semantic
fields is a well known attempt to capture one aspect of the
organization of LSEM. Let me briefly return in this connection to the above mentioned alternative of meaning postulates
and semantic decomposition.

   Without going into the details, it should be clear in principle, how componential analysis, to which I have subscribed,
copes with the systematic integration of elements of LSEM.
Basically, semantic relations between words are captured by
their combinatorial make up from identical or distinct semantic primes, just as phonological relations among words are
captured by shared phonetic features in corresponding positions. Moreover, as mentioned above, the general combinatorial ("syntactic") principles of SEM are proliferated down
into the semantics of words; hence the inferential rules
that hold for SEM in general, are immediately sensitive to
word internal structures. Given for example the analysis of
melt proposed in (4) and (5), it directly follows, that *the
gold melted* can be inferred from *John melted the gold* by the
general rule of detachment. And from *the gold melted* by the
axioms defining the prime GO *the gold was rigid* and *the gold
became liquid* can be derived. In general, then, the combinatorial principles of semantics (specified essentially by the
system of categories) together with the system of primes define the structure of LSEM.[3]
   The meaning postulate approach, in contrast, would have to
assume that the elements of LSEM are not interrelated by
their structure, but rather by rules or axioms that have to
be stated additionally. Thus, the two readings of *melt*

would be totally different items exhibiting no greater similarity than the various readings of *bank* or *port*. Let MELT
represent transitive and TLEM intransitive *melt*. There would
then be a meaning postulate

16) X MELT Y---➤ Y TLEM

relating the two semantic representations. Further postulates
would be required to relate TLEM (and hence MELT) to LIQUID
and RIGID, stipulating these to be the readings of *liquid*
and *rigid*.

Assuming that the two approaches are equivalent as to their
formal principles (both need a system of primes as well as
axioms interrelating the primes and rules of inference),
there is a certain trade-off in terms of the information to be
specified: Componential analysis yields complex lexical
entries and simple (universal) rules, meaning postulate
approaches have simple lexical entries, but rather complex
rules of inference. The problem is not a purely quantitative
one, though. Different predictions follow with respect to
language acquisition. Componential analysis would predict
that the acquisition of transitive *melt* implies the identification of the reading of intransitive *melt* as a possible
lexical structure. It furthermore predicts that the acquisition of one correlated pair of verbs consisting of a causative verb and the corresponding inchoative verb implies the
disposal of the missing counterpart as a potential lexical
item as soon as a separate inchoative or causative verb is
acquired. No such prediction follows, however, from the
meaning postulate approach, as any such pair in this account
must be acquired (or may be triggered) and interrelated
separately.

In discussing the alternative in question, Fodor *et al.*
(1980) point out an apparent difficulty for componential
analysis, namely that meaning postulates can easily cope with
asymmetrical inferences, while componential analysis is on
principle doomed to definitional equivalence. Thus, while
(17) would be a fairly plausible meaning postulate interrelating *red* and *coloured*, there does not seem to be a reasonable
analysis of *red* in terms of say, RED and P which is not circular, as P now must be defined as the full disjunction of
possible colour primes.

17) RED X - - - ➤ COLOURED X

18) [/red/; A; X̂ [COLOUR X RED]]

19) [/coloured/; X̂ [∃Y [COLOUR X Y]]]

From (18) and (19), a rule corresponding to (17) follows as
a case of independently needed rule of existential generali-

zation. Although this analysis certainly needs further
clarification, it is not a mere makeshift. I would rather
claim that something like the sem^le of (19) is the characteristic pattern of the semantics of colour terms. And it
predicts, moreover, that the meaning of *coloured* is likely
to be developed as an existential generalization with respect
to true colour terms.

One might argue now, that what I have said in this section
is just as much a matter of conceptual as semantic structure.
That brings me to the second remark.

Although I have made no explicit claims as to the formal
character of CON, it should be obvious that there must be a
systematic relation between SEM and CON. In a similar vein,
however, semantic and syntactic structure, which I have
assumed to be based on autonomous principles, exhibit relevant similarities, and there are, incidentally, certain dependencies also among syntactic structures and the prosodic
aspect of phonetic representations. It thus remains to be
shown whether and in which way LSEM and LCON differ as to
their principles. In this respect, I will mainly refer to
the examples already discussed in Section 3 above. The
point, though, can now be sharpened a bit by means of what
has been said about concepts.

Many of the cases that I have called (conceptual) indeterminateness clearly violate the predicability condition, if
applied to lexical entries. Here is one illustration:

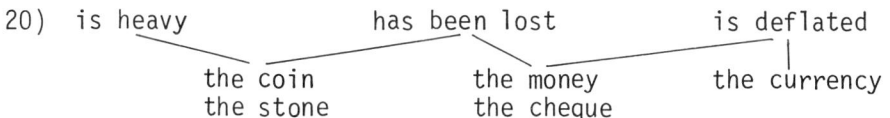

20) is heavy   has been lost   is deflated

            the coin   the money   the currency
            the stone   the cheque

As the predication *the money has been lost* is actually subject
to two possible interpretations: on one reading, money goes
with *coin*, on the other *money* goes with *currency*. Yet neither
lose nor *money* is ambiguous. They rather "co-vary" as to
predicability connections. These are not marginal cases,
but rather instances of a widespread phenomenon. It also
comprises such apparent paradoxes as:

21) (a) The temperature is ninety;
     (b) the temperature is rising;
     (c) hence ninety is rising.

22) (a) The colour of the water is green;
     (b) the colour of the water is (sometimes) changing;
     (c) hence green is (sometimes) changing.

As Jackendoff (1979) points out, the paradox involved in these
inferences cannot be adequately resolved by merely assigning
different intentions to the two occurrences of *temperature* or

colour, it rather requires different types of predicate, one of identification, one of change. Co-varying with this predication is the type of *temperature*: once it is a fixed value of a function, once it is a sequence of values.

Although LSEM is in a sense more abstract than LCON, SEM must not be taken as merely a coarsened reflection of CON. It is rather based on different principles. To illustrate an opposite effect, where CON is in a sense simpler than SEM, consider the representation of *my father*. A tentative semantic analysis of *my* would be something like (23):

23) $\hat{X}$ [DEF X [∃R [[R SPEAKER Y] ∧ [X Y]]]]

Here X is the variable to be substituted by the reading of the noun that *my* combines with to give a noun phrase denoting an individual, specified by the definiteness-operator DEF. The crucial point is that *my* involves some relation R that obtains between the speaker and the individual Y bound by DEF. Clearly R can be specified in many ways according to the context in which it denotes a relation: inalienable possession in *my hand*, alienable possession in *my car*, producer-product relation in *my recent book*, position in *my seat*, origin in *my country* etc. Taking CAR as a simplified representation of *sem* of *car*, we get (24) as the reading of *my car*:

24) DEF Y [∃R [[RR SPEAKER Y] ∧ [CAR Y]]]

Consider next a simplified, though plausible analysis of father:

25) $\hat{X}$ [∃Z [[PARENT X Z] ∧ [MALE X]]]

That accounts for the fact that *father* is a relational noun. Combining (23) and (25), i.e. inserting (25) for X in (23), we get the following representation for *my father*:

26) DEF Y [∃R [[R SPEAKER Y] ∧ ∃Z [[PARENT Y Z] ∧ [MALE]]]]]

Rough paraphrase: the Y to whom the speaker has a relation and who is male and for whom there is a Z whose parent Y is. That sounds clumsy, but is in effect quite straightforward. The interesting point is that we get the primary, natural interpretation of *my father* only if we interpret PARENT as an instantiation of R and SPEAKER as an instantiation of Z. It seems plausible to assume that in CON these duplications do not occur. Rather a representation that amounts to (27) would seem to be indicated, where the circle marks definiteness, and an arrow connects a predicate with an argument.

27) male————(▸y◂————— parent ————▸ ego

Again, this is not a curiosity of the particular example, but rather a general phenomenon.

   In short, then, SEM reflects the structure of CON, but not
like a mirror, but rather like a display filtered through a
coloured and structured glass. Or to use an even closer analogy, SEM reflects CON as a score reflects what a violinist
intentionally performs: it leaves out a large number of highly
specific graduations, intended distinctions, and added structural values; but at the same time it makes systematic distinctions not appearing in the performance at all by representing a certain note as, say, E flat rather than D sharp
etc. The differences follow from the different principles
organizing the two levels of representation.
   My third remark concerns the problem of delimiting the borderline between semantic and conceptual phenomena. Just as
with the distinction between syntax and semantics, we have
no *a priori* criteria for drawing the boundary. Some properties
of word meaning are clearly due to conceptual principles,
others are clearly semantic. (Thus the ambiguity of *score*
between number of points and codification of a composition
belongs to LSEM, while the differentiation of the latter into
a copy, an edition, the (invariant) content of several edi-
tions etc. belongs to LCON.) Many phenomena, however, are
not at all clear in advance. Let me point to two types of
cases.
   First, as is well known, temporal relations are to a large
extent expressed by spatial semantic units, prepositions like
at, in, before, adjectives like *long* and *short*, nominals like
extension, point, interval being obvious examples. Further
"exportation" of spatial structure can be observed in many
places. Given the distinction between SEM and CON, two possibilities are to be considered: (a) different conceptual domains based on different structural principles (time, space,
social rank, exchange value, etc.) are represented (accessed)
by invariant semantic elements, abstracting away from the
particular conceptual conditions of the different domains;
(b) the conceptual structure itself is organized according to
highly abstract representational schemes that are imposed
on different domains of experience, such that e.g. time is
conceptualized as a one-dimensional space, and semantic elements represent these abstract conceptual patterns. The
alternative cannot be decided in advance, but is subject to
empirical investigation. Different predictions with respect
to the developmental aspect would follow: according to (a)
the development of invariant patterns across space, time,
value, etc. would be a consequence of language acquisition,
according to (b) it would be an independent (possible innate)
condition on conceptual development.
   The second class of phenomena, loosely connected to the
former, relates to the status of selection restrictions. Is

it a matter of lexical structure, that *eat* requires a living
subject, *melt* a physical, rigid object, *count* a countable set
as object? This at least has been assumed by most linguistic
analyses so far. Consider, however, a theory, according to
which there are no (or at least much less) lexical selection
restrictions, to the effect, that *His heart melted* does not
constitute a semantic violation, but rather a problem of finding a mental model that interprets the sentence. Again, we
have no *a priori* intuitions as to what is the right solution.
Different predictions follow and can, eventually, be subject
to empirical investigation.

This then concludes my provisional answer to question (I).
Expanding on the partial answer (I') given at the end of
Section 2, we might now say that the knowledge underlying
the use or interpretation of a word w with respect to a
context c_i involves the following specifications:

(*p*, *syn*, *sem*) con_j $perc_k$ where *perc* is the perceptual
structure that can (but need not) be related to the conceptualization con_j.

(I) can now be answered somewhat more completely by

I'') (a) The specification of *p*, *syn*, *sem*, *con* and *perc*, if
          perception is involved.
     (b) The connection between *p*, *syn* and *sem*.
     (c) The mapping determined by *sem* and c_i into *con*.

Each of the structures in (a) is embedded in and therefore
determined by its respective system of organization. The
connection in (b) and the structures it connects are determined
by the knowledge of language (in a particular interpretation
of this term). The connection in question is to a large extent, although by no means completely, determined by convention,[4] it constitutes the famous "arbitrariness of signs".
The mapping in (c) is not part of the language in the narrower
sense, it is based on the rules (15) constituting the function
V, and it is not determined by convention but rather by universal principles and primes.

7. SEMANTICS AND PRAGMATICS

Before turning to the question II concerning the "How" of
acquisition, I will add two remarks about how all this relates
to pragmatics. Pragmatics is itself a highly indeterminate
term. What is usually covered by it can best be referred to
two different domains. (See Stalnaker (1972) for a short and
clear exposition in this respect.)

One domain of problems concerns the context dependency of
utterance meaning, down to the interpretation of particular

words, with so-called "contextuals" as borderline cases, such as *the steak* meaning "the guest who ordered the steak". Problems of this kind are captured in principle by assigning to *sem* a conceptual interpretation con_j according to the context c_j. As I have already said, I have confined myself to variations that are still in the range of literal meaning, and a number of intricate problems will arise if this range is extended. Metaphoric interpretation, induced by analogy — i.e. by construing one domain in terms of the structure of another domain — and indirect reference, i.e. referring to a salient characteristic instead of the object itself, are two general mechanisms to be invoked in this connection. They may be considered as extensions of the rules constituting the interpretation function V assumed in (D 3') above. Alternatively they might be construed as functions that operate within the domain of CON itself. Whatever the appropriate way to look at these issues might be, their place in principle should be clear. They are part of the meaning of words and sentences as characterized previously. Hence I have nothing to add with respect to the first domain of pragmatics. I would merely conjecture, that initial steps in the development of word meaning are likely to turn on variations within the range of literal meaning, although the mechanisms of analogy and indirect reference are certainly available right from the beginning and might thus be exploited in relevant ways, especially in constructing new words. (See Clark (this volume) for pertinent observations and analyses.)

The second domain of pragmatics comprises the problems dealt with mainly in speech act theory, i.e. the character and functioning of illucutionary forces. I will not be concerned with this domain in this paper for two reasons.

First, the illocutionary force — or the communicative sense, as I would rather say — is a problem of utterances, not of words, even if in particular cases one-word utterances are realized with a particular illocutionary force, as in *thanks!*, *cheerio!*, *where?*, *leftwards!*, *attention!* etc.

Second, illocutionary force must be accounted for in a much broader context, namely that of interpersonal relations, and social interaction including communication, and especially verbal communication, as a particular domain (for further discussion see Bierwisch (1980b)).

8. WHAT DOES IT MEAN TO LEARN A WORD?

It is commonplace that words are learned. A child's mental lexicon depends on the input information the child comes across. In this respect, learning to talk is different from learning to walk. The obvious difference must not ob-

scure the equally important similarities. Chomsky (1980)
has argued that the usual notions of learning are rather inappropriate to account for the process of language acquisition,
which is in essential respects determined by highly structured
internal dispositions. Language acquisition, he claims, consists essentially in the activation of these dispositions, the
emerging differences between different languages being due to
the specification of certain free parameters according to the
actual experience coming from the child's environment. It
remains to be seen whether these basic ideas can account not
only for the development of grammatical rules, but also for
that of lexical items. There appears to be a problem in this
respect, as the vocabulary of a language is notoriously characterized by idiosyncratic peculiarities rather than by uniform and general structures holding for all possible languages.
One might even go on to argue that within a single language
community there are no two individuals with exactly the same
lexical knowledge. All this might be true and still only in
apparent conflict with the view that linguistic knowledge —
including the mental lexicon — develops according to internal,
uniform dispositions. Much of the previous discussion should
pave the way for a solution to that problem. In other words,
our provisional answer to (I) not only indicates the complexity of what is to be acquired, but points also to the
underlying principles that render the acquisition possible.
The rest of this paper attempts to spell out the consequences
of (I) for an answer to question (II).

Let me start with the almost trivial claim that word meanings are acquired both *piecemeal* and *holistically*. To put it
less paradoxically, words and their meanings are acquired as
items that are to be inserted into, or rather developed within
systematically organized structures. To highlight the purport
of this claim, I will briefly contrast three conceptions of
word learning which are not only related to different underlying assumptions as to the nature of learning, but as a consequence of these assumptions concentrate also on different
aspects of the overall process. I have briefly characterized
the three conceptions in Section 1 as Association, Accretion
and Projection.

Association comprises a family of more or less related conceptions that can be characterized by the following assumptions:

A 1) (a) A word w consists basically of a pair (p, m), where
p is the phonetic form and m the meaning of w.

(b) The acquisition of w consists in establishing an associative link between p and m.

(c) p and m are introduced and discriminated from other
words essentially by the fact that they are associated
to each other.

(A 1) is clearly the core of behaviouristic theories of language. There is, however, a wide variety of less strict conceptions that also rely in one way or the other on (A 1). Besides the fact that it is a much too simplified view that the meaning of a word can be identified as a simple m subject to associative connection, (A 1) does not provide any reasonable basis for an explanation of the origin of p and m. The possibility of their existence is not considered as a real problem, its solution is simply taken for granted. It should be clear by now, that (A 1) is wrong in all relevant respects, except that some connection between p and all the rest must be established. I will argue that the latter requirement, though obviously true, plays a by far less important role than (A 1) makes it appear.

   Accretion is a much more sophisticated conception, which grew out of a number of exciting experimental and observational findings indicating that the meaning of a word is not simply to be taken for granted but goes through systematically determined developmental stages. The essentials of this view can be summarized as follows:

A 2) (a) A word w consists of a syntactically classified phonetic form p to which its meaning m is assigned.
   (b) The meaning m consists of a systematically accruing structure of semantic primes.
   (c) The development of words and their meanings proceeds by mutual delimitation and specification within systematically determined domains.

(A 2) too comprises a number of variants whose differences need not be spelled out. Its most perspicuous version is certainly that of the seminal work of Clark (1973). It represents a fundamental improvement over (A 1) in at least the following respects: (a) Word acquisition is based on a systematic theory of linguistic structure according to which lexical items are determined by their place and role within that structure. (b) The existence of m is not simply taken for granted. Its origin and properties are explained in terms of semantic primes, principles of their combination, and developmental processes and strategies governing their gradual creation. (c) It proposes a systematic account for a range of empirical facts that cannot plausibly be captured by (A 1). Facts of this kind are the following: words are not acquired in an arbitrary sequence, but rather according to principles of systematic development within certain domains, with respect to increasing degrees of refinement, and according to universal dimensions or parameters. The meaning of an individual word is not fixed once and for all, but goes rather through a potential sequence of increasing specificity.

Overgeneralization and its later restriction is the best known phenomenon resulting from this developmental sequence. I will return to these problems below.

Projection does not seem to be an explicitly distinguished conception so far, but it is implicit in or at least compatible with a number of studies of which Carey (1978) is to my knowledge the clearest exposition of what I mean by projection. There is, however, no simple and clearcut borderline between accretion and projection. It is merely for the sake of clarification that I will exaggerate the difference, which is by far less deep than that between (A 1) and the rest.

A 3) (a) A word w consists of a syntactically classified phonetic form p interpreted with respect to the various aspects of meaning.

(b) All the components of w develop within the systems of representation which they belong to.

(c) Individual words are created as marked points within projections in terms of which levels of representation are related to each other.

The core of (A 3) is the claim that the acquisition of any single word depends on conditions emanating from all the levels of structure in which it participates. It is in this sense that acquisition of words proceeds holistically. It is piecemeal in two respects. In a trivial sense, each lexical unit is to be created as a particular coincidence between a phonetic form and the various layers of interpretation. In a far more intricate sense, new pieces of information can be added to the lexical system if one or the other level of structure provides them. Thus if a new phonetic distinction is triggered within the phonological system, a whole set of lexical items can be affected. Similarly for syntactic classification and semantic specification. By the same token, lexical specifications can be extracted from the individual words, once a certain generalization is captured in terms of redundancy and other grammatical rules. In general, then, it is the lexical system rather than the individual words that is acquired. It should by now be obvious that, although the individual links between the different aspects of meaning are indispensible, their role is by far less predominant in the development of words than the growth of the structures to be linked.

Before turning to a discussion of certain consequences following from (A 3) with respect to our question (II), I would briefly point to some more general aspects of (A 3).

It should be obvious that (A 3) must be construed as a special aspect of a more general position concerning language

development. (A 3) merely specifies the consequences of that
position with respect to lexical knowledge. In fact, (A 3)(b)
explicitly presupposes the autonomous (though interacting)
development of the various levels of representation. Consider in this respect once more the positions (P 1) and (P 2)
— Formalism and Functionalism — discussed in Section 2.
What has been argued there with respect to syntactic categories, is actually a much more general problem. Much
analysis and argument concerning language acquisition can be
grouped around the problem of how syntax and semantics are
related. One line of argument is that syntax develops out of
semantic (or rather conceptual) relations, i.e. that actor-
action is turned into subject-verb, action-object into verb-
object, and so on. A second line of argument tries the opposite way, considering more differentiated semantic relations
as an increasing refinement of initially fixed syntactic
patterns and categories. This view is even less plausible,
given the sophisticated differentiation of conceptual connections exhibited by the child's preverbal behaviour. Both
lines of argument erroneously attempt to reduce one level of
structure to another. There is, of course, no need for such
a reduction. It might very well be (and most certainly is)
the case that the child's two- and three-word utterances
are organized according to situationally determined conceptual
structures. There is, however, no need whatsoever to construe
these relations as the roots out of which syntax grows. They
may be a precondition, but not the origin of syntactic rules,
just as, say, sitting precedes standing and standing is a precondition of walking, though none is an early phase of the
other.
  Another general problem concerns the question of what can
be acquired in the first place. For obvious reasons, learning
is based on prerequisites that cannot themselves be learned.
It is an empirical question what these prerequisites are with
respect to a certain domain. Let us suppose that for each
level of structure its primes and general combinatorial principles constitute the innate basis of learning.[5] Halle (1978)
has summarized the pertinent arguments with respect to the
phonological level, Fodor (1975) provides a principled discussion with respect to semantic and/or conceptual structure.
He argues, in particular, that in order to acquire a concept,
we must already dispose of the means to form a hypothesis
concerning the concept in question. That means that the
principles of conceptual structure cannot be learned, but must
be innate. That much can hardly be doubted. One might now
argue that, as the principles must be given in advance, such
that we already know all possible concepts, we do not really
learn any of them. There is a crucial ambiguity in the notion

of learning involved here. In one sense, the argument is
right, in another sense, it is wrong. It is right in the
sense in which we know all the prime numbers, once we know
the definition of prime number. It is wrong in the sense that
we must decide whether 89 is prime or not. Thus we can learn
that 89 is a prime number, although we already know all possible prime numbers. Notice that this type of learning is
neither a mere triggering of preconditions, nor a process that
affirms already acquired knowledge. It nevertheless is
strictly dependent on the preconditions in question and (in
this case) previously acquired knowledge. It is this type of
development that constitutes the overwhelming part of processes addressed by our question (II).

Turning now to the more specific problems, we might say
that the mental lexicon and the information assigned to the
individual lexical items result from the solution of a number
of tasks shaped in the way just discussed by the different
structural systems. According to the previous discussion,
we might distinguish the following tasks:

a) Developing phonological distinctions in terms of which
   word forms are structured and distinguished.
b) Developing conceptual distinctions in terms of which mental
   models are built up.
c) Determining the semantic structure of lexical items.
d) Determining the syntactic categories to which word forms
   are to be assigned.
e) Mapping semantic structures on the appropriate conceptual
   distinctions.
f) Connecting semantic structures to syntactically categorized
   word forms.

This enumeration is neither complete nor does it imply a
temporal order in which the tasks are faced and solved. It
merely indicates the complexity of processes that replace the
simple formation of a form-meaning association stipulated by
(A 1). It is in fact a crucial point of the answer I wish to
propose for question (II), that the different tasks are by no
means solved all at once, but that their solution may rather
grow out at different times as the various levels of structure
develop.

It is obvious that an initial phonetic matrix p^i must be
created on the basis of and placed within the phonological
system. In a sense, the child has grasped the definition if
it identifies the sounds of cat by means of p^i and assigns
it to con^i (con^i = the child's initial concept based on and
placed within LCON).

Eventually, p^i will develop into p^{le}; syn^{le} and sem^{le} will
be created and assigned to it; and con^i will develop into

the family of concepts accessed by the pertinent *sem*. The
sequence of steps leading to that result is by no means determined by the first acquaintance with the word. Many of
them may result from developments that have nothing to do with
the particular word involved, but are created by independent
phonetic, syntactic, or semantic achievements.

9. THE SEMANTIZATION TASK

Ignoring the source and development of p and *syn*, we are left
with the following tasks. Using our earlier terminology,
they can be restated as follows:

a) Identification of *con* with respect to a given *c*.
b) Determining *sem* such that $V(sem, c) = con$.
c) Determining V such that $V(sem, c) = con$.
d) Establishing (p, syn, sem).

I will call (a) the *Conceptualization Task*, (b) and (c) the
different aspects of the *Semantization Task*, and (d) the
Mapping Task, which will be taken up in the next section.
    As to (a), I will make the simplifying assumption that its
solution is to be taken for granted, i.e. that the relevant
conceptual distinctions are already established. In other
words, the situation(s) must already be understood in the
relevant respects in order to relate a word to some of the
distinctions involved. The conceptualization task is a prerequisite for the rest, and the basis for its solution is
clearly not linguistic.
    The two aspects (b) and (c) of the Semantization Task are
closely interrelated for obvious reasons. According to (D 3)
above, which takes *sem* to be a function from contexts into
concepts, they would in fact constitute just one task. According to the view expressed by (D 3'), which I have adopted,
they are different in an interesting respect: whereas (b),
the determination of *sem*, has to be accomplished for any
particular word, albeit on the basis of general principles
underlying SEM, (c), the determination of V, is a task not
bound to individual lexical items. Assuming that V is based
on rules and principles, the solution to (c) is more like
discovering a morphological rule, for example, than establishing a particular morpheme.
    In the simplest case, (c) might have a trivial solution by
construing V as a constant function which allows for collapsing
sem and *con*. Whether and to what extent that is really the
case for a certain initial phase, is an empirical issue, that
is difficult to explore. Notice that the distinction emerges
only to the extent to which the same word is applied to sys-

tematically varying contexts yielding different conceptual interpretations for the same word. I doubt that the simplifying conjecture is correct, but for the time being I will take for granted the solution to (c) in one way or the other and explore some problems concerning (b).

One of the main empirical findings in word acquisition turns on various types of overgeneralization, that is, lack of discrimination compared to the adult's lexicon. Clark (1973) provides a wide variety of instances. These phenomena gave rise to the missing feature hypothesis, that is a core part of the conception of Accretion, according to which features are gradually added up. Within the present framework, the phenomena in question may be traced to two sources: incompleteness with respect to the conceptualization task, or incompleteness as to the semantization task (i.e. lack of conceptual or semantic distinctions). As I have neutralized the problem connected to (c), I will deal only with potential lack of semantic distinctions, making the slightly simplifying assumption, that any specification in sem corresponds to a (possible) differentiation in con, but not necessarily vice versa. In other words, I will leave open whether there are conceptual distinctions in the child's mental world that do not show up in his language. (Actually, I am sure that there are many.)

10. THE MAPPING TASK

Suppose that the solution of the conceptualization and semantization task provides the meaning m of a word w. I will take m to be specified in various degrees of completeness and stability with respect to sem and con. We can now consider (d), which I have called the mapping task, as connecting m to a syntactically categorized word form p. The mapping task comes in two forms, which can simply be stated as:

T 1) What can p denote?

T 2) How can m be expressed?

As a rule, (T 1) specifies the problems encountered in language understanding, (T 2) specifies the problems to be solved in speech production. The ways in which these tasks are solved are fairly different, for obvious reasons: (T 1) relies heavily on contextual information in determining the actual meaning on the basis of which the semantic structure can eventually be identified. (T 2) exploits instead the available grammatical mechanisms and lexical knowledge acquired so far in order to come up with a word form p that according to this knowledge is related to m. Lexical knowledge is the converging outcome of solutions to both types of task. However, although both are involved in the acquisition of word meaning, they play fairly different roles in the overall process.

Before turning to some remarks on these differences, let me emphasize a general point concerning both ways of mapping. Remember that according to the conception of Association, the purport of the mapping task is the core of word acquisition. As I have already pointed out, establishing the connection between p and m occupies a far less central position according to the Projection-view. The reasons should be clear by now. Not only is the framework that provides potential conceptual, semantic, and phonetic representations a rich structure that deprives the mapping task of the atomistic character inherent in the isolated formation of associative links. It also crucially facilitates the mapping itself, as the range of items to be considered in the task is systematically restricted by the rules determining the candidates to be connected and even the connection itself. (For example, although semantic and syntactic structures are following different principles, they highly constrain their mutual options. Hence the syntactic context can drastically reduce the number of options available for a particular instance of (T 1).)

What is even more important, however, is this: although the mapping task replaces in a sense the formation of associative links, it does not replace it with something similar, but with a radically different type of connection. In order to see the distinction, consider the well-known cases of confusion like *left* instead of *right*, *tomorrow* instead of *yesterday* and similar frequent phenomena. The confusion that shows up during a certain period does not merely affect arbitrary items, as say *yellow* instead of *left*, but rather well-defined pairs or small sets. Clearly, association between p and m could not account for such systematic confusion. It is precisely this difference that I had in mind in replacing Association by Projection.

Returning to the different role of (T 1) and (T 2), let me first note in passing that it relates in part to the obscure problem of active and passive knowledge. Speaking and understanding, recognition and recall are some of its facets. I have nothing to add to the poor state of present knowledge. Let me merely point out that because of this difference a child (or a speaker in general) is not infrequently confronted with (T 2) although the conventionally appropriate lexical item is already part of his mental lexicon.

Trivially, tasks of the type we are considering are not

faced consciously. Usually, the child is not aware whether
he faces a task and which one. In particular, the child does
not discriminate conventional vocabulary from new creations
produced according to (T 2). (Occasionally, of course, reactions produce awareness, but that is not the general case.)
In general, then, success on both tasks increases the system
of lexical entries. Notice, however, that unpredictable,
new information relevant to the mapping task can be achieved
only by solutions to (T 1). That is trivial, but important.
In order to solve instances of (T 2), the child brings to
bear innate and/or previously acquired knowledge. Only (T 1)
can eventually yield decisions the outcome of which was not
previously known. In other words, only (T 1) provides access
to external information. This must not obscure, of course,
the importance of the internal structure in terms of which
the new information is to be interpreted. In so far as the
internal structure on all pertinent levels is the precondition
without which no sense could be made of external information,
efforts according to (T 2) are no less important than those
released by (T 1). Still, there remains the asymmetry I have
indicated.

Notice finally, that in solving (T 2) type tasks, the child
(unconsciously) decides whether analogy, word formation,
compounding, or whatever might provide the desired solution,
while the solution of a (T 1) type task does not leave these
options.

To conclude, the discussion of the question (II) can be
summarized by the following provisional answer:

II') Word meanings develop within the framework indicated by
    (I"). The development proceeds according to various
    tasks, in particular:
    (a) the conceptualization task, constructing possible
        denotata;
    (b) the semantization task, connecting language and the
        mental world;
    (c) the mapping task, relating form and meaning.

This is, of course, a programme rather than an answer. More
concrete questions, leading to more specific answers, can
easily be derived.

11. REPRESENTATION AND OPERATION

The previous discussion of question (II) is, by and large,
an attempt to arrange questions and proposals that have been
pursued in the literature according to a certain perspective.
I will now add a consideration that, as far as I can see, has
not been made explicit so far.

Let me begin by explaining the following distinction:

a) Disposal of a representation
b) Operation over a representation

I say that a person disposes of a certain internal representation if he is able to create and entertain it and to behave
according to it, whatever type of behaviour is pertinent.
In a sense, disposal is the necessary and sufficient condition
for implicitly knowing the representation. Thus, you dispose
of a phonetic representation p if you are able to pronounce
it or to recognize it if presented with an appropriate acous-
tic signal. Operation over a representation is a rule-governed
mental activity by which the representation is affected or
modified in one way or the other. Operation over a representation presupposes, of course, disposal of it. There may be,
moreover, different types of operations available with respect
to the same class of representations.

The crucial point of the distinction is that disposal of a
representation does not automatically imply the ability needed
for a certain operation over it.

Let me illustrate the point by some examples. You may dispose of a tune or melody, if you are able to recognize it,
to differentiate it from other tunes, and (at least approximately) to sing it. Imagine now a number of operations, such
as inverting the intervals, inverting the order or intervals,
leaving out the up-beat, changing the rhythm, and so on. Your
disposal of the tune does not imply that you may perform these
operations or to recognize them if you are presented with
their result.

Before I apply the distinction of representation and operation
to the development of word meaning, two problems should be
cleared away. First, the distinction is to be relativized with
respect to a given system of representation. Thus from a purely
phonological point of view, to assign a syntactic structure to
a phonetic sequence might be taken as an imposed operation. In
the same vein, the semantization task may be thought of as imposing certain operations on the mental world. Hence, if we
were to consider separately the different levels of organization involved in language understanding and production, we
should construe the whole process as a mixture of disposing of
and operating over certain representations. I will therefore
assume that in a sufficiently clear sense, disposal of linguistic structures involves all and only the levels of representation discussed above. More specifically, disposal of the representation of a word w relative to a context c involves p, syn,
sem, and con. That is, in fact, what it means to know a word.

Secondly, for obvious reasons, but in a way that is anything
but clear, a representation must itself be created by certain

operations. Thus language understanding as a process results in the creation of an internal representation of the phonetic, syntactic, semantic, and conceptual structure of the perceived utterance. This process consists in a highly complex sequence of operations. We therefore have to distinguish between operations that create representations, and operations that operate over representations. Let us call the former "disposing operations" and the latter "affecting operations". Given the relativization just discussed, it should be clear that what is a (sequence of) disposing operations from one point of view, may be an affecting operation from another point of view. To some extent, language development can even be regarded as a process that gradually turns affecting operations into (automatized sequences of) disposing operations, which are, of course, relativized to more complex systems of representation. Anyway, for a given state of development, disposal of a word can be distinguished from operations affecting it. As I am interested here only in the affecting operations, I will continue to use the simple term operation.

The point I would like to make should now be obvious: language acquisition consists in the first place in developing the disposal of the pertinent representations. This disposal is then embedded into or supplemented by various systems of operations, some of them permanent and systematic — like logical inference, poetry, or alphabetic writing — others only occasionally and unsystematic — such as different types of language games (in the narrower, not the Wittgensteinian sense), performing tasks in the psychologist's lab, etc.

On this background, the following conjectures seem to be fairly natural:

1) For a given system of representations, different operations can apply with different degrees of reliability.

2) One and the same operation may apply to different structures or items of a given system of representation with different degrees of reliability.

Both claims are fairly vague and can be specified in various directions. As to (1), operations can be ordered according to certain types of complexity and, what is more relevant in the present context, related to certain developmental stages. As to (2), at least two directions can be pursued. First, different representational subsystems might differ as to accessibility for certain operations. Logical inference, for example, seems to be easier to apply to conceptual representations than to semantic ones, and easier to semantic than to strictly syntactic representations (provided that

conceptual, semantic, and syntactic inference is the same type
of operation). Secondly, within the same level of representation, different items or types of structure may be
easier to access than others.

We may now think of language acquisition in general and
development of word meaning in particular in both a narrower
and a wider sense. In the narrower sense, it comprises
merely the disposal of representations, in the wider sense, it
includes the gradual accessibility of representations for various types of operations.

It seems to me now that studies of language acquisition in
a number of cases suffer from failing to distinguish between
the wider and the narrower sense of language acquisition. More
precisely, in many cases reliability of the application of
certain operations is (erroneously) identified with the disposal of representations. Although the distinction might
sometimes be fairly subtle, and difficult to assess, it should
be clear enough in principle. It can actually be related
directly to a methodological problem: as mere disposal of a
representation is difficult to reveal, most experimental studies are addressed to representational disposal plus something
more. To take just two of the more frequently used paradigms:
the antonym word game clearly requires representation plus
the application of an additional rule specified by the task.
The acting-out-paradigm requires representation plus trans-
position into an action that, first, is organized according
to its own rules and representations, and secondly, is under-
or overdetermined in the crucial respect serving as the experimental variable. Therefore, all that can be claimed on the
basis of such tasks is this: if the task is performed correctly,
the representation in question can be assumed to be disposed
of. If the task fails, this might be due to the lack of representation or to the lack of accessibility for the operation
in question. Hence accessibility for operations, not necessarily disposal of representation, is tested in tasks like
acting out, antonym games, sorting of words, and all the other
understanding-plus-something-tasks. This does by no means
deprive these paradigms of their dignity and importance. It
merely clarifies what they reveal.

If one element in a representation presupposes the occurrence
of another one, the former may be more basic than the latter
one. Thus, according to the analysis of colour terms proposed
above, [COLOUR X Y] is more basic in this sense than any of
the values GREEN, RED etc. that may occur as a specification
of the variable Y. Notice that RED and [COLOUR X Y] are not

ranked to each other in anything like the predicability
tree, just because they are of different semantic categories.
In a similar vein, the polarity-part in the semantics of
spatial adjectives like *big, small, long, short* and the rest
would be more basic than the specification of the various
dimensions involved. For empirical evidence to that effect,
see the work reported in Carey (1978).

Furthermore, the stability of an element might depend on its
marked or unmarked character according to the markedness asymmetry.
That would account in particular for the *more/less*-type confu-
sions, if the preference of the unmarked term is in fact
due to semantic conditions, and not, as experimental results
of Carey (1978) suggest, to a less specific bias in favour of
the positive direction of a scale. If Carey's account is
right, the *more/less*-problem is in fact not due to an asymmetry between words but rather between alternative outcomes
of a strategy followed in a task that goes beyond mere understanding. The same consideration would apply to the asymmetries
in the interpretation of *in, on,* and *under* revealed by Clark
(1973a) in a task that required manipulation of objects relative to containers and surfaces.

What all this comes down to, is simply the following:
the development of the semantic aspect of word meaning is
determined by two interacting, though asymmetric developmental
processes. The first is accomplished by coping with the
semantization task proper providing disposal of the pertinent
semantic components. The second is the gradual growth of
stability providing access to the established semantic configurations for an increasingly varied number of operations.
Flores d'Arcais (this volume) provides interesting evidence
bearing on this aspect by demonstrating how connectives
become available for more and more special tasks during a
fairly long developmental path.

Although operational potential seems to me a crucial and
systematic parameter in language development (and cognitive
growth in general), it is still far from clear, how its substantial characteristics could eventually be specified.

12. TYPES OF LEXICAL ENTRIES

So far, I have talked in a rather unifying way, suggesting
that the acquisition of word meanings follows more or less
the same route for all types of lexical items. This is
obviously wrong in various respects. Before commenting on
some of the more obvious differences let me emphasize, however, that the unifying perspective must still be taken as
corresponding to essential conditions in the subject matter
itself and not merely as a matter of presentation. Linguistic

knowledge in general and word meanings in particular develop,
according to the Projection-view, on the basis of inherent
principles organizing the structure of interacting modular
components. Each of these components does not only provide
the margin for variations according to particular structural
properties, developmental conditions, and individual experience,
but above all the integrating framework that determines the
eventual make-up of the overall structure as well as the place
and character of its parts. In this sense, the development
of words and their meanings is in fact a unified process where
none of the pieces is acquired independently of the developing
whole.

Keeping in mind this unifying framework, we may now turn
to the piecemeal aspect of the growing mental lexicon. Even
here, we have to consider the interaction of specializing
conditions and factors that do not affect lexical entries
in isolation but rather systematically determined groups and
substructures. It is commonplace that the growing numerical
size of the mental lexicon is a very raw indicator of actual
development. What is more important: the quantitative aspect
often obscures the crucial qualitative differences between the
various developmental achievements.

To begin with, the phonological, morphological, syntactic,
semantic, and conceptual systems of representation develop,
as I have repeatedly pointed out, according to autonomous,
though interacting principles. Thus on the one hand, representational devices are released by their respective matura-
tional schemes, and their partial correspondence during initial
phases need not reflect their final interrelation. That does
not only apply to the more obvious independence of initial
developments in phonetic and conceptual structures, but also
to syntax, semantics, and morphology. On the other hand, once
a certain structural device is established on one level, it
may induce or shape the development on other levels. Thus
the development of syntax sets the stage for accomplishing
the semantization task, e.g. for connectives. In a similar
vein, acquaintance with certain templates of word formation
clearly facilitates the second half, i.e. (T 2), of the
mapping task. Such dependencies must not be oversimplified,
though. Often the different ingredients of a certain phenomenon are difficult to disentangle. Let me give a single
illustration.

German children, according to simple and widespread observation, come up with utterances like (28) during the two-word-
phase:

28) (a) Auto um! "Das Auto ist umgefallen" (The car toppled
        over)

(b) Strumpf an. "den Strumpf anziehen" (put on the stocking)
(c) Mantel zu. "den Mantel zuknöpfen" (button up the coat)

To put it as simply as possible: prefixed verbs are reduced
to the prefix.[6] At least the following conditions must be
taken into consideration:

Phonology: Separable prefixes of verbs have primary stress.
Morphology: Prefix + Stem is a fixed template for possible
verbs.
Syntax: Separable prefixes have a fixed, clause final position; Noun - Prefix (Verb) combinations like (28) systematically correspond to Noun - Verb combinations like *Puppe
schlafen* (doll sleep) and Noun-Particle combinations like
Knopf ab (button (is) off) of the child's language.
Semantics: The meaning of the prefix is the more salient
part, which is, moreover, the invariant of a set of related
verbs like e.g. *umfallen, umkippen, umstürzen* etc.
Lexical: Verbal prefixes correspond to homophonous adverbial
particles with closely related meanings.

   Which of these factors are relevant for the phenomenon
illustrated in (28) is by no means obvious. From the point
of view of the adult grammar, they are not independent at
all, although they are governed by different rules belonging
to separate components of the grammar. From the point of
view of the child's developing knowledge, it is difficult
to decide which paves the way for which (if any).
   Taking these considerations as a permanent background, let
us turn to the more specific problems of different conditions
for the development of word meaning. A well known distinction
is that between so-called content words on the one hand, i.e.
the major lexical categories, and all types of grammatical
words on the other. Flores d'Arcais (this volume) gives
revealing evidence that nouns and connectives are relatively
different with respect to developing stability in the sense
discussed above, i.e. with respect to different operations as
required in lexical decision tasks or sorting tasks for isolated words. It goes without saying, however, that this
characteristic does not hold in a uniform manner with respect
to other dimensions of development, especially the mere
disposal of meaning, nor for all subclasses of the two large
categories of lexical items. In the remainder, I will consider some determinants that may give rise to developmental
specifications.
   I need not emphasize that this can be done only by way of
selective exemplification, since even a rough account of the
relevant factors would have to be based on a sufficiently
detailed theory of semantic representations, including the

choice of primitive terms, combinatorial categories, semantic rules, and all the rest. I will ignore, furthermore, the problems involved in the conceptualization task; I will simply assume that what is to be verbalized must have been distinguished conceptually. Although this is certainly contrary to fact in many cases, it seems to me a reasonable idealization, that is factually true, moreover, for a relevant class of cases. By the same token I presuppose that perceptual structures have been established in advance, at least insofar as they are involved in the interpretation of lexical items.

The following exemplifications will be ordered along the following conditions: (a) demonstrability, (b) lexical autonomy, (c) hidden parametrization, (d) token-reflexivity. These are merely hints for orientation that will be explained in turn. They are not independent of each other, and they are not meant, in particular, to characterize disjoint classes of lexical entries.

(a) By *demonstrability* I mean the possibility to introduce a word, at least in principle, by demonstration (pointing or acting out). Two points should be clear in advance. First, even though demonstration or ostension, i.e. co-occurrence of a phonetically structured signal and a (conceptualized) percept seems to be the simplest and most direct basis to acquire a new word, it requires a rich structure of prerequisites. Second, even if we grant a fairly generous interpretation of demonstrability, there is a large amount of vocabulary that is not amenable to demonstration on principled grounds. *Tomorrow, cheap, true, also, seldom, or* is an arbitrary selection pointing to different limits of demonstrability. Let us first briefly consider the prerequisites for ostensive definition (in a fairly wide sense, which does not necessarily involve explicit sentences of the form *That is...*).

a) The relevant percept must have been formed and conceptualized in pertinent respects. (Otherwise *ball* or *tomato* would not be distinguished from *red* or *round*, for example.)
b) A semantic scheme or template must be available to shape the semantization task.
c) The relevant semantic primes must be activated in order to fill or specify the scheme of (b) in accordance with the conceptualization presupposed in (a).
d) The appropriate syntactic categorization must be determined according to which the lexical entry functions in complex expressions.

This still incomplete list is neither meant to indicate a temporal or logical order between (a) to (d), nor does it suggest that the conditions must be met all at once. As I

pointed out earlier, certain aspects might develop according
to the inherent time schedule of the levels involved. (a)
to (d) merely indicate the conditions necessary to arrive at
a complete lexical item on the basis of perceptual demonstration. There is a certain amount of evidence, however, according to which (a) to (d) are usually met rather early and are
probably interactive right from the beginning (reviewed in
Carey (1978), for example). It comes from experiments and
observations showing the following: first, at the age of
seventeen months, girls systematically discriminate between
proper names and common nouns by interpreting sentences like
There's Corgi and *There's a corgi*, respectively; see Katz *et
al*. (1974). Hence syntactic information can be used long
before it shows up in speech production. Secondly, at the
age of two years, words introduced in isolation to name
either an object or an activity are automatically assigned the
category noun and verb, respectively, as exhibited by their
subsequent use; see Braine (1971). Expanding on these observations, Carey concludes that syntactic and semantic specifications develop in parallel.

Turning now to lexical entries that cannot be introduced
by demonstration, one easily realizes that the difference
is by far less drastic than might be expected at the first
glance. The prerequisites differ only with respect to
(a), which now ceases to refer to percepts and might be
replaced by (a'):

a') The relevant concept must have been formed.

This condition does not exclude, however, that the concept
in question is at least partially related to perceptual
structures also for nondemonstrable words. Consider cases
like *learn, task, solution,* or even *word*.   There is no perceptual invariant for the concept of learning or of a task,
although there are plenty of perceivable events instantiating
learning or situations instantiating a task. Hence demonstrability determines a scale, rather than a disjunctive alternative: words with ostensible meaning require conceptualization, and non-ostensible words may be related in various
ways to perceptual instances. Differences in acquisition of
word meaning related to this dimension may therefore be dependent more on the development of conceptual organization in
the mental world than on demonstrability as such.

(b) By *lexical autonomy* I mean the possibility to determine
the meaning of a word independently of its syntactic integration into larger expressions. The property in question
establishes a scale, ranging from fully autonomous words
like proper names through words that require more and more
linguistic context like transitive verbs and prepositions to

those that are fully dependent on syntactic embedding like determiners, particles such as *even, only,* or connectives like *and, if, because*. The distinction between autonomous and dependent lexical items corresponds to some extent to that between autocategorematic and syncategorematic elements. It is also related (but not identical) to the distinction between lexical and grammatical words and a number of other distinctions of a similar type. I will not attempt to make the notion fully precise, as this would require more formal machinery than necessary for the purpose at hand. The main point in the present context is simply this: the semantic and conceptual specification of different words is entangled in different degrees into the structure of utterances they may occur in. In this sense, you can pull out more easily, for example the meaning of *Bill* than that of *still* from an utterance of *Bill was still waiting*. On the background of this provisional characterization, I will briefly comment on three points.

First, the less autonomous a word is, the more is the acquisition of its meaning not only influenced by the interaction of conceptual, semantic, and syntactic structure beyond the word in question, but does actually depend on these structures. It would thus be a plausible conjecture, that dependent items are more difficult to learn, that they develop later than autonomous words. Plausible, but wrong. I have already mentioned that children distinguish fairly early between proper and common nouns by coping with the presence or absence of a determiner. Notice, that this does not only indicate the child's syntactic classification of nouns, but also his at least partial (and possibly almost complete) disposal of the syntactic and semantic representation of determiners.

Secondly, even if the onset of the development of strictly dependent items might not be essentially later than that of autonomous words, we still have the fact that their further development is considerably slower in certain respects. See again the results of Flores d'Arcais (this volume) for evidence from sentential connectives. This observation can now be interpreted in still another respect. Suppose that it is natural for dependent items to be at the disposal within their appropriate syntactic and semantic context. The fact that they are less available than autonomous words outside their context, would then be an automatic consequence. In other words, it is more difficult to apply the same operation (lexical decision, sorting, etc.) to a dependent than to an autonomous word, if the task requires isolation from context.

Third, there seems to be a systematic affinity between lexical autonomy and demonstrability: Autonomous words are more readily introduced by simple ostension than dependent

words. This affinity is only a rather partial one, however.
On the one hand, there are words that are fairly easily
demonstrated, although they are not autonomous at all. Spatial prepositions like *in*, *at*, *under* are a simple case in
point. It is easy to show by means of two objects, what it
means for one of them to be in, at, or under the other, although propositions are not autonomous at all. (Notice that autonomy in the sense discussed here can be related to some extent to the possibility to be questioned by a Wh-word. As
is well known, there is no way to question a preposition, but
only a prepositional phrase, e.g. by means of *where*. On the
other hand, it should be obvious that there is a large number
of autonomous words that are not amenable to demonstration.
(Even proper names are often not introducable by direct
acquaintance.) Hence lexical autonomy and demonstrability
are independent, albeit related dimensions.

Notice in passing that natural paraphrasing, which might
come into play in explaining the meaning of new words, is
closely bound to lexical autonomy. The more the meaning of
a word is dependent on its linguistic context, the less can
it be defined in a direct explicit way.

(c) By *hidden parametrization* I mean the occurrence of a
variable in the semantic structure of a word whose value
must be specified in order to grasp its meaning, although
it is not in general indicated in the linguistic context.
There is a wide variety of such latent variables. Let me
illustrate the problem by three different types of examples.

The first is the class of so-called relational adjectives,
like *long*, *short*, *old*, *expensive*, etc., which relate an object with respect to a certain dimension to the standard
or norm of its class. Thus, formally they contain a component like [NORM X], where X is an explicitly specified variable,
and NORM is a function that has as value the standard object
of the class from which X is selected. It requires the
identification of the class in question and the standard representative.

The second example is that of relational nouns like *friend*,
father, *sister*, *neighbour*, *top*, *front*, *end* etc. They are all
based on a semantic scheme of the following type:

29) $\hat{X}$ [$\exists Z$ [[R X Z]...]

where R is a relation characteristic for the different lexical entries. The hidden parameter is the variable Z to which
X is related by R.

The third example is that causative verbs, which are based
on the scheme (30):

30) $\hat{X}$ [$\hat{Y}$[∃Z[DO Y Z] ∧ [CAUSE Z [... X ...]]]]

The entry (9) for *melt* is a concrete example. Here the hidden parameter is Z, the event by means of which the actor Y causes the effect on X.

Further types of implicit variables can easily be added. The shared property of all these cases, specified reference to implicit entities, has fairly different consequences for the development of word meaning. Whereas reference to the implicit norm seems to be caputred very early (see Carey 1978), the relational character of kinship terms is notoriously difficult and develops only gradually (see Haviland and Clark 1974; Deutsch, 1979).

(d) By *token-reflexivity* I mean the fact that the meaning of a word is dependent on one or the other aspect of the uttered token of the word. Thus the meaning of *I* depends on who utters it, the meaning of *here* and *today* depends on where and when the words are uttered, etc. In other words, token-reflexives — which Jakobson (1957) called "shifters" and which are treated in formal semantics as "indexicals" and in linguistics as "deictic expressions".

There is a fair amount of work dealing both with the structural and developmental aspects of deictic expressions. Although it has become sufficiently clear that these items exhibit specific developmental properties (see de Villiers and de Villiers 1978 for a brief survey), it is by no means obvious which factors are responsible for which phenomena. Consider for example the interesting study of personal pronouns of Deutsch and Pechmann (1978).

Using a naming task in a situation with four participants — speaker, addressee, a male and a female observer — Deutsch and Pechmann found the following developmental ordering:

mir > dir > uns_3 > uns_1 > uns_2 > euch > ihm > ihr > ihnen

a > b means 'a has more correct responses than b'. uns_3 refers to all four participants, uns_1 to speaker and addressee, uns_2 to speaker and one observer. Deutsch and Pechmann interpret these by means of three coordinates in terms of which the situation can be structured, namely the coordinates having Proximal, Speaker, and Singular as their respective unmarked or neutral value, and the following general principles:

a) The unmarked value is less complex than the marked one.
b) Additional specifications increase the complexity.
c) The Speaker coordinate is less complex than the Proximal coordinate, which in turn is less complex than the Singular coordinate.

With the exception of uns_3 this analysis yields a fairly close correspondence between complexity and order of development, where (a) and (b) confirm principles that have been found valid in other domains as well (e.g. spatial adjectives); thus only (c) must be stipulated specifically for the present domain. Besides certain problems with the proposed analysis,[7] the following questions might be raised in the light of our previous discussion: first of all, the naming game is one of the disposal-plus-something-tasks, which do not provide direct evidence of the semantic and conceptual structure that is at the child's disposal. Second, the particular difficulties with third person pronouns might be due either to their complexity roughly along the lines of (a), (b) and (c), or to their special deictic interpretation required in the four-person-naming-game and thus be an instance of shifters in a two-fold sense, in that they are either token-reflexive or relative to a different point of reference. And third, the ordinary deictic, i.e. token-reflexive character of I, we and you, may or may not be a crucial factor in the task at hand, as the game was played with dolls, which involves an additional identification of the speaker and the addressee with their respective dolls. In short, the pattern of data reflects a certain developmental aspect of pronouns, but it allows no direct inference with respect to the role of the token-reflexive nature of pronouns. This discussion of pronouns can easily be extended to other deictic expressions (see Bierwisch 1980b).

Let me conclude these considerations by two more general remarks. First, it should be obvious that none of the four properties I have considered in this section provides a simple and direct developmental dimension. They rather served to elucidate a heuristic framework which the actual conditions underlying developmental peculiarities of different types of lexical items may in part coincide, in part contrast with.

Secondly, I hope to have given some reason for the claim that results that go beyond description in the domain of acquisition of word meaning will only be forthcoming to the extent to which the full range of linguistic, and especially semantic theorizing is taken into account, i.e. the systematic analysis of semantic structures is taken as a crucial part of language acquisition research. The need for an integrated research is on both sides: semantic theorizing is still badly in need of empirically justified constraints, to which language development gives a particularly revealing access; language acquisition research needs semantic theorizing, since only on its basis can revealing questions be formulated. Over and above the principles of semantic structure, however, specific developmental parameters and their interaction with structural

conditions must be identified. I have tried to isolate some
of these potential parameters in terms of types of tasks to
be faced by the learner, types of information that can be
used, and modes (or stability) of representation with respect
to disposal and operation. Given this interaction of various
conditions and the presumed relative autonomy of the developing systems, it should be clear enough that no simple and
direct observability of the explanatory factors is to be
expected.

13. CONCLUDING REMARKS

The gist of my survey and of the projection view I've advo-
cated might be summarized by a simple anecdote illustrating a
well-known, recurring observation. I once heard my three-
year-old nephew saying:

31) Guck mal, Mami, der Ball is genau so rot wie meine Hose!
    (Look, mummy, the ball is just as red as my trousers!)

both being clearly blue. Obviously, little Thomas was not
colour blind. Based on normal visual perception, he presumably had developed a proper system of colour categories.
He knew, moreover, that there are particular lexical items
referring to these categories. He even knew which lexical
items (of his vocabulary) these are. Thus he must be supposed
to dispose of the following correlated informations:

a) RED, GREEN, BLUE, YELLOW, BROWN ... refer to basic colour
   categories;
b) $\hat{X}$ [COLOUR X V] is the semantic scheme of colour terms,
   with V to be specified by one of the values in (a);
c) /ro:t/, /grü:n/, ... are the phonological representations
   of colour terms;
d) syntactically, colour terms are [+ Adjective]

Thus in some sense, he had fully developed the meaning, both
the semantic structure and the conceptual units, of colour
words. And he furthermore knew that objects can be compared
with respect to the properties expressed by these terms, and
that this comparison is going to be realized in a particular
syntactic way. All that was left, was to fix the proper
correspondence between phonetic and semantic representations.
Everybody knows that errors of that type are characteristic
for a certain stage of development and that they are by far
more likely to occur than, say (32),

32) Look, the ball is just as red as the tomato!

meaning that the ball and the tomato are both round or of

the same size. A theory beyond description should be able
to explain such typical phenomena on principled grounds.

NOTES

1 For more detailed discussion of the problems involved, see
   Chomsky and Halle (1968) with respect to phonology, Chomsky
   (1965) with respect to syntax, Jackendoff (1975) with respect to semantic and morphological regularities, and Bierwisch (1967) with respect to inflectional rules.
2 These informal remarks can easily be made precise in one
   way or the other. See Lewis (1972) for a perspicuous discussion of categorial systems of the type envisaged here.
3 Although it seems to be plausible to construe the system
   of primes to be innate in its essentials, we need not claim
   innateness for all particular primes occurring in a given
   language. If we denote by PRIME the initially fixed system,
   from which primes of SEM are to be drawn, PRIME might well
   contain certain dimensions or parameters that can be specified according to triggering experience. Thus although
   RED, GREEN, BLUE etc. might be irreducible primes of SEM,
   it might be sufficient that PRIME contains a dimension of
   colour values that can be specified in a number of ways
   (which still are probably not arbitrary, as the results
   of Berlin and Kay (1969) indicate).
4 See Cooper and Ross (1975) for a discussion of markedness
   phenomena restricting the mere conventionality of the relation between *p* and *sem*. According to their observations,
   semantically unmarked items tend to be phonetically unmarked, other things being equal. Thus *long* is "shorter"
   than *short*, etc.
5 This is an oversimplification in several respects. First,
   as I have argued above with respect to conceptual structure,
   it may be domains rather than primes that must be given in
   advance. Secondly, it might be more than just combinatorial
   principles, which must be given besides the inventory of
   primes. (See Wexler and Culicover (1980) for an extensive
   discussion of this problem with respect to syntax.) For
   the present purpose, however, the simplified assumption
   will do.
6 This might, of course, be a totally misleading formulation,
   as the category verb might not yet, have been emerged, and
   reduction is not involved in any serious sense. The formulation is not relevant, though. What is at issue is
   merely the fact that particular elements that eventually
   become verbal prefixes are selected.
7 Without going into details, let me mention just two points.

First, the plural of first person pronouns is neither conceptually nor semantically identical to the plural of other
noun phrases, as *we* is not simply a set of speakers, but
rather a set including the speaker. Secondly, it is at
least dubious, whether we_1, we_2, and we_3 are semantically
distinct. It is more likely that *we* invariably denotes a
set that includes the speaker, the difference between the
various roles of the other members of the set being a matter of conceptual interpretation relative to a particular
context. (This is, of course, different for languages
that formally distinguish inclusion or exclusion of the
addressee.) On that account, the difference between uns_1,
uns_2, and uns_3 would not correspond to a difference in
complexity of the semantic structure, but rather to a difference in the mapping from semantic structure to conceptual
structure.

REFERENCES

Berlin, B. and Kay, P. (1969). "Basic Color Terms: Their
     Universality and Evolution". Berkeley and Los Angeles:
     University of California Press.
Bierwisch, M. (1967). Syntactic features in morphology:
     general problems of so-called pronominal inflection in
     German. *In* "To Honor Roman Jakobson", pp. 239-270. The
     Hague: Mouton.
Bierwisch, M. (1980a). Utterance meaning and mental states.
     In "Memory and Cognition" (F. Klix and J. Hoffman, eds.).
     Berlin: Deutscher Verlag der Wissenschaften.
Bierwisch, M. (1980b). Semantic structure and illocutionary
     Force. *In* "Speech Act Theory and Pragmatics" (J.R.
     Searle, F. Kiefer and M. Bierwisch, eds), pp. 1-35.
     Dordrecht: D. Reidel.
Bierwisch, M. (1981). Semantische und konzeptuelle Reprä-
     sentation lexikalischer Einheiten. Berlin: Akademie der
     Wissenschaften, Manuskript.
Bierwisch, M. (in press). How on-line is language understand-
     ing? *In* "The Process of Language Understanding" (G.B.
     Flores d'Arcais and R. Jarvella, eds). London: Wiley.
Bowerman, M. (1974). Learning the structure of causative
     verbs: a study in the relationship of cognitive, semantic
     and syntactic development. *Papers and Reports on Child
     Language Development* (Stanford University) $\underline{8}$, 142-178.
Braine, M.D.S. (1971). The acquisition of language in infant
     and child. *In* "The Learning of Languages: Essays in Honor
     of David H. Russell" (C. Reed, ed.). New York: Appleton
     Century Crofts.

Carey, S. (1978). The child as a word learner. *In* "Linguistic Theory and Psychological Reality" (M. Halle, J. Bresnan and G.A. Miller, eds). Cambridge, MA: MIT Press.

Chomsky, N. (1965). "Aspects of the Theory of Syntax". Cambridge, MA: MIT Press.

Chomsky, N. (1980). "Rules and Representations". New York: Columbia University Press.

Chomsky, N. and Halle, M. (1968). "The Sound Pattern of English". New York: Harper and Row.

Clark, E.V. (1973). What's in a word? On the child's acquisition of semantics in his first language. *In* "Cognitive Development and the Acquisition of Language" (T. Moore, ed.), pp. 65-110. New York and London: Academic Press.

Clark, E.V. (1973a). Non-linguistic strategies and the acquisition of word meanings. *Cognition* 2, 161-182.

Cooper, W.E. and Ross, J.R. (1975). World order. *In* "Papers from the Parasession on Functionalism" (R.E. Grassman, J.L. San and T.J. Vance, eds), pp. 63-111. Chicago: Chicago Linguistics Society.

de Villiers, J.G. and de Villiers, P.A. (1978). "Language Acquisition". Cambridge, Mass: Harvard University Press.

Deutsch, W. (1979). The conceptual impact of linguistic input. *J. Child Language* 6, 313-327.

Deutsch, W. and Pechmann, T. (1978). Ihr, dir, or mir? On the acquisition of pronouns in German children, *Cognition* 6, 155-168.

Fodor, J.A. (1975). "The Language of Thought". New York: Crowell.

Fodor, J.A., Garrett, M.F., Walker, E.C. and Parkes, C.H. (1980). Against definitions, *Cognition* 8, 263-367.

Halle, M. (1978). Knowledge unlearned and untaught: what speakers know about the sounds of their language. *In* "Linguistic Theory and Psychological Reality" (M. Halle, J. Bresnan and G.A. Miller, eds), pp. 294-303. Cambridge MA: MIT Press

Haviland, S.E. and Clark, E.V. (1974). "This man's father is my father's son": a study of the acquisition of English kin terms, *J. Child Language* 1, 23-47.

Jackendoff, R.S. (1975). Morphological and semantic regularities in the lexicon, *Language* 51, 638-671.

Jackendoff, R.S. (1978). Grammar as evidence for conceptual structure. *In* "Linguistic Theory and Psychological Reality", (M. Halle, J. Bresnan and G.A. Miller, eds), pp. 201-228. Cambridge, MA: MIT Press.

Jackendoff, R.S. (1979). How to keep ninety from rising, *Linguistic Inquiry* 10, 172-177.

Jakobson, R. (1957). "Shifters, Verbal Categories, and the Russian Verb". Cambridge, MA: MIT Press.

Johnson-Laird, P.N. (1979). "Formal Semantics and the Psychology of Meaning". Paper delivered at Symposium on Formal Semantics and Natural Language, University of Texas, Austin.

Johnson-Laird, P.N. (1980). Mental Models in Cognitive Science, *Cognitive Science* 4, 71-115.

Katz, N., Baker, E. and McNamara, J. (1974). What's in a name? A study of how children learn common and proper names, *Child Development* 45, 469-473.

Lewis, D. (1972). General semantics. *In* "Semantics of Natural Language" (D. Davidson and G. Harman, eds), pp. 169-218. Dordrecht: Reidel.

Miller, G.A. and Johnson-Laird, P.N. (1976). "Language and Perception". Cambridge, MA: Harvard University Press.

Nunberg, G. (1979). The non-uniqueness of semantic solutions: polysemy, *Linguistics and Philosophy* 3, 143-184.

Osherson, D.N. (1978). Three conditions on conceptual naturalness. *Cognition* 4, 263-289.

Putnam, H. (1975). The meaning of "meaning". *In* "Minnesota Studies in Philosophy of Science" (K. Grunderson and G. Maxwell, eds), vol. 6. Minneapolis: University of Minnesota Press.

Searle, J.R. (1980). The background of meaning. *In* "Speech Act Theory and Pragmatics" (J.R. Searle, F. Kiefer and M. Bierwisch, eds), pp. 221-232. Dordrecht: Reidel.

Stalnaker, R.C. (1972). Pragmatics. *In* "Semantics of Natural language" (D. Davidson and G. Harman, eds), pp. 380-397. Dordrecht: Reidel.

Wexler, K. and Culicover, P.W. (1980). "Formal Principles of Language Acquisition", Cambridge, MA: MIT Press.

SUBJECT INDEX

Acquisition of syntax, 17-18,
  21-24, 29-30, 35
Acquisitional mechanisms, 78
  communicative pressure, 4
  failure in understanding, 145
  induction, 10, 248-256, 259
  internal dispositions, 362,
  365-366
  internal problem space, 4
  resource allocation, 27
Acting out task, 152, 158, 192,
  267-268, 373
Action, 28, 60, 63-65, 68, 330-
  331, 334, 339
Assimilation
  of Instrument into Agent,
  227-228
  of Manner into Instrument,
  228-229
  of new category members, 251-
  252
  of Patient into Agent, 229-
  230
Awareness, 370

Case roles, 9, 202, 208
  Actor/Agent, 70, 104, 107-
  108, 111, 117, 136, 156,
  158-159, 177, 187-188, 202-
  209, 213-214, 217, 219,
  225-226, 231-232, 240, 250,
  254, 258, 260

Experiencer, 136, 203-205,
  224-225, 231-238, 254, 260
Instrument, 205-206, 208, 219
Object, 205-206, 208-209, 213-
  215, 217, 219
Patient, 189, 202, 204-205,
  213-214, 250
Recipient, 216-217, 219
Subject of Attribution, 209-
  213, 219
Transferred Object, 216-217,
  219
User, 219
Categorial evolution
  transformation-over-time-theory,
  246, 256-258
Category formation, 241
Category monitoring, 8, 171-173
Cognitive development, 249, 338,
  359
Cognitive style, 333
Cohesion
  intralinguistic, 130, 135, 138
  semantic, 162-163
Colour terms, 356-357, 384
Comprehension
  of language, 122-123, 125, 159,
  368, 371-372, 374
  sentence processing strategies,
  123, 191, 194
  non-linguistic strategies, 269
  strategies in processing connectives, 278-279, 293

Verb category, 257-258, 384
Verbal games, 62-63

Word(s)
  definition of, 342-343
  content words, 265, 286, 295,
    376, 379
  frequency of, 286-288
  function of, 265, 271
  function (grammatical) words,
    286, 294, 376, 379
  notion of wordness, 285-294
  semantic knowledge of, 267-
    268, 329-330
Word form, 342
Word formation devices, 299-
  301
  compounding, 316-321, 343
  conversion, 317, 319, 323
  principle of productivity,
    11, 312, 315-319
  principle of regularization,
    11, 313, 319-323
  principle of semantic trans-
    parency, 11, 313, 319-323
Word meaning
  accretion view, 363, 368
  ambiguity, 347-348
  association view, 362-363

componential analysis, 344-
  345, 355-356
demonstrability, 377, 380
development of, 361, 373, 375
judgments of similarity, 279-
  283
hidden parametrization, 380
indeterminateness, 347
lexical autonomy, 378-380
meaning postulates, 344, 355-
  356
pre-emption by homonymy, 310-
  311
pre-emption by synonymy, 309-
  310
progressive differentiation
  of, 270, 278-279
projection view, 364-365, 375
semantic complexity of, 269
token reflexivity, 381
vagueness, 347
Word monitoring task, 8, 165-
  166, 169
Word order, 104, 155-156, 159,
  177, 190-192, 195
  pragmatic constraints of, 7,
    103, 105, 113-114
Word recognition, 169

Zero anaphora, 131, 137